CHESTERFIELD AND HIS CRITICS

To

THE RIGHT HON. J. M. ROBERTSON

IN DEEPEST GRATITUDE

CHESTERFIELD
AND HIS CRITICS

BY
ROGER COXON

LONDON
GEORGE ROUTLEDGE & SONS, LTD.
BROADWAY HOUSE : 68-74 CARTER LANE, E.C.
1925

Printed in Great Britain by Fox, Jones and Co., Kemp Hall Press, High Street, Oxford.

PREFACE

MUCH has been written concerning the Earl of Chesterfield—more, perhaps, than the importance of his life and work would seem to justify. Within the last eighty years there have appeared two biographies, four lengthy memoirs in editions of his works, and at least half a dozen essays of considerable length by eminent critics.

If, therefore, an excuse must be made for adding to the list of books on Chesterfield, it is to be found in the fact that, in spite of—or in many instances because of—what has been written hitherto, the popular conception of his character remains a profoundly mistaken one. A mass of misunderstanding has gathered round his name, and there exists no complete sketch of his personality which can be said to conform to the evidence of his life and writings. But apart from neglect, suppression, distortion, and even invention of evidence by the critics, another reason for the misconception of Chesterfield's character arises in the undue importance that has always been attached to the *Letters to his Son*—the only work of his known to the majority of his readers. Those whose knowledge of Chesterfield is confined to this collection of letters must of necessity form an opinion of their author in which certain aspects of his character are unduly exaggerated, and others ignored altogether.

In this book I have tried to place the *Letters to his Son* for the first time in their true perspective with Chesterfield's other letters, his essays, his speeches, and his conduct generally in public and private life. The result is an estimate of his character which cannot be said to concur with any previously recorded. As the title implies, my aim has not been to write a biography in the ordinary sense of the word : on matters which are authenticated and not in dispute I have not dwelt for long, whereas it has been necessary to deal at some length with questions on which the commentators' opinions are contrary to the evidence or at variance. My conclusions have been reached independently of the weight of critical opinion, and are based entirely on the best available evidence, which will be found reviewed throughout the book. The reader may or may not agree with all these conclusions, but he will at least be in possession of the facts, and will not be asked to accept anything on trust.

Much of this evidence has been unearthed from the Public Record Office and the MSS. Room of the British Museum, and now appears in print for the first time. Other important new material, shedding fresh light on certain aspects of Chesterfield's character, has been revealed in the course of the last fifty years, chiefly by the Royal Historical MSS. Commission. This, together with certain long-forgotten contemporaneous evidence, I have set out in some detail, since none of it has been discussed in any previous work on Chesterfield.

In support of the opinion expressed in these pages that Chesterfield has never been accorded his rightful place as an English essayist, I have added eleven of his essays, reprinted in each case from the original paper. Other reprints, particularly those in editions of Chesterfield's works, contain numerous inaccuracies.

I have enquired into the authenticity of all Chesterfield's

essays (see pp. 213–220) and endeavoured to prove that he was not the author of several ascribed to him by Horace Walpole, Mr. Walter Sichel, and other writers. The authenticity of much of his verse has been discussed by his biographers, but since little of it is of any literary value I have deemed further enquiry unnecessary.[1]

At the end of this book will be found a collection of twenty-seven personal letters of Chesterfield's, hitherto unpublished. Certain of these, as well as other letters quoted in the text, the originals of which are in the possession of the Earl of St. Germains, were kindly placed at my disposal by the courtesy of the Hon. Montague Eliot, to whom I am much indebted. To Chesterfield's correspondence with Sarah, Duchess of Marlborough, in the archives at Blenheim, I have been unable to obtain access.

Considerable pains have been taken to make this record of Chesterfield as accurate as possible. The MS. and proofs have both been most carefully revised by my friends J. M. Robertson and Eric Leadbitter, for whose invaluable help, extending over many months, I am more deeply grateful than it would become me here to express.

---

[1] It may, however, be worth mentioning that there are strong reasons for doubting whether Chesterfield would have written, still less allowed to get into circulation, the Epitaph on Queen Caroline which is ascribed to him by Mahon in his *History of England* (chap, xvii). Mahon gives no authority for his statement, and implies his unfamiliarity with the lines which, he says, " were circulated at the time, but which I have not been able to recover." They were found many years later in Colonel Towneley's MSS. (see Hist. MSS. Comm. vol. iv, Part i, p. 414) and reprinted by Lord Carnarvon at the end of the *Appendix to Chesterfield's Letters to his Godson* No other writer on Chesterfield refers to them.

CONTENTS

CHRONOLOGICAL TABLE

OF THE PRINCIPAL EVENTS IN CHESTERFIELD'S LIFE

1694.—September 22. Birth.

1712.—Enters Trinity Hall, Cambridge.

1715.—Appointed Gentleman of the Bedchamber to the Prince of Wales. Enters the House of Commons as M.P. for St. Germains.

1723.—Appointed Captain of the Guard.

1726.—Succeeds to the Earldom of Chesterfield on the
* death of his father, the third Earl.

1728.—April 23. Appointed Ambassador at the Hague.

1730.—June 18. Installed Knight of the Garter.
June 19. Appointed Lord Steward towards end of ten months' leave of absence.

1732.—Birth of his son.
Returns from the Hague, end of February.

1733.—April 13. Dismissed from office in consequence of his opposition to Walpole's Excise Bill. Enters Opposition.
September 5. Marries Melusina de Schulenberg.

1739.—Begins Series of *Letters to his Son*.

1742.—Fall of Walpole and formation of Carteret's Government. Chesterfield remains in Opposition.

1744.—December. On fall of Carteret is appointed Lord Lieutenant of Ireland and Ambassador to the Hague on Special Mission.

1745.—January 11. Arrives at the Hague.
May 20. Leaves the Hague.
August 20. Arrives in Ireland.

1746.—April 23. Leaves Ireland.
November. Resigns post of Lord Lieutenant and becomes Secretary of State.

1748.—February 6. Resigns Secretaryship of State.

1751.—Carries Reform of the Calendar.

1752.—Begins to suffer from deafness.

1755.—Practically retires from public life owing to deafness.
November 28. Birth of his godson and successor, Philip Stanhope.

1757.—Effects reconciliation and coalition between Newcastle and Pitt.

1761.—Begins Series of *Letters to his Godson*.

1768.—November 16. Death of his son.

1773.—March 24. Death.

I

ESSAYIST

THE extent of critical influence on broad movements in art must always remain a matter for speculation. Movements, Schools, Periods, Waves, come and go, rise and fall, subject to historical and other causes over which the critics have little or no control. Criticism at its worst may hinder, and at its best hasten the rejection of a bad or the acceptance of a good trend in art ; but, beyond this four-fold function, in the light of history criticism seems to have done little more, so far as broad movements are concerned. The *Quarterly's* attack on Keats, Ruskin's on Whistler, to take perhaps the two best-known instances, prove the impotence of accredited criticism to destroy wholesome values in art.

The effect of criticism upon individual writers is, however, not so limited in extent. Whereas a movement will eventually stand or fall according to the accepted canons of art, criticism of the individual is subject to personal prejudices outside the range of art, whose adverse effects may be as arbitrary and capricious as they are tenacious and far-reaching. No matter how exemplary the private life of a writer, how impeccable the doctrines he preaches, his works, if mediocre, will not survive. It would be unfortunate for our literary standards were it otherwise. It is equally unfortunate that a writer of surpassing merit may suffer neglect on account of a persistent critical attack upon his morals.

Probably no English writer has been more injured by this effect of adverse criticism than the Earl of Chesterfield. The *Letters to His Son* were published during the period of a moral reaction against the laxity of the preceding half-century, and, though too buoyant to be actually submerged, were carried out to sea on an angry wave of criticism. Johnson's unjust verdict, " They teach the morals of a whore and the manners of a dancing master," softened though it is by the more impartial remarks of

Boswell, will never be forgotten. The outcome of personal prejudice, it is one of those sayings which, despite a lack of truth, remain unfortunately memorable by reason of their terseness and vigour.

Johnson having given Chesterfield a bad name, lesser writers proceeded to hang him. The ephemeral fulminations of William Crawford, Thomas Hunter, and Jackson Pratt were followed by Cowper's powerful lines in the *Progress of Error*, where Chesterfield is thus apostrophized :

> " Thou polish'd and high-finish'd foe to truth,
> Grey-beard corrupter of our list'ning youth,
> To purge and skim away the filth of vice
> That, so refin'd, it might the more entice,
> Then pour it on the morals of thy son,
> To taint *his* heart, was worthy of *thine own* !
> Now, while the poison all high life invades,
> Write, if thou canst, one letter from the Shades."

For well over half a century attacks on Chesterfield persisted. To hold up one's hands at the moral deficiencies of a celebrity is an easy method of seeking credit, and even Dickens joined the chorus of execration by lampooning him as Sir John Chester in *Barnaby Rudge*. In 1870, however, Sainte-Beuve started a critical reaction in favour of Chesterfield, which was augmented by the publication twenty years later of the *Letters to his Godson and Successor*, a series similar in character to the earlier letters to his son. This publication, received favourably by Austin Dobson and other critics, gave rise to a revised estimate of Chesterfield by Churton Collins, which still remains the final authoritative verdict. In this admirable study Chesterfield at last appears in his true light, the following summary of his philosophy being as unimpeachable in substance as it is eloquent in manner :—

" The charm of Chesterfield lies in his sincerity and truthfulness, in his refined good sense, in his exquisite perception of the becoming, finding expression in seriousness most happily tempered by gaiety. Of no man could it be more truly said that he had cleared his mind of cant. A writer more absolutely devoid of pretentiousness or affectation cannot be found. Of moral and intellectual frippery he has nothing. Sophistry and paradox are his abhorrence. All he has written bears, indeed, the reflection of a character which is of all characters perhaps the rarest—' the character of one '—it was what Voltaire said of him— ' who had never been in any way either a charlatan or a dupe of charlatans.'[1] He is one of the very few writers who never wear a mask, and in whose accent no falsetto note can ever be detected. In his fearless intellectual honesty he reminds us of Swift, in his pellucid moral candour he reminds us of Montaigne. To contemplate life, not as it presents itself under the glamour or the gloom of illusion and prejudice, as it presents itself to the enthusiast or the cynic, but as it really is ; to regard ignorance as misfortune and vice as evil, but the false assumption of wisdom and virtue as something far worse ; to be or to strive to be what pride would have us seem, and to live worthily within the limits severally prescribed by nature and fortune—all this will the study of Chesterfield's philosophy tend to impress on us."[2]

In the light of Professor Collins's criticism, supplemented by that of Mr. C. Strachey in 1901, Johnson's epigram, Cowper's sonnet, " the unspeakable vulgarity and absurdity of Dickens's caricature and travesty " [3] are sufficiently exposed, and a further defence of Chesterfield's *Letters to his Son* becomes superfluous. One important point, however, may be mentioned. It has often been remarked of the *Letters* that the greater number attach more importance to manners than to morals, and accordingly suffer from lack of ideals. The same objection might be made with almost equal justice and irrelevance to a manual of instruction on golf ; for it must be remembered that the principal motive of the later letters was purely technical, namely to improve the manners of an honest young man who lacked outward grace and polish. The objects of the *Letters* are very clearly set out in that of November 3rd, 1749, which begins as follows :—

[1] " Votre philosophie n'a jamais été dérangée par des chimères, qui ont brouillé quelquefois des cervelles assez bonnes. Vous n'avez jamais été dans aucun genre, ni charlatan, ni dupe de charlatan, et c'est ce que je compte pour un mérite très-peu commun, qui contribue à l'ombre de félicité qu'on peut goûter dans cette courte vie."—Voltaire to Chesterfield, 24th October, 1771—Maty, *Chesterfield's Miscellaneous Works*. Vol. II, pp. 292, 294. (Each was then in his seventy-eighth year.)

[2] *Essays and Studies*, pp. 256, 257.

[3] *Ibid.* p. 200.

" DEAR BOY,

From the time that you have had life, it has been the principal and favourite object of mine to make you as perfect as the imperfections of human nature will allow : in this view I have grudged no pains nor expense in your education ; convinced that education, more than nature, is the cause of that great difference which we see in the characters of men. While you were a child I endeavoured to form your heart habitually to virtue and honour, before your understanding was capable of showing you their beauty and utility. Those principles, which you then got, like your grammar rules, only by rote, are now, I am persuaded, fixed and confirmed by reason. And indeed they are so plain and clear, that they require but a very moderate degree of understanding, either to comprehend or practise them.

" Lord Shaftesbury says, very prettily, that he would be virtuous for his own sake, though nobody were to know it ; as he would be clean for his own sake, though nobody were to see him. I have, therefore, since you have had the use of your reason, never written to you upon those subjects : they speak best for themselves ; and I should now just as soon think of warning you gravely not to fall into the dirt or the fire, as into dishonour or vice. This view of mine I consider as fully attained.

" My next object was sound and useful learning. My own care first, Mr. Harte's afterwards, and *of late* (I will own it to your praise) your own application, have more than answered my expectations in that particular ; and, I have reason to believe, will answer even my wishes. All that remains for me then to wish, to recommend, to inculcate, to order, and to insist upon, is Good-breeding ; without which, all your other qualifications will be lame, unadorned and, to a certain degree, unavailing. And here I fear, and have too much reason to believe, that you are greatly deficient. The remainder of this letter, therefore, shall be (and it will not be the last by a great many) upon that subject."[1]

It should be borne in mind that these letters were never intended for public perusal, but are and will always remain private personal documents to be read, if read fairly,

---

[1] Bradshaw, *Lord Chesterfield's Letters*, vol. I, p. 263.

in the light of the recipient's character, as the best letters are always written. Professor Collins asserts that " the literary fame of Chesterfield must rest on the letters to his son."[1] Nevertheless, a literary estimate of Chesterfield founded solely on his letters will be inadequate. It is hard to believe that the writer himself would not have preferred his literary fame to rest on what he wrote for the general public, and in particular his later contributions to the *World*.

This weekly periodical, though it had a large circulation during its four years' existence and was reprinted in book form more than once during the eighteenth century, has for many years remained in comparative obscurity. Its neglect, which is certainly not merited, is perhaps partially due to an unfortunate passage in Macaulay's essay on *Horace Walpole's Letters to Sir Horace Mann*. He is accusing Walpole (not unjustifiably) of allowing snobbery to affect his literary judgment, and instances the opinion expressed by him in a letter to Mann of October 6, 1753, that many of the earlier numbers of the *World* were by " our first writers." Macaulay then proceeds with more indignation than judgment to exclaim :—

" Who, then, were the first writers of England in the year 1753 ? Walpole has told us in a note. Our readers will probably guess that Hume, Fielding, Smollett, Richardson, Johnson, Warburton, Collins, Akenside, Gray, Dyer, Young, Warton, Mason, or some of those distinguished men, were in the list. Not one of them. Our first writers it seems, were Lord Chesterfield, Lord Bath, Mr. W. Whithed, Sir Charles Williams, Mr. Soame Jenyns, Mr. Cambridge, Mr. Coventry. Of these seven personages, Whithed was the lowest in station, but was the most accomplished tuft-hunter of his time. Coventry was of a noble family. The other five had among them two seats in the House of Lords, two seats in the House of Commons, three seats in the Privy Council, a baronetcy, a blue riband, a red riband, about a hundred thousand pounds a year, and not ten pages that are worth reading. The writings of Whithed, Cambridge, Coventry, and Lord Bath are forgotten. Soame Jenyns is remembered chiefly by Johnson's review of the foolish Essay on the Origin of Evil. Lord Chesterfield stands much lower in the estimation of posterity than he would have done if his letters had never been published."

[1] *Essays and Studies*, p. 230.

Of this last sentence Mr. C. Strachey aptly remarks that it " is a good example of that form of reasoning known as *muddying the waters*. But although it has no point in the argument of which it forms a part, it is interesting as an admission that the popular conception of Chesterfield —the clever and heartless dissembler, the odious apostle of profligacy—has been the result of inferences drawn from the contents of the *Letters*."[1] A recent authority[2] on eighteenth-century periodical literature says of Macaulay's judgment as a whole that it " is lacking in true historical perspective and is not a just summing up of the value of the *World* as an essay periodical."

Horace Walpole's remark taken quite literally is perhaps indefensible, but, as one critic[3] has pointed out, " It is clear that he was speaking with reference to the matter in hand. It did not occur to him that great historians and poets would be likely or suitable contributors to a series of light papers." Nor do we think it would have occurred to Macaulay in a less heated moment. Of the authors cited by him, eight never wrote for a periodical paper in their lives, and Richardson's contributions consist only of one paper for the *Rambler* (1750) and possibly one for the *True Briton* (1723). Hume was then absorbed in his History at Edinburgh, and Collins wrote nothing after 1749, owing to softening of the brain. Of those remaining, Fielding abandoned literature at the close of the *Covent Garden Journal* (November, 1752) two years before his death ; Akenside edited and contributed to Dodsley's *Museum* (1746), after the expiration of which he devoted himself almost entirely to the medical profession for the next ten years ; Joseph Warton, whose name Walpole probably omitted accidentally, wrote twenty-four numbers for the *Adventurer* and one for the *World* ; Thomas Warton, who was then only twenty-five, is said to have written for various papers, including the *World* ; Johnson was then mainly engaged in the preparation of his Dictionary and at that time would have been regarded by very few as one of our first writers.

It is our opinion that most of the essays written by Chesterfield, Jenyns, and Cambridge for the *World* are not

---

[1] Introduction to *Letters of the Earl of Chesterfield to his Son*, p. vii.
[2] G. S. Marr in *The Periodical Essayists of the Eighteenth Century* (1923) p. 143.
[3] L. B. Seeley in *Horace Walpole and His World*, p. 25.

inferior in literary merit to, and distinctly more readable than, those by the periodical writers in Macaulay's list ; an opinion which we feel it would be easier to maintain than the statement that these three writers have not written ten pages that are worth reading. Dr. G. S. Marr in a detailed survey of some hundred and fifty eighteenth-century periodicals ranks " one or two essays by Johnson, the inimitable creations of Goldsmith, his *Beau Tibbs* and his *Man in Black* ; and some of the *World* articles of Chesterfield and Walpole " with the *Spectator* as providing the most varied and pleasant reading in the whole of the eighteenth-century periodicals ; [1] an opinion to which we would heartily subscribe, with the substitution of the names of Soame Jenyns and R. O. Cambridge for that of Horace Walpole. It may be noticed that the same writer gives more praise to the essays by the two former than he does to those of Walpole in his subsequent account of the *World*,[2] of which he states (p. 142), that it " was eagerly read, exercised considerable influence at the time, and remains easily the best example of the *lighter* eighteenth-century periodical " ; and again (p. 149), " Taken as a whole, the *World* is one of the most readable of the eighteenth-century periodicals. Its lightness and crispness and wealth of ironical suggestion are features all its own. The *World* marks a distinct advance towards our modern magazines, and the rank of its main contributors, their style and treatment, all unite to give the *World* a unique place in this progression of periodical literature."

As stated by its editor, Edward Moore, in the first number, the design of the *World* was " to ridicule with novelty and good humour the fashions, follies, vices and absurdities of that part of the human species which calls itself the WORLD, and to trace it through all its business, pleasures and amusements." Here, then, is for Chesterfield a medium at once broader and more congenial than that of instructor. He is no longer restricted by the motives to which the letters to his son and godson so conscientiously adhere. Admonition gives place to entertainment, technical instruction to general charm. The ever-present shadow of " My dear friend "—who must have been a dull dog at his best—disappears, and the writer emerges in his true brilliance, exhibiting at times an ebullition of spirit by

[1] *The Periodical Essayists of the Eighteenth Century*, p. 31.
[2] *Ibid.* pp. 141–149.

which the reader is transported, as it were, to his radiant mood, and enjoys in sympathy what must have been the thrill of inspiration.

For the most part the didactic manner is abandoned, though it appears conspicuously in the essay on Civility and Good-breeding,[1] which is an epitome of much that Chesterfield was at such pains to teach his son. The phraseology is, in fact, at times identical with that of the *Letters*.

To give one short example :

" Courts are unquestionably the seats of good-breeding ; and must necessarily be so ; otherwise they would be the seats of violence and desolation."—*The World*.[2]

" Courts are unquestionably the seats of politeness and good-breeding ; were they not so, they would be the seats of slaughter and desolation."—Letter to his son.[3]

The fact that this latter sentence was written rather more than six years before the former tells how clearly the system of manners must have been engraved in Chesterfield's mind.

This essay is in one sense the least typical of Chesterfield's contributions to the *World*, savouring as it does more of the magisterial style of the *Letters*. In order that so much ground might be covered in the compass of a short paper its form is throughout almost epigrammatic, and it is perhaps for this reason that it was written unwillingly,[4] for Chesterfield had a dislike for and distrust of epigrams *per se*. When sending his son a list of " Maxims or Observations on Men and Things," he is careful to state ; " I am no system-monger ; and, instead of giving way to my imagination, I have only consulted my memory ; and my conclusions are all drawn from facts, not from fancy. Most maxim-mongers have preferred the prettiness to the justness of a thought, and the turn to the truth ; but I have refused myself to everything that my own experience did not justify and confirm."[5]

It may be remembered how in *De Profundis* Oscar Wilde

[1] See p. 247 *post*.
[2] October 30, 1755. See p. 248 *post*.
[3] August 21, 1749, Bradshaw, vol. II, pp. 232, 233.
[4] See p. 247 n. *post*.
[5] Letter of January 15, 1753, Bradshaw, vol. II, p. 569.

is tempted by a Tennysonian alliteration to describe
himself as a " lord of language," a phrase which will serve
as well as some others of his own creation to indicate
that in reality language was his lord. But to no writer
could this same title be applied with more justice than to
Chesterfield, whose handling of words is so apt that his style
is almost epigrammatic in its natural flow, and whose
sincerity was yet so intense that the most tempting turn of
a sentence would not cause him to deviate one hair's breadth
from the truth.

It may be suggested, in passing, that it was probably
this very passion for sincerity that provoked the advice
to his son which proved so disastrous to the father's
reputation. Times and customs being what they were,
did he not feel obliged to abandon as impracticable the
thought that his son would lead a chaste life abroad ? To
shirk the question would have been easy, excusable, and
insincere. Once the hypothesis was accepted, Chesterfield's aversion from all forms of grossness, augmented in
this particular case by the well-founded fear of physical
danger, naturally led him to guide his son into the safer,
if no less immoral, paths of " gallantry." Analogous
advice on the subjects of gambling and drinking occurs
constantly in the Letters. Unpleasant, worldly, unpaternal,
unideal, certainly ; but let the moralist ask himself these
questions. In rerum natura, was the hypothesis a fair one ?
If so, was the advice thereupon unjustifiable ? We have no
wish to discuss the ethics of this question : the reader must
form his own opinion.[1]

It is possible that Chesterfield would have been treated
more leniently by the moralists and their followers had he
dealt less severely with the faults of his own countrymen,
living as he did in one of those periods when our country
had become unduly self-conscious of its nationality and
intolerant of criticism from within. While other writers
in the World contented themselves with ridiculing current
foibles and follies, Chesterfield would occasionally go further
and expose national faults and vices. The Englishman's
insularity is treated admirably in No. 29, where a father

---

[1] Chesterfield has been defended at length on this point by Abraham
Hayward in Edinburgh Review, September, 1845, vol. LXXXII, p. 439 ;
Churton Collins in Essays and Studies, pp. 221–23 ; Charles Strachey,
Introduction to Chesterfield's Letters to His Son, pp. lxv, lxix–lxxv ;
W. H. Craig, Life of Lord Chesterfield, pp. 286–292.

discusses the unprofitable use his son is making of the " grand tour," and quotes a letter he has received from him at Rome, beginning :

" In the six weeks that I passed at Florence, and the week I stayed at Genoa, I never had time to write to you, being wholly taken up with seeing things, of which the most remarkable is the steeple of Pisa : it is the oddest thing I ever saw in my life ; it stands all awry ; I wonder it does not tumble down."

The remainder of the letter describes the writer's life in Rome, spent entirely with his English friends, " nine or ten as smart bucks as any in England . . . We none of us speak Italian, and none of those signors speak English ; which shows what sort of fellows they are," and petitions for leave to return, " as if I were not to live and die in Old England, and as if good English acquaintance would not be much more useful to me than outlandish ones."

Snobbery will always be a target for satire, but it has seldom been treated more effectively than by Chesterfield in No. 114 of the *World*.[1] The sentiments expressed in that essay occur frequently in his letters to son and godson, and in his will he gives two years' wages to his servants, " whom I consider as unfortunate friends, my equals by nature, and my inferiors only by the difference of our fortunes."

Chesterfield's contempt for pride of birth found expression in more than one sly dig at the low intellectual level of the nobility, not only in his essays, but even in the House of Lords itself. In his speech against the Bill for the licensing and regulation of theatres he says :—" Wit, my Lords, is a sort of property ; it is the property of those who have it, and too often the only property they have to depend on. It is indeed but a precarious dependence. *Thank God! we, my Lords, have a dependence of another kind ; we have a much less precarious support, and therefore cannot feel the inconveniences of the Bill now before us ;* but it is our duty to encourage and protect wit, whosoever's property it may be."[2]

[1] See p. 239 *post*.
[2] Maty, vol. I. *Miscellaneous Pieces*, XLVI, p. 239. *Cf.* also : " I make no doubt but that there are potentially, if I may use that pedantic word, many Bacons, Lockes, Newtons, Cæsars, Cromwells and Marlboroughs, at the plough-tail, behind counters, and perhaps even among the nobility." —*World*, No. 120 (see pp. 243, 244 *post*).

It is a confession that might easily have come from the candid mouth of Lord Mountararat in *Iolanthe*. Here is another shaft of irony directed at the upper classes.

" The middling class of people in this country, though generally straining to imitate their betters, have not yet shaken off the prejudices of their education ; very many of them still believe in a Supreme Being, in a future state of rewards and punishments, and retain some coarse, home-spun notions of moral good and evil. The rational system of materialism has not yet reached them ; and in my opinion, it may be full as well it never should ; for as I am not of levelling principles, I am for preserving a due subordination from inferiors to superiors, which an equality of profligacy must totally destroy."[1]

It would be a mistake, however, to assume from these attacks on the Philistinism then prevailing that Chesterfield had not his country's interests very closely at heart. In order to give a reason for his unpopularity Professor Collins builds up a powerful case in support of the theory that " Chesterfield is, of all English writers, if we except Horace Walpole, the most essentially un-English."[2] The truth of this theory is, however, more apparent than real. Chesterfield in a political capacity showed an unselfish devotion that was in his day surpassed by no one. With the exception of Pitt he was perhaps the only politician —certainly the only well-known one—who can be said to have earned the name of *Patriot*, a party appellation which, soon after Walpole's fall, became deservedly a term of derision. But Chesterfield's patriotism was not of the insular jingoistic type, manifesting itself in a wilful refusal to recognize the faults, or a vulgar glorying in the perfections of one's country : it was of that higher order whereby consciousness of imperfections promotes not so much an impulse to cast them into oblivion as a desire to effect a remedy by their exposure ; to which the cynic might reply, not without some truth, that since this type of patriotism is itself essentially un-English the theory is merely given so much the more support. The conclusion at which Professor Collins arrives is that " The Philistines have had their revenge. The injustice of which he was un-

[1] *World*, No. 189 (see p. 258 *post*).
[2] *Essays and Studies*, p. 234.

doubtedly guilty in not sufficiently recognizing their robust virtues as well as their deficiencies, they have repaid by magnifying his foibles into vices and his vices into crimes." [1]

This result it would be difficult to dispute, though Chesterfield was probably as fully conscious of his country's virtues as of its deficiencies. That he devoted little attention in his writings to the former was simply because he felt it his duty to expose the latter. As a public writer, in fact, his attitude towards his country, though less rigorously defined, was identical with that towards his son as expressed in the letter quoted above. [2]

The main principles of virtue are taken for granted. His objects are to fill up the gaps, to remedy the imperfections, to adorn with exterior graces the structure of which he is convinced the foundation is essentially sound. But because, in his efforts to achieve these objects, he frequently cites the French as his model, it does not follow, as Professor Collins asserts, that " in the French character and temper he saw the foundation of human perfection." [3] Rather was it the coping-stone of French manners that he endeavoured to place upon an English foundation of character; or, as he says in a letter to Madame de Monconseil about his son, " Mon idée est de réunir en sa personne ce que jusqu'ici je n'ai jamais trouvé en la même personne ; je veux dire, ce qu'il y a de meilleur des deux nations."[4] And again in the *World*, No. 148,[5] "I am sorry to be obliged to confess that my native country is not perhaps the seat of the most perfect good-breeding, though I really believe that it yields to none in hearty and sincere civility, as far as civility is (and to a certain degree it is) an inferior moral duty of doing as one would be done by. If France exceeds us in that particular, the incomparable author of *L'Esprit des Loix* accounts for it very impartially, and I believe very truly, ' If my countrymen,' says he, ' are the best-bred people in the world, it is only because they are the vainest.' "

Chesterfield was continually ridiculing the English habit of aping French manners and customs, a habit to which he objected partly on economic grounds. The following passages are scarcely the sentiments of one who in the

[1] *Essays and Studies*, p. 236.
[2] P. 4 *ante*.
[3] *Essays and Studies*, p. 234.
[4] June 24, 1745. Bradshaw, vol. II, p. 787.
[5] See p. 249 *post*.

opinion of Professor Collins was " in genius, in sympathy, in culture far more French than English."[1]

" If it be so genteel to copy the French, even in their weaknesses, I should humbly hope it might be thought still more so to imitate them where they really deserve imitation, which is, in preferring every thing of their own to every thing of other people's. A Frenchman, who happened to be in England, at the time of the last total eclipse of the sun, assured the people whom he saw looking at it with attention that it was not to be compared to a French eclipse : would some of our fine women emulate that spirit, and assert, as they might do with much more truth, that the foreign manufactures are not to be compared to the English, such a declaration would be worth two or three hundred thousand pounds a year to the kingdom, and operate more effectually than all the laws made for that purpose."[2]

" If a man would be well received in good company, he must eat, though with reluctance, according to the laws of some eminent glutton at Paris, promulgated here by the last-imported French cook, wishing all the while within himself that he durst avow his natural taste, for good native beef and pudding." [3]

The subject is treated at some length in No. 93 of *Common Sense*,[4] the following extract from which indicates broadly Chesterfield's sentiments with regard to the French.

" I behold with indignation the sturdy conquerors of France shrunk and dwindled into the imperfect mimics, or ridiculous *caricaturas*, of all its levity. The *travesty* is universal ; poor England produces nothing fit to eat, or drink, or wear. Our clothes, our furniture, nay, our food too, all is to come from France, and I am credibly informed that a poulterer at Calais now actually supplies our polite tables with half their provisions.

[1] *Essays and Studies*, p. 234. Craig, on the other hand, states (p. 95, n. 1) that " His lordship's *dislike of France* peeps out frequently in his letters and his miscellaneous works " ; but this extreme would be as difficult to defend as that of Professor Collins.
[2] *Common Sense*, No. 4, February 26, 1737.
[3] *Common Sense*, No. 54, February 11, 1738. See p. 222 *post*.
[4] November 11, 1738. See p. 228 *post*.

" I do not mean to undervalue the French ; I know their merit ; they are a cheerful, industrious, ingenious, polite people, and have many things in which I wish we did imitate them. But, like true mimics, we only ape their imperfections, and awkwardly copy those parts, which all reasonable Frenchmen themselves contemn in the originals."

There are countless little touches in Chesterfield's essays which go to prove that the satire they contain is a medium of instruction rather than an object in itself. It is never of a malicious order, and often, after the faults have been exposed, a guiding hand appears to point the better way. Thus, a series of pungent essays on the subject of " soaking " ends with the following description of his friend and fellow-contributor to the *World*, Richard Owen Cambridge :

" Cantabrigius drinks nothing but water, and rides more miles in a year than the keenest sportsman, and with almost equal velocity. The former keeps his head clear, the latter his body in health. It is not from himself that he runs, but to his acquaintance, a synonymous term for his friends. Internally safe, he seeks no sanctuary from himself, no intoxication for his mind. His penetration makes him discover and divert himself with the follies of mankind, which his wit enables him to expose with the truest ridicule, though always without personal offence. Cheerful abroad, because happy at home ; and thus happy, because virtuous."[1]

An essay on affectation in women concludes in an almost Addisonian strain with a companion picture of ideal womanhood, and goes far towards modifying the charge of crude misogyny commonly preferred against Chesterfield.

" How amiable may a woman be, what a comfort and delight to her acquaintance, her friends, her relations, her lover, or her husband, in keeping strictly within her character ! She adorns all female virtues with native female softness. Women, while untainted by affectation, have a natural cheerfulness of mind, tenderness and benignity of heart, which justly endears them to us, either to animate our joys or soothe our sorrows ; but how are they changed, and how shocking do they become, when the rage of

[1] *World*, No. 92.   October 3, 1754.

ambition, or the pride of learning, agitates and swells those breasts, where only love, friendship, and tender care should dwell !

" Let Flavia [1] be their model, who, though she could support any character, assumes none. Never misled by fancy or vanity, but guided singly by reason, whatever she says or does is the manifest result of a happy nature and a good understanding. Though she knows whatever women ought, and, it may be, more than they are required to know, she conceals the superiority she has with as much care as others take to display the superiority they have not. She conforms herself to the turn of the company she is in, but in a way of rather avoiding to be distanced, than desiring to take the lead. Are they merry, she is cheerful ; are they grave, she is serious ; are they absurd, she is silent. Though she thinks and speaks as a man would do, she effeminates, if I may use the expression, whatever she says, and gives all the graces of her own sex to the strength of ours ; she is well-bred without the troublesome ceremonies and frivolous forms of those who only affect to be so. As her good breeding proceeds jointly from good nature and good sense, the former inclines her to oblige, and the latter shows her the easiest and best way of doing it. Woman's beauty, like men's wit, is generally fatal to the owners, unless directed by a judgement which seldom accompanies a great degree of either : [2] her beauty seems but the proper and decent lodging for such a mind ; she knows the true value of it, and far from thinking that it authorizes impertinence and coquetry, it redoubles her care to avoid those errors that are its usual attendants. Thus she not only unites in herself all the advantages of body and mind, but even reconciles contradictions in others; for she is loved and esteemed, though envied by all."[3]

If the ideal of womanhood here expressed denies to

[1] "Lady Francis Shirley "—Horace Walpole's MS. note on this passage in Maty, vol. I, *Miscellaneous Pieces*, p. 71. We think, however, that Horace Walpole was mistaken (as in several other of his notes), and that if Chesterfield had any living person in mind it was Lady Hervey (the celebrated Molly Lepel). See a description of her in a letter to his son of October 22, 1750, conforming to the above in many respects ; notably : " She has all the reading that a woman should have ; and more than any woman need have ; for she understands Latin perfectly well, though she wisely conceals it."—Bradshaw, vol. I, p 361.

[2] *Cf.* " A wise man will live at least as much within his wit as within his income."—Chesterfield to his Godson. See p. 183 *post.*

[3] *Common Sense*, No. 32. September 10, 1737.

the weaker sex certain attributes which at the present day it is universally admitted to possess, is the omission to be regarded as a serious blemish in Chesterfield's character ? We suggest that the contemporary readers of *Common Sense* would regard the ideal as a high one, and lacking nothing. Chesterfield has been too frequently judged by modern standards. What faults he had were the faults of his day, and to that extent deserve palliation. Though his vast historical knowledge enabled him to see into the future of politics, to make, for example, a remarkable prediction of the French Revolution in a letter to his son dated December 25, 1753, he cannot be described as a man ahead of his time. It would in any case have required more than human prescience for an eighteenth-century writer to foresee the growth of the Woman's Movement. But Chesterfield was too closely interested in life as he found it, to be concerned with speculations about the future. He portrayed life as it really was, and it is in the observation of human nature that he excels. The weapon of satire is then laid aside, and an acute analysis reveals man's fallacies and follies under a light so strong and clear that after a time we become conscious less of the object revealed than of the light itself ; of the force of Truth as an absolute rather than a medium. Fragmentary quotations, in which of necessity the persistence of his analysis cannot appear, do not suffice to illustrate this effect ; but it can hardly fail to be recognized in Nos. 120 and 196 of the *World*.[1]

" Plain English," in his own phrase, was Chesterfield's medium for the presentment of his common-sense and truth, and it was the aptest medium he could have chosen ; nay more, in view of the attainment of his object, the only medium ; for truth in its purest form can only be presented in the clearest light, and his style is freer from impurities and excrescences than any other English writer's. He is chary of employing any figure of speech except occasional irony. Metaphors are rare in his writings : similes almost non-existent. So clear is his meaning that their use would be pleonastic, and pleonasm he avoids as he would hyperbole. His style is, in fact, almost entirely without adornment : its beauty is the beauty of nakedness, and, while it scarcely admits of analysis, is as difficult to

[1] See pp. 243 and 262 *post.*

imitate as it would be impossible to travesty. It is the product of art, as all style must be, but it is art not so much revealed as transcended.

Though Chesterfield always wrote to his son from a definite personal standpoint—not, let it be remembered, the paternal one, but, to use his own words, " as a friend "—in his essays it is only on the rarest occasions that the personal element peeps through the veil, and then only to express its diffidence. Take, for example, the following sentence :—

" If I loved to jingle, I would say that human nature has always been invariably the same, though always varying ; that is, the same in substance, but varying in forms and modes, from many concurrent causes, of which perhaps we know but few."[1]

Paradox he eschews, as though it were a dangerous weapon, harmful to the purest truth : hence his exposure of the artifice while employing it, and the implied suggestion that the truth of what he writes is too sacred to be given the appearance of cleverness.

Effective as his style invariably is, nothing that he wrote was ever written for effect. In an age when Latin quotations besprinkled the pages of every educated writer, he seldom makes use of them in his essays ; while Greek he only quotes with a blush, as " The Greeks (to display my learning) said ἱματιον ἀνηρ, or, the dress shows the man."[2] Or " Cicero in his offices makes use of the word *decorum* . . . to express what he tells us the Greeks signified by the word (I will not shock the eyes of my polite readers with Greek types) ' *to prepon.* ' "[3]

It is as though Chesterfield were not satisfied with his own natural view of the truth ; but, feeling that its presentation in anything but a purely objective form might rouse suspicion in the mind of the reader, he rigorously suppresses every trace of the personal. One can almost hear him saying, " I must not let the reader think that this passage was written to exhibit my cleverness." Or, " This alliteration may suggest that sense has been sacrificed to sound. It must be altered." It is hard to

[1] *World*, No. 197, see p. 268 *post*.
[2] *Common Sense*, No. 4.
[3] *World*, No. 189, see p. 257 *post*.

C

conceive a more severe censorship of style. And the amazing thing is that what is left is style at one of its highest pinnacles : not Pope's

> " True wit is Nature to advantage dressed ;
>   What oft was thought ; but ne'er so well expressed " :

but something transcending wit, and far greater in its purity and simplicity.

In present-day writings Truth seldom appears undisguised. Perhaps we have become too sensitive for it to be revealed to us in its naked purity, and prefer to see glimpses of its form through the veil of Chesterton's paradox or Shaw's *épatement*. Or perhaps these writers have done us an injustice by assuming that they could not gain our ear except by expounding Truth in a fanciful strain. Be that as it may, assuming that their motive in writing is to reveal the truth to us, the question is how far have they actually succeeded ? Are our final thoughts those of unalloyed conviction, or are we searching instinctively (though perhaps sometimes quite unnecessarily) for a grain of salt, because—well, because we feel : " This is Chesterton," or " This is Shaw " ? The corresponding effect after reading Chesterfield is simply " This is Truth." His style is too simple, too pure to give rise to any subsequent sense of destructive suspicion, and the substance of what he writes is itself such " plain common sense " that to question its truth never occurs to the reader.

The ideal of " plain common sense " may not be perhaps the highest, but it is one which is attained by him as few ideals ever have been attained in literature. He does not press it beyond its natural limitations.

> " I look upon common sense to be to the mind what conscience is to the heart, the faithful and constant monitor of what is right or wrong. And I am convinced that no man commits either a crime or a folly, but against the manifest and sensible representations of the one or the other." [1]

He is, however, conscious of its rarity in practice.

> " I take common sense, like common honesty, rather to

[1] *Common Sense*, No. 31. September 3, 1737.

be called common, because it should be so, than because it
is so. It is rather that rule, by which men judge of other
people's actions, than direct their own ; the plain result
of right reason, admitted by all, and practised by few." [1]

There are some writers whose anxiety to be impartial
is such that their work, overburdened with conscientious
qualifications, amounts to little more than a negative
conflict between the tedious opponents of a dual personality. The truth of what Chesterfield preaches is,
however, so manifest in its presentation that the suggestion
of partiality never arises. Understatement is as odious
to him as overstatement, and his dicta are presented not
with the persuasiveness of an advocate, but with the
confidence of a judge. In his non-political essays it is
never felt that he is making out a case : he is merely stating
one, but stating it so fairly and truthfully that he can
afford to be forcible without rousing the suspicion of
advocacy. The few essays, however, in which he does take
a definite side, testify, as clearly as do his speeches in the
House of Lords, to his power of controversy on occasion.
In an attack on the ministry formed after Walpole's resignation in 1742, the broadsword is substituted for the rapier,
and used with most telling effect. Chesterfield had spent
the best years of his life in opposition to Walpole, and with
Carteret had done almost as much in the Lords as Pulteney
and Pitt in the Commons to effect the Prime Minister's fall.
It is not difficult then to imagine his mortification when the
Pelhams, after secret negotiations with his two colleagues,
received them into their party, with the result that, though
Walpole was ruined, his policy persisted, against, moreover,
a broken opposition. Though, for the most part, this
attack is maintained in a spirit of dignified if scathing
restraint, indignation breaks through even Chesterfield's
sense of decorum in this picture of the turncoat Carteret :—

" A man who, when in the opposition, even his sincerity
could never beget confidence, nor his abilities esteem ;
whose learning is unrewarded with knowledge, and his
experience with wisdom ; discovering a haughtiness of
demeanour, without any dignity of character ; and possessing the lust of ambition and avarice, without knowing the
right use of power and riches. His understanding blinded

[1] *Common Sense*, No. 1. February 5, 1737.

by his passions, his passions directed by his prejudices, and his prejudices ever hurrying into presumption; impatient even of an equal, yet ever requiring the correction of a superior. Right as to general maxims, but wrong in the application; and therefore so intoxicated by the prospect of success, that he never is cool enough to concert the proper measures to attain it." [1]

Severe as these strictures are—and they are less violent than the contemporaneous diatribes of Pitt against the same statesman—the verdict of history offers little towards their qualification. Certain points it is difficult to accept—notably " the lust of avarice " for, in Chesterfield's own words, Carteret " had a great contempt for money " [2] but, broadly speaking, Chesterfield's resentment, which was in no degree personal, but due to a genuine concern for the safety of his country, has not rendered the portrait inaccurate. It is probably not less true to life than the more softened judgments passed by himself and Pitt after Carteret's death.[3] As a specimen of concise, pungent English prose it would be hard to find its superior, containing as it does all the force of rhetoric without any of its weakening attributes. A sonority of effect is obtained simply by threading abstract substantives on participles, each one of these substantives the more powerful for being bereft of epithet. By reason of their multifarious endings, abstract nouns form perhaps the richest instrument in the orchestra of our language, and few, if any, English writers have handled them with the dexterity of Chesterfield.

Let it be remembered, however, that this portrait of Carteret is not typical of Chesterfield as a writer. It is the voice of the statesman thundering in the House of Lords, rather than of the student of human nature in his library at Blackheath, whither ill-health and deafness caused him to retire from public life in 1752. Though, as Mr. Frederic Harrison observes, " it was a cruel chance that this able

---

[1] *Old England*, No. 1.   February 5, 1743.   This passage which we have transcribed from the original paper has been more often quoted than anything Chesterfield ever wrote.   It may, then, be worth mentioning that in Maty's transcription, upon which all subsequent commentators have relied, the first sentence ends thus: " possessing the lust of avarice, without knowing the right use of power and riches."   The omission of the words " *ambition and* " before " avarice," besides disturbing the perfect balance of the sentence, renders the antithesis incomplete.

[2] *Character of Lord Granville* by Chesterfield. Bradshaw, vol. III, p. 1418.

[3] See article on Carteret in the *Dictionary of National Biography*.

and honest man was permanently debarred from office by incurable deafness,[1]" it is by reason of this very chance that the best of Chesterfield's essays came to be written. And the cruelty of the chance is softened by the reflection that these treasures, neglected though they be, are perhaps of more value to us to-day than would be the fruits of his work had he served in office under Pitt. Chesterfield reaches his highest standard in his contributions to the *World*, which were written while he was living in semi-retirement, deprived by deafness of the society which he used to adorn. Why they are not more in number is explained to a certain extent by him in the following letter to Dayrolles :—

" You fine gentlemen, who have never committed the sin or the folly of scribbling, think that all those who have, can do it again whenever they please, but you are much mistaken : the pen has not only its movements, but its hours, its days of impotence, and is no more obedient to the will, than other things have been since the fall. Unsuccessful and ineffectual attempts are in both cases alike disagreeable and disgraceful. It is true, I have nothing else to do but to write, and for that very reason perhaps I should do it worse than ever ; what was formerly an act of choice, is now become the refuge of necessity. I used to snatch up the pen with momentary raptures, because by choice, but now I am married to it. . . . Though I keep up a certain equality of spirits, better I believe than most people would do in my unfortunate situation, yet you must not suppose that I have ever that flow of active spirits which is so necessary to enable one to do anything well. Besides, as the pride of the human heart extends itself beyond the short span of our lives, all people are anxious and jealous, authors perhaps more so than any others, of what will be said of them, at a time when they cannot know, and therefore ought not reasonably to care for, either. Notwithstanding all these difficulties, I will confess to you that I often scribble, but at the same time protest to you that I almost as often burn. I judge myself as impartially, and I hope more severely than I do others ; and upon an appeal from myself to myself, I frequently condemn the next day, what I had approved and applauded the former. What will finally come of all this I do not

[1] *Chatham* p. 45.

know ; nothing, I am sure, that shall appear while I am alive, except by chance some short trifling essays, like the *Spectator's*, upon some new folly or absurdity that may happen to strike me, as I have now and then helped Mr. Fitz-Adam in his weekly paper called the *World*."[1]

The self-censorship revealed here does not seem to accord with Maty's statement that these essays were all written " offhand, without any rasure or interlineation."[2] That Chesterfield's opinion of their trifling quality was due to false modesty is improbable ; and it must be admitted that with one exception (that on " Men of Honour and Gentlemen ")[3] the five contributions he had made to the *World* at the time this letter was written are not of any particular value. As he himself indicates, they are of a topical nature, and it is in the more general subjects that he excels. The essays on Birth and Descent ; Affectation ; Civility and Good Breeding ; Fashion ; Decorum ; Passion ; and The Supposed Degeneracy of Human Nature are undoubtedly his best, and with one other topical subject comprise his last eight contributions to the *World*. It is a thousand pities that the paper should have ceased to exist at the very time when Chesterfield, aged sixty-two, was at the height of his achievement as an essayist. Nor was there any successor to the *World* before Chesterfield's death, except Johnson's *Idler*, to which for obvious reasons Chesterfield could not contribute.

It is unnecessary to dwell for long on what history has rendered Chesterfield's most celebrated contribution to the *World*, that is his puff of Johnson's *Dictionary*,[4] which appeared shortly before its publication, and the famous letter from Johnson which it provoked. The main facts of the story are set forth by Boswell, though in a characteristically partial manner. A fuller and more truthful account can be found in Mr. Charles Strachey's Introduction to *Chesterfield's Letters to his Son*[5] beginning with the following personal apology :—

[1] January 1, 1754. Bradshaw, vol. III, pp. 1082–83. Fitz-Adam was the *nom de guerre* of the editor, Edward Moore.
[2] See p. 247 n. *post*.
[3] See p. 233 *post*.
[4] Nos. 100 and 101, November 28 and December 5, 1754.
[5] Pp. lix–lxiv, founded on Lord Brougham's article in the *Quarterly Review*, September, 1845. Brougham's account is an elaboration of Croker's defence of Chesterfield that appeared in his edition of Boswell's *Life of Johnson*.

" It cannot be doubted that in their famous encounter Johnson was in the wrong. This has already been demonstrated so clearly[1] that it seems rather like flogging dead horses or bursting open open doors to go into the question at all. But as popular beliefs die hard, and as Boswell's *Life of Johnson* has a thousand readers to the commentators' poor ten, the commentators must try by reiteration to make up for their inability to secure successive generations of readers."

Mr. Strachey concludes with this apology for Johnson :—

" The result of the whole matter may be stated thus : Chesterfield really did nothing to justify Johnson's famous letter, but that letter is in itself such an excellent piece of work that we are not disposed to inquire too closely into its origin. The controversy—if so it may be called—is rescued from insignificance by the letter, and our admiration for Johnson is only increased by the skilful manner in which he has contrived to come out of the affair with all the *literary* honours on his side."

It is perhaps invidious to comment on a criticism which is manifestly intended not to be taken quite seriously, but it seems rather unseemly to suggest that Johnson should be admired for a piece of intellectual impertinence and humbug, which has had, moreover, the effect of irretrievably damaging an honest man's reputation. Johnson's letter undoubtedly falls into that category of literature where style is so closely wedded to substance that the two must stand or fall together. Irrespective of the underlying facts, it is natural to assume, as Sir E. Gosse does, that unusual simplicity of style betokens intense sincerity of feeling.[2] But when we have enquired into the origin of the letter ; when we recognize how unjustifiable it all was ;

---

[1] For example in the *Quarterly Review* (September, 1845) and in Mr. Ernst's *Life of Chesterfield.* (Strachey's note.)

[2] " The author is singularly moved ; his English, though always stately and formal, is lifted out of the sesquipedalian affectation of magnificence which has amused the world so much, and which was beyond question a serious fault of Johnson's style . . . In the letter to Chesterfield he is simple, terse, and thrilling, and, as the occasion was a private one, we may take it that in the extraordinary fire and pungency of the sentences we have something like a specimen of that marvellous power in conversation which made Johnson the wonder of his age."—*A History of Eighteenth-Century Literature*, p. 289.

when we know that it contained a deliberate accusation against Chesterfield, the untruth of which Johnson, on his own subsequent admission, was conscious of at the time he penned it ; do not the simple periods (themselves so untypical of Johnson) strike a falsetto note ? If the letter is not heartfelt it is not anything—certainly not " an excellent piece of work." As for " the skilful manner in which Johnson contrived to come out of the affair," there was nothing to come out of, no controversy at all, since Chesterfield declined to join issue. The only possible skill which can be attributed to Johnson, apart from the plausibility of the letter itself, lay in his accurate surmise that Chesterfield would be too proud to demean himself by pointing out the falsity of the charges it contained. Perhaps it is as well to give Boswell's account of Chesterfield's conduct.

" That Lord Chesterfield must have been mortified by the lofty contempt, and polite, yet keen, satire with which Johnson exhibited him to himself in this letter, it is impossible to doubt.   He, however, with that glossy duplicity which was his constant study, affected to be quite unconcerned. . . . Dodsley . . . told Dr. Adams that Lord Chesterfield had shown him the letter.   ' I should have imagined,' replied Dr. Adams, ' that Lord Chesterfield would have concealed it.'   ' Poh ! ' said Dodsley, ' do you think a letter from Johnson could hurt Lord Chesterfield ? Not at all, sir. It lay upon his table, where anybody might see it. He read it to me ; said, " this man has great powers," pointed out the severest passages, and observed how well they were expressed.'   This air of indifference, which imposed upon the worthy Dodsley, was certainly nothing but a specimen of that dissimulation which Lord Chesterfield inculcated as one of the most essential lessons for the conduct of life."

It surely requires the blind partiality of a Boswell to regard such conduct as consistent with an uneasy conscience ; or, as Mr. Strachey puts it, " I do not think Boswell will find many readers to agree with him. Chesterfield's behaviour was altogether in accordance with his matter-of-fact, critical, and almost exasperatingly serene temperament."[1]

[1] In a letter to the *Morning Post* of March 5, 1924, the Hon. Stephen

There are certain characters both in history and in fiction whom we love almost as much for their faults as for their virtues, and Johnson is as certainly one of these as Chesterfield assuredly is not. Until we encounter Chesterfield as a pathetic figure in old age we find it difficult to extend to him the sympathy that Johnson's personality extracts from us so readily. We can tolerate most things that Johnson does wrong, because he is Johnson ; but while few would disagree with Mr. Strachey's dictum that " he undoubtedly surpassed Lord Chesterfield in greatness of soul as much as in bigness of body ", there is little doubt which of the two exhibited the greater soul in this unfortunate affair. Johnson was too human not to indulge at times in spite and vindictiveness ; too impulsive always to consider whether the thoughts that sprang from his over-fertile mind were either true or fair, before he uttered them. Chesterfield was too impersonal for any form of malice to enter his nature at all ;[1] had far too great an abstract love for honour and justice ever to allow an uncalculated statement, still less an untruth, to escape the censorship of his lips or pen.[2] An impartial analysis of the two characters as ultimately formed will reveal but little difference between them, in spite of a disparity of natural temperament.[3] The reason is that while Johnson was indifferent to self-control, it was to Chesterfield his religion. The character of Johnson underwent but little change from youth onwards : Chesterfield's life from early manhood consisted of a curiously self-detached, deliberate, self-critical process of character-formation. This idea of self-influence he endeavoured to implant in his son's mind, and we believe that it was only the consciousness of its effect on his own character that led him, in the face of manifest

Coleridge puts forward the tentative suggestion that Chesterfield's silence was due to the fact that he never actually received Johnson's letter. The writer points out in the course of a somewhat lengthy argument that there is no first-hand evidence that the letter was ever sent to Chesterfield. For our part we feel it impossible to regard Boswell's story as a pure invention on the part of himself, Adams, or Dodsley which is the only other alternative.

[1] " Hatred, jealousy, or envy make most people attentive to discover the least defects of those they do not love ; they rejoice at every new discovery they make of that kind, and take care to publish it. I thank God I do not know what those three ungenerous passions are, having never felt them in my own breast."—Letter to his Son ; March 11, 1751. Bradshaw, vol. I, p. 415.

[2] His attack on Carteret (see pp. 19-20 *ante*) is the one exception to this practice that we have found.

[3] This point is discussed at greater length on p. 107 *post*.

discouragement, to make such persistent efforts towards the moulding of his son's.

It is, moreover, important to notice that, whereas Johnson lives in our minds more vividly than any other character, with the possible exception of Pepys, Chesterfield's personality for the greater part of his life is elusive and intangible. Though, from the later letters to his friends, we get a vivid picture of him as a lovable old man struggling successfully against the most cruel adversities, we never *see* him in his prime. His political life is as impersonal as his essays, and his very individuality sunk in conformity to a hard and fast ethical code, a conformity so rigid, so fanatical almost, that the mere suggestion of temptation is strangled at birth. And with the virtual exclusion of temptation departs also the resistance to temptation and its successive attributes, until Chesterfield may be said to have ultimately become no longer his natural but his ideal self.

II

DIPLOMATIST

BEFORE we proceed to discuss the operation of Chesterfield's moral code upon his political career it will be advisable to dwell for a time on his work as Ambassador at the Hague (1728–32). The facts with regard to this epoch in his life are not in dispute, and to relate them in detail would mean not only covering well-trodden ground but wandering along by-paths of European History remote from the study of Chesterfield's character. His skill as an ambassador, his zeal and assiduity, are admitted by the severest of his critics, though to get a true realization of these faculties one must read through fifteen volumes of official correspondence in the Holland State Papers, a task which we recommend to our readers, with no more enthusiasm than Carlyle recommended a perusal of the Reichenbach-Grumkow Correspondence in the Prussia State Papers of the same period.

Carlyle complains in his loudest voice of the distastefulness of his task, which he terms " an adventure, never to be spoken of again, when once *done !* " ; and on giving a few pages of extracts from the " Nosti-Grumkow Correspondence " exclaims :—" What fractional elements, capable of gaining some vestige of meaning when laid together in their cosmic order, I could pick from the circumambient immensity not cosmic, are here for the reader's behoof." [1] But this intercepted correspondence does not amount to one-thirtieth of that contained in the Hague Papers during Chesterfield's term of office, and being of a personal nature makes much less tedious reading. Reichenbach's letters especially contain many " human " touches, and are in parts often unconsciously entertaining, an epithet which is the last that can be applied to the Hague correspondence. Nevertheless, it must be admitted that even in the dullest of Chesterfield's despatches one is soothed by his graceful periods and balanced sentences, while the less

---

[1] *History of Frederick the Great*, Book VII, chap. ii.

27

formal letters, especially those to the Under-Secretary George Tilson, are occasionally adorned with ironical touches such as the following :—

" The King of Prussia in the oath he prepared for the Prince to swallow, among many other things, has made him swear that he will never believe the doctrine of Predestination ! A very unnecessary declaration in my mind for anybody who has the misfortune of being acquainted with him to make, since he himself is a living proof of free-will, for Providence can never be supposed to have pre-ordained such a creature." [1]

The main impression, however, which a studied perusal of this correspondence will leave on the reader is not so much admiration for Chesterfield's diplomatic skill as a strong realization of his modesty, conscientiousness, and unlimited patience—three qualities which we shall find constantly exhibited throughout his later life, though little credit for them has been given him by the critics.

In these days it is often said that a person is generally accepted at his own valuation—a belief whose truth would certainly seem to be manifested in the business world, and to a lesser extent in that of politics. To what degree it was true concerning the world in which Chesterfield moved is impossible to determine ; nor is it easy to say how far it can be generally applied to our country to-day. The statement presupposes in our nature a degree of credulity which, to be perfectly frank, we know in our heart of hearts does not exist. Whether the valuation expressed is a high or a low one we make allowances : in the former case because we are not really such credulous fools ; in the latter because a certain convention is commonly accepted, or, if it be preferred, because of a distinctive trait in our national character concerning which we are, in reality, no less conscious than reticent. We would even go so far as to suggest in a whisper that it is possible for us to feel secretly gratified when the more primitive American is awestruck at some casual revelation of our cultured lack of self-esteem.

[1] Chesterfield to Tilson, December 12, 1730. Bradshaw, vol. II, p. 709. The just contempt which Chesterfield expressed more than once for Frederick William was not extended to his son. Frederick the Great and Chesterfield had for each other the deepest respect. See Maty, vol. I, sect. iv., pp. 100, 101 and 307.

Now this national characteristic—one of the component factors of what is expressed by the word " gentleman "— is not of long-standing ; and it is our belief that if Chesterfield did not actually plant it in our soil he did more than anyone to promote its growth. We have no wish to labour the point, which of necessity does not admit of definite proof ; but a comparison of the polite conventions of his time, as revealed in contemporary memoirs and letters, with those more delicate attributes which by his preaching and practice he superimposed upon society will show that it is no mere surmise ; especially when it is remembered that Chesterfield was held as the ideal of a gentleman for at least one generation to follow. Modesty is a quality which he constantly impresses on his son, and which is frequently revealed in his private letters and conversation. In these official letters, however, when he is writing in effect to the king through the medium of a Secretary of State, the official subservience of an eighteenth-century subject seems at times to carry his self-depreciation to the point of servility. We confess occasionally to have been reminded of the studied extravagance of Mirabell's speech to Lady Wishfort in Congreve's *Way of the World* : [1]

" If a deep sense of the many injuries I have offered to so good a lady, with a sincere remorse, and a hearty contrition, can but obtain the least glance of compassion, I am too happy.—Ah, madam, there was a time !—but let it be forgotten—I confess I have deservedly forfeited the high place I once held of sighing at your feet. . . . "

If, however, his diplomatic letters sound at times obsequious it must be remembered that they are written in the language of eighteenth-century officialdom, a language which Chesterfield by some miracle of style contrives to make graceful in its very stiltedness. Was self-depreciation ever expressed, for instance, more eloquently than in the following passage ?

" I cannot express the sense I have of his Majesty's goodness to me in excusing the ill success that my endeavours for his service sometimes meet with here. Could any thing add to that zeal with which I shall always endeavour to obey his Majesty's commands, it would be that

[1] Act V, Sc. 2.

indulgence he is pleased to show to my want of abilities to execute them." [1]

As we shall see in the course of his career, Chesterfield was far too conscientious ever to be guilty of servility. It was, in fact, probably the want of it more than anything else that led to his appointment at the Hague in 1728. During the later years of the reign of George I he had been a fairly consistent supporter of the Prince, and it was expected that when the latter came to the throne his chief favourites would be singled out for preferment. As is well known, however, George II to everyone's surprise chose wisely to retain Walpole in office, and ten months elapsed before Chesterfield obtained his appointment at the Hague. Maty says with regard to this delay :—" Whether the earl's attachment was thought so strong as not to require any immediate encouragement, or whether a want of obsequious-ness, even at that early period, diverted for some time the course of royal favors from him, is uncertain. His name, however, was not in the list of promotions ; he kept only his post of lord of the bed-chamber, and was not even restored to the place of captain of the yeomen of the guard." [2]

The first of Maty's conjectures—with regard to the earl's attachment not requiring encouragement—may be dis-missed on the ground of puerility, and we prefer to rely on the second one, which in a subsequent note he says himself is rendered " not improbable " by the following information received from that excellent authority the Bishop of Water-ford, Chesterfield's chaplain and correspondent for so many years :—" At the beginning of the reign of George II, a person told Lord Scarborough, Lord Chesterfield, and Lord Lonsdale, that the king intended to closet them with regard to something that was to be proposed to the house of lords : but they all three requested that his majesty

[1] Chesterfield to Townshend, May 3, 1729. Public Record Office. State Papers Foreign (Holland), vol. CCCIV, f. 70. (Where the letter appears in Bradshaw the latter is given as a reference. If the reference is to State Papers or to MSS. in the British Museum it may be understood that the letter, as in this case, is here printed for the first time.)

[2] Vol. I, p. 46. " He was in 1723, while Lord Stanhope, made Captain of the Gentlemen Pensioners, which he resigned in 1725, on some difference with Sir Robert Walpole, which, as well as a speech of his to the King, I presume on the same occasion, made a noise at the time. The details have not reached us. See *Suffolk Correspondence*, i. 183."—Croker's note to *Lord Hervey's Memoirs*, vol. I, p. 98.

would not do it, for it would have no influence upon them ; but, on the contrary, make them so much the more upon their guard, being determined to vote according to their own way of thinking, as their honor and conscience directed them."[1]

The most authentic account of Chesterfield's appointment is given by Hervey, who says, " When the distribution of places, changes, and promotions was making at the beginning of this reign, the King told Sir Robert Walpole he would have something done for Chesterfield. Sir Robert, who did not dislike removing so declared an enemy to a little distance from the king's ear, proposed sending Lord Chesterfield ambassador to Holland ; and Lord Chesterfield, afraid to act against Sir Robert, and ashamed to act under him, gave in to this proposal, thinking it would allow people time to forget the declarations he had made of never forgiving Sir Robert, and save him from a little of that ridicule which the laughers of his acquaintance would be apt to lavish upon him when they saw him listed again under the banner of a man he had formerly deserted, and against whom he had so long fought with his wit, that only weapon with which he cared for fighting."[2]

Hervey's well-known animus against Chesterfield makes us chary of attaching much weight to his remarks concerning the latter, but the substance of this account so far as Walpole is concerned is doubtless correct. The Prime Minister had good cause for not wanting so independent a man as Chesterfield to serve under him in England ; had already sufficient influence over the king to choose the majority of his own subordinates, and was not sorry to have this particular one out of the way. Accordingly we find Chesterfield, then in his thirty-fourth year, installed at the Hague, whence he writes his first official letter to Townshend on May 7, 1728, ending characteristically as follows : " I cannot conclude this letter without recommending myself most humbly to the King's indulgence that he will graciously be pleased to pardon the many faults that my want of both Experience and Abilities must necessarily make me committ. I tremble every step I take, and my only hope is in His Majesty's Goodness which I have so often experienced though so little deserved, and in Your

[1] Maty, vol. I, sect. iii., note 1, p. 286.
[2] *Memoirs*, vol. I, pp. 97, 98.

Lordship's friendship which I most earnestly begg the continuance of."[1]

Chesterfield's main achievements during his first three years at the Hague consist of the prevention of war with Prussia which seemed inevitable after the idea of a personal duel between George II and Friedrich Wilhelm had been abandoned ; his management of the preliminaries to the marriage between the Prince of Orange and the Princess Royal ; and his secret negotiations with Count Sinzendorf (Austrian Envoy at the Hague) and the Pensionary of Holland which led to the signing of the Second Treaty of Vienna.[2] Though full justice for all these achievements, especially the last, has scarcely been done to Chesterfield by the historians, his biographers are as justly liberal in their praise of his ability as George II was on the various occasions on which his valuable services were rendered. The State Papers in revealing the skill which those services involved do little more towards shedding fresh light on Chesterfield's character. We shall therefore pass these quickly over and, after dealing with one or two minor points, direct our main attention to the last year of his Embassy which has been barely noticed by the historians owing to its lesser historical importance, and by his biographers because none of them has ever troubled to consult the original records for details of this period of his life.

Chesterfield's term of office at the Hague falls into two periods of eighteen months each, between which he spent ten months in England on leave of absence, though in full correspondence with his German Secretary, Charles Holzendorf, who was left in charge at the Embassy. It is commonly supposed that this holiday was engineered by Townshend, who wanted to make his position in the " firm of Walpole and Townshend " more secure by having his fellow Secretary of State, the Duke of Newcastle, then little more than a tool in Walpole's hands, supplanted by Chesterfield. From the conversation that took place between Walpole and Chesterfield on the latter's return it is evident that Chesterfield was an innocent accomplice in this

---

[1] State Papers (Holland), vol. CCC, f. 11.

[2] March 16, 1731. See Chesterfield's note to his Account of the Government of the Dutch Republic, Bradshaw, vol. I, p. 619 ; his letters from the Hague, ibid., pp. 707–713 passim, and State Papers (Holland), vols. CCCIX and CCCXI, Maty, vol. I, sect. iii., note 34, pp. 61, 62 and 293; Marchmont Papers, vol. I, p. 62.

intrigue,[1] the subsequent failure of which is said to have been one of the main causes of Townshend's resignation in the following May.

It would have been a strange stroke of irony had Chesterfield succeeded Townshend; yet we believe this event was for some time by no means an improbability. George II doubtless would have liked it to take place, but the combined opposition of Caroline and Walpole was too strong for him. Hervey, it is true, tells us that " Lord Townshend having positively declared to the King in the winter that he would quit, Sir Robert Walpole had got the King's leave to tell Mr. Stanhope [2] that he should succeed Lord Townshend as Secretary of State."[3] It is hard to believe, however, that Harrington had quite such an easy passage into office. With regard to his ambition for the post, Coxe's opinion is that " he had to struggle as well against the ill-will of the king, who was highly displeased with his brother Charles Stanhope, as against the prejudices of Sir Robert Walpole, who, deeply impressed with a recollection of the conduct of earl Stanhope at Hanover, had taken an aversion to the very name. It required all the influence of the duke of Newcastle, and the friendship of Horace Walpole,[4] to surmount these obstructions."[5] Moreover, Reichenbach in a letter from London to Grumkow of March 13-24, 1730, says, " On ne sçait pas encore qu'il [qui] viendra à la place de *Townshend* [6] en cas que quelque changement devroit arriver, mais les Pretendans y sont *Horace Walpole, Lord Harrington,* et *Lord Chesterfield* sans qu'on puisse dire positivement qui de ces Mrs. emportera la Victoire " ; and again four days later, " On

---

[1] See p. 79 *post.* No evidence exists for the contrary view which has in fact seldom been suggested ; though Sir Sidney Lee, in his article on Chesterfield in the *Dictionary of National Biography*, mentions that he " canvassed the possibility of becoming Townshend's colleague as Secretary of State." This statement may, however, be disregarded, since the account given by this writer of Chesterfield's embassy at the Hague is one mass of confused dates and inaccuracies. On similar grounds may also be rejected the statement of Philarète Chasles that " une intrigue fut tramée entre lord Townshend et l'ambassadeur à la Haye, pour renverser et remplacer le duc de Newcastle, peut-être Robert Walpole lui-même."—*Revue des Deux Mondes* (December, 1845), p. 914.

[2] Then in Paris engaged in concluding the Treaty of Seville, for which service he was shortly afterwards created Lord Harrington.

[3] *Memoirs*, vol. I, p. 141.

[4] Robert Walpole's brother ; not his son the well-known letter-writer.

[5] *Memoirs of Sir Robert Walpole*, Chap. XXXVI, vol. II, p. 375.

[6] The names in italics appeared in cipher in the original correspondence but were deciphered on its interception.

D

croit à present que *Lord Chesterfield* emportera contre *Lord Harrington, Lord Chesterfield* ayant fait sa Paix avec Robert Walpole, car ils ont été auparavant fort mal ensemble."[1]

Though Carlyle has described these letters as a " sordid mass of eaves-droppings, kitchen-ashes and floor-sweepings,"[2] we do not think the evidence they contain can be summarily disregarded, when it is remembered that Reichenbach was then Prussian Ambassador in London and in personal communication with the highest of our officials.[3] That these particular rumours amounted to something more than mere court gossip is evident from the following passage in Coxe's *Memoirs of Sir Robert Walpole*,[4] his authority for which is " a communication of Sir Robert Walpole " in the Etough Papers.

" The earl of Chesterfield . . . had long coveted the post of secretary of state, and an arrangement had been made in his favour. After an audience of the queen, to which he was introduced by Walpole, and thanking her for her concurrence, he had the imprudence to make a long visit to the mistress. The queen was informed of the circumstance, and his appointment did not take place."

Exactly when Chesterfield " made his peace " with Walpole is not known, but we are told by Hervey that on being appointed Lord Steward he " made the warmest professions to Sir Robert Walpole that it was possible to utter, acknowledging that his attachment this winter to Lord Townshend gave him no right to expect this favour, and he concluded with saying, " I had lost the game, but you have taken my cards into your hand and recovered it."[5] What truth there may be in this we know not, but it can be surmised that the Steward's Staff and the Garter, which he received on the previous day, were given Chesterfield partly by way of compensation for his not being offered the Seals.

There is no evidence to show that he made any personal

---

[1] State Papers, Foreign (Prussia), vol. 27.
[2] *Frederick the Great*, Book VII, chap. ii.
[3] A comparison of his letters with the contemporaneous and authoritative *Diary of Lord Egmont* (vol. I, Hist. MSS. Comm., 1920) will often show a surprising similarity of detail in reference to current political secrets.
[4] Vol. II, p. 282.
[5] *Memoirs*, vol. I, p. 143.

effort either to supplant Newcastle or to succeed Townshend
when the latter's resignation was imminent. His letter to
Townshend asking for leave of absence certainly sounds
innocent and reasonable enough.

"Hague, October 7, N.S., 1729.
" MY LORD,

" When I had the honour of seeing his Majesty at Helvoet
Sluys, I had not time humbly to beg his permission to pay
my duty to him in England some time this winter, where
not only my own inclinations call me upon that account,
but where also my own private affairs render my presence
very necessary. I must therefore beg of your Lordship to
use your interest with his Majesty, that he will be graciously pleased to give me leave to come to England for
some time this winter. It is now above a year and a half
that I have been here, and have not stirred one day from
my post ; so that I hope his Majesty will not think this
request unreasonable ; nor, indeed, have I any reason to
suppose that my presence anywhere can be of importance
enough for his Majesty's service to suffer in the least by
my absence from hence."[1]

By the same post he writes as follows to the Under-
Secretary, George Tilson :—

" I enclose in this my letters to Lord Townshend, which
I begg you will deliver to his Lordship himself if he is in
Town ; if not to keep them till he comes. One of them is
to ask his Majesty's leave for me to go to England for a
little time, both upon account of my own private affairs,
and of my health, for my leggs still continue in a way that
I should be very glad of better advice for them than any I
can have here."[2]

We believe that this latter was a genuine reason for
Chesterfield's return, and one to which he refers in a letter
to his son of November 16, 1766, when, advising him upon
a similar trouble, he says :—

" I will therefore tell you my own case, in 1732 [sic],
which may be something parallel to yours. I had that year

[1] Bradshaw, vol. II, p. 704.
[2] State Papers (Holland), vol. CCCV, f. 207.

been dangerously ill of a fever in Holland ; and when I
was recovered of it the febrific humour fell into my legs
and swelled them to that degree, and chiefly in the evening,
that it was as painful to me as it was shocking to others.
I came to England with them in this condition, and consulted Mead, Broxholme, and Arbuthnot, who none of them
did me the least good ; but, on the contrary, increased the
swelling by applying poultices and emollients. In this
condition I remained near six months. . . ."[1]

Our opinion is that when writing this letter Chesterfield
was thinking of his return on leave in October, 1729, the
date of which he confused with that of his permanent
return in 1732. During the few weeks he spent at the Hague
in that latter year there is no mention of any illness in his
official communications, and the longest lapse of time
between the writing of any two consecutive letters is only
four days.[2] In 1729, on the other hand, a few weeks before
writing to Tilson as above, he ends a letter to Townshend
with these words :—" A Fever that I have had these three
or four days hinders me from troubling your Lordship any
longer at present than while I assure you that I am " etc.[3]
The following day his Secretary, Holzendorf, writes to
Tilson :—" You will see in the Dispatch to My Lord Townshend that His Excellency complains of a feaver ; I cannot
help adding that he is a good deal out of order with it.
He has had two severe fitts of it, and just now has another
strong attack which hinders him from acknowledging the
honour of his Lordship's letter. . . . His Excellency will
begin to-morrow to take the Quinquina by the help of
which we hope the return of his ague and feaver will be
prevented."[4]
In his next letter to Townshend, Chesterfield, apologizing
for his delay in executing the king's commands, says that
" The attacks of my fever have been so very violent and
lasted so long that I was not able to go yesterday to talk
with the Pensionary and Greffier " ;[5] in reply to which
Townshend writes :—" His Majesty expressed great con-

---

[1] The letter proceeds to relate how he was then cured by means of a
brine remedy in three weeks.—Bradshaw, vol. III, p. 1351.
[2] State Papers (Holland), vol. CCCXVI.
[3] August 12. *Ibid.*, vol. CCCV, f. 29.
[4] See also Holzendorf's letter of the same date to Newcastle's Under-
Secretary Delafaye : *ibid.*, ff. 31 and 33.
[5] August 16. *Ibid.*, i. 37.

cern at the ill state of your health," and in another letter of the same date, " I am infinitely concerned at the accounts I have had of your Lordship's indisposition, and hope before this time it will have entirely left you."[1]

If, then, these facts are considered enough to support our surmise, it would account to a large extent for Chesterfield's inordinate length of leave. But whether, in writing to his son, he had the year 1729 in mind or not, the State Papers of 1732 prove beyond all doubt that his mention of that year was a slip ; and in consequence the reason concerning his ill-health which Maty gives, amongst other suggestions, for his final departure from the Hague, supported as it is by this one authority only, falls to the ground. So also must be discarded the deductions from it made by Ernst (p. 70) with regard to Chesterfield's absence from the House of Lords in that year ; [2] as well as the following pathetic picture by Craig, which will serve as a good illustration of his method of embroidering plain facts. He begins by saying definitely, though without authority, that Chesterfield " applied for his recall upon the ground of his failing health, which was indeed a sufficient one, as we find in one of his letters to his son " ; after quoting from which he proceeds :—" Such was his condition, in fact, that humanity as well as expediency demanded that his request should be granted, nor need we speculate with his biographer, Dr. Maty, that ' the very reason which had procured him his appointment, the fear of his acquiring too great an interest with his sovereign,'[3] may have been

---

[1] August 10–21. *Ibid.*, ff. 41 and 43. The illness did not last long. From a note in the handwriting of James Dayrolles, dated August 19, we learn that " My Lord Chesterfield se trouve tout à fait délivré de sa Fievre, est sorti ces jours-ci, et agit comme auparavant."—State Papers ; Foreign Newsletters (Holland) ; Bundle 69.

[2] This is one of the few inaccuracies in Ernst's biography, which consists for the most part of a careful and well-arranged précis of Chesterfield's letters and Maty's *Life*. He seldom ventures an opinion or even a deduction of his own. Had he taken the trouble to verify this particular one by consulting the *Journals of the House of Lords* he would have found that Chesterfield, so far from being prevented " from taking any part in the Debates that year," was present at forty-four of the sixty Sittings of that House between the date of his return in February and the end of the session on June 1st, 1732. A short account of a speech he made on behalf of the Government at the end of the session is given in Lord Egmont's Diary, vol. I, p. 278. (Hist. MSS. Comm., 1920.)

It may be mentioned that during his ten months' leave from the Hague (1729–30) he was absent from fifty of the seventy-six Sittings of the House of Lords ; which figures would tend to support our surmise that it was at that period that he was in the doctors' hands.

[3] Vol. I, p. 63.

the motive for granting it.   Amid general regrets he left Holland, a helpless invalid. . . ."[1]

We agree, though for different reasons, with Craig, and also with Ernst (p. 70), in regarding Maty's conjecture as unnecessary. If Walpole was afraid " of his acquiring too great an interest with his sovereign," in the capacity of Ambassador at the Hague, especially when English affairs there had been reduced to a state of quiescence in which they seemed likely to remain for some length of time,[2] why should he be anxious for Chesterfield to take up the more intimate duties of Lord Steward, to which post he had been appointed in June 1730 ? The following personal letter from Chesterfield to Harrington has more bearing on the point than any other, and since it is of a less official nature than most of his from the Hague we will quote it in full.

" Apart.

" Hague, Jan. yᵉ 29th, N.S., 1732.

" MY LORD,

" As I now foresee a near and certain period to the Uneasy situation I have been in here so long, I think it necessary to trouble your Lordship with this letter to begg that you will endeavour to know his Majesty's pleasure as to my future destination.

" When the treaty is once sign'd I shall be entirely useless and a very unnecessary expence to his Majesty here ; so that I could wish his Majesty would permitt me to return to the employment he has honour'd me with near his person, which as yett I have neither deserv'd nor executed.

" I reckon the treaty will be sign'd about this day fort-night ; but the ratification, which is meerly a matter of

---

[1] *Life*, pp. 129, 130. The unreliability of Craig's lengthy biography is not confined to mere " embroidery." His authority is too frequently that of his own imagination, as for example when he says on p. 136 that Chester-field " in the strongest terms denounced the Excise scheme from his place in the House of Lords," in which Chamber it was never debated : (see p. 58 *post*). On the other hand, his comments often show remarkable insight into Chesterfield's character, and he has the gift of summing up a situation with considerable fairness and clarity.

We confess to a feeling of sympathy with Craig for the reason that throughout his book he consistently spells the name of the Bishop of Waterford as " Chevenix," an error which we have ourselves found it requires the greatest strength of mind to avoid committing.

[2] As a matter of fact, for eleven months after Chesterfield's departure our interests at the Hague were conducted entirely by the Resident, James Dayrolles.

form, will take up at least two months here ; so that I
presume, if his Majesty approves of my return to England,
it will not be necessary that it should be delay'd till after
the exchange of the Ratifications which may equally be
done by whoever his Majesty is pleas'd to send here in my
room ; or, if no body comes, by old Dayrolles, who has
exchang'd ratifications here for these last fifty years.

" I must desire your Lordship to represent all this to the
King, and to lett me know his Majesty's commands, which,
whether they be to return, to stay here, or to go to any other
part of the world, will always be most chearfully and
exactly obey'd by

" Your Lordship's most humble and most obedient
servant,

CHESTERFIELD.

" P.S.   If his Majesty permitts me to return, your Lordship will be pleas'd to think of my letter of revocation."[1]

We would also reject the suggestion made by the editor
of the *Suffolk Letters*[2] that " Lord Chesterfield was recalled from the embassy to the Hague in 1732 on the pretence of ill-health ; but his opposition to the measures of
Walpole, and particularly the part he took against the
Excise bill, lead us to suspect that there was some political
cause for his recall."   As Chesterfield himself is at pains to
point out in his letter to Harrington of January 2, N.S.,
1731, his granted " leave to return " did not amount to
a *recall* :—" I cannot conceive upon what Monsieur Hop
founds his assertion of my being uneasy at being recalled,
as he terms it, and of my attributing it to the ill-will of the
two brothers, as he is familiarly pleased to call Sir Robert
and Horace[3] . . . "   Moreover, as shown by Ernst (p. 70),
the conjecture is " inconsistent with Lord Chesterfield's
own letters . . . and also with chronology ; for the Excise
scheme—his opposition to which led to his dismissal from
his post of Lord Steward—was not brought on till the
following year."

If, then, these various reasons and conjectures must be
dismissed, why was it that Chesterfield left the Hague ?
We believe the main reason, which no one has suggested,

---

[1] State Papers (Holland), vol. CCCXVI, f. 110.
[2] Vol. II, p. 63, Croker's note.
[3] Bradshaw, vol. II, p. 714. See further quotations from this letter
on pp. 41, 42 *post*.

though there is ample support for it in his letters, was simply that he was tired of the work there.

Mahon's opinion of Chesterfield's term of office at the Hague is that " public business though at first strange and unwelcome, soon became easy, nay delightful, to him "[1] —an opinion almost entirely contrary to the evidence expressed in the letters of Chesterfield from the Hague which Mahon himself was the first to publish. It is, in fact, a distinctive trait which we shall see frequently manifested in Chesterfield's character, that official duties of any sort, whether those of Ambassador, Opposition Leader, Irish Viceroy, or Secretary of State, palled on him in a very short space of time. Nevertheless, when duty called upon him to perform a task, conscience never permitted him to scamp the work. However distasteful it may have been to him, however anxious he was for a rest, while actually at the oar he always pulled his hardest. Chesterfield never expressed any enthusiasm for his work at the Hague, and went back there in August, 1730, on the full understanding that his stay would be only for a few months. Within a month of his return we find him suggesting in a letter to Harrington, Townshend's successor, that the time might be made still shorter. He is speaking of the negotiations with Austria which led to the second Treaty of Vienna, and says :—

" I look upon our negotiation with the Emperor as begun ; but I look upon it, too, as very far from being ended, and I foresee the many difficulties that will arise in the course of it. . . . But as these difficulties will take up a good deal of time, and probably not be discussed here, or, if they were, as I am both unfit and unwilling to be concerned in them, I submit it to your Lordship, whether it is not time to think of a successor for me here, who will require some time to get ready, and who it may be proper should be here before I go. There is now a little more than three months to the sitting of the Parliament ; and since I am to be back by that time, I confess I should be glad it were as soon as possible. I therefore beg your Lordship will mention this affair to the King, in what way you think properest, whether as from yourself or me."[2]

[1] *History of England*, chap. xxx.
[2] September 19, N.S., 1730. Bradshaw, vol. II, pp. 707–8.

Writing to Tilson on November 7 upon the same subject, he says :—" Whatever may be the events of this Negotiation, I heartily wish myself out of it, and in St. James's Square." [1] Shortly afterwards he applied formally for leave to come home, which was granted in a letter of November 27 from Harrington, who mentions that the King " has named Mr. William Finch who was before in Holland to return thither in quality of his Minister Plenipotentiary to take care of his Majesty's Affairs upon your quitting that employment." [2] In acknowledging this letter, after thanking the King for granting his request, Chesterfield adds characteristically :—" I could have wished that my Services here had deserved the rewards they have already met with, or could entitle me to ask the continuance of his Majesty's favour to me ; but I am sensible how unequal they were to the former, and how insufficient a claim they would be to the latter." [3]

There was no doubt that Chesterfield was by now in many respects weary of his life at the Hague, and we find him again writing to Tilson on December 12, N.S., 1730 :—" I find I shall have the pleasure of seeing you soon in England. Without pretending to be fatigued with business, I have had enough on't to desire no more, and to be very glad to be quiet in St. James's Square." [4] A week later, however, he tells Harrington :—" I am very willing to stay here till this affair be determined one way or other, and the more so, because should the Emperor agree, I foresee there will be some difficulties in finishing here, where, from the nature of the government, every wrong head or heart has a right of opposition, and can do hurt, though not good." [5]

Having learnt that Monsieur Hop at the Hague had informed his brother the Dutch Ambassador in England that Chesterfield had been " recalled " owing to the displeasure of Sir Robert Walpole and his brother Horace, the earl writes with some indignation to Harrington :—

" Your Lordship very well knows that when I came back here last summer, it was declared by their Majesties, and understood by me and every body else, that I was to return

---

[1] Chesterfield's home in London. State Papers (Holland), vol. CCCVIII, f. 164.
[2] *Ibid.*, vol. CCCIX, f. 79.
[3] December 15, 1730. *Ibid.*, f. 131.
[4] Bradshaw, vol. II, p. 709.
[5] December 19, N.S., 1730. *Ibid.*, p. 712.

for good and all by the meeting of the Parliament ; so that my writing to your Lordship lately upon that subject was only reminding you of a thing fixed, and not desiring any thing new when I came here.   I told every body I should return to England after Christmas, and that the employment the King had done me the honour to give me[1] required my attendance in England ; so that my return was universally expected here, and is nothing new, nor can consequently be attributed to any of Monsieur Hop's surmises.   If Monsieur Hop interprets my saying that I am personally sorry to leave this place, to be discontent, I cannot help it.   It is true I have said that to every body here, and it is no more than what common civility, and even truth, requires from me.   I have all the reason in the world personally to regret leaving this place, but that is no argument for my being discontented at my return.

" As I suppose the King has seen this letter of Monsieur Hop's I must desire your Lordship will be pleased to set this matter right with his Majesty, who would have very great reason to be offended, if he could believe that while on one side I beg his leave to return, on the other I complain and am dissatisfied with obtaining it.   I should be extremely sorry at my return to England to meet with any ill-will or suspicions ; for I solemnly declare I shall bring none with me.   I desire to live in friendship with all that are in his Majesty's service ; it was upon that foot that I took the employment I have, and upon that foot only will I keep it."[2]

This matter was soon cleared up, as we learn from a letter to Harrington a fortnight later which begins :—
" I was extremely glad to find by your Lordship's letter *apart*[3] that the trouble I had given both you and myself about Monsieur Hop's intercepted letter was unnecessary ; and, indeed, I should never have thought it necessary to have taken the least notice of any of that gentleman's surmises, had I not found by Mr. Walpole's letter that, at least, they had made some impression upon him."[4]

By this time preliminaries were practically settled with Austria, and consolation for the tedious delays was afforded

[1] Lord Steward of His Majesty's Household.
[2] January 2, N.S., 1731.   Bradshaw, vol. II, pp. 714–5.
[3] This letter does not appear in the State Papers.
[4] January 16, N.S., 1731.   Bradshaw, vol. II, p. 715.

by the immediate prospect of St. James's Square, its comforts and its pleasures. Chesterfield writes to Harrington at the end of February :—

" If Mr. Finch is impatient to come here,[1] I am sure I am not less so to return to England ; and if he has a mind to take the trouble of bringing the Republic into the treaty of Vienna, in case it be concluded, I will most cheerfully resign to him both the trouble and the credit of doing it. I have staid here till now not by choice but by obedience ; and I shall be gladder to see Mr. Finch here whenever he comes than he can possibly be to come." [2]

Little did the writer of this letter know that it would be a whole year before his hopes were fulfilled. There is certainly an implication that the task " of bringing the Republic into the Treaty of Vienna " would prove no light one, but even Chesterfield had not then more than an inkling of the trouble it would involve. Though the concurrence of the Republic may strike us to-day as being of little historical importance, it presented a different aspect to George II and his ministers at the time, and they were doubtless justified in believing that Chesterfield, who was held in such high esteem at the Hague, and had proved his diplomatic skill on so many occasions, was the fittest man to accomplish it.

This task was no mere diplomatic work in which his wits were opposed to other ambassadors'—he had already won over to his side the Pensionary of Holland and Count Sinzendorf, the Austrian Envoy. What these three men were confronted with throughout was the uncontrollable mechanism of a republic whose constitution rendered international diplomacy almost an impossibility. Had Holland then been under the rule of a Stadtholder, the Treaty of Vienna would doubtless have been concluded by all the countries at the same time, and no subsequent Act of Concurrence would have been necessary. As it was, however, ridiculous delays occurred which prolonged the negotiations for eleven months.

The concurrence of Holland was a task which could not

---

[1] There was certainly ground for Finch's impatience. A yacht had been ordered for him in which to sail to Holland at the end of December. See Chesterfield to Harrington ; December 26, N.S., 1730.—*Ibid.*, p. 712.

[2] February 27, N.S., 1731. *Ibid.*, p. 721.

be expected to bring credit commensurate with its difficulty to those who accomplished it ; while an unfair amount of odium was bound to attach to those officially concerned should it fail. Though it was by no means the most important achievement in Chesterfield's life, it was without any doubt the most difficult, and for that reason we propose to give brief extracts from the letters written by him during the progress of the negotiations, in the hope that they will afford the reader some idea of the qualities which are revealed in a perusal of the whole correspondence. In order, however, to indicate the main difficulties involved it will be advisable first to cite the opening passages from *Some Account of the Government of the Republic of the Seven United Provinces*,[1] which according to Mahon was drawn up by Chesterfield at the Hague.[2]

" The Government of the Republic of the Seven United Provinces is thought by many to be Democratical ; but it is merely Aristocratical, the people not having the least share in it, either themselves, or by representatives of their own choosing : they have nothing to do but to pay and grumble.

" The Sovereign Power is commonly thought to be in the States General, *as they are called*, residing at the Hague. It is no such thing ; they are only limited Deputies, obliged to consult their Constituents upon every point of any importance that occurs. It is very true that the Sovereign Power is lodged in the States General ; but who are those States General ? Not those who are commonly called so ; but the Senate, Council or *Vrootschaps*, call it what you will, of every town in every Province that sends Deputies to the Provincial States of the said Province. These *Vrootschaps* are in truth the States General ; but, were they to assemble, they would amount, for aught I know, to two or three thousand ; it is, therefore, for convenience and despatch of business that every Province sends Deputies to the Hague, who are constantly assembled there ; who are commonly called the States General ; and in whom many people falsely imagine that the Sovereign Power is lodged. These Deputies are chosen by the *Vrootschaps* ; but their

---

[1] Bradshaw, vol. II, pp. 618–624.

[2] " It was found among Mr. Philip Stanhope's papers, and had, no doubt, been sent to him for his instruction."—Mahon's note ; *ibid.*, p. 618.

powers are extremely circumscribed ; and they consent to nothing without writing, or returning themselves to their several constituent towns for instructions in that particular case. They are authorised to concur in matters of order ; that is, to continue things in the common, current, ordinary train ; but for the least innovation, the least step out of the ordinary course, new instructions must be given, either to deliberate or to conclude.

" Many people are ignorant enough to take the Province of Holland, singly, for the Republic of the Seven United Provinces ; and, when they mean to speak of the Republic, they say *Holland* will or will not do such a thing ; but most people are ignorant enough to imagine that the Province of Holland has a legal, a constitutional power over the other six ; whereas by the Act of Union the little Province of *Groningen* is as much Sovereign as the Province of Holland. The Seven Provinces are seven distinct Sovereignties, confederated together in one Republic ; no one having any superiority over, or dependance upon any other. . . .

" The unanimity, which is constitutionally requisite for every act of each Town, and each Province, separately, and then for every act of the Seven collectively, is something so absurd, and so impracticable in government, that one is astonished that even the form of it has been tolerated for so long ; for the substance is not strictly observed."

With this introduction, then, we will proceed to give an epitome of the tedious tale of difficulties and delays, of Chesterfield's successive hopes and disappointments, his persuasive powers and modesty, his patience, irony and common-sense.

To Harrington

April 13, 1731.
" I now experience in perfection, and labour under the inconveniencys and absurditys of a Republic Government ; for tho' they are all well inclined to the Treaty in general, yet every one to shew he is Master thinks he must make his own difficultys and objections, most of which require more patience to hear than abilitys to answer."[1]

---

[1] State Papers (Holland), vol. CCCXII, f. 89.

To Harrington.

April 20.

" There being now two Posts due from England, I have no orders from your Lordship to acknowledge, and very little to trouble you with from hence, for to give a particular account of my negotiations here now would be as voluminous as unnecessary, and I should even be ashamed to repeat to your Lordship the absurd reasonings and difficultys I am obliged to hear from the many petty Sovereigns of this Republick. Some have arisen from their not understanding Latin, others from their understanding nothing at all, and a third sort, which is the hardest to overcome, is the effect of almost an English Spirit of discontent that makes them oppose the Treaty for no other reason than because they imagine that the Ministers here (the Pensionary and Greffier[1]) had a hand in the making of it, and without their Participation. Next week when the States of Holland meet, all these difficultys will be ascertained, and I shall be able to give your Lordship an account of what will finally be insisted upon and what not, and I am in hopes they will be reduced to a few, and those not insurmountable."[2]

Harrington to Chesterfield.

April 9, O.S.

" Tho' the objections generally made are low and triffling, yet we should be glad to have those points of which your Excellency believes they intend to make additional separate Articles."[3]

To Harrington.

April 24, N.S.

" I should have acquainted your Lordship with the many objections made here to the Treaty and with which the Pensionary and I are pelted every day, if they had been less numerous and more important, and if I could have known which of them would have been finally insisted upon, which I shall not know before Saturday. However, since your Lordship orders me, I will venture to give you my guesses upon these points that I believe they will chiefly insist upon. . .

[1] The Pensionary corresponded to our Prime Minister : the Greffier was a sort of Secretary of State.
[2] State Papers (Holland), vol. CCCXII, f. 113.
[3] *Ibid.*, f. 111.

" These are the chief of the many Objections that are raised here. Some proceed from the natural attention of People here to Trifles, and a spirit of chicane and Distrust inseparable from a Republican Government : others arise from Patriots (for we have admirable Patriots here as well as in England) who because they think the Pensionary and Greffier were concerned in the Treaty, and consequently interested in the success of it, have a mind to show that those two Ministers have been negligent of the interests of the Republick which they themselves have so much at heart." [1]

To Thomas Robinson.[2]

May I.

" If your Patience was tryd in treating with four or five Ministers at Vienna, I can assure you mine is almost worn out in treating with two or three hundred Sovereigns here, whose various Tempers, Reasonings and Interests produce such strange effects that one wonders how a Government so constituted can ever dispatch any business at all."[3]

To Thomas Robinson.

May 11.

" . . . The Imperial Ministers will very probably say that all these remarks are very easily answer'd, to which I agree ; but tho' the objections will admitt of answers, the heads that made them will not so easily admitt of reasonings. Let them consider the unfortunate mould of this Government, where Unanimity is required, and consequently where the wrongest head or the worst heart can obstruct the wisest and the justest measures. They must take this constitution as it is, and if they will have its concurrence they must make allowances for its defects."[4]

To Harrington.

May 15.

" Notwithstanding my endeavours to bring this affair to a speedy conclusion, and the labours of the Pensionary and Greffier, all the unlucky accidents possible have con-

[1] *Ibid.*, f. 117.
[2] At that time Minister at Vienna. He was appointed Secretary of State in 1754, and in 1761 created Lord Grantham.
[3] British Museum ; Add. MSS. 23781, f. 394.
[4] *Ibid.*, f. 432.

spired to retard it. The business of the Pensionary of
Horn consumed three weeks entirely. The States of
Zeeland have quarrell'd among themselves about a trifle,
and are separated in a fury, and don't assemble again 'till
the beginning of next month, so that 'till that time we
cannot have their concurrence ; and the Pensionary is now
so ill in bed of the gout and a feaver that he is incapable of
any business." [1]

To George Tilson.

May 18.

" I believe you think us slow here, but in recompense
we are sure ; and if you will make the proper allowances
for the worst form of Government that I believe was ever
contriv'd, you will think that if a Treaty communicated
here in April is concluded in June, we have been pretty
expeditious. The Accession to the Hannover Treaty took
ten months, and the Accession to the Quadruple Alliance
is not yett done. I shall at least reap one benefitt from
this Negotiation, which is that it will have taught me
patience ; for one must have a good provision of it to treat
with these gentlemen here." [2]

To Harrington.

June 12.

" I press dispatch and reasonableness as much as is
possible, and I must do the Pensionary and Greffier the
Justice to say they do so too ; but this Government is such
a many headed Monster that one can no more judge what
they will do than most of them are capable of judging what
they ought to do." [3]

To George Tilson.

July 27.

" Having received no commands from Lord Harrington
by this post, I will not trouble him with a letter, and, indeed,
I am both weary and ashamed of sending him nothing from
hence but ridiculous causes and useless complaints of
delays. The province of Holland has not yet, in form,
confirmed the act of concurrence, because the towns
of Dort and Leyden had some notable scruple which

---

[1] State Papers (Holland), vol. CCCXII, f. 187.
[2] Ibid., f. 209.
[3] Ibid., vol. CCCXIII, f. 41.

they wanted to consult their principals upon. However, the sentiments of Holland are enough known to point out to the other provinces what they ought to do. In two or three days Count Sinzendorf expects the arrival of his courier here, and with a satisfactory answer ; if so, you may look upon the affair as done.

" It is impossible for any body who is not very well acquainted with this form of government to have a notion of the strange delays and absurd difficulties that have arisen in the course of this negotiation ; but to give you some image of it, represent to yourself an English Minister endeavouring to carry a point by the single merit of the point itself, without the assistance of reward and punishments, through what our patriots would call an independent and unbiassed House of Commons, that is, an assembly of people influenced by every thing but by the Court ; and then judge how soon and how easily it would pass ! This is the case of the Pensionary and Greffier ; with this difference, too, that here unanimity is necessary. Without the power of either hopes or fears, they must labour to unite a great number of heads, many of them incapable of judging at all, and yet obstinately pretending to it ; many of them incapable of judging right, but yet obstinate in the wrong ; and others who always lay hold of such public occasions to extort private advantages for their towns, themselves, and their families. This being the nature of this government, it is rather to be wondered at that any thing is done here at all, than that it is long a doing. For my own part, if I would teach any body the Christian virtues of patience, forbearance, and long-suffering, I would send them to negotiate a treaty here ! " [1]

The hopes expressed in this and the preceding letters were unfulfilled, and not long afterwards we find three letters from Chesterfield in which the moods change from half-amused apprehension to angry impatience, and thence to sheer despair. The first two of these are addressed to one of his most intimate Dutch friends, Baron Frederick Willem Torck, who held various important posts in Gelderland, which province he also represented in the States General. Chesterfield is beginning to get concerned about the objections raised by a certain Monsieur de Linden, presum-

[1] Bradshaw, vol. II, pp. 724–5.

E

ably Deputy for Utrecht, of whom he writes to Torck on August 17, 1731 as follows :—

" Il est a cette heure tout herissé de doutes et de difficultez sur le traitté meme ; il tremble aux dangérs des garanties ; et il ne considere point que les dangers seroient les mêmes, et peut etre plus grands, si on ne les donnoit point, et enfin touttes les raisons qui le portoient si fort pour le traitté, les trois premiers mois apres la signature, sont evanouiës, et sont remplacées, par des raisonnemens tout contraires." [1]

A week later he writes again :—

" A propos du Traitté, il faut que je vous dise un beau projet, que l'imagination fertile de Monsieur de Linden a formée pour vous presentér a votre prochaine Assemblée. C'est de vous proposér d'autorisér Vos Deputez de consentir au traitté a condition seulement que touttes les autres Provinces y consentent unanimement ; Or comme il prevoit, que la Province d'Utrecht selon la louable coutume n'y consentira que tard, ou peut étre point du tout, il espere indirectement accrochér l'Affaire, de cette maniere la. J'espere qu'on ne donnera point dans ce panneau, et il me semble que vous devez vous fiér plutot a vos propres jugemens sur le traitté, que de vous en rapportér a ceux de la Province d'Utrecht ; Si le traitté vous est avantageux consenter y, s'il vous est désavantageux, au nom de Dieu rejettez le, mais jugez toujours pour vous memes.

" Adieu, le bon Dieu vous aye en sa sainte garde, et continuez toujours votre amitié au plus fidele de vos amis et serviteurs—Chesterfield." [2]

By this time matters have become really serious, as is shown by the following letter to Robinson of August 31.

" I plainly see the Court of Vienna is very indifferent as to the Concurrence of the Republick, and will not stirr one Step to procure it ; so that I look upon the affair as entirely broken off ; and if no further concessions are made, when Count Sinzendorf communicates the answer, I shall

[1] " Some Unpublished Letters of Lord Chesterfield."—*Nineteenth Century*, August, 1912, p. 284. (Chesterfield's spelling.)
[2] *Ibid.*

prepare with all speed for my departure, knowing very well how useless and even ridiculous my stay here would be afterwards.

" You may easily imagine how mortifying this Disappointment is to me upon all accounts, as well for my own sake as for the sake of the Confusion that I see will ensue ; for the Republick must and will throw itself into the Arms of France, and I can't help saying it is the Emperor's fault, for tho' I admitt that what the Republick asks is trifling and not worth asking, by the same rule I am sure it is not worth refusing." [1]

Even if allowance is made for a certain amount of diplomatic bluff in the above passage, this letter may be regarded as probably the most pessimistic that ever came from Chesterfield's pen. Of the many hundreds of his letters, private and official, published and unpublished, that have come before our notice, this is the only one in which despair untempered by philosophy is reflected. Optimism was perhaps the strongest of his natural characistics, and forms the bedrock upon which his philosophic conduct of life was based ; but the task of treating with the Republic of the Seven Provinces was enough to try the temper of the most cheerful philosopher, as the following letters will show.

To Harrington.

October 26, N.S.
" My Letters now are so many confessions of my own unskilfullness, since I cannot acquaint your Lordship that an affair in which I am employ'd, and in some measure referred to by both Partys, is yet adjusted ; but while I can't send his Majesty the account I could wish, I must continue to begg the indulgence I want. . . .

" The last draft of a Declaration that I offer'd, which Count Sinzendorf has agreed to, and which the Pensionary, the Greffier and I are endeavouring to bring the Deputys to sign, is as follows :—

" 'Sacra Caesarea et Catholica Majestas, Sacra Regia Majestas Magna Brittaniae et Celsi et Praepotentes Domini &c. hisce declarant, combinationem binarum partium Articuli quinti et praefixum in fine terminum, nullum alium

[1] Add. MSS. 23782, f. 499.

habere scopum quam prospicere Juri ; quod ex Tractatibus anterioribus, aequitate, vel rei natura resultat. '

" These words, as your Lordship sees, mean nothing, and yet I am in hopes will be accepted. Such is the nature of this Government, to give more attention to such nonsense in such Latin than to things of the greatest consequence."[1]

To Harrington.

October 30, N.S.

" I am sensible what a silly figure I make here in the mean time, labouring in vain for above Six Months to get the Republick into measures which for their own interest they ought to have come in to in six days : but I have not to do here with Ministers and People of Sense, but with a tumultous, ignorant, and obstinate multitude."[2]

To Harrington.

November 9, N.S.

" I received on Wednesday last the honour of your Lordship's letter of the 22nd October O.S. which brought me fresh instances of His Majesty's goodness and indulgence in not imputing to me the extraordinary and unaccountable delays of this Republick. I wish I could judge as favourably of myself, but when I consider how much time has been spent, and hitherto in vain, to bring the Republick into a measure to which their own interest so manifestly invites them, I cannot help thinking but that I must some how or other have been in fault."[3]

Harrington to Chesterfield (in reply).

November 2, O.S.

" I am sorry for the uneasy situation your Excellency seems to be in. No body certainly could have done more in that place than you have done, and I hope your Anxietys will be at an end very soon."[4]

To Robinson.

January 15, N.S., 1732.

" No body can be more persuaded than I am of your indefatigable endeavours to prevail with the Court of Vienna to facilitate the concurrence of this Republick

[1] State Papers (Holland), vol. CCCXV, f. 39.
[2] Add. MSS. 23783, f. 275.
[3] State Papers (Holland), vol. CCCXV, f. 97.
[4] Ibid., f. 102.

by shewing some complaisance ; and at the same time I am sensible how they have been frustrated by the Stiffness, or what they always call the Dignity, of that Court, of which I have seen many instances. I don't know whose Situation is the most disagreeable, yours or mine : you have to do with obstinate and able People, I with obstinate and ignorant ones ; yours won't hear reason, mine can't understand it if they hear it.

" I can't imagine what the Imperiall Ministers call the domineering of the English, unless they mean by it that we won't let them domineer over us, which I hope we never shall submitt to. Nobody wished more than I did to see the present system brought about, and nobody can wish more than I do to perpetuate it, but at the same time it must be continued upon the foot of equall friendship and not of dependance, and if the Court of Vienna aims at the latter I can easily prophesy that they will loose the former."[1]

Matters were now within a few weeks of actual conclusion, and the rest of the correspondence is largely taken up with the customary apologies on the part of Chesterfield, and felicitations to and from all concerned, of which the following extracts will serve as examples.

Harrington to Chesterfield.
January 25, O.S., 1732.

" As to the share your Excellency has had in the management and Conclusion of this important affair I must repeat to you that the King is entirely satisfyed with your Conduct, and is convinced that if it had been possible for any Body to have brought it to a speedier Issue your Excellency would have done it. And his Majesty is so far from imputing the inevitable Difficulties and Delays which have attended the whole Negociation to any Fault in your Excellency that He thinks it chiefly owing to your great application and abilitys that it is finished so happily, and even so soon." [2]

Chesterfield to Harrington.
February 20, N.S., 1732.

" Thus is this affair at last finish'd after a very tedious and probably a very unskilfull negotiation on my part. Its

[1] Add. MSS. 23784, f. 95.
[2] State Papers (Holland), vol. CCCXVI, f. 120.

own weight and his Majesty's great Credit and influence here have alone carried it through and overcome the many difficultys that wrong judgements, private Interests, personal picques, and the poor remains of an expiring French Party had raised to obstruct it till now. I am happy in having been the Instrument the King has employ'd to put the last hand to the Settlement of the present Tranquillity and future Security that he has procured for Europe. But I am still happier in the assurances your Lordship has given me of His Majesty's gracious approbation of my conduct, when all I could hope for was only his forgiveness of my faults."[1]

It would be pleasant to end this correspondence with Harrington's final letter of unqualified praise from the King,[2] or with Chesterfield's official letter of farewell to the States General,[3] in which the personal touches of affection and sorrow are suggested with such delicacy, yet strength of conviction, that to doubt their sincerity were as difficult as to reconcile them with certain expressions in the letters we have just read. Equally pleasant would it be to conclude this section with the thought of Chesterfield's enjoying a well-earned rest at St. James's Square, for whose comforts he had expressed such longing soon after his return to Holland in the Autumn of 1730. Happiness is, however, not always obtained in the realization of long-felt desires ; and, after full allowance has been made for conventional flattery, there remains a keen sense of disillusionment in the following letter to Torck written a few days after his return to England :—

" 3 Mars, V.S., 1732.
" Le peu de tems que j'ay été icy a été employé a des ceremonies tres fatiguantes, c'est a dire a recevoir et a faire de tres mauvais complimens, et il faut que je dise que jusqu'icy mon sejour de Londres ne m'a dedomagé en rien d'avoir quitté celuy de la Haye ; Et franchement vous autres,

---

[1] State Papers (Holland), vol. CCCXVI, f. 157. *Cf.* Chesterfield's letter to Robinson of February 21, N.S., in which he congratulates him " upon the compleating of a work that you begun with so much creditt and reputation, but which the tedious length of the Negotiations here denies me any pretensions to."—Add. MSS. 23784, f. 209.

[2] State Papers (Holland), vol. CCCXVI, f. 166.

[3] *Ibid.*, f. 173.

vous m'avez gaté pour les manieres Angloises, et mes chers compatriotes ne me ragoutent nullement. Sans mentir je regrette infiniment la vie de la Haye, qui m'accomodoit bien mieux que celle que je mene icy." [1]

Chesterfield had not yet learnt entirely to master disillusionment and disappointment. His philosophy was of gradual growth ; but disillusionment was not perhaps entirely what marred the happiness and peace of his return. He had left behind at the Hague many life-long friends, the record of difficult work successfully accomplished, and a European reputation for diplomatic tact and skill which survived his death. He had also left behind a young French governess, Madame du Bouchet, who, within a few days of his departure, became the mother of his son, and soon afterwards followed the father to England, where she lived with her child upon an allowance which he made her.

[1] " Some Unpublished Letters of Lord Chesterfield."—*Nineteenth Century*, August, 1912, p. 285.

III

IN OPPOSITION

CHESTERFIELD'S code, as we shall see, was not the fashionable code of honour then prevailing; and, while the strongest personality was required for its self-imposition in the first place, the strongest will was required to conform to it in the second. Too deliberately framed to come under the heading of conscience (by which is rather suggested a spontaneous bias, over whose advent we have no control, however much we may disregard its monitions) his code might be best termed a self-manufactured conscience, functioning in all respects like the real one, and, except in regard to relations with the opposite sex, of a not less exacting standard.

" He avowed no rule of conduct outside the urbane conventions of polite society." [1]

This statement of Sir Sidney Lee's will serve as a good example of the every-day conception of Chesterfield's moral code, unfairly based as it is on the *Letters to His Son*.[2] Its entire inaccuracy is exposed in No. 49 of the *World*,[3] wherein not only are the conventions of polite society ridiculed,[4] but a rule of conduct is avowed, lofty enough in its ideal to satisfy the sternest moral teacher :—

" The word Honour, in its proper signification, doubtless implies the united sentiments of virtue, truth, and justice, carried by a generous mind beyond those mere moral obligations, which the laws require, or can punish the violation of. A true man of honour will not content himself with the literal discharge of the duties of a man and

---

[1] Article on Chesterfield in the *Dictionary of National Biography*.

[2] It appears word for word with no more discretion than acknowledgment as the original utterance of Mr. Gordon Dorrance, obtruding itself as the only well-turned sentence in his introduction to a recent American publication on Chesterfield.—*The Pocket Chesterfield*, p. xxii. (Philadelphia : Dorrance & Co., 1920.)

[3] See p. 376 *post*.

[4] Note in particular the exquisite play on the word *gentle* in Chesterfield's footnote to the word *gentleman*.

a citizen ; he raises and dignifies them into magnanimity. He gives where he may with justice refuse, he forgives where he may with justice resent, and his whole conduct is directed by the noble sentiments of his own unvitiated heart ; surer and more scrupulous guides than the laws of the land, which, being calculated for the generality of mankind, must necessarily be more a restraint upon vices in general, than an invitation and reward of particular virtues."

This passage surely speaks for itself ; and yet the moral attitude of its author has been summed up by another eminent critic in these words :—

" We do not think of his Lordship as precisely immoral, but as afflicted with a kind of colour-blindness which prevented him from paying attention to the moral side of things in general."[1]

For reasons already stated, the subject of honour is not one with which Chesterfield was deeply concerned in the *Letters to his Son ;*[2] but the high standard of his moral code is manifested in his political letters, and, what is far more, in his political career, which may be not unfairly summarized as one long, consistent effort to keep to the path of honour, regardless of injury to self. Mr. Strachey has done good service in exposing once and for all, by a series of plain facts, the misconception (again founded on the *Letters to his Son*) of Chesterfield as a self-seeking politician with all the tricks of statecraft at his fingers' ends.

" Strange as it may appear to those who have been used to think of him as a supple courtier and unscrupulous schemer, Chesterfield had a positive genius for exasperating those whom he should have been at pains to conciliate, and for alienating sympathies which it was to his interest to secure. . . . He never went out of his way to please a possible patron."[3]

We do not think that Chesterfield's genius for exasperating possible patrons, or, as Craig terms it (p. 143), " his fatal tendency to the inopportune where his own personal

---

[1] Sir Leslie Stephen in the *Cornhill Magazine*, July, 1871, p. 97.
[2] See that of November 3, 1749, quoted on p. 4 *ante.*
[3] Introduction to *Letters of the Earl of Chesterfield to his Son*, p. 1.

interests were concerned," was simply a kink in his character, a mere personal caprice, as these writers, apparently at a loss for an explanation, would seem to suggest. If Chesterfield is judged, as he nearly always has been, from a purely personal standpoint, his political behaviour is for the most part inexplicable. Let him be regarded, however, in that impersonal light in which he invariably appears in the letters to his son and his essays, and there is at once a complete and consistent explanation of his conduct as a statesman.

Chesterfield, as is clearly indicated in almost every one of his speeches, was by nature a democrat, and, for the greater part of his period of opposition (1733–1744), England was governed by three people, Robert Walpole, Caroline, and George II, under as autocratic a sway as occurs in the whole of our modern history. Only twice during this régime, namely in the opposition to Walpole's Excise Bill, and the clamour for war with Spain in 1739, was the temper of the people asserted, and it is not to be wondered at that Chesterfield was tempted to use the first of these outcries as a means to rid the country of one whom he fervently believed to be a dangerous autocrat with a corrupt electorate at the end of his purse-strings.

Exactly what Chesterfield did on this occasion is not known, but in common with several other peers, including Scarborough, Cobham, Stair, Marchmont, and Montrose, he is said " to have declared against " the Bill.[1] Mahon tells us that " some sarcasms upon it were ascribed to himself " ;[2] Maty goes further and states that " he expressed in the strongest terms his disapprobation of the scheme."[3] He did not, as Craig asserts (p. 136), speak against the Bill in the House of Lords, since the measure never reached that House ;[4] but he is supposed to have persuaded his three brothers to vote against it in the House

[1] See Letters from Colonel the Hon. Charles Howard and Sir Thomas Robinson to Lord Carlisle, April 10 and 14, 1733.—*Carlisle Papers.* Hist. MSS. Comm., 15th Report, Appendix Part VI, pp. 107 and 110. In Robinson's letter may be found a most interesting and graphic account of the final debate on and dramatic abandonment of the Excise Bill.

[2] *History of England*, chap. xvi. vol. II, p. 169.

[3] Vol. I, p. 65.

[4] Philarète Chasles in a lengthy but inaccurate account of Chesterfield in the *Revue des Deux Mondes* (December, 1845), says of the Excise Bill that he "le foudroyait à la chambre des pairs." Carnarvon makes a similar mistake in mentioning Chesterfield's " vote on the Excise Bill."—*Letters to his Godson*, p. lxxxi.

of Commons. The fact that they did so vote was evidently regarded as significant at the time, for in a semi-official letter to the Earl of Essex, then Envoy at Turin, the Under-Secretary, Charles Delafaye, after giving a holograph account of the debate on the Excise Bill, adds in cipher, " It is observed that Lord Chesterfield's Brothers voted against the Majority."[1] The most interesting version of Chesterfield's attitude is to be found in the *Diary of Lord Egmont*,[2] who was at that time in close touch with Walpole, and can be regarded as a conscientious and impartial chronicler :—

" I was assuredly informed that Sir Robert made complaint to the King that my Lord Chesterfield's brother [brothers ?] voted against the Tobacco Bill, whereupon the King resenting it determined to turn John Stanhope (one of them) out of his place, and my Lord Chesterfield likewise ; but my Lord Wilmington, the Duke of Dorset, and Earl of Scarborough went straight to his Majesty and declared if he did so, they would lay down their places. This made his Majesty pause, and he ordered a meeting of them all with Sir Robert Walpole to reconcile matters, at which meeting Lord Chesterfield refused to be present, so ill he resented this affair. But the conclusion was that he should not be turned out, and he afterwards declared he would not lay down [*i.e.*, resign], purely to spite Sir Robert who wished he would."

Such, then, is the small amount of evidence we have been able to bring together on this important event in Chesterfield's life, and we trust it is not doing him an injustice to deduce from it that his opinions on the Excise Bill were sufficiently clearly indicated to justify Walpole in removing him from his post as Lord Steward.[3] This was done on

[1] April 5, 1733. Add. MSS. 27732, f. 147. (*Essex Papers.*) Though the Bill was ultimately abandoned there was never an actual majority against it in the House of Commons.

[2] Hist. MSS. Comm. (1920). Diary of Viscount Percival, afterwards First Earl of Egmont. Vol. I, p. 357.

[3] We have purposely omitted Horace Walpole's account of Chesterfield's disgrace, which he ascribes to the Queen's displeasure at the earl's intimacy with Lady Suffolk (Mrs. Howard). See his *Reminiscences of the Courts of George I and George II* in the *Letters of Horace Walpole* (edit. 1840), vol. I, p. lxxxii. His story is adopted by Coxe in his *Memoirs of Sir Robert Walpole*, vol. II, pp. 282, 283. Its manifest absurdity was first exposed by Croker in his addition of the *Suffolk Letters*, vol. II, p. 84 ; and Brougham

Incorrect ref; - 1798 ed.
Is their a later ed. of Coxe?

April 13, 1733, to the fury of the heated London populace, with whom he became for the time being a popular martyr.[1] Maty tells us that when the Duke of Grafton by order of the King demanded " the surrender of his white staff, his lordship chearfully complied ; and, without attempting any apology for his conduct, begged of his grace to assure his majesty that he was ready to sacrifice every thing for his service, except his honor and conscience."[2]   According to Hervey, " Lord Chesterfield wrote the King a letter next morning of which he gave me the following copy.[3]   The King sent him no answer ; and Sir Robert Walpole, to whom the King showed it, and who did not know I had seen it, told me that Chesterfield had written the King a letter, extremely laboured, but not well done."[4]

The *Craftsman*, after reporting Chesterfield's dismissal, added the following comment :—" The World seems greatly astonish'd at so unexpected an Event, and those who are most zealous for the present Royal Family grieve to see so *able* and *faithful a Servant* dismiss'd in so critical a Conjuncture."[5]   This passage was severely attacked in a Government publication, *The Free Briton* (April 26), on the grounds of disloyalty ; and a controversy ensued of which Maty gives a very fair summary.[6]   Not content, however, with censuring the *Craftsman*, the *Free Briton* hinted that, were it not a Breach of Privilege, certain underlying reasons could be given for Chesterfield's dismissal :—" Suppose that we were acquainted with more

tears it to shreds in the *Quarterly Review* of September, 1845, in which he states that, " This story has since been repeated in we know not how many books and essays ; and yet we must say that we think the editor of the *Suffolk Letters* disposed of it in the most conclusive manner more than twenty years ago." Coxe is subjected to a castigation as severe as it is merited. " The heaviest of Archdeacons never chuckled over a more palpable mare's nest ; but how he came to imbed it in the stiff clay of his own historic text without having taken the slightest trouble to compare the charmingly precise and particular *anecdote* of a Horace Walpole with the dates of about the most prominent events in Lord Chesterfield's public career is a specimen of incompetency for the study of affairs such as Clarendon himself could hardly have prognosticated for a Cathedral Close."

[1] See *Egmont Diary*, vol. I, p. 363.

[2] Vol. I, p. 66.   See also *Egmont Diary*, vol. I, p. 369, in which Chesterfield's actual words are cited thus, " I insist that you tell his Majesty my place and all I have in the world is at his Majesty's service, except my honour."

[3] " Unfortunately this was not preserved."   Croker's note.

[4] *Memoirs of the Reign of George II*, vol. I, p. 211.

[5] No. 355, April 21 ; not No. 354, April 14, as Maty states.

[6] Vol. I, pp. 66, 67.

than meerly *royal Will* and *Pleasure* as operating in this Affair ; suppose we knew by the *most authentick Information* that the noble Lord, by *Misbehaviour* or *Mistake*, be it better or worse, had imposed the Necessity on his Royal Master to remove him from his Service." Chesterfield at once sent a message to the editor giving him *carte blanche* " without any apprehensions of Breach of Privilege, or Actions of *Scandalum Magnatum*," to state these reasons. This challenge was not accepted.[1]

We should be chary of condemning Chesterfield's action as unprincipled, since the indictment is not clear and his defence has been lost. To our mind the strongest point in his favour is that Hervey, who never misses an opportunity of traducing Chesterfield, in the lengthy, first-hand account he gives of the whole affair, mentions nothing to his discredit beyond reporting Walpole's criticism of his letter to the king. A subsequent explanation of Chesterfield's conduct is to be found in a letter to the Duchess of Marlborough signed " S,"[2] and written in the year 1737. After highly praising the characters of Montrose, Chesterfield and Marchmont, the writer goes on to say : " These were the gentlemen that at the time of the Excise scheme first set up the standard against Sir Robert's measures with the advice and assistance of Lord Cobham, a very good Whig with a great deal of knowledge and a very good understanding. . . . They all opposed the Excise scheme as bringing too much power to the Crown, although they should lose the King's favour. They did not do this with a view to get into office."[3]

Craig[4] sums up the matter thus :—" That he may have acted upon conscientious grounds, and from a sincere belief in the dangers of the scheme, is of course possible ; but it is difficult to understand how the nature of the measure could have raised such apprehensions in a statesman of his experience, knowledge, and judgment. . . . It is not easy to discern the scruples by which so able a man as Chesterfield was led to oppose it." But unless Chesterfield subsequently changed his mind, he cannot be said to have objected *in theory* to Walpole's Excise Scheme, for in a long and impartial account of Lord Bute's Administration,

---

[1] See *Craftsman*, May 19, June 9 ; and *Free Briton*, May 24, etc.
[2] Possibly Lord Scarborough ?
[3] *Marlborough Papers*, Hist. MSS. Comm., 8th Report, Appendix Part I, p. 18.
[4] P. 136.

written in the year 1764, he discusses the Excise Scheme of thirty years afterwards (opposed so violently by Pitt)[1] as follows :—" Amongst the Ways and Means to raise the supplies of the year, an excise was laid upon cyder ; though the thing was right, the name was odious ; and Lord Bute, if he had had more experience, and known the temper of the people, would have known that even right things cannot be done at all times, especially at that dawn of his administration."[2]

It is surely possible that Chesterfield felt much the same in 1733, and that this was not the occasion for passing what he believed to be a sound measure. The country was almost unanimously opposed to the Bill, and its temper was thoroughly roused. Had it become law, the disorder occasioned by the debates upon it in Parliament might have reached serious extremes. There is certainly no evidence for supposing that Chesterfield's attitude towards the Bill differed from that of his friend Lord Scarborough, who, according to Hervey, two days before the second reading, " came to Sir Robert Walpole, to let him know that he found the clamour so hot and so general, that it was his opinion the Administration ought to yield to it ; that, for his own part, how right soever he might think this scheme in an abstracted light, yet, considering the turn it had taken, he was determined not to continue to cram it down the people's throats ; and came to tell Sir Robert that, if it should be forced through the House of Commons, and brought into the House of Lords, he would oppose it there. . . . The soldiers, he said, had got a notion that it would raise the price of tobacco, and upon this notion were so universally set against the scheme, that they cursed the Administration and the Parliament, murmured treason even under the walls of the palace, and were almost as ripe for mutiny as the nation for rebellion."[3]

---

[1] " In the House of Commons Pitt thundered against the intrusion of hired officers into private dwellings, and quoted the proud old maxim that every Englishman's house, was or should be his castle . . .

" In the Upper House it drew forth keen attacks from Lords Hardwicke, Lyttelton, and Temple ; and thirty-nine Peers recorded their votes against it ; the first time it is said when that branch of the Legislature ever divided on a money-Bill."—Mahon's *History of England*, chap. xli., vol. V, pp. 15–17.

[2] Bradshaw, vol. III, p. 1434.

[3] *Memoirs of the Reign of George II*, vol. I, pp. 189, 190. Hervey proceeds to relate his own attempts to persuade Walpole that Scarborough's action was the outcome of Chesterfield's influence over him.

We have no wish to press this suggestion beyond reasonable limits, but feel, in fairness to Chesterfield, that it should be considered together with our former surmise that he was also influenced by opportunist motives, and regarded the Bill as a convenient means of effecting Walpole's downfall.

Concerning Chesterfield's opposition to Walpole, which dated from his dismissal, Mr. Strachey observes :—

" Opposition to Walpole might conceivably have been carried on without completely breaking with King George —that is to say, such an ingenious feat might have been accomplished by Chesterfield had he really possessed the exceptional combination of slyness and selfishness with which he is often credited. . . . Ordinary prudence, which it would be ridiculous to regard as dishonourable, would have led even the least self-seeking of politicians to avoid, at least, any behaviour personally offensive to the King." [1]

Excellently stated ; but it must be remembered that Chesterfield's opposition was not merely opposition to Walpole. It was something more than personal opposition, more even than democratic opposition to an arbitrary ruler indulging in corrupt practices. There was not, in fact, very much in Walpole's own policy for Chesterfield to oppose. What he did mainly oppose, what he resented from pure patriotic fervour, was the Hanoverian policy imposed on Walpole, and afterwards upon Carteret, from the throne ; opposition to which could not be dissociated from personal offence to the King. Throughout Chesterfield's speeches and political pamphlets runs a note of solicitous regard for the interests of his country. He resented George II's spending English money on Hanoverian schemes in gratification of his personal whims ; objected, as he put it, to " the vessel of Great Britain being steered by the Hanoverian rudder." [2] " Ordinary prudence " would have allowed such objections to remain unstated, and whether Chesterfield, feeling as he did for his country, would have regarded silence on such points as dishonourable, must be left to the opinion of the reader. It is certain, however, as we shall see, that his standard of honour was a remarkably high one, and that he did not allow himself

---

[1] *Letters to His Son.* Introduction, vol. I, pp. li, lii.
[2] *Case of the Hanover Forces*, p. 10. Maty, vol. III, p. 48.

as a politician to be influenced by considerations of even ordinary prudence.

So long as George II was king there was always the danger of England being involved in European wars on account of the Electorate, and against this danger Chesterfield, both in the House of Lords and in the Press, acted as a salutary and constant guard. How much he *achieved* it is of course impossible to estimate, but it may at least be said that in the main his opposition was wholesome for the country, and ethically superior to the blind party opposition which characterized his times. There seem to be only two occasions on which it is difficult to acquit it entirely from the charge of factiousness.

The first is his advocacy of the war with Spain in 1739, which developed into the Continental War eventually concluded by the Treaty of Aix-la-Chapelle in 1748. Mahon's condemnation of the instigators of this war is for him remarkably heated.

" To inflame a headstrong resentment—to kindle an unjust and unprofitable war—to serve their party at the expense of principle—and to wound their antagonist through the sides of their country—such was the conduct of those who arrogated the name, but forsook the duty of PATRIOTS ! These noisy bawlers with NO SEARCH as their favourite cry, who exclaimed that unless that right were explicitly renounced by the Spaniards there should be no alternative but hostilities ; these very men, only ten years afterwards, cheerfully concurred in a peace that left the Right of Search altogether unnoticed and secured ! "[1]

Upon some of the counts in this severe indictment, Chesterfield must be acquitted. How far the war was unjust is a historical question to discuss which would take us too far from the subject of these pages. That it was misguided in its inception is generally agreed, but the national feeling was so strong, so unanimous, that it seems almost straining a point to censure its advocates as inspired by nothing more than party faction. That the war was an unprofitable one cannot be laid to the charge of all its instigators, least of all perhaps to Chesterfield, who never ceased to oppose the dilatory manner in which it was carried on, first by Walpole and afterwards by Carteret

[1] *History of England*, chap. xx., vol. II, pp. 282, 283.

and Newcastle. Had the war been concluded, as Chesterfield strongly urged, in 1743, when generous terms were offered by the Emperor of Austria and the French, it might be regarded to-day as an adornment to instead of as a dark blot on the pages of our history.

The second instance of Chesterfield's apparently factious opposition was his support of the Bill to indemnify witnesses giving evidence in the Secret Committee Enquiry into Walpole's administration, from penalties to which they might become liable by their disclosures. This Bill has been freely attacked by the historians on ethical grounds.[1] Despite their partiality, it is perhaps worth quoting Coxe's censures :—

" Many words are not required to show the fatal tendency of a Bill, calculated to suborn witnesses, to multiply accusations, to encourage villains to accuse a person who was innocent, or at least, should be deemed innocent, until he was proved guilty, to bribe men to give evidence to save their own lives and estates ; a bill in which the enquiry was uncertain, and the indemnity as uncertain as the discovery which the witnesses might make. For it did not lay down any specific object of which the earl of Orford was supposed guilty, it did not offer the payment of a certain sum of money, or the pardon of any particular crime ; but the persons who gave evidence were to be indemnified for *all* the sums which they might lose, and receive a pardon for *all* the crimes which they might disclose, in giving evidence against the earl of Orford. It was holding up the ex-minister as a public felon, and converting the House of Commons into a tribunal of blood. . . .

" The reader . . . will turn with horror from the malignant comparison of Chesterfield, who endeavoured to prove, that *such an indemnity was not a new thing in our constitution, because rewards were daily offered to highwaymen and murderers, for the discovery of their accomplices.*"

Writing to Mann on May 14, 1742, Horace Walpole characteristically observes : " It is so absurd a bill that there is not the least likelihood of its passing the Lords.[2]

[1] Coxe's *Memoirs of Sir Robert Walpole* (edit. 1816), chap. l, vol. IV, pp. 289–292. Mahon's *History of England*, chap. xxiv., vol. III, p. 122. J. M. Robertson's *Bolingbroke and Walpole*, pp. 203, 204.
[2] It was rejected in the House of Lords on May 25, by 109 to 52. See Horace Walpole to Mann, May 26, 1742.

F

By this bill, whoever are guilty of murder, treason, forgery, etc., have nothing to do but to add perjury, and swear Lord Orford knew of it, and they may plead their pardon."

It is difficult at first glance to imagine the support of such a bill to be inspired by any motives other than those of rancour and malignity ; yet such evidence as we have seems to indicate that Chesterfield felt no *personal* ill-feeling towards his late political enemy.   We learn from Horace Walpole that when the fallen minister took his seat in the House of Lords, three months before Chesterfield's speech on the Indemnity Bill, " The Bedford, Halifax, Berkshire, and some more [*sic*] were close by him, but would not bow to him.   Lord Chesterfield wished him joy."[1] Again, six months after Chesterfield's speech, the same writer tells his friend that at a levee the new Earl of Orford " had a long, laughing conversation with my Lord Chesterfield, who is still in Opposition."[2]   Moreover, the speech itself, in which Chesterfield disclaimed any sentiment of pique against Lord Orford, is argued, if vehemently, in a purely impersonal spirit.   The opening words, containing a graceful compliment to Carteret, who had opposed the Bill in a particularly brilliant speech, are worth quoting :—

" I have so long honoured the abilities, and so often concurred with the opinion of the noble lord who began the debate, that I cannot, without unusual concern, rise up now to speak in opposition to him ; nor could any other motive support me under the apparent disadvantage of a contest so unequal, but the consciousness of upright intentions, and the concurrence of the whole nation."[3]

Odious as the Bill was in its nature, the Commons and country knew that without some such legislative aid the Secret Committee could not proceed.   Witness after witness had refused to commit himself.   There was a growing feeling in the country against the amount of jobbery and peculation which was known to exist, and which it was hoped the Secret Enquiry would expose, and in exposing destroy.   No one loathed bribery more than Chesterfield, and it would perhaps have been too much to expect him to refrain from supporting so distinct an effort (misguided

[1] Letter to Horace Mann, February 18, 1742.
[2] Letter to Horace Mann, November 15, 1742.
[3] Maty, I, p. 112.   12 *Parl. Hist.* 650.

though it was) in the direction of political purity. Among the many charges made justly or unjustly against Chesterfield, that of humbug cannot be found even in the attacks of his bitterest opponents, and it is hard to convict him in this instance of humbug or even self-deceit in his avowed " consciousness of upright intentions." Rather would it seem that as he did not allow self-interest to hinder him from pursuing the straight path, neither would he allow consideration for others so to move him. His attitude towards this question is, in fact, as consistent with his policy as a statesman, as his action in welcoming Walpole to the House of Lords was with his every-day conduct as a gentleman.

We have thought it necessary to dwell for some time on these two instances because they are the only ones in the eleven years of Chesterfield's opposition, against which the charge of faction can be reasonably preferred. His own views on faction are clearly expressed in the first number of his paper *Old England or the Constitutional Journal*.[1]

" All experience convinces me that ninety men out of a hundred, when they talk of forming principles, mean no more than embracing parties, and, when they talk of supporting their party, mean serving their friends, and the service of their friends implies no more than consulting self-interest. By this gradation, principles are fitted to party, party degenerates into faction, and faction is reduced to self. For this reason I openly declare that I think no honest man will implicitly embrace any party, so as to attach himself to the persons of those who form it. I am firmly of opinion that, both in the last and present age, this nation might have been equally well served either by whigs or tories ; and, if she was not, it was not because their principles were contrary to her interest, but because their conduct was inconsistent with their principles."

To these views he adhered after retiring from office, for on March 26, 1750, he writes to the young Earl of Huntingdon as follows :—

" Your notion of our parties is so just that one would think you must have been concerned with them all, to know them so well ; but yet as things are circumstanced here, it

---

[1] February 5, 1743. Maty, vol. I, *Miscellaneous Pieces*, p. 109. See also W. Sichel's *Bolingbroke and his Times*, Vol. II, p. 278.

will be impossible for you not to adopt to a certain degree some one. In business one must have connections, and party forms those connections ; the difference is that a fool embraces with zeal the errors of his party, a knave, the guilt, but a man of sense and virtue the general principle only, and therefore he adopts that party whose general principle he knows to be right. The natural rights and liberty of mankind are the true objects of Whiggism, for which reason your own good sense and virtue made you adopt that party in spite of all the prejudices of a West-minster[1] and Oxford education, but not without seeing the knavery, or the folly of most of the individuals, who either bubbled or bribed, often act directly contrary to the right principles which they profess.''[2]

In the main, therefore, we think that Chesterfield's opposition policy was as free from faction as from self-interest, and the only possible motives remaining would seem to be those of either high principle or personal pique, with neither of which is it *prima facie* inconsistent. This latter motive Lord Rosebery regards as the chief directing force in Pitt's policy from the time he first entered Parliament in 1735 until Carteret's fall in 1744 [3]—a policy which, during those years, was almost identical with Chesterfield's. But whatever reasons Pitt had for pique they were almost negligible compared with those of the elder statesman.

It is, in fact, impossible to read Chesterfield's political essays in *Common Sense* without recognizing a trace of personal feeling. Except for the letters to his friends they are, without doubt, the least impersonal of any of his writings. But if it is impossible entirely to defend them, they become at least softened upon investigation. The anti-Hanoverian case was a sound one from a patriot's point of view, and was presented in its serious aspect by Chesterfield and Waller in their three lengthy and well-reasoned pamphlets, *The Case Against the Hanover Forces,* etc.[4] But when presented in a racy paper by an acknow-ledged wit, was it not likely that nasty little hits at the Hanoverians, naughty little allusions to George II should

---

[1] *Cf.* " Westminster school is, undoubtedly, the seat of illiberal manners and brutal behaviour.''—Letter to his Son, January 18, 1750.   Bradshaw, vol. I, p. 313.
[2] *Letters of Lord Chesterfield to Lord Huntingdon,* p. 9.
[3] *Chatham,* pp. 189-191.
[4] Maty, vol. III, pp. 43-170.

occur ? Malicious would be perhaps too strong a term to employ, because the wit is throughout carefully directed against George the Elector, not against George personally, still less against George the King. In this respect his contributions differ from those of the other writers in *Common Sense*, whose antagonism to the King suggests more the angry unreasoned cry of the people. Chesterfield, though himself a keen anti-Jacobite, believed that the Whigs, in their extreme anti-Jacobitism, were paying an unnecessary price for a Protestant king ; whereas it was a simple matter to keep George's Hanoverian policy in check. In the third number of *Old England* he claims that, " This royal family has not a more faithful and loyal subject in the kingdom than myself ; and if I may borrow an expression I have long admired, it is under this royal family alone that I think we can live free, and that I hope we are determined to live free." [1]

Chesterfield's antipathy to the Court was exhibited perhaps most openly when he declined to observe the order issued in respect of mourning for Queen Caroline, who died on November 20, 1737.[2] But even on this occasion his prevailing motive seems to have been not one of personal feeling, but of objection on principle to what he considered arbitrary conduct on the part of the Crown, as can be seen from the following letters to Lyttelton, which serve well to illustrate his independence of spirit and jealousy of encroachments upon individual liberty.[3]

" Bath. November 28, 1737.
" Pray what do those Peers, who are neither paid for voting nor mourning, intend to do with regard to this silly

---

[1] February 19, 1743. Maty, vol. I. *Miscellaneous Pieces*, p. 116. The expression is " borrowed " from the last paragraph of the Lords' Protest in 1737 against the defeat of the motion for settling £100,000 per annum on the Prince of Wales. " We thought it more incumbent upon us to insist upon this motion, for the sake of this Royal Family, under which alone we are fully convinced we can live free ; and under the Royal Family we are fully determined we will live free." See Hervey's *Memoirs of the Reign of George II*, vol. III, pp. 88–90. This protest " was signed, if not penned, by Lord Chesterfield." Maty, vol. I, p. 84.

[2] " I have heard nothing remarkable of late from England. Lord Chesterfield is neither gone into Mourning nor has he been at Court to make a Compliment of Condoleance."—E. Hamilton, writing from Leyden to the Duke of Ormonde, January 27, 1738.—*Weston Papers*. Hist. MSS. Comm., 10th Report, Part I, p. 513.

[3] *Cf.* Chesterfield's reference to " this long mourning, by which trade has suffered so immensely," in *Common Sense*, November 11, 1738. See p. 230 *post*.

Order of Council for putting coaches and servants in mourning ? It seems to me indecent to comply with it after one has observed the Order of Council of 1728[1] in cases where one should otherwise have shown the highest regard. Lord Winchelsea, for instance, in obedience to that Order, did not put his liveries nor coaches in mourning for his wife nor his father, and ought he then to do it upon this occasion ? To me, this new Order of Council seems to be a declaration that no public marks of regard, tenderness, and affection shall be shown in this kingdom but for the sacred persons of the Royal Family. I would in this, as in everything else, avoid singularity, but if any number of Peers will have spirit enough not to comply, I will be one of them ; in all events, I'll stay till I get to town before I take any step in this matter." [2]

" Bath. December 12, 1737.
" As to the mourning, I shall observe the King's order of 1728, and not My Lord President's of 1737. It might be very proper, in consequence of an arrêt de par le Roy in France, to overturn all the rights of blood, friendship, and regard for any but the sacred persons of the Royal Family, to whom alone, to be sure, they are due, but here, in my opinion, it is *yet* a meanness to do it, and I will be one of the last to come into it.

" I am sorry it did not occur to my Lord President to propose a Deification of her late Majesty, and that the Bishops should be ordered to perform the ceremony of her Apotheosis in the true Pagan manner ; if it had, I make no doubt but it would have been readily ordered and religiously complied with. I am not the least afraid of having my chariot or liveries insulted for being out of mourning ; besides, at this time of year the black would show *dirt* more than the blue."[3]

[1] This Order was dated 14th November, nearly eighteen months after the death of George I. After referring at some length to " the Hardships and Discouragements that so many of His Majesty's Trading Subjects labour under in respect of the long Continuance both of public and private Mournings," the Order declares that " for the future upon any Publick or Court Mourning His Majesty will not require or expect that any persons whatsoever should put their Coaches, Chairs, or any of their Servants into Mourning, and that the time for the continuance of all such Publick or Court Mourning be no more than one half of the time that has been usuall and customary on those occasions."—Public Record Office. Privy Council I, 4, bundle 23.
[2] Mahon, vol. V, pp. 431–2.
[3] *Ibid.*, pp. 433–4.

Chesterfield's brother, John Stanhope, writing from Paris to Lady Denbigh, discusses the matter in a less bitter spirit :—

" I might I fancy as well tell you Queen Elizabeth is dead as that Queen Caroline is so ; to be sure so important an event is come to your knowledge long ago ; all the English here have follow'd the example of Lord Wald-grave, have taken the deepest mourning for her yesterday, both men and women. The ambassador puts all his ser-vants, equipage and apartments in black. The time of mourning is a year, the first six months deep. You will believe me when I tell you I am really sorry for her death, for now the Lyon coat must lie by a great while ; I have never wore it. I have another apprehension about me, which is that, since it's necessary to mourn so very strictly out of the kingdom, when I come to London perhaps I may be ordered to black my face, who can tell ? " [1]

But though Chesterfield's opposition may have been influenced to some extent by personal pique, it is obvious from his letters to the Scottish peers that in the main it was guided by considerations for his country. Towards the end of Walpole's administration, when the less disin-terested members of the opposition were scenting office in the near future, he writes as follows to Lord Stair:—

December 3, 1739.
" The Bill to limit the number of place-men in Parlia-ment is to be brought in after the holidays, and will, I suppose, be as soon rejected. . . . To tell you the plain truth, many of the Opposition do not in their hearts greatly relish the place-bill, which they think might prove a clog upon their own Administration . . . If the whole Opposition meant the same thing as you and I do, they would most certainly entertain this measure, which is the only one that can recover the constitution ; all others are but temporary palliatives ; for while the Houses of Lords and Commons are absolutely in the power of the Crown, as they visibly now are, we have no constitution, and the Crown alone is, without a mystery, the three branches of the Legislature.

[1] December 16, 1737. *Denbigh Papers* (Part V), Hist. MSS. Comm., (1911) p. 225.

But unfortunately, I doubt, this is what many people desire as heartily as you and I wish the contrary.

" Sir Robert's health is thought to be very precarious, and there are many of us who already anticipate in their thoughts the joyful moment, which they think not remote, of coming into power ; and consequently, far from desiring to make shackles for themselves, are rather willing to continue those upon the people which Sir Robert has forged for them. This, I own, is a melancholy case ; but I fear it is too much the case. The persons you allude to, that you think might be prevailed with to act against Sir Robert, are not to be moved. They have been tried, and their own interest in so doing has been manifestly shown them, but to no purpose. They consider money as their only interest, and would not venture the suspension of a quarter's salary, to save the whole nation. This, my dear Lord, is our wretched situation, from whence, I think, little good can arise. Union among ourselves cannot be expected, where our views are so widely different. This Sir Robert knows, and triumphs in. I despair of either doing good or seeing any done ; yet while I live, I assure you, I will endeavour it. I wish my country well, and upon that principle alone must wish you so ; but many other considerations concur to make me honour and esteem you as I do, and to form that attachment and friendship with which I shall ever be, My dear Lord, etc." [1]

And again, five months later :

" My DEAR LORD,
" I wish I had anything better than thanks to return you for your several letters ; but, unfortunately, I can send you no accounts from hence, that I can write or you read with satisfaction. The Opposition is, in truth, become no Opposition at all—is looked upon already in that light by the Court, and I am afraid, will soon be so by the whole nation. The views of the individuals are too different for them to draw together. Some few mean the public good, and they are for acting and pushing of constitutional measures ; but many more mean only their private interest, and they think public inaction and secret negotiations the most conducive to it. They consider Sir Robert's life as a bad one, and desire, by their submission and tame-

[1] Bradshaw, vol. II, pp. 752, 753.

ness, to recommend themselves to be his successors. The Court, they say, is too strong to be overcome by Opposition; that is, in truth, they think it would be too strong for their impatience for power upon any terms. In this distracted state of the Opposition, you will not be surprised that nothing is done, and that the Court triumphs . . .

If all meant as well as you do, I should, with more hopes and better spirits, take what little part I am able ; but I confess that, in the present situation of things, I rather content myself with not doing ill, than hope to do any good. I will keep my conscience and my character clear, wish what I should, and do what I can ; *et pour le reste, alors comme alors.''* [1]

A year later we find him on the eve of a holiday abroad in an unusually despairing mood, ill in health and sick at heart over the self-seeking faction of the Opposition and their anti-patriotic actions, writing to Lord Marchmont a letter in which he concludes :—" The curiosity of knowing what becomes of one's country, and one's friends, is natural ; nay, the want of it would be blameable ; but beyond that, I protest, the melancholy prospect before us has sunk me into such an indifference as to public matters, that I should neither trouble my friends nor myself about them. I want[2] those two great prevailing springs of action, avarice and ambition ; and being convinced that, as the world goes, a man that will enjoy a quiet conscience must lead a quiet life, I most cheerfully embrace an honest, however contemptible obscurity." [3]

Six weeks later he writes to Lyttelton from Aix-la-Chapelle :—" If I recover my health and spirits, they shall be at the service of my friends, to employ as they think proper, and as occasions allow. If not, the honest comforts of a private life shall be my determination, as they have long been my wish." [4]

How, we wonder, has it come about that Chesterfield is so often credited with an over-weening degree of political ambition, since every particle of evidence on the question

[1] May, 1740. Bradshaw, vol. II., pp. 754–756.
[2] *I.e.* " I lack."
[3] April 24, 1741. Bradshaw, vol. II, p. 761.
[4] June 6, 1741. Mahon, vol. V., p. 441. See also his letter to Lyttelton of August 1, 1741—*Ibid.*, pp. 442, 443.

points to the exact contrary ? Would it not be more natural to accept this want of ambition, and, remembering his recurrent periods of ill-health and oft-expressed desire for a quiet life, to regard his political services as governed by purely altruistic motives ? It is at least certain that to the sentiments expressed in these letters he remained perfectly true on the dissolution in 1742 ; for, although Walpole's fall was as much due to Chesterfield as to anyone, he declined to join in the general scramble for office, and, in fact, remained in opposition for nearly three more years.

Mr. Charles Whibley, drawing somewhat rash conclusions from the more pessimistic of Chesterfield's letters written during his holiday abroad in 1741, states that " he wandered further and further away from public affairs, and fell out of humour with the controversies which once engrossed him . . . Whether the lack of interest came from philosophy, or idleness, he did not determine. But true it is that his withdrawal was complete, and not even the retirement of Sir Robert Walpole nor that broken leader's accession to the House of Lords availed to bring Chesterfield back into the cockpit of politics." [1] This statement entirely lacks foundation, and is, in fact, contradicted on the same page by Mr. Whibley himself, who remarks that, " From 1732, the year of his return from his first embassy, until 1745, when he went to Ireland as Lord-Lieutenant, he was busily engaged in fighting Walpole." To be strictly accurate, Chesterfield's opposition to Walpole began when he was dismissed from office in April, 1733, and ended with the debate on the Secret Enquiry Bill after Walpole's fall in March 1742. " That broken leader's accession to the House of Lords " is of no material importance, since he only spoke once in the Upper Chamber.

The simple facts are that Parliament was dissolved at the end of April, 1741, and did not sit again until December. Chesterfield, to recover his health, left for the Continent in May, and returned in five or six months "restored to vigour and active at his post." [2] Horace Walpole writing to Mann on December 10, 1741, mentions that " Lord Chesterfield made a very fine speech against the Address, all levelled at the House of Hanover," and from that time

[1] *The Criterion*, April, 1924, p. 245.

[2] Mahon's *History of England*, chap. **xxiii**, vol. III, p. 92.   See also Pitt to Chesterfield, Aug. 6 and Sept. 10, 1741.   *Chatham Correspondence* vol. I, pp. 1–4.

until his appointment in 1744 Chesterfield was never absent from " the cockpit of politics." His motives for remaining in opposition after Walpole's fall are clearly expressed in a letter written to Dr. Chenevix at that time.

" I need not tell you, I am sure, how much I wish to be able to contribute to the advantageous change of your situation, but I am sure, too, that I cannot tell you when I shall ; for, till I can do it consistently with my honour and conscience, I will not do it at all, and I know you do not desire I should. The public has already assigned me different employments, and among others that which you mention ; but I have been offered none, I have asked for none, and I will accept of none till I see a little clearer into matters than I do at present ; I have opposed measures not men ; [1] and the change of two or three men only is not a sufficient pledge to me that measures will be changed ; nay, rather an indication that they will not ; and I am sure no employment whatsoever will prevail with me to support measures I have so justly opposed. A good conscience is in my mind a better thing than the best employment, and I will not have the latter till I can keep it with the former ; when that can be I shall not decline a public life, though in truth, more inclined to a private one."[2]

---

[1] " Measures, not men, have always been my mark."—Goldsmith : *The Good-natured Man* (1768). Burke, in his *Thoughts on the Causes of the Present Discontents* (1770), attacks the cant of " not men but measures." —Bradshaw's note.

[2] March 6, 1742. Bradshaw, vol. II, p. 768. See also letter to Lord Stair, January 6, 1743. Appendix p. 299 *post*.

IV

IN OFFICE

WHEN eventually Chesterfield did obtain office his political conduct remained as disinterested as it had been throughout his opposition and in his previous posts. In his last letter to his godson [1] he wrote :—

" If you should ever fill a great station at Court, take care above all things to keep your hands clean and pure from the infamous vice of corruption, a vice so infamous that it degrades even the other vices that may accompany it. Accept no present whatever ; let your character in that respect be transparent and without the least speck, for as avarice is the vilest and dirtiest vice in private, corruption is so in public life. I call corruption the taking of a sixpence more than the just and known salary of your employment, under any pretence whatsoever. Use what power and credit you may have at Court, in the service of merit rather than of kindred, and not to get pensions and reversions for yourself or your family, for I call that also, what it really is, scandalous pollution, though of late it has been so frequent that it has almost lost its name."

The course he preaches here was practised by him to the letter. The only recorded instance of Chesterfield's being offered a bribe was in George I's reign, when efforts were made to induce him to join the King's party, where his kinsman, General Stanhope, who was then chief minister, would have been of the greatest service to him. The reward offered was a dukedom for his aged father, and Chesterfield, at the cost of annoying both parent and kinsman, refused to accept the offer. [2] When he was appointed Captain of the Yeomen of the Guard in 1723,

[1] ' To be delivered after his own Death.'—Bradshaw, vol. II, p.657.
[2] Maty, vol. I, pp. 26, 27.

his predecessor, Lord Townshend, who had not availed himself of the patronage which the post entailed, advised him to make it more profitable than he himself had done, by disposing of the places. Chesterfield's reply was, " I rather, for this time, wish to follow your Lordship's example than your advice." [1]

Chesterfield carried his hatred of corruption to the extent of refusing all rewards for public services. On his resigning the Seals of Secretary of State in 1748, George II offered him the alternative of a dukedom or a pension, both of which he declined. He also refused the red ribbon of the Bath, which was offered as a reward for his services as Captain of the Yeomen. His action in this instance has been attributed to less worthy motives. It is thought by some writers [2] that he considered the reward unworthy of his rank. Others suggest that he feared it might be a bar to the Garter. There is no direct evidence in support of either opinion, and neither motive is consistent with his public character. That he was anxious to obtain the Garter is certain, but his motives are expressed with as much reason as importunity in a letter to Lord Townshend, written from the Hague on August 31, N.S., 1728.

". . . By the death of the Duke of York there are now two Garters vacant that probably will not long remain so, and your Lordship knows by the former applications I have troubled you with on that score, how desirous and ambitious I am of that honour. Your Lordship knows too, that, though it is at all times a mark of honour and his Majesty's favour, yet it can never be of so much (or indeed of any real) use to me, as now, that I have the honour to be in the station I am in. In the first place the thing itself is much more considered abroad than in England ; in the second place, such a mark of favour is much more necessary for those who have the honour of being employed abroad, than for those who have the advantage of being at home ; and I am sure every body will agree that I can never have it so advantageously for myself (especially in this country) as at a time when it must be known to be entirely owing to your Lordship's friendship and recommendation. It may possibly be

[1] Maty, vol. I, pp. 30, 31.
[2] Abraham Hayward and Lord Carnarvon.

owning a great weakness when I confess to your Lordship that I would rather have this one mark of his Majesty's and your favour than any one other thing that your Lordship can recommend to, or the King dispose of ; but at the same time I hope it may in some measure excuse the great earnestness with which I beg leave to recommend this request to your protection ". . . [1]

To this letter Townshend made an encouraging reply on September 6, O.S., followed by three more in the same month[2] to the effect that the vacant Garters were not going to be bestowed in the immediate future, but that Chesterfield could live in hopes. The third of these four letters is perhaps worth quoting to show George II's opinion of Chesterfield at that time.

" Windsor, September 13, 1728.

" My Lord,

" My Lord Lincoln being lately dead, and a third Garter being thereby become vacant, I this morning took an opportunity of laying your Lordship's request in that matter before the King, which I can assure you His Majesty received in a most gracious and favourable manner, and with as particular a regard for your Lordship as you could wish. His Majesty told me that I knew his Intention was not to dispose of these vacant Garters at present, that he had seen your desire in that behalf by the Letter you had wrote to me, that he was sensible of your zeal for his service, that he was well pleased with your behaviour, and that you might be assured he would have you in his thoughts in the bestowing of these favours, not doubting but that you would continue to serve him with the same application, good conduct and ability you had hitherto done.

" I am etc   TOWNSHEND."

On March 25, N.S., 1729, Chesterfield, " being informed that the vacant Garters are to be disposed of before the King leaves England," renewed his application to Townshend who replied on March 18, O.S., that their disposal was still in abeyance, but that he would do his best for him.[3] As things turned out, however, Chesterfield did

[1] Bradshaw, vol. II, pp. 684, 685.
[2] State Papers (Holland), vol. CCCI., ff. 278, 282, 306; vol. CCCII, f.24.
[3] *Ibid.*, vol. CCCIII., ff. 235 and 237.

not receive the honour until after Townshend's downfall, reasons for which can be found in the following interesting information communicated to Maty " by one of Lord Chesterfield's intimate friends " :—" The first time he appeared at court on his return to London (the 24th of October, 1729),[1] Sir Robert Walpole took him aside and told him, ' I find you are come to be Secretary of State.'

" ' Not I,' said his Lordship, ' I have as yet no pretensions, and wish for a place of more ease. But I claim the Garter, not as a reward for my late services, but in virtue of his majesty's promise while prince of Wales. I am a man of pleasure, and the blue ribband would add two inches to my size.'

" ' Then I see how it is,' replied Sir Robert, ' it is Townshend's intrigue, in which you have no share ; but it will be fruitless : you cannot be Secretary of State, nor shall you be beholden for the gratification of your wishes to any body but myself.' "[2]

The authenticity of this conversation, which is in substance characteristic of both men, does not seem open to dispute, but for reasons which will shortly appear it would be wise to take the last sentence of Chesterfield's reply with a grain of salt. The motives which the unassuming statesman was at times pleased to ascribe to his public conduct are to be regarded with suspicion.[3] His contempt for birth and rank was far too deeply ingrained for us to believe that his desire for the Garter was prompted by motives of personal vanity. He was doubtless conscious of his rather unfortunate physical exterior, and felt that " the blue ribband " would do more than anything to give him that standing on the Continent that was necessary to his work. If, moreover, he felt entitled to it by virtue of a promise, he was the last person to surrender what he considered his moral due. His code of right and wrong was so unbending in its application that he seldom gave way to personal considerations whether of convenience or inconvenience

A trivial but illuminating instance of this uncompromising and impersonal course of action occurred during

[1] He had left the Hague on leave only four days previously.
[2] Maty, vol. I, sect. III., note 30, pp. 291-2. See also p. 33 *ante*.
[3] Note in particular the reasons that he gives for accepting the Lord Lieutenancy of Ireland, reasons that are modest to the point of gross insincerity, and Craig's excellent comment thereon,—(p. 89 *post*).

his first Embassy at the Hague when the Grand Pensionary, the Austrian Envoy (Sinzendorf), and himself were at their wits' end to make Holland a party to the Second Treaty of Vienna. By way of expediting matters Chesterfield had persuaded the Deputies of the States General to allow him to be present at their Conferences on the Treaty—an unusual proceeding, and one which showed their trust in him. What then, could have been more advisable for all three parties than the simultaneous presence of Sinzendorf at the Conferences? The Deputies did not object : Chesterfield wanted it, and so did Sinzendorf. The two envoys had for each other not only deep respect but a fellow-feeling amounting to more than ordinary friendship. There was, however, one objection to the plan : it involved the surrender of a portion of England's national prestige— not a very considerable portion, but Chesterfield's first duty was to safeguard his country's dignity, and the following rigmarole taken from one of his letters to Harrington will show how he did it.

" As soon as this Conference was over I went to Count Sinzendorf, and told him what had passed at it, and asked him if he had any difficulty as to my assisting at those Conferences. He answered that he should be extreamly glad of it in all respects but one in which he was not the Master, which was the Precedency, but that if I appeared at those Conferences he must immediately produce his full Powers wherein he is styled *Legatum Nostrum Extraordinarium*, after which he said he supposed I would not contest the rank with him. I told him that I supposed no such thing, for that his Title of Ambassador Extraordinary in his full Powers was only for the signing of the Treaty, and not for the previous Negociations; and that unless he was *accredité* to the Republick as Ambassador Extraordinary I could by no means give him the *Pas*.

" I immediately acquainted the Members of the Conference with this incident, and we have agreed that our Conferences shall be separate ; but that if a case should happen wherein it may be necessary we should both be present, that the Members of the Conference shall come out to us in another room without Chairs, and confer standing without any ceremony or precedency." [1]

---

[1] 19th June, 1731, N.S. State Papers (Holland), vol. CCCXIII, ff. 74–5.

Puerile and contemptible as this must sound to the
modern ear, let us not be in too great a hurry to condemn
Chesterfield as a small-minded stickler for details, a touchy,
pettifogging snob.   This letter was written by a man who
had a personal dislike for ceremony, who, three years
before, had pleaded with the eloquence of a schoolboy to
be excused from making a " public entry " into the Hague ;[1]
and who afterwards resigned the Lord Lieutenancy of
Ireland probably on account of his dislike for the regality
it involved more than for any other reason.   He had
nothing to gain by his action except George II's possible
approval.[2]   There was on the other hand a fair amount
to lose—the risk of offending Sinzendorf and all that that
might involve, and a certain loss of time which could only
redound to his own discredit and inconvenience.   As
things turned out little harm was done, and we learn from
a letter to Torck that Sinzendorf was admitted to a Conference the very day after Chesterfield had written to
Harrington.

" Les Conferences ont commencez, et Mercredi passé
(June 20th) Mr. Sinzendorf en eut une qui dura trois
heures . . . Je n'ay pas assisté a cette Conference a cause
du Ceremoniel entre Sinzendorf et moy ; Mais comme vos
Messrs veulent absolument que j'y assiste a l'avenir, on a
trouvé un Expedient pour le Ceremoniel."[3]

The reader must form his own opinion of this action :
we have recorded it only as an interesting application
of Chesterfield's inviolable rule in life—Duty before
Expediency.

A somewhat similar instance occurred in 1745, though
in this case it was Chesterfield's own dignity and not his
country's that was involved.   After Newcastle and others
by the utmost skill and persuasion had made the King
submit to granting Chesterfield Office under the Broad
Bottom Administration, the Earl risked upsetting all
their plans by insisting, against the strongest royal opposition, on being received in the closet by George before

---

[1] See his letter to Townshend of June 30, 1728, and the latter's reassuring
reply ;   State Papers (Holland), vol. CCC., ff. 289, 301.

[2] This was, as a matter of fact, formally expressed in Harrington's reply.

[3] June 22, 1731.   " Some Unpublished Letters of Lord Chesterfield."—
Nineteenth Century, August, 1912, p. 281.

G

proceeding on his embassy to the Hague;[1] apropos of which Horace Walpole writes to Mann on January 14, 1745 :—" Lord Chesterfield is set out for the Hague : I don't know what ear the States will lend to his embassy, when they hear with what difficulty the King was brought to give him a parting audience ; and which, by a watch, did not last five-and-forty seconds." If ever there was an occasion when a point of ceremony might have been waived, this was one. It was a small right to insist upon, but it was a right, and therefore had to be observed.

The same uncompromising attitude was adopted by Chesterfield a month later in his first action as Lord Lieutenant of Ireland, of which Maty gives the following version :—

" Lord Chesterfield had long wished for an opportunity of rewarding the services of his chaplain ; and this opportunity offered while he was at the Hague. A vacancy having happened in the bench of bishops in Ireland, Lord Chesterfield wrote to Lord Harrington, who was then with the King at Hanover, recommending doctor Chenevix to the vacant see. He received a polite answer, rejecting in civil terms the recommendation. Lord Harrington at the same time assured Lord Chesterfield that his Majesty would accept of any other person he should name, and therefore advised him to *look out* for another bishop ; to which Lord Chesterfield replied, that he begged his lordship would desire the king to *look out* for another lord lieutenant. The reply had its effect ; doctor Chenevix was made bishop of Killaloe, and a few months after translated without opposition to the see of Waterford."[2]

The story appears in fuller detail in Chesterfield's letters to Dr. Chenevix[3] and in the Newcastle Papers,[4] from which we will quote the following extract as expressing Chesterfield's attitude particularly clearly in a letter from him to Newcastle :—

" I am very glad your Grace approves of a resolution which I can never depart from, I mean that of not suffering

[1] Maty, vol. I, p. 138.
[2] *Ibid.*, pp. 146, 147.
[3] March 12, April 27, and May 12, N.S., 1745. Bradshaw, II, pp. 782–784.
[4] Add. MSS. 32804, ff. 24–326, *passim;* from which Ernst quotes at some length on pp. 220–243 *passim.*

an indignity. And I look upon it as the highest, the most distinguished indignity, to have my recommendation to the dirtiest Bishopric in Ireland refus'd. Dr. Chenevix is without blemish as to his life and character, and if his attachment to me is to be, as it must be, the only objection to him, that objection doubles the indignity. I am therefore determin'd that if Dr. Chenevix is not Bishop of Chlonfert, I will not be Lord Lieutenant of Ireland. I know the plan with regard to myself very well ; I am to be very ill us'd with one hand, and very well offer'd with the other, in order to make me accept the latter. But those who know me little enough to imagine that that is the way of dealing with me, will find themselves mistaken. I will resent the indignitys and I will despise the offers."[1]

In reading these letters we are filled with pity for poor Newcastle, negotiating between the obstinacy of George and the inexorableness of his Lord Lieutenant. There is also the continuous thrill of excitement. Is not Chesterfield stretching the cord too tight ? Surely the strain is too much, this time, for human nature, for Hanoverian nature, to stand ! It is with a gasp of relief that we come to Newcastle's final letter saying " this day his Majesty was pleased to consent to the Irish Bishoprics."[2]

When it is remembered that Chesterfield had been in opposition for over eleven years ; that these letters were written only a few weeks after the stupendous difficulties that had occurred in his obtaining office ; and that he was genuinely anxious to retain office in order to do his utmost to secure peace with France and Spain, we are left wondering at the extraordinary risks he took. His action seems to have been dictated no more by self-sacrifice for his friend on the one hand than by personal pique on the other. Rather was it the inevitable result of driving a quixotic code of right and wrong through the maze of court compromise and intrigue ; an action magnificent in its disinterestedness but not statesmanlike. If it was successful, it was chiefly the wiles of Newcastle that made it so ; and this aversion from compromise must be regarded as a serious blemish upon Chesterfield's earlier political career.

The most conscientious man cannot apply the same

[1] April 13, N.S., 1745. Add. MSS. 32804, ff. 290, 291. Ernst, pp. 240, 241.
[2] April 23, O.S., 1745. *Ibid.*, f. 309. Ernst, pp. 242, 243.

inflexible ethical code to his political actions that he can to his private life. In the latter case he is not concerned with ultimate advantages to self, for the highest advantage to self is, *ex hypothesi*, the moral quietude obtained by adherence to his principles : nothing else counts. A statesman is concerned with the ultimate material advantages to his country, to obtain which he must often, on the grounds of expediency, tolerate, perhaps even advocate, individual injustices, ethical imperfections. In short, his policy must be one of continual compromise—the adjustment of an individual mind to the composite mind of a party or cabinet.

Though Chesterfield had his country's interests as closely at heart as anyone then living, he was unable to serve his country at the expense of his conscience. His normal test was not, " Will this action ultimately be the best for my country ? " but " Is this action ethically right or wrong ? " In matters of broad, vital policy such an attitude is unimpeachable : in questions of detail it becomes just as indefensible on the ground of practicability.

To such a character, discipline, other than self-imposed discipline to the code, is unknown, and, as a young politician Chesterfield had no compunction in voting against his party, both in the House of Commons and afterwards in the House of Lords. Even had circumstances placed him, as Pitt was placed, in virtual control of a set of nonentities in the cabinet, we cannot conceive his achieving much success, for in George II's reign it was necessary for a Prime Minister to serve both King and Country, and this Chesterfield could never have done when the two interests conflicted. It was because Walpole could and did perform this double feat that he towers above Chesterfield as a statesman, though inferior to him in many forms of ability. A study of Chesterfield's political career suggests that at times he carried his hyper-conscientiousness to the point of reckless imprudence by not practising the art of dissimulation that he preached to his son. Since so many of his detractors have magnified this eminently wise advice into the teaching of dishonesty, it is as well to quote at length from the letter in which dissimulation is most fervently advocated.

" *Volto sciolto con pensieri stretti* [1] is a most useful maxim

Literally : " The face open ; the thought closed." This phrase

in business. It is so necessary at some games, such as *Berlan, Quinze, etc.*, that a man who had not the command of his temper and countenance would infallibly be undone by those who had, even though they played fair ; whereas in business you always play with sharpers, to whom at least you should give no fair advantages. It may be objected, that I am now recommending dissimulation to you ; I both own and justify it. It has been long said *Qui nescit dissimulare nescit regnare* ; I go still farther, and say, that without some dissimulation no business can be carried on at all. It is *simulation* that is false, mean, and criminal ; that is the cunning which Lord Bacon calls left-handed wisdom, and which is never made use of but by those who have not true wisdom. And the same great man says that dissimulation is only to hide our cards ; whereas simulation is put on in order to look into other people's. Lord Bolingbroke, in his ' Idea of a Patriot King,' [1] which he has lately published, and which I will send you by the first opportunity, says, very justly, that simulation is a *stiletto* ; not only an unjust, but an unlawful weapon, and the use of it is rarely to be excused, never justified : whereas dissimulation is a shield, as secrecy is armour ; and it is no more possible to preserve secrecy in business, without some degree of dissimulation, than it is to succeed in business without secrecy. He goes on and says, that those two arts of dissimulation and secrecy are like the alloy mingled with pure ore : a little is necessary, and will not debase the coin below its proper standard ; but if more than that little be employed (that is, simulation and cunning), the coin loses its currency and the coiner his credit."[2]

We cannot help feeling that when writing these words Chesterfield was conscious of certain occasions in his political life when a little dissimulation would have been more profitable than some of his ultra-frank outbursts in

occurs very frequently in the letters to his son. According to Churton Collins its origin " is to be found in Wotton's Letter to Milton prefixed to some of the editions of *Comus*, where it is attributed to one Alberto Scipione." (*Essays and Studies*, p. 208.) In this letter, however, it occurs in a different form, " *pensieri stretti, ed il viso sciolto*," and there seems no reason for supposing that it was not a recognized proverb, even in Wotton's day.

[1] Published in 1749. See letter to his son, December 12, 1749. Bradshaw, vol. I, pp. 290, 291.

[2] Letter to his son, May 22, 1749 : *ibid.* pp. 213, 214.

the Press and House of Lords. We do not suggest from this that Chesterfield practised a higher moral standard than he preached to his son, because we do not consider the advice in this letter subversive of morality in any way. What, however, we do maintain is that he had two moral standards, one for political and another for his private life; and of these the first, though it should have been the more elastic, was without doubt the more rigid.

As Lord Lieutenant of Ireland he allowed himself no personal indulgences whatsoever. Prior to his rule the post had been regarded as an ornamental sinecure. He converted it into one of active exertion.[1] A long letter written by him a month before taking up his duties, concerning a scheme for introducing French Protestants into Ireland, ends as follows :—

" If it is generally lik'd in Ireland, and call'd for, I am not only ready to co-operate but contribute, and the people shall be forthcoming. If not, I shall rest content with my good intentions for that kingdom, which surely wants, and in my opinion might make, great improvements ; getting people from abroad, and keeping their own money at home, would be two very considerable ones, and are both in their own power. I heartily wish my administration might be an Æra of some National benefit : whoever can suggest any, will be welcome ; whoever can bring it to bear will be still welcomer to
" Your faithfull friend and servant, CHESTERFIELD." [2]

Three months after arriving in Ireland he writes to his friend David Mallet from Dublin Castle,

" The business of this place, such as it is, is continual ; and as I am resolved to do it while I am here, it leaves me little or no time to do things I should like much better." [3]

Ireland needed reform in many ways. " Neglect and bad example in the highest quarters had served to form, or to encourage, evasion of responsibilities, and the *laissez faire* of popularity-hunting viceroys had served to establish

[1] Maty, vol. I, pp. 151, 152.   Craig, pp. 237-240.
[2] July 23, 1745.   *English Historical Review*, October, 1889, vol. IV, p. 753.
[3] November 27, 1745.   Bradshaw, vol. II, p. 790.

the very evils which they were sent to correct. Chester-field, on the other hand, determined to initiate reform by his own example ; nor was he the sort of man to be influenced in any line of conduct which he thought fit to pursue by the consideration of how other people might like it. By way of discontinuing extravagance he took care that, whilst the viceregal establishment was maintained with becoming splendour, there should be no waste, no mere vulgar display, no disorderly excess, or facilities of ruin. He, the veteran punter of White's, to whom play must have been as the very breath of his nostrils, did not allow any gambling to take place at the Castle during his tenure of office ; he discountenanced excess of every kind, especially in wine, at his own table, and, so far as lay in his power, at such hospitalities as he accepted. To do this required considerable courage ; for at that time drinking was the fashionable vice—wine-drinking especially, in the very nature of things, being the privilege of the wealthier classes."[1]

This account of Chesterfield's good services in Ireland is confirmed by the two following short extracts from letters typical of Irish opinion at the time of his departure.

Dublin. April 19, 1746.

" To the universal regret of all sorts and conditions of men, our good Lord Lieutenant is preparing for England and will sail with the first fair wind, and it is doubted whether he will return to us any more . . . As the Parliament is now prorogued, the members are hurrying out of town. I suppose many of them with very light purses, though the Lord Lieutenant did all in his power to encourage parsimony, and to his immortal honour (though fond of play) he discontinued the groomporters, that bane to youth; and to make amends to the keeper, instead of profits which might arise by the table, has settled forty pounds a year on him during life." [2]

Dublin. May 29, 1746.

" It will be now too late to tell you of our gaiety and our sobriety whilst Lord Chesterfield was here, and un-

[1] Craig pp. 234, 235.
[2] Edmund Spencer to Francis Price. (*Puleston Papers*.) Hist. MSS. Comm., 15th Report, Appendix, Part VII, p. 334. Chesterfield actually sailed on April 23rd.

necessary to tell you we are returning to old habits now he is gone. This I must say, his example has convinced that people may be cheerful, though sober."[1]

To promote temperance was a measure after Chesterfield's heart, as can be seen from his essays on " Soaking " (Nos. 90, 91 and 92 of the *World*).[2] To court unpopularity by so doing was scarcely in accordance with the advice he gives to his son,[3] and, if we are to believe his letters, must have caused him considerable moral effort. The prohibition of gambling must have involved a still greater effort, but Chesterfield during his tenure of office, both as Lord Lieutenant and afterwards as Secretary of State, maintained his self-restraint in this respect, though " the very day he bad farewell to the cares of administration, he renewed his evening visits at White's, which had been interrupted for four years "—a fact which Maty [4] feels " obliged to mention, not without much concern."

How then are we to regard Chesterfield ? As a pleasure-loving libertine, governing himself by supreme self-control, overcoming his natural predilections at the occasional calls of an inconvenient conscience : or as a hard-working, hyper-conscientious patriot posing to the world as a man of pleasure ? It is hard to say which was his real nature, and which was imposed, but we feel that his true character lies in one or possibly both of these alternatives ; and that the facts of his life will not be found to conform to any formula differing widely therefrom.

Possibly both alternatives are true ; that he began life as a man of pleasure, and, having risen to the position of an acknowledged wit and leader of society, was loth to abandon that position at the sterner call of patriotism. There is ample evidence that he did obey the summons almost to its fullest extent, but it is clear that he disliked

---

[1] Lord Chief Baron Bowes to George (Bubb) Dodington. (*Matcham Papers*.)   Hist. MSS. Comm., Report on MSS. in Various Collections, vol. VI, p. 68.

[2] *Cf.* Letter to Bishop of Waterford, June 18, 1747 ; and Letter to Faulkner, April 13, 1754. Bradshaw, vol. II, pp. 822, 1102 ; also several letters to his son and godson.

[3] *Cf.* especially this passage in the letter of June 24, 1751. " With a passionate desire of pleasing every body, I came by degrees to please some ; and I can assure you that what little figure I have made in the world has been much more owing to that passionate desire I had of pleasing universally, than to any intrinsic merit or sound knowledge I might ever have been master of."—Bradshaw, vol. I, p. 461.

[4] Vol. I, p. 186.

to appear in the light of a hard-working conscientious patriot.

Lord Marchmont tells us that when he asked Chesterfield for information concerning the places in the Broad Bottom Administration, " He said, as to himself he had chosen Ireland for a reason I would laugh at, which the Duke of Shrewsbury gave him ; that it was a place wherein a man had business enough to hinder him from falling asleep, and not so much as to keep him awake."[1] Upon which Craig justly observes, " This manner of putting things is eminently characteristic of a man who uniformly disclaimed all motives for his conduct which were not founded upon the most absolute selfishness, whilst never failing to carry out the work set before him with an ardour of self-sacrifice that was perhaps unexampled among his compeers."[2]

For a gentleman to evince a passion for hard work—it was hardly possible : for the reigning wit, whose latest *bon mot* was ever the talk of the town, to confess an ardent desire to serve his country—out of the question ! It may be vain, affected, insincere, but it is eminently English ; and on this ground we are willing to forgive him. Of the thousands of men who entered our Army in 1914, how many confessed to being prompted by the highest motives ? When we read of Chesterfield's administration of Ireland, which nearly all historians acknowledge to have been the most successful and happiest in the history of that unhappy country, we cannot believe that his actions were entirely the outcome of a calculated self-control, the practising of an ideal of conduct that he preached to his son. They would seem to embrace something more than the imper-

---

[1]*Marchmont Papers*, vol. I, p. 91. See p. 92 *post*.

In a long letter of August 13, 1745, from Chesterfield to Robert Trevor, Minister at the Hague, after stating the efforts he is making for peace and the difficulties in the way of securing it, he adds, " In five or six days I shall leave, and without regret, this busy disagreeable scene for one much better suited to my temper and inclination." He then quotes Shrewsbury's saying which he terms " a pleasing description to a half lazy man as I am."— *Trevor Papers*. Hist. MSS. Comm., 14th Report. Appendix Part IX, p. 127. See also letter to Mme. de Monconseil, June 24, 1745. Bradshaw, vol. II, p. 785.

That Chesterfield had other motives for choosing the post of Lord Lieutenant appears from a letter from J. de Pesters to his cousin Lady Denbigh, dated November 29, 1744, in which he says, " On veut envoier un homme de poids en Hollande pour demander une reponse decisive, et cet homme-la sera, je crois, Lord C[hesterfiel]d ; savoir si apres cela on luy donnera cette lieutenance que vous savez qu'il ambitionne ; c'est une question."— *Denbigh Papers* (Part V), Hist. MSS. Comm. (1911), p. 186.

[2] *Life of Lord Chesterfield*, p. 214.

sonal rule of an able, impartial minister. Is it possible that in this additional factor is to be found the real Chesterfield showing through the veil; not the hard, self-controlled, impersonal machine, but a keen reformer with a real love for the people he governed, a love, moreover, which was returned by the Irish to a degree that they have not felt nationally for an Englishman before or since ?

In a letter to the Duke of Newcastle of 26th April, 1746, announcing Chesterfield's departure from Ireland, Bishop Raphoe says : " 'Tis almost impossible to exceed in describing the universal love and Respect that has been expressed on every occasion to the Lord Lieutenant by every degree of people, or the obliging manner in which they were accepted and returned. There are very few of any Station, but have received some distinguishing mark of his notice and favour."[1] There were endless tributes in the form of verse and studied compliments from the higher authorities in Ireland, but the most eloquent and spontaneous of all came from the lower classes. To quote Craig, " The poor unlettered folk who had no money to spend on effigies, and were no adepts in verse-making, gave their benefactor all they could, their gratitude. When the day arrived on which he was to take ship for England, with the understanding that his absence was to be only temporary, large crowds collected round the Castle gates from an early hour (the embarkation was to take place at 9 a.m.) to bid him farewell. Ordinarily the departure of a Viceroy is attended with some pomp and more precaution ; but on this occasion the Earl dispensed with both, displaying to the last that perfect confidence in his subjects which had so large a share in securing their goodwill. As if reluctant to shorten the time of his stay among them, he did not even use a carriage on the occasion ; but, accompanied by his Countess, walked slowly to the place of embarkation, whilst the sympathetic multitude, consisting of persons of all ranks and denominations, followed them to the water's edge, where they remained while the ship that took them away was in sight, praising and blessing and entreating him and the good-natured Melusina, after the passionate Irish fashion, to 'come back soon.'"[2]

That he did not come back is a fact to be deplored. Lord Brougham describes Chesterfield's exchanging his

[1] Add. MSS. 32707, f. 106.   Ernst, pp. 300, 301.
[2] *Life of Lord Chesterfield*, pp. 247, 248.

Lord Lieutenancy for the seals of Secretary of State as
" A change alike unfortunate for himself, for his sovereign,
and, we are most seriously persuaded, for the permanent
interests of the empire . . . Had he continued in Ireland
for but a few years more—heartily animated as he was
with an interest in the country, a warm love of the people,
a thorough conviction that a course of steady impartial
government, a fixed discountenancing of jobs of every
sort and kind, and the cordial promotion of national industry in all departments—the whole administration conducted
on the principle of fostering whatever was at once Irish
and good, and of discouraging whatever needlessly irritated
the prejudices of a naturally generous and affectionate
race of men—had Lord Chesterfield been allowed to remain
in Dublin for ten years in place of eight months, we think
it almost impossible that he should not have accomplished
more for the civilization of the people, the improvement
of the country's resources, and the obliteration of its long-
descended feuds and bitternesses, than could have been
looked for from twenty years of any Lord Lieutenant since
the Revolution. It was a grievous blunder that removed
from Ireland, which needed a first-rate man, a first-rate
man for whom the first place was not open in England,
and who could nowhere be satisfied long to fill any place
but the first."[1]

Interesting as Lord Brougham's speculations may be,
they depend on a very slender hypothesis. It was not a
question whether Chesterfield was allowed to remain in
Ireland, but whether he chose to do so. To put it shortly,
Chesterfield himself, more than anyone, seems to have
been responsible for the " grievous blunder."

Critics are unanimous[2] in agreeing with Mahon that
" Lord Chesterfield consented much against his own inclination to exchange the Lord Lieutenancy of Ireland for
the Seals of Secretary of State."[3]   Evidence for this may
be found in An Apology for a Recent Resignation[4] and also
in the Marchmont Papers. Lord Marchmont states in
his diary that Chesterfield told him on August 30th, 1747
(ten months after Chesterfield had become Secretary of
State), that on his arrival from Ireland " the Duke of

---

[1] Quarterly Review. September, 1845.
[2] With the exception of Bradshaw ; see p. 95 n. post.
[3] Mahon's Preface to his edition of Chesterfield's Letters. Vol. I, pp. xii,
and xiii, cf. also vol. III, ibid., p. 182 n.
[4] Ibid., vol. V, pp. 58–86.

Newcastle had spoke to him of being secretary, if Lord Harrington quitted, or was turned out ; and that he had refused it, saying he would keep Ireland, as long as he was in place, for he liked it, as it just answered Lord Shrewsbury's description ; it had business enough to keep a man awake, and not enough to hinder him from sleeping."[1] But of what value is this evidence when confronted with the following correspondence between Newcastle in London and Chesterfield in Ireland ?[2]

Chesterfield to Newcastle.

November 25, 1745.

" I am in place, and heartily wish to be out of it. I am out of the opposition, and do not wish to be in it."[3]

Newcastle to Chesterfield.

January 6, 1746.

" The Duke of Bedford and my Lord Gower act hand and heart with us ; and my Lord Gower told me the other day he really thought we could form an administration, if the King desired we should, exclusively of those whom we wish'd to have but could not have ; Mr. Pitt, etc. With this the King seem'd pleased. I ventured to tell him I believed Lord Chesterfield would not hurt this scheme when he came over ; to which he answered that he would do everybody justice,—that Lord Chesterfield had done extremely well in Ireland ; that his notions were very right as to England and should be followed . . . I must beg that you would think of coming to England as soon as you can finish your affairs on the other side of the water : we want your advice, we want your assistance and support. *If we go on we cannot go on without you. If we go out we* [4] For my own part I can most truly say, I have the utmost confidence in, and reliance upon, your opinion and judgment ; and the marks you have given me of your friendship have been such as have unfeignedly attach'd me to you." [5]

Chesterfield to Newcastle.

January 11, 1746.

" You did very right to tell the King that I would not

---

[1] *Marchmont Papers*, vol. I, p. 183.   See also the repetition of this story, *ibid.*, p. 91 (p. 89, *ante*).
[2] Much of which is here printed for the first time.
[3] Add. MSS., 32705, f. 379.   (Ernst, p. 277.)
[4] These words in italics are erased in the MSS.
[5] Add. MSS., 32706, f. 17.   (Ernst, p. 283.)

disturb such a scheme of Administration ; I shall not
disavow you if Gower and the Duke of Bedford continue
in ; and if they don't I shall disturb no scheme, nor be
concern'd in any ; but be quiet for the rest of my life.

" Nothing can be more obliging than your desiring me to
return to England as soon as possible, and the reasons you
give for desiring it, but I assure you I do not want pressing
for that. And I will not stay one moment longer than
necessary. My drudgery here is uninterrupted and intolerable to one naturally so lazy as I am."[1]

Chesterfield to Newcastle.

February 18, 1746.

" I am convinc'd I need not tell you that the day after
my arrival in London I shall most certainly resign my
employment . . .

" The rest of my stay here shall be as short as I can
possibly make it, though it cannot be half so short as I
wish it . . . In the mean time my situation is extremely
disagreeable ; and God knows when it will end, for I have
no great hopes that the Council in England will give much
attention or dispatch to my Irish Bills."[2]

Newcastle to Chesterfield.

February 18, 1746.

" In all situations your presence is most agreeable to
your friends. In our present circumstances it is absolutely
necessary, and therefore I must conjure you to make what
haste you can to us ; for, tho' your Irish subjects will
detain you as long as they can, I should hope you would
think near seven months royalty sufficient."[3]

Chesterfield to Newcastle.

February 27, 1746.

" Though I am obliged to you for wishing me in England,
I assure you you need not invite me there. I have had
Royalty enough, God knows, and am very impatient to
return to the state of an English subject. Your return of
my bills from the Counsil determines mine to England.
I will hurry 'em through the Parliament as soon as possible,
and then in a most gracious speech prorogue it. Don't

---

[1] Add. MSS., 32706, f. 35. Ernst p. 285.
[2] *Ibid.*, f. 176. Ernst, pp. 288, 289. Bradshaw, vol. II, pp. 791, 792.
[3] *Ibid.*, f. 164. Ernst, p. 287.

think by this that I imagine I can be of any use to you in England ; rather the contrary ; and very possibly some silly accident may happen to me at my arrival, for in the present situation of mind in which I take his Majesty to be he may probably be glad to ease himself upon one whose resentment could be of no consequence."[1]

Newcastle to Chesterfield.

March 5, 1746.

" I really hope and believe you will find yourself under a mistake. I think things are greatly alter'd ; and if you suffer now, I really believe it will be not for your own sins but for ours. But I can never think upon your subject without congratulating myself and my brother upon the acquisition of the most honourable and the most estimable friend that ever two men had.

" I will get my Lord President to post back to you your Irish Bills, so that I will flatter myself that we shall have the honour and pleasure of seeing you here soon. For indeed we want you, to add weight, solidity and firmness to our system ; and to connect us all thoroughly together ; and in what immediately relates to my own Department, I really want your opinion and advice."[2]

Chesterfield to Newcastle.

March 11, 1746.

" I count the days with impatience till I can have the pleasure of seeing you in England."[3]

Chesterfield to Newcastle.

March 20, 1746.

" I assure you I will not stay here one moment longer than is absolutely necessary : the return of the Bills from England will fix that moment. If you knew the life I lead here, you would not suspect me of prolonging it one instant."[4]

Chesterfield to Newcastle.

April 22, 1746.

" I wait the first favourable gale to carry me from hence, where from concurrent reasons you will easily judge how

[1] Add. MSS., 32706, f. 221.   Ernst, pp. 291, 292.
[2] *Ibid.*, f. 247.   Ernst, pp. 292, 293.   Craig regards these words as tantamount to a virtual recall, if not exactly to an actual one. p. 257 n.
[3] *Ibid.*, f. 286.   Ernst, p. 295.
[4] *Ibid.*, f. 323.   Ernst, pp. 295, 296.

disagreeable my present situation must be. I need not therefore tell you how impatient I am to assure you in London, that no man there is more faithfully and inviolably yours." [1]

Is it possible to reconcile this evidence with Lord Marchmont's ? We think not, and we feel certain that if, instead of only Chesterfield's letter of February 18, 1746, the whole correspondence had been available to Lord Mahon, he would not have preferred [2] the second-hand evidence of Lord Marchmont to the incontrovertible first-hand evidence of the Newcastle Papers.

In the face of this correspondence it is difficult to regard Chesterfield's action in leaving Ireland as inspired by altruistic motives. The plain truth seems to be that he was frankly bored, partly with the " drudgery " and partly with the " royalty " that his office involved. He had guided Ireland safely through a very dangerous period of her history—the Jacobite Rebellion of 1745 ; he had tasted the fruits of high office, found them not too palatable, and longed for a rest. It was not, as we have seen, by any means the first occasion on which he had expressed hankerings after a private life : even within a month of his arrival in Ireland he wrote in a letter to Andrew Stone, the Under-Secretary, " As to myself, I most sincerely wish at my return from hence to be at liberty and quiet."[3]

Nevertheless, it is doubtful whether, on leaving Ireland, Chesterfield did much to obtain the liberty and quiet for which he seemed to have been so anxious. From letters to Robert Trevor it would appear that the danger in which the country lay during the continuance of the war was what chiefly concerned him—a patriotic feeling which ranked higher in his mind than any personal desire. To turn back for a moment ; the exact status of a Lord Lieutenant of Ireland at that time with regard to cabinet councils is difficult to determine, but there seems no doubt that from the time Chesterfield accepted the office in December, 1744, he was able to bring his influence to bear on foreign affairs. In January, 1745, he was appointed

---

[1] Public Record Office. State Papers Domestic (Ireland), 409.

[2] As, curiously enough, Ernst (p 322) and Craig (pp. 259, 260) have done. Bradshaw notes the conflicting evidence in commenting on Mahon's note to Chesterfield's letter to Sir Thomas Robinson, October 31, 1746 (vol. II, p. 802 n.).

[3] September 30, 1745. Add. MSS. 32705, f. 233. Ernst, p. 266.

Envoy at the Hague, where he remained until May 20. Between that date and his landing in Ireland on August 31, he wrote to Robert Trevor at the Hague eight letters[1] of length on Continental matters which show that he was working hard in the cause of peace. The last of these begins as follows :—" My journey to Ireland now draws so near that a thousand necessary though frivolous details plague me one half of the day, and business of a more important nature, though God knows, and so do you, of a very disagreeable one, employs the rest."[2] In writing to Madame de Monconseil he excuses his delay in answering her letter on the grounds of " ma part à la régence d'ici, et les affaires d'Irlande, où je vais en six semaines."[3] Even while he remained in Ireland the correspondence between him and Newcastle is not unconcerned with foreign affairs.

Chesterfield returned to England in April, 1746, and, Parliament having been prorogued, the government of Ireland was left in the hands of a Commission of three Lords Justices. Accordingly he had little to do as Lord Lieutenant, though there are a few official letters written to and by him in this capacity between the months of June and November.[4] What work, if any, he did in the Council Chamber during this period is not known, but that he was in touch with foreign affairs is clear from a letter to Trevor of May 20. Writing to him again on August 5 he says :—

" Lord Sandwich will, I believe, set out for Holland this day sevennight, but whether authorised and instructed as it is there expected he should be is another point. I was much pressed, as you have probably heard, to make you a visit, [i.e. to the Hague] but I believe, in a very little time, neither you nor any of my friends in Holland will be surprised that I declined it. I can submit to the opinions of others, but I cannot act against my own. I was and am still convinced that the Dutch are very unwilling to conclude with France without us. But I am as much convinced too, that when a new Minister shall appear (if that should be the case) to have no new instructions, no

[1] Trevor Papers. Hist. MSS. Comm., 14th Report, Appendix Part IX, pp. 113–128 passim.
[2] August 13, 1745—ibid., p. 127.
[3] June 24, 1745. Bradshaw, vol. II, p. 785.
[4] Public Record Office. State Papers Domestic (Ireland), 409.

ultimatum, no specific points, by way of basis for a pacification, the Dutch will not delay much longer the signing what,
I believe, has for some time been agreed upon between
them and France. If things have lately changed a little
to our advantage, I think we ought to avail ourselves of
those favourable moments, to mend the conditions of
the pacification rather than to delay the conclusion of it.
But this opinion of mine is not the prevailing opinion
here."[1]

Soon after the date of this letter Chesterfield had a
" long and dangerous illness."[2] To recover his health he
went to Bath, whence he returned to London on the last
day of October, and " was sent for to come to a meeting
[of the Council] that very evening, but begged to be excused,
for his absence for three months hindered his being *au fait
des affaires*."[3] On the following day Chesterfield was
appointed Secretary of State, Newcastle having irritated
Harrington out of office, as he did Chesterfield himself
fifteen months later, and Chesterfield's successor, the Duke
of Bedford, in 1751.

It is doubtful whether his acceptance of the Seals was
purely voluntary. According to the version he gave Lord
Marchmont ten months later, he was more or less pushed
into the post by George II and the Pelhams. This account
is distinctly entertaining, and affords an excellent example
of Newcastle's absurd jealousy of his brother, the Prime
Minister, but is too long to quote in full. Concerning
Chesterfield the main points are as follows :—The King
said he thought Harrington's successor must be Chesterfield,
and asked if he would take the seals, for he was the fittest,
if he was willing . . . The Duke of Newcastle pressed him to
accept, being frightened lest on his refusal Lord Granville
should be named. Chesterfield desired that he might be
allowed to the next day to turn himself round, and consider
of it. Mr. Pelham told him that he must accept, or else
he could not continue in, for, if any other was put in, he
must resign, as he could trust no other. For this reason

[1] *Trevor Papers*, p. 146.

[2] See letter from him to Thomas Prior, September 23, 1746. Bradshaw,
vol. II, p. 801. He was absent from the Cabinet Meeting of August 12,
and there is no record of his having attended one between those of August
6 and November 4.

[3] Diary of Lord Marchmont, August 30, 1747. *Marchmont Papers*,
vol. I, p. 183.

H

Chesterfield did accept of the seals, but desired to go in to the King alone.[1]

In a letter written to his son less than six weeks after his appointment, he says : " The post I am now in, though the object of most people's views and desires, was in some degree inflicted upon me ; and a certain concurrence of circumstances obliged me to engage in it ; but I feel that it requires more strength of body and mind than I have, to go through with it."[2]   It certainly was not a particularly tempting prospect to become joint Secretary of State with Newcastle, and, as most writers suggest, it seems only his patriotic desire to effect a peace that persuaded him to take the post.   In any case he did so not without misgivings for the future, and insisted on a private interview with the King, at which " Lord Chesterfield said he must take the liberty to capitulate with his Majesty ; that as he came in to serve his Majesty, and not himself, he desired, that whenever he found his service not agreeable, or not useful to him, he might take the liberty to resign the seals, without it being taken for an affront or disgust at the particular time ; to which the King answered, ' Then take the seals, for I can believe *you* ; ' which expression the King has often repeated since with particular emphaticalness."[3]

The misgivings felt by Chesterfield were doubtless shared by others, and are expressed with considerable freedom in a tract of the times entitled *An Expostulatory Letter to a certain Right Honourable Person upon his late Promotion.*[4] The remarkable prescience exhibited in this long-forgotten pamphlet, which forecasts in detailed accuracy the ineffectiveness of Chesterfield's tenure of office, compels us to attach some weight to the conjectures it expresses concerning the reasons for his promotion.   We quote from it with the more confidence since it is of a less adulatory nature than most of the contemporaneous writings on Chesterfield, and evinces a sincerity and impartiality which are only too rare in such political tracts.

" When your Lordship went to Ireland the whole British Nation were pleased to know his Majesty was so well

---

[1] *Marchmont Papers*, vol. I, pp. 183-186.
[2] December 9, 1746.   Bradshaw, vol. I, p. 45.
[3] *Marchmont Papers*, vol. I, p. 186.
[4] 1747 (32 pp).

represented ; and the Esteem of the Irish, which they had at first for your Name and Character, grew into Love and Veneration, which were every Day increasing thro' the new Benefits you were meditating for them. Why then, my Lord, did you slight the Affection of a People that was growing to the highest Pitch of Fondness,[1] and among whom you had no Controuler or Associate, to accept a Charge which at best is burthensome and envied ; in which you were not sure either that your Opinion would prevail, or that you might not, undesignedly to be sure on your Side, but by your new Friends maliciously contrived, bring a Cloud upon your bright Character, and incur the Displeasure of a People, whom you had both Will and Capacity to scrve, but was defeated of all the Means, and cramp'd in every Opportunity ?—But perhaps it was not a Matter of Choice, but only the Effect of too easy Compliance. Let us see then, if we can find a better Reason for this Transposition of Office.

" The Lustre that would have attended your Irish Administration, they foresaw, if protracted to the same length that of late years has been granted to other Administrators, could not have been looked upon by some Eyes without painful Dazzling and unwelcome Shame. It was not proper that a whole Nation, long accustomed to Variety of *Masters*, with little Variation of *Sorrow*, should be suffered to make too close Comparison between distant Extremes. An Irish Viceroy with a great Soul and great Abilities might have an Opportunity of making himself adored ; but an *English Minister of State* with the same valuable Qualities, will be sure, in such Company as he must be obliged to keep, to lose some of the Character he brings with him into Office. Since they cannot rise to a Level with him, they will either bring him down to a Level with them, or vote

---

[1] " High stations furnish great opportunities of doing good where there is a head to discern and a heart to apply. Your Excellency is eminent for both. Since your arrival in this kingdom you have acquired a thorough knowledge of its interests, which you apply to the service of his majesty and the public in such a manner that your administration will be always remembered with gratitude and honour. Your management, so generous of your own, and so frugal of the public treasure, joined with a conduct so open and sincere, without the least tincture or suspicion of private views, leave us at a loss to determine which to admire most, the true policy or the probity of our governor."—This footnote to the pamphlet is taken from the dedication to Chesterfield of Thomas Prior's *Authentic Narrative of the Success of Tar-Water* . . .(1746).

him out of the Society with some Brand of Ignominy invented by themselves. This, my Lord, makes me fear that they have been too hard for you in the late Change. Your quick imagination and ready Zeal to serve your Country in the best Manner laid you open to the Delusion of your Enemies. As they acted in this Manner towards another tow'ring Genius,[1] why was you not cautious, why did you not suspect the Trickery when they held forth the Temptation ? " (pp. 8–10).

Before we discuss Chesterfield's experience as Secretary of State, it will be as well to consider his position at this period when he was at the zenith of his public career. To arrive, however, at even an approximate contemporary estimate of Chesterfield, of anyone, in fact, at that time is by no means easy, owing to the inaudibility of the people's voice. Nevertheless, if we listen carefully to the public and private expressions of the times, a faint echo of the truth can be heard.

After making the fullest allowance for party prejudice on both sides, we are left with the belief that the universal love expressed by the Irish for Chesterfield was shared more or less generally by the English ; no doubt to a lesser, but still to a large degree. Or, perhaps it would be more accurate to say that where the Irish felt genuine affection, the English felt unbounded trust ; for trust is undoubtedly the keynote of contemporary public sentiment towards Chesterfield. It has been our duty in the course of this enquiry to read through many tedious encomiums addressed to Chesterfield by admirers of his time—it would have been the easiest task, indeed, to prepare a laudatory anthology in verse alone—and throughout all, underlying the complimentary froth, runs a note of extreme confidence in him as a public servant. The sentiment is too recurrent to be suspected of insincerity ; but, apart from these expressions, we find Chesterfield commanding that same confidence in his dealings with individuals. At the Hague, for example, the aged and experienced Pensionary, the astute Greffier, Count Sinzendorf, the Austrian Envoy are almost immediately won over by the young ambassador's honesty and open dealing ; while at home, Townshend and his successor Harrington express in numerous letters the confidence in him which they share with the King.

[1] *I.e.* Carteret (from the context).

Walpole, it is true, found him an untrustworthy subordinate, but this exception is one which goes far towards proving the rule ; for, as we have seen, it was Chesterfield's conscientiousness and sincerity that made him too independent to be the slave of party. What doubtless helped to strengthen the public trust in Chesterfield throughout his period of opposition was the unswerving democratic policy he expressed with such reckless disregard of self on paper and in Parliament ; [1] but in any case it would have been strange if a man of his position, who always put his country's interests before his own, and was manifestly above all the jobbery and corruption of his time, had not commanded the nation's confidence. The voice of the people may have been inarticulate, but the actions of a man of Chesterfield's personality could not fail to impress their judgment. Shortly after Walpole's fall, the Duchess of Marlborough wrote to Lord Stair as follows :—
" I have been told that Lords Chesterfield and Gower are to have nothing in the government, which I think a very ill sign of what is intended ; because that can be for no reason but because you are all such men as are incapable of ever being prevailed on by any arts to act any thing contrary to honour and the true interests of our country." [2] We believe that in these words is expressed the general sentiment of the people towards Chesterfield throughout his public career.

How then did it come about that this man, whose disinterested patriotism was regarded by the country as a model of public virtue, who was recognized in his day as the fountain of honour, should, within a generation, become the type of dissimulation and insincerity ? In the first place it must be remembered that Chesterfield's reputation for integrity was founded on no striking political achievement likely to survive in the fickle memory of the public, but simply on a disinclination to serve his own ends, sufficiently unusual to gain notoriety at the time. It has also already been mentioned that the *Letters to his Son* were published during a period of national feeling unfor-

---

[1] *Cf.* " Your Lordship's Politeness as a Nobleman was never doubted ; but as a Patriot we remember you were always zealous against too much Party Adulation to the Throne."—*An Expostulatory Letter*, p. 19.

[2] February 16, 1741. Mary Berry's *Extracts from the Letters of Sarah, Duchess of Marlborough to the Earl of Stair, illustrative of Horace Walpole's ' Reminiscences '*—*Letters of Horace Walpole* (edit. 1840) vol. I, p. cxxi.

tunate for their reception,[1] and the charge of dissimulation, was simply thrown in to weigh down the scale still further in his disfavour. But the moralists who poured abuse upon the *Letters to his Son* have long been forgotten, and with their names might also have perished this false charge of insincerity and cunning, had it not been for the publication of Boswell's *Life of Johnson*. This was the event which set the seal on Chesterfield's ultimate reputation in the public mind, and it seems that nothing that has been said or written since will ever do much to disturb it. Here was a vivid character who commanded instant sympathy and respect from the public ; but since Chesterfield figured in Boswell's pages as the man from whom Johnson received most injustice, general opinion, already prejudiced against him, became still more antipathetic. The laurels he had gained at such self-sacrifice during his public career were cast aside : his posthumous characteristics were stamped thus :—exquisite manners ;—unkindness to Johnson ;— unnatural parental advice to an illegitimate son whom he endeavoured to train in the arts of immorality and dissimulation. What, on the other hand, did Johnson stand for ? A rough exterior, underlying which lay a tender heart and deep sincerity. Why, the very antithesis ! Chesterfield thus came to be regarded as the moral negative of Johnson, and, consciously or unconsciously, it is this fortuitous conception of him that has survived in the public mind to this day.

The antithesis of Johnson, we repeat, is what most accurately describes the present every-day conception of Chesterfield, so far as such a conception exists. The general public—and here we speak from personal experience gained during the preparation of this work—has no conception of Chesterfield at all. It knows two facts concerning him ; that he often wrote letters to his son ; and that once, while entertaining Colley Cibber, he kept Johnson waiting in an antechamber. There is considerable

---

[1] See p. 1 *ante*. Sir Edmund Gosse accounts for this national wave of feeling as follows :—" There was a strong reaction at that moment throughout English society in favour of enthusiasm and passion. Rousseau was in the air ; the asceticism of the Wesleys was rousing the emotions of the public. The torpor of the preceding age was being shaken up with violence in religion, in the arts, in literature, in the canons of conduct. To widely opposed sections of society the Frenchified *Laissez-faire* of the past generation had grown detestable. No victim to the new zeal could be found more acceptable than the cool and unsentimental Chesterfield, and he was offered up on every altar."—*Sunday Times*, November 25, 1923.

excuse for the *popular* belief in this story, though Boswell has stated distinctly that "*Johnson himself assured me that there was not the least foundation for it.*" But seeing is believing, and for every one person who has read Boswell there are at least a hundred who must have seen the fictitious incident portrayed in a rather melancholy steel-engraving. Apropos of Johnson's denial of the story, Strachey alludes to it as one " which Boswell, nevertheless, cannot resist repeating and which the popular love of dramatic effect still keeps alive." Later, he adds, " But Boswell is manifestly unjust. We have seen how reluctantly he discredits the story about Cibber, when his duty was to have given it the *coup de grâce*." [1] But this is being " manifestly unjust " to Boswell. Reluctant he may have been, but the fact remains that he did deliver the *coup de grâce*, a task which would have been difficult to accomplish had he not first repeated the story.

Johnson's denial, then, stands in Boswell's text to-day, where it has stood since 1791, for those who wish to read it. But despite this fact, the fiction has a vitality which is in some respects inexplicable. We can understand its hold on the popular mind. We can understand Craig, who is a clever intuitive critic, but not a conscientious biographer, being unable to resist the temptation of adopting it. [2] What we cannot understand is how the fiction found its way into Lord Brougham's defence of Chesterfield, [3] a defence based on that of Croker in the latter's edition of Boswell. Both Croker and Boswell himself are frequently quoted. The facts are marshalled with the care and justice we should expect from an eminent laywer ; the points made with a practised advocate's eloquence and skill. Yet this one adverse point, whose truth is so clearly denied by his principal witness, is overlooked ; and, instead of being able to use its negation in his favour, he merely counters it by exclaiming, " Kept waiting !— Samuel Johnson had not much experience of Whitehall." Equally remarkable is the oversight of Lord Carnarvon

[1] Introduction to *Chesterfield's Letters to his Son*, vol. I, pp. lx, lxiii.

[2] *Life of Lord Chesterfield*, p. 322. He must have known the truth, for Johnson's denial is stated clearly by Ernst (p. 467), whose account of the whole Chesterfield-Johnson episode, *with this one exception* is reproduced (without acknowledgment) almost word for word by Craig.

[3] *Quarterly Review*, September, 1845. It is this defence upon which Ernst and Strachey have both founded their judgments, and which will always remain the standard authority.

whose critical conscientiousness is apparent on every page of his *Memoir*. After relating the Cibber story, he is at pains to suggest numerous excuses for Chesterfield's conduct. The last one of these he takes direct from Boswell, citing the full reference in a footnote.[1] Had he only read on to the very next sentence on the page referred to he would have seen Johnson's denial in clear print, and saved himself the trouble of all his laborious conjectures.

The persistence of this story would seem, then, at times, to be not merely inexplicable but uncanny. Vitality has doubtless been given to it by the words in Johnson's letter to Chesterfield : " Seven years have now past since I waited in your outward rooms or was repulsed from your door ; " a charge which Ernst answers as follows ; (p. 468) :—

" The respective social positions of Chesterfield and Johnson seem always to have been overlooked. In 1747, Chesterfield was Secretary of State, and persons who visit Secretaries of State were liable then, as now, to be ' kept waiting.' As to the words ' repulsed from the door,' they can only be a rhetorical flourish.

" Johnson was not then the Johnson as we know him in the pages of Boswell : he was a comparatively unknown man : he had published nothing of importance but his *London*, and his *Life of Savage*."

Johnson's letter forms the *literary* support to the *anti-Johnson* conception of Chesterfield, and we will cite one example of the length to which critical, as apart from popular, prejudice on this matter has been carried. Sir Leslie Stephen in his biography of Johnson states that " the letter is one of those knock-down blows to which no answer is possible, and upon which comment is superfluous." [2] These words were written in 1878, long before which time both Croker and Brougham had made remarkably effective replies to all the definite charges it contained. Whether Stephen had encountered Brougham's defence we cannot say : it is inconceivable that a biographer of Johnson could have been unaware of Croker's. But fact and argument count for little when opposed to an apparently facile antithesis of character. The same critic's

---

[1] *Chesterfield's Letters to his Godson*, p. xl.
[2] *English Men of Letters Series*, p. 46.

lengthy estimate of Chesterfield, an estimate so biassed as
to be entirely worthless, ends as follows :—

"Dr. Johnson, the 'respectable Hottentot,' as his
lordship calls him,[1] has got the best of it in the long run.
His letter to Chesterfield remains as a splendid specimen
of hard hitting, or, as Mr. Carlyle calls it, a 'far-famed blast
of doom,' proclaiming to the listening world that patronage
should be no more, and conferring a kind of immortality
on its victim. The fine gentleman was unlucky in coming
into collision with that rough mass of genuine manhood ;
and yet the fact that he received a fair knock-down blow
from Boswell's hero is, perhaps, his best title to be remembered by posterity."[2]

The effect of Johnson's letter on Chesterfield's
posthumous reputation could scarcely be better expressed !
But we have already had occasion to discuss the letter in
its broad aspects[3] and are unwilling to weary the reader
with its details. Since Croker and Brougham exposed the
falsity of Johnson's charges, the fatuousness of his
complaints, other writers, including Ernst, Carnarvon,
Craig, and Strachey have added so much weight to their
arguments that any further remarks we could make would
be superfluous.

Leaving the unfortunate affair in the hands of this array
of critics, whose judgments upon it have never been
impeached,[4] let us see what remains to justify the *anti-
Johnson* prejudice against Chesterfield. To quote Boswell
again :—"He told me that there never was any particular
incident which produced a quarrel between Lord Chester-

[1] For the inaccuracy of this statement see next page.
[2] *Cornhill Magazine*, July, 1871, p. 101.
[3] pp. 22–26 *ante*.
[4] There have been two feeble attempts to overcome the difficulty caused
by Boswell's insertion of Langton's note on the inaccuracy of Johnson's
statement that not "one act of assistance" had been rendered by Chesterfield. Carlyle in his review of Croker's *Boswell* (*Fraser's Magazine*, No.
28—1832) tries to bluff the reader in a footnote, beginning, "Were time
and printer's space of no value, it were easy to wash away certain foolish
soot-stains dropped here as 'Notes.'" Dr. Birkbeck Hill endeavours to
refute Croker by proving (?) that Johnson's words were, in point of time,
strictly accurate ; forgetting apparently that it was Johnson himself who
made the admission and, in Langton's words, "when he gave me this copy
of his letter, desired that I would annex to it his information to me, that
whereas it is said in the letter that 'no assistance has been received,' he
did once receive from Lord Chesterfield the sum of ten pounds . . ."

field and him ; but that his Lordship's continued neglect was the reason why he resolved to have no connection with him." Brougham's comment on the charge of neglect is that, " Nothing but the inveterate mania of toadyism and lionizing could have made a gentleman born like Boswell adopt the notion that men of literary or scientific eminence have a right, merely as such, to be cultivated as private acquaintance by either Secretaries of State or Earls of Chesterfield ;—that they or their friends for them should ever condescend to complain of what Boswell in this story over and over calls ' neglect,' is to our view most melancholy and most degrading." [1]

With this view we agree in substance ; but, apart from whether Johnson had or had not any right to resent Chesterfield's " neglect," what he told Boswell was surely no less than the truth. The two characters pursued their lives along parallel paths : there was practically no contact between them—the one episode of the *Dictionary*, and nothing more. Since, then, Johnson scarcely enters into the drama of Chesterfield's life, is it not farcical that he should still play so large a part in the tragedy of Chesterfield's reputation ? Brougham wrote in 1845 of the unfortunate encounter as one " with which Boswell's narrative still connects in the popular mind impressions bitterly adverse and (we think) quite unjust to Lord Chesterfield." That these words are no less true to-day is clear from the most recent occasion on which Chesterfield has appeared before the public eye—we refer to the discovery and publication in 1923 of his *Letters to Lord Huntingdon*. The notices of this book in the " popular " papers [2] made practically no mention of the interesting fresh material revealed, but consisted almost entirely of the stale, raked-up Chesterfield-Johnson garbage ;— Johnson's two fatuous epigrams upon Chesterfield ; Johnson's letter to Chesterfield, almost as unfair ; Johnson waiting in the ante-chamber ; Chesterfield's description of Johnson as a respectable Hottentot, which has been conclusively proved to apply solely to Lyttelton. [3]

---

[1] *Quarterly Review*, September, 1845.
[2] We do not refer to the better-class weeklies.
[3] See Boswell's *Life of Johnson* (edit. Birkbeck Hill), p. 267 ; Birkbeck Hill's *Dr. Johnson : His Friends and his Critics* (p. 214). Lord Carnarvon (*Memoir* p. xlii) rejects Dr. Hill's conclusion on the sole ground that Boswell believed Chesterfield intended the description to apply to Johnson ! All other modern authorities accept it.

Lamentable as it all is, it is still more amazing that so much falsehood, falsehood that has been exposed time and again by the highest literary authorities, should still continue to exist on what is really so slender a basis. The contrast between the two characters is for the most part superficial. Social position, manners, sexual morality ; these are the main points on which the differences are manifest. Disregard the exteriors, and it will be found that in most respects the characters are remarkably alike. Churton Collins wisely remarks that Chesterfield " has much of the sterling good sense of Johnson, and, if we penetrate below the surface, much also of Johnson's seriousness and solidity."[1] Is it unfair to describe them both as wise, honourable, affectionate, hard-working, conscientious, intellectual Englishmen, each living up to his own ideals—ideals that were not in the main dissimilar ; each bearing with philosophic fortitude a heavy load of sorrows?[2]

Having endeavoured to trace the *popular* conception of Chesterfield from his day to our own, let us return to the better-informed contemporary opinion which we believe for the most part differed in no marked degree from the comparatively recent estimates of such careful appraisers as Churton Collins, Lord Carnarvon and Charles Strachey. What the modern critic does not realize, and can only dimly imagine is the influence of Chesterfield's magnetic personality, with which contemporary opinion was clearly imbued. To attempt to analyse this personality is, we confess, a task beyond our powers. That he was endowed with certain natural gifts—notably those of oratory and charm of manner—we feel compelled to believe, in spite of the constant efforts on his part to impress on his son that they were laboriously acquired. The truth is probably that what nature gave him he was at pains to cultivate, and that what was not innate he was at equal pains to acquire. Whether he was as naturally inclined to laziness as he would seem to have wished his friends to believe is again doubtful. What we do know, however, is that he

---

[1] *Essays and Studies*, p. 257.

[2] " He never complains ; he makes the best of things, like the gallant man that he was ; and he never tires of the amiable didacticism which was in his blood and bone, and which he gladly acknowledged for a foible, like the candid and honest man that he was." This passage, in some respects so applicable to Johnson, forms the conclusion to a critical article on Chesterfield in the *Times Literary Supplement* of February 7, 1924.

was physically at a natural disadvantage. His presence was scarcely commanding, his exterior positively unattractive ; moreover, he was afflicted with recurrent periods of ill-health which became more and more frequent until his condition during the last twenty years of his life was that of a hopeless invalid. To overcome these handicaps, apart from sheer will-power and determination, there must have existed some extraordinary personal magnetism. One indication of its force is to be found in the deep respect with which he was regarded by such commanding personalities as Montesquieu,[1] Voltaire,[2] and Frederick the Great.[3] Chesterfield was not profoundly intellectual, certainly no self-advertiser ; and what had he actually *achieved* to command such respect from notabilities outside his own country ? Surely very little in point of actual performance; but he was apparently held in high esteem on the Continent before he had had time or opportunity to achieve that little. This we gather from a curious side-issue in one of the intercepted letters from Reichenbach to Grumkow. It is dated April 7, 1730, and was written while Chesterfield was on leave from the Hague, having spent eighteen months there in which he had certainly done good sound work, but accomplished nothing of considerable importance.

" C'est une affaire bien étrange qu'on a une Idée trop petite icy des Allemands, et que nous autres Allemands avons une Idée trop vaste et magnifique des Anglois, et croyons que c'est un Ange même qui vient, par exemple Lord Chesterfield passe icy pour un bon homme qui est en crédit auprès de Sa Majesté Brittanique mais on n'a pas pourtant une Idée si extraordinaire de Luy icy, comme on a de Luy en Allemagne." [4]

It is perhaps worth while giving Carlyle's rendering of this passage with his accompanying comments.

---

[1] " Montesquieu, after the publication of *L'Esprit des Lois*, wrote to the Abbé de Guasco, who was then in England—' Tell my Lord Chesterfield that nothing is so flattering to me as his approbation ; but that, though he is reading my work for the third time, he will only be in a better position to point out to me what wants correction and rectifying in it ; nothing could be more instructive to me than his observations and his critique.' " —Critical Essay by Sainte-Beuve in *Letters, Sentences, and Maxims by Lord Chesterfield*, p. xii.

[2] See extract from Voltaire's letter to Chesterfield, October 24, 1771 ; cited on p. 3 n. *ante.*

[3] See Maty, vol. I, sect. IV, pp. 100, 101, and 307.

[4] State Papers (Foreign) Prussia vol. 27.

"Singular enough, how these English are given to undervalue the Germans ; whilst we in Germany overvalue them. There is, for instance, Lord Chesterfield, passes here for a fair enough kind of man, and is a favourite with the King " (not with Walpole or the Queen, if Nosti knew it) ; " but nobody thinks him such a prodigy as you all do in Germany,"—which latter bit of Germanism is an undoubted fact ; curious enough to the English, and to the Germans that now read in extinct Books." [1]

The truth of Carlyle's " undoubted fact " we cannot accept. That Chesterfield was regarded with deep, even with prodigious, admiration by many of his contemporaries in England can be seen from the numerous encomiums to which we have already referred. It was not a case of a prophet in his own country, though certain fortuitous circumstances might lead the casual reader to that conclusion. Let us consider for a moment which of Chesterfield's contemporaries bore him the most personal animosity. The names that readily occur are those of Horace Walpole, Hervey, Caroline, Sandwich, and possibly Carteret. Is it not an unfortunate coincidence that for the most vivid records of his times we are almost entirely indebted to two of these personal enemies ? It is true that the historians have had considerable recourse to a third chronicler, the Earl of Marchmont, who was a friend of Chesterfield ; but his *Diary* is of an entirely impersonal nature, and written in a style that is almost unreadable. Marchmont's statements—he expressed no opinions—are resorted to for truth rather than pleasure. Hervey, on personal issues, is as unreliable as he is entertaining. Horace Walpole was a man to whom Chesterfield's personality would naturally make a strong appeal, and his early animosity towards him was purely the result of filial devotion ; but while he can be readily excused on that ground, his prejudiced utterances are rendered none the more trustworthy.[2] Towards the end of Chesterfield's life, Walpole seems to have become genuinely fond of him ; but his affection was not enough to prevent his joining in the chorus of abuse that greeted the publication of the *Letters to his Son*.

In the pages of this book will be found a number of quotations from contemporary sources which may tend to

---

[1] *Frederick the Great*, Book VII, chap. II.
[2] His MS. notes on Maty's *Chesterfield* are, moreover, full of inaccuracies.

counteract the partial observations of Hervey and Walpole ;
but it will be perhaps as well to give in full one example
of what we believe to have been the general current estimate
of Chesterfield.   The passage selected occurs in Thomson's
Seasons (*Winter*), and has, we believe, never previously been
cited in Chesterfield's favour.

> " O Thou, whose wisdom, solid yet refin'd,
> Whose patriot-virtues, and consummate skill
> To touch the finer springs that move the world,
> Join'd to whate'er the Graces can bestow,
> And all Apollo's animating fire,
> Give thee, with pleasing dignity, to shine
> At once the guardian, ornament, and joy
> Of polish'd life ; permit the rural Muse,
> O Chesterfield, to grace with thee her song !
> Ere to the shades again she humbly flies,
> Indulge her fond ambition, in thy train,
> (For every Muse has in thy train a place)
> To mark thy various full-accomplish'd mind :
> To mark that spirit, which, with British scorn,
> Rejects the allurements of corrupted power ;
> That elegant politeness, which excels,
> Ev'n in the judgment of presumptuous France,
> The boasted manners of her shining court ;
> That wit, the vivid energy of sense,
> The truth of Nature, which with Attic point
> And kind well-temper'd satire, smoothly keen,
> Steals through the soul, and without pain corrects.
> Or rising thence with yet a brighter flame,
> O let me hail thee on some glorious day,
> When to the listening senate, ardent, crowd
> Britannia's sons to hear her pleaded cause.
> Then dress'd by thee, more amiably fair,
> Truth the soft robe of mild persuasion wears :
> Thou to assenting reason giv'st again
> Her own enlighten'd thoughts ; call'd from the heart,
> The obedient passions on thy voice attend ;
> And ev'n reluctant Party feels a while
> Thy gracious power : as through the varied maze
> Of eloquence, now smooth, now quick, now strong,
> Profound and clear, you roll the copious flood."

Highly eulogistic as these lines are, the reader must
be warned against accepting them with a shrug of the
shoulders as mere laudatory froth.   They do not give a
complete picture of Chesterfield it is true ; but a careful

perusal of them will reveal that they contain little more than the truth. The parenthesis "For every Muse has in thy train a place" can be rejected, and a few of the expressions softened. It would be difficult to do more without injustice to Chesterfield. If the description of his oratorical powers be considered too flattering, let us not forget Mahon's tribute :—

"Whether from such studies, or from natural genius, Chesterfield's speeches became more highly admired and extolled than any others of the day. Horace Walpole had heard his own father ; had heard Pitt ; had heard Pulteney ; had heard Wyndham , had heard Carteret ; yet he declares, in 1743, that the finest speech he ever listened to was one from Chesterfield." [1]

Exactly when Thomson wrote these lines it is impossible to say, but they appear in the 1744 edition, and, from the allusion to Chesterfield's rejection of "the allurements of corrupted power," were probably written after Walpole's fall in 1741 when the earl preferred to remain in opposition. After Chesterfield's success in Ireland, his popularity became for the time still greater, but we must be content with quoting this one earlier eulogium, and proceed to the final and less glorious episode in his public career.

Of Chesterfield's period of office as Secretary of State not much appears in the histories. All writers (including Horace Walpole) are agreed that Newcastle's petty and jealous conduct rendered it impossible for him to retain his post. George II and Newcastle were both opposed to his peace policy ; and against Newcastle and his wiles Chesterfield had little chance. He could not descend to the Duke's methods, and the odds were too heavy against him. As Craig remarks (p. 272), "It was, in fact, impossible for a self-respecting Minister to continue in office then if his views did not happen to coincide with those of the omnipotent Duke." And again (p. 270), "To a man of Chesterfield's stamp such a position was intolerable ; he determined to vacate it on the first opportunity." But this is exactly what Chesterfield did not do. It is easy enough to understand why he resigned his position. What no one has attempted to explain is why "a man of his

[1] *History of England*, chap. xxx, vol. III, p. 326. Horace Walpole to Mann, December 15, 1743.

stamp " tolerated the indignities of such a position for
almost exactly twice as long as he endured the pomp and
drudgery of an Irish Viceroyalty. It was entirely contrary
to the independence of character shown in his earlier
political life, and may have been partly due to the tolerance
which we should expect to increase with age and experience
in the life of a wise man. A year after he had accepted
office, Chesterfield wrote to Dayrolles : " You judge
very right in thinking that it must be very disagreeable
to tug at the oar with one who cannot row, and yet will
be paddling so as to hinder you from rowing. I think
I have had a great deal of patience already, and how
much longer it will hold, God knows ; to do any good
I would bear a great deal, but as I find that impossible,
and that we are to be ruined by incapacity, I do not much
care to share in the reproach when I know I am free from
the guilt." [1] The author of these sentiments was no longer
the man who had boasted, two and a half years before,
of " a resolution which I can never depart from, I mean
that of not suffering an indignity."[2]

Though altruistic patriotism, assisted by a growing
tolerance, was doubtless the main factor in the change,
it may be that Chesterfield's conduct was at least partly
due to the fact that his son was at this time within measur-
able distance of entering public life. The father's letters
are beginning to contain references to young Stanhope's
future career, for the success of which Chesterfield reveals
more ambition than he had ever displayed for his own.[3]
It would be obviously impossible to attain the objects
he then had in view for his son were he to be in disfavour
with the highest in the land, and he made it clear on
resigning the Seals that he would on no account go into
opposition.[4]

Though the circumstances of Chesterfield's tenure of
office and his subsequent retirement shed little light on
his character, it is worth while examining them, since
they throw a strong side-light on the amazing way in which
foreign affairs were conducted at this period of our history.
The diplomatic correspondence of the years 1746-48,

[1] October 23, 1747. Bradshaw, vol. II, p. 840.
[2] See his letter to Newcastle, pp. 82-83 ante.
[3] Bradshaw, vol. I, pp. 45, 80, 83.
[4] Marchmont Papers, vol. I, p. 273, and Letters to Dayrolles. See also
Newcastle's letter to Sandwich, February 9, 1748; p. 122 post.

contained in several volumes of the Newcastle Papers, reads like a travesty of history—a tragic farce, in which statesmen's reputations, soldiers' lives, and national fortunes are played with and heedlessly sacrificed, not to the ambitions of great men like Pitt or Napoleon, but to the personal whims and petty jealousies of incompetent politicians like Newcastle and Sandwich.

At the time Chesterfield left Ireland, Henry Pelham was Prime Minister, Hardwicke Lord Chancellor, Harrington Secretary of State for the Northern and Newcastle for the Southern Department. The exact provinces of these Departments were changed from time to time, but the Northern always embraced our affairs with Holland, to which country Sandwich, as we have seen, was appointed Envoy Extraordinary in August, 1746. He immediately began a secret correspondence with Newcastle, to the natural annoyance of the Northern Secretary, Harrington, who resigned in consequence two months later. On Chesterfield's succeeding him at the end of October, 1746, things went smoothly for the first seven months. The only approach to a hitch occurred when Sandwich failed (for a few days) to appreciate the omnipotence of Newcastle, who accordingly wrote him the following typical letter.

November 14, 1746.

My dear Lord,

You must allow me to be a little angry with you, and to express both my surprise and concern that I have not had one word of answer from your Lordship, either to my publick or private letters upon the great alteration which has lately happen'd in the Secretary's Office. This is an event so considerable in itself, so material to the publick, and so agreeable to me (as I find it is to your Lordship by your publick and private letters to Lord Chesterfield), that indeed I did expect to hear from you upon it. You have all imaginable reason to be pleased with your new Correspondent ;[1] but I have the vanity to think you have [sic] the obligation entirely to me ; for the King was not only so gracious as to offer me several times to make anyone Secretary of State whom I should recommend (and determined upon My Lord Chesterfield upon my recommendation) but His Majesty was pleased for some days, to press me

---

[1] Chesterfield.

I

in the strongest manner, to take the Northern Department, alledging to me how necessary it was that I should have the pen in my own hands, and how much trouble I had had in combating and disputing the works of others ; [1] to all which I answer'd that that would be no longer the case, that Lord Chesterfield and I should perfectly agree, that in that respect it would be the same thing who had the Northern Department, and that, for many reasons, it was most for His Majesty's Service that I should remain where I was, however flattering the change might be to me. And, indeed, Lord Chesterfield is so good, in writing all the letters in concert with me, that it is just the same thing who has the pen ; and Your Lordship sees the publick letters from the Office now are entirely agreeable to the private thoughts I used to fling out to you in our private correspondence, and, for that reason, I shall not trouble you with any business."[2]

Trouble began when, to further the cause of peace, Chesterfield had his friend Solomon Dayrolles appointed King's Resident at the Hague under Sandwich. The latter was not quite thirty years of age, full of importance in his first post, and not unaware of the fact that he was Newcastle's latest pet. Perhaps Dayrolles's appointment was not made in the most tactful manner ; but whether the slight was intentional or not, Sandwich chose to take deep offence, and wrote as follows to Newcastle :—

" I have wrote privately to My Lord Chesterfield. I wish he may shew you my letter, in which I hope I have just given him reason to see that I did not think I deserved from him what he has thought proper to do in sending one to be a spy upon my actions. I have touched it so gently that he must look very close to see that I understand the meaning of Mr. Dayrolles' mission ; tho' I own I have had difficulty to hide my opinion, since the manner of doing it without giving me the least previous intimation, and the secret foundation which I am satisfied it was built upon . . . have, I own, touched me so nearly that it will not be easy for me to get rid of the impression it has made."[3]

[1] Harrington in particular.
[2] Add. MSS. 32806, f. 203. This and the following extracts are now printed for the first time. (It may be added that Newcastle's letter procured from Sandwich the meek and servile reply that was required.)
[3] May 23, N.S., 1747. Add. MSS., 32808, f. 196.

On the same day,[1] Newcastle had written to re-assure Sandwich :

"Dayrolles' appointment perhaps surprised you : I will tell you plainly how it happened. Lord Chesterfield sent him to me one morning to ask my concurrence in his being appointed Second Minister at the Hague, as his uncle was ; which was now the more necessary, as you were so pressing to come away for a short time. Dayrolles is a very honest fellow ; a great friend of many of my friends, and an old acquaintance of mine. Upon this, I readily agreed to it ; and the rather, as I thought his nomination might prevent a more disagreeable person being sent, in case you come away for never so short a time."

The rest of the letter is little more than a series of covert suggestions that Chesterfield was trying to negotiate a peace on his own account through the agency of Marshal Noailles, and the true Newcastle note is struck in the following passage : " I wish a good Peace as much as any body, and might content myself with an indifferent one, when all means to better it have been tried, and proved unsuccessful . . . But I neither think it right for the Publick, nor reputable for the persons concerned, that negotiations for Peace should not go thro' the same hands that have conducted the measures of War ; or, to speak more plainly to your Lordship, that those who have had the chief hand at home in advising and carrying on the measures of War should not have the same concern in and means of deliberating upon those of Peace." And again, towards the end of the letter : " It would be odd if those who have borne the burden of the day should not be thought the properest persons to be entrusted with conducting the measures for the conclusion of it." [2]

These sentiments are typical of Newcastle's petty-mindedness, of his supreme egoism. Even when his country's fortunes were at stake his mind seemed unable to travel beyond the limits of the personal. If Macaulay had had the opportunity of perusing the three hundred and fifty volumes of the Newcastle Papers, comprising as they do something like a quarter of a million pages

[1] May 12, O.S., 1747. The difference in the two styles must be remembered in reading this correspondence.
[2] Add. MSS. 32808, ff. 199–201.

of letters, we doubt if he would have found it necessary to alter one word of his well-known summary of the Duke.

" No man was ever so unmercifully satirised. But in truth he was himself a satire ready made. All that the art of the satirist does for other men, nature had done for him. Whatever was absurd about him stood out with grotesque prominence from the rest of the character. He was a living, moving, talking caricature. His gait was a shuffling trot ; his utterance a rapid stutter ; he was always in a hurry ; he was never in time ; he abounded in fulsome caresses and in hysterical tears. His oratory resembled that of Justice Shallow. It was nonsense effervescent with animal spirits and impertinence. Of his ignorance many anecdotes remain, some well authenticated, some probably invented at coffee-houses, but all exquisitely characteristic. ' Oh—yes—yes—to be sure—Annapolis must be defended—troops must be sent to Annapolis—Pray where is Annapolis ? '—' Cape Breton an island ! wonderful ! —show it me in the map. So it is, sure enough. My dear sir, you always bring us good news. I must go and tell the King that Cape Breton is an island.'

" And this man was, during near thirty years, Secretary of State, and, during near ten years, First Lord of the Treasury ! His large fortune, his strong hereditary connexion, his great parliamentary interest, will not alone explain this extraordinary fact. His success is a signal instance of what may be effected by a man who devotes his whole heart and soul without reserve to one object. He was eaten up by ambition. His love of influence and authority resembled the avarice of the old usurer in the *Fortunes of Nigel*. It was so intense a passion that it supplied the place of talents, that it inspired even fatuity with cunning . . . It was as dangerous to have any political connection with Newcastle as to buy and sell with old Trapbois. He was greedy after power with a greediness all his own. He was jealous of all his colleagues, and even of his own brother. Under the disguise of levity he was false beyond all example of political falsehood. All the able men of his time ridiculed him as a dunce, a driveller, a child who never knew his own mind for an hour together ; and he overreached them all round." [1]

---

[1] Essay on Horace Walpole.

For the following nine months, *i.e.* from May 1747 until February 1748, our most important foreign affairs remained under a dual control. Chesterfield, as Secretary for the Northern Department, supported by Henry Pelham and the whole of the Cabinet with the exception of Newcastle and Bedford, conducted an official correspondence with Sandwich, the main object of which was to procure peace as soon as possible. Simultaneously, this object was being delayed at every turn by the clandestine correspondence of Newcastle and Bedford, supported by the Duke of Cumberland and, less actively, by George II in England, with Sandwich and the Bentincks, supported by the Prince of Orange and the War Party in Holland.

Sandwich, who knew he could gain no prestige if the French terms were accepted, staked everything on a successful prosecution of the War with the help of the Dutch. Either through blind optimism and self-deceit, or by calculated overstatement, he presented the future extent of the Dutch co-operation in such a rosy light to Newcastle that the latter, only too anxious to be convinced, remained opposed to peace right to the bitter end. Only occasionally did he allow himself to become sceptical. Thus, in a letter to Sandwich of July 28, 1747, he writes :

" My difficulties encrease every day. I will endeavour to do for the best, but I cannot answer for events. I have had a most desponding letter from the Duke.[1] In these circumstances what can we do but make peace, with our allies, if we can get a tolerable one ? If Bergen-op-Zoom is taken all the World will cry out for Peace. The impractibility of carrying on the war was insisted upon by *Every Body* [2] last night, but myself. It was affirm'd we had no resources ; that Holland could not pay the expenses of the present year ; that great clamours and discontents were rising against the new Government, etc. ; and if the Stadtholder does not shew he can *act* as well as write, and that the Republic has *Power* as well as Will, all will signify nothing." [3]

Newcastle's most illuminating letter, however, is one written to Sandwich on December 18, 1747, in which the

---

[1] *I.e.* of Cumberland.

[2] *I.e.* in the Council Chamber. Present : Lord Chancellor, Henry Pelham, Dukes of Newcastle and Dorset, and Earl of Chesterfield.

[3] Add. MSS. 32809, f. 111.

views of both parties are stated with considerable clarity and fairness.

" You must not be uneasy that I make my complaints to you of the conduct of our allies, and particularly of the Stadtholder, from whom *We* [1] expected such resolution, activity, and forwardness as would have silenced those who represented the state of affairs in Holland as miserable for themselves and incapable of giving relief or assistance to us. You would not be surprised at me if you knew the heavy charge that is daily levell'd at *Me* singly. It has been represented even to His Royal Highness that I am the only *one* that talks to the King in the Closet of this opinion, and that I differ with all my relations, confidents, and friends, and, I think, with every honest and sensible man in England.

" The chief difference of opinion between my Colleagues and myself has been this. They thought we should conclude Peace now, on such terms as we could get ; since in their opinion it would be impracticable to get an army in Flanders, and another in Italy which would be able to show their faces against the French ; so that we must be in a worse condition than we are now, after eleven millions expended for the next campaign, and running the risk of having the whole Republic of Holland swallow'd up, this winter, which they still think not only possible but probable. My opinion was that the Peace we could get now was so bad that we ought to be at any expense, and run some risks to try to get a better, which I thought might be very practicable by the armies we might form in Flanders and Italy. Towards this I depended much upon the alteration that has happen'd in Holland, both as to the inclinations and power of the Republic, of which we had the most solemn assurances ; to which, you know, some here would not give the least credit.

" I am sorry to say my expectations, if not disappointed entirely in this respect, are at least suspended ; but I am yet willing to hope such measures may be taken by your rowzing up the attention of the Stadtholder, and representing to my good friend Bentinck the alarms we have here from their inactivity, that our fears will be in some measure removed." [2]

[1] By this Newcastle probably meant George II and himself.
[2] Add. MSS. 32810, ff. 373, 374.

A month later, Newcastle's last supporter, the Duke of Bedford, deserted him for the peace party, which event he relates at some length to Sandwich in a letter of January 19, 1748, adding that "nothing but H.R.H.'s great and powerfull protection could enable me to go on." [1] Even Sandwich had now become pessimistic, as appears from his letter to Newcastle of January 23, N.S., 1748.

"I am far from saying things are well. I own there are hardly any parts of this government [2] that do not want amendment. Their weaknesses are very numerous, and I am sure you will do me the justice to own I have never endeavoured to hide them to my friends. All I contend for is that they are not so bad as they are represented to be by some designing people. It is very natural for those who think Marshall Saxe's plan [3] an admissible one to endeavour to describe our affairs as being in a desperate condition, because nothing but our being in a very desperate state indeed can ever render that plan fit to be listened to with patience. My opinion is, and allways will be, different from the promoter of those principles.[4] He may have private views of advantage that I have no business to enter into, but as I consider them chiefly to turn upon the desire of encreasing his power, as I am no ways inclined to contribute to that purpose, I have no inducement, either publick or private, to conceal my real sentiments." [5]

Perhaps Sandwich revealed his *real* sentiments here more fully than he was aware of. They do not strike us as being of a particularly creditable order. There is certainly no evidence whatsoever in support of the charges he brings against Chesterfield, and we know of no other occasion on which this charge of selfish ambition has been made against him.

By this time circumstances were becoming intolerable for Chesterfield. Apart from the annoyance caused him by the Newcastle-Sandwich correspondence, he had

[1] Add. MSS. 32811, f. 85.

[2] The Dutch.

[3] Which, according to Sandwich, involved "the restitution of Cape Breton, an establishment for Don Philip, and the restoring the fortifications of Dunkirk." See Letter from him to Newcastle, January 30, N.S., 1748. Add. MSS. 32811, f. 92.

[4] Chesterfield.

[5] Add. MSS. 32811, ff. 38, 39.

recently received deliberate slights from the King, who tacitly refused to grant a colonelcy to his cousin George Stanhope,[1] despite Chesterfield's warm support.[2] After Stanhope's name had been passed over on five occasions, Chesterfield told his friend Lord Marchmont, in the course of a long conversation concerning his resolution to resign office, that Newcastle " was so jealous of the favour of the closet, that he could not endure any one should have credit there ; and therefore if he, Lord Chesterfield, wanted to have anything, it was sure to be opposed in every way possible ; that he was not inclined to take Colonel Stanhope's affair in a high way ; but he saw it was done to shew that he had no credit, and to tell everybody not to apply to him, if they wanted anything ; that in his situation what must the world think, but that he continued in for the sake of £5,000 a year ; that besides he was every day setting his hand to what he disapproved, carrying on measures he condemned, and acting as the Duke of Newcastle's *commis*, whilst his Grace played the part of sole minister, and was safe." [3]

Other reasons appear, as we shall shortly see, in his general correspondence, and, after drawing up " an able memorial, setting forth the dangers of the war, and the necessity of taking serious measures to close it " ; [4] Chesterfield resigned the Seals on February 6, 1748.[5]

Six days later Newcastle sent Sandwich his official instructions [6] to make peace at the Aix-la-Chapelle Conference, with the result that preliminaries were signed there at the end of April. Of this event Chesterfield writes to Dayrolles on May 3rd as follows :—

" My prophecy, as you observe, was fulfilled *sonica*,[7]

[1] See Chesterfield to Lord Essex, June 21, 1733 ; p. 296 *post*.

[2] *Marchmont Papers*, vol. I, pp. 225–227. See also Chesterfield to Stone, Add. MSS. 32709, f. 29 ; Ernst, pp. 309, 310, 331, 332.

[3] *Marchmont Papers*, vol. I, p. 263

[4] Mahon's *History of England*, chap. xxx, vol. III, pp. 339, 340.

[5] A full account of Chesterfield's resignation and its causes is to be found in a letter from Henry Fox to Sir. C. H. Williams, of February 17, O.S., 1748, quoted in Coxe's *Pelham Administration*, vol. I, pp. 389, 390. Fox suggests that one cause that led to Chesterfield's failure to obtain the supreme power he aimed at was his studied and prolonged attempts to gain influence through the medium of Lady Yarmouth, the King's mistress.

[6] Add. MSS. 32811, f. 148.

[7] *I.e.*, promptly, at once. The term is taken from the game of basset, where it signifies a card having an immediate effect on the game. *Cf.* " The Knave won *Sonica*, which I had chose."—Pope, *The Basset Table*, i. 51. (New English Dict.)

which I heartily congratulate both you and myself upon, for, had not that part of my predictions come to pass in the moment that it did, the other part would, which was inevitable ruin. Had not the French politely signed the preliminaries when they did, but resolved to profit of the advantages which they had in their hands, we were undone. Most people here are astonished at the moderation of the French Court, and cannot account for it from any known rules of policy. Deep and profound historians, who must assign some great and political cause for every event, will likewise, I believe, be at a loss to assign such a one for this. But I, who am apt to take things in a more simple light, and to cook for their causes more in the weaknesses than in the wisdom of mankind, account for it in this manner. The King of France is a quiet, unambitious Prince, was weary of the war, and particularly of a camp life, which, as he had once adopted, he could not well lay aside while the war lasted. The French Courtiers are not so unskilful as not to advise what they know their Prince wishes, no matter whether it be consistent with, or contrary to, the public interest. This very principle, if you do but change the word *Peace* to War, accounts likewise for our continuing the War, so long after it was plain that we were not able to carry it on. But be the causes what they will, our escape is surely great in general, and the escapes of four people in particular, are almost miraculous. The Duke of Cumberland has escaped defeat and disgrace. The Prince of Orange has escaped being deposed, and the Duke of Newcastle and Lord Sandwich, being————.[1] I do not therefore wonder in the least at the general joy, which you tell me is expressed at the Hague upon this occasion, from the Princess and the Baron, to the fisherman at Scheveling. Must not Bentinck now confess that either he lied like a tooth-drawer while he was here, or else that he knew nothing at all of the state of his own country ? And must not Lord Sandwich confess himself a dupe, if he will not acknowledge himself to be something worse ? " [2]

And again to Dayrolles on May 13th :—

" You answered the Prince of Orange's question, concerning me, perfectly well ; far from blaming the peace,

[1] Thus in the MS.—Mahon's note.
[2] Bradshaw, vol. II, pp. 864, 865.

I am heartily glad that it is made. I was for making it sooner, and consequently better. I foresaw and foretold our weakness this campaign, and would have prevented, by a timely negotiation last October, those evident dangers to which it must necessarily expose us, and which we have escaped more by our good fortune than our wisdom. I may add, that my resignation made this peace, as it opened people's eyes with relation to the imminent dangers of the war, and made the continuation of it too strong a measure for our Minister to stand. As a proof of this, I resigned on the 6th of February last, and on the 9th Lord Sandwich had orders sent him to make the best peace that he could, but to make any rather than none. The Republic is saved by it from utter ruin ; and England from bankruptcy." [1]

How much truth Chesterfield's boast contains it is impossible to say. His " proof " is scarcely logical, and not even strictly accurate, as Sandwich's orders were not sent until the 12th.[2] There is no actual evidence on the point to be gleaned from the Newcastle Papers, but the Duke's letter to Sandwich, telling him of Chesterfield's resignation, is not without interest.

" February 9th, 1747-8

MY DEAR LORD,

You will see by my publick letter the great event that happened here on Saturday last.

Tho' there had been, some time, reason to expect it, yet it came pretty suddenly upon us, and before we were prepared for it. I must do My Lord Chesterfield the justice to say that he left the King's Service with great duty and decency to his Majesty and with the strongest assurance of his resolution to support the King's measures to the utmost of his power. I hope and believe we shall have no farther alterations, but things will not go on thoroughly well except we can agree perfectly in the measures to be pursued, which I do not despair of. The only thing which is yet done in consequence of this is His Majesty's having order'd me immediately to take the Noithern Department, as you will see by my publick letter. Who will be join'd with me in the Secretary's Office I cannot yet say. The Town has named a great many, the Duke of Bedford, yourself, my Lord Gower, Mr. Pitt, and Mr. Fox. Who

[1] Bradshaw, vol. II, p. 866.
[2] Add. MSS. 32811, f. 148.

it will be, or who it should be, in the present circumstances, I cannot pretend to say. But who I wish it should be and could be I very well know, and I hope you know too I think I shall be able to write clearer by the next post." [1]

Newcastle writes to Sandwich three days later that " the pacifick party in the House of Commons . . . were so alarm'd at the resignation of the pacifick Lord Chesterfield, and had such a dread of another warlike Secretary that they express'd such apprehensions and uneasiness at the supposed design in your favour that very ugly consequences were flung out." He then proceeds to break the news that in the circumstances Bedford has been appointed to the Southern Department, and that Sandwich is to succeed Bedford.[2]

A fortnight later Newcastle's disillusionment with regard to the value of Dutch assistance was rendered complete. Charles Bentinck, who had for several months been acting in the closest co-operation with Sandwich and Newcastle to defeat " the pacifick Lord Chesterfield," was sent by the Prince of Orange on a special mission to England for the purpose of borrowing a million pounds, his credentials being contained in a " Mémoire pour servir d' Instruction à Monsieur Le Comte C. de Bentink allant faire un tour en Angleterre " ;[3] apropos of which Newcastle unburdens himself thus to Sandwich :—

" February 26, 1747–8.

MY DEAR LORD,
I am really at a loss upon what to say upon the most extraordinary scene which the *Mémoire instructif* communicated to me here in confidence by Charles Bentinck has opened to us. The most plain and direct contradictions to every thing that has been wrote by the Prince of Orange himself, or represented by his several ministers by his order. And you will allow me to say that this state of the circumstances of the Republic, authenticated by the hand of the Stadtholder, is so different from all the accounts that you have ever given of it, either publick or private, that I cannot but own I am most extremely grieved for the sake of the public, for my own sake, and for yours,

[1] Add. MSS. 32811, f. 197.
[2] As First Lord of the Admiralty. Add. MSS. 32811, f. 213.
[3] Add. MSS. 32811, f. 235–238.

to see such a paper, so verified, come at this time. What have we been doing if this is the state of our case ? What have we depended upon from Holland, if they are not able, without an impracticable loan of a Million here, to keep their heads above water ? Or why did we reject M. Saxe's proposals, or were encouraged, or indeed forced to do it by the Stadtholder and his friends, if, notwithstanding the alteration of some circumstances in our favor, we cannot hope to better our conditions of peace by the next campaign ?

In short, the Paper is the language, and almost the words that have been preached here all this Winter. It will be a great triumph to them, and all we can say is they were more in the right than we could have imagined. You must not wonder if I am astonished that such a Paper should be brought over by Mr. B.; but what is much worse, that this should be in any degree the case, and I in no degree informed of it. Had this come out a few days sooner,[1] what would then have been the consequence of it ?

Ever yours, Holles Newcastle."[2]

This letter is surely as complete a vindication of Chesterfield's pacific policy as his staunchest supporter could desire, and will serve as a fitting epitaph to his period of office, a period which reflects little credit on him, if credit is to be measured by achievement, and still less on our country in general. The statesmanlike essentials of wisdom, foresight, patience, industry and patriotic fervour were all exhibited by him to a considerable degree. What he lacked was ability to cope with Newcastle. But this deficiency it is impossible to express in terms of abstract qualities. Such qualities might be speculatively summed up as involving a kind of super-cunning that was ethically abhorrent to Chesterfield's code of honour. On the other hand we may imagine them in terms of some magnetic force not possessed by Chesterfield or possibly by any statesman that has ever lived.[3] It is possible,

---

[1] By this we imagine Newcastle means prior to Chesterfield's resignation.
[2] Add. MSS. 32811, f. 287.
[3] Pitt, it is true, worked successfully in coalition with Newcastle for over four years—a coalition which without Chesterfield's consummate tact would never have come into existence. It must be remembered, however, that at the time of its inception Newcastle was over sixty years of age, and to a certain extent a spent force. Moreover, George II, who, next to Newcastle, proved Chesterfield's greatest political handicap, was

granted certain favourable conditions, to conceive Chesterfield as a great statesman ; but, speculation apart, the
fairest thing that can be said of him in office is that his
failure to achieve success was due to no subjective cause.

Except for occasional appearances in the House of Lords
—notably his proposal and carrying of the Bill for the
Reformation of the Calendar in 1751—Chesterfield's public
career was now at an end ; but, before we review the last
twenty-five years of his life, it may be as well to quote at
some length from the letters he wrote at the time of his
resignation, the story of which they tell with convincing
sincerity. They afford, moreover, an excellent bridge
between his public and private life, and display Chesterfield's extraordinary faculty for instantly adjusting
his mode of living, even his temperament, to altered
conditions objectively imposed ; his determination successfully to practise the philosophy he preached to his son,
culled largely from the *de Officiis* of Cicero. Chesterfield,
though naturally of a pleasure-loving disposition, had
felt himself bound to devote the best years of his life to
the service of his country. "Iis qui habent a natura
adjumenta rerum gerendarum, abjecta omni cunctatione,
adipiscendi magistratus et gerenda respublica est." [1] He
now felt that he could conscientiously consider himself
as coming under the category of those, "qui aut valetudinis
imbecillitate, aut aliqua graviore causa impediti a republica
recesserunt cum ejus administrandae potestatem aliis
laudemque concederent." [2]

Just as Chesterfield's letters to his son and godson are
for the most part an expansion of the chapters which deal
with the fourth division of the *honestum* in *de Officiis*, lib. i,
so these letters are founded throughout on the earlier
chapters 20 and 21. In particular, the following passage
must surely have been ringing in his head when he wrote
them.

" Nec vero imperia expetenda, ac potius aut non
accipienda interdum, aut deponenda nonnumquam.
Vacandum autem omni est animi perturbatione, tum
cupiditate et metu, tum etiam aegritudine et voluptate

then an old man and had lost nearly all his power. He died a year before
Pitt resigned from the coalition.

[1] *De Off.*, I, 21.

[2] *Ibid.*

nimia et iracundia ; ut tranquillitas et securitas adsit, quae affert cum constantiam, tum etiam dignitatem.''[1]

We will begin this short series [2] with a letter written eleven days before Chesterfield's resignation.

To Solomon Dayrolles,

London, January 26, O.S., 1748.

" . . . Neither the state of foreign nor domestic affairs will permit me to continue much longer in my present situation. I cannot go on writing orders, of which I see and foretell the fatal tendency. I can no longer take my share of either the public indignation or contempt on account of measures in which I have no share. I can no longer continue in a post in which it is well known that I am but a *Commis* ; and in which I have not been able to do any one service to any one man though ever so meritorious, lest I should be supposed to have any power and my colleague not the whole. And lastly, I tell you very truly, I long for rest and quiet, equally necessary to my present state both of body and mind. Could I do any good, I would sacrifice some more quiet to it ; but, convinced as I am that I can do none, I will indulge my ease, and preserve my character.[3]

" I have gone through pleasures while my constitution and my spirits would allow me. Business succeeded them ; and I have now gone through every part of it, without liking it at all the better for being acquainted with it. Like many other things, it is most admired by those who know it the least. And this one consideration would alone disgust one of it, even if one had the sole power ; which is, that in this country one must, for political reasons, frequently prefer the most unworthy to the most worthy, and prostitute to importunity and undeserving greediness the rewards of merits. Thus weary of business, you will easily imagine, that in retiring from my present business, I shall not engage in any other ; but far from embarking upon any account in cabals and opposition, whenever I do take any part in the House of Lords, it shall be in support of the Government. Do not think neither that I mean

---

[1] *De Off.*, I, 20.

[2] Bradshaw, vol. II, pp. 845–854.

[3] *Cf.* " Commutato autem genere vitae, omni ratione curandum est, ut id bono consilio fecisse videamur."—*De Off.* I. 33.

a sullen retirement from the world; on the contrary, my retreat from business will give me both more time and better spirits for the enjoyment of social life, from which I will never withdraw myself."

To Solomon Dayrolles.

London, February 9, 1748.

" *Le sort est jetté* : you receive this letter from a sincere friend, but not from a Secretary of State ; and I know you to be so true a friend too, that I am sure you value it more in the former character than in the latter. Last Saturday [1] I resigned the Seals into the King's hands, who parted with me in the most gracious manner possible. My health, my spirits, and my character, all concurred in this measure, and made it absolutely necessary for me. I retire without any personal quarrel with any man whatsoever ; and if I disapproved of measures, it was by no means upon account of their authors. Far from engaging in opposition, as resigning Ministers too commonly do, I shall, to the utmost of my powers, support the King and his Government ; which I can do with more advantage to them, and more honour to myself, when I do not receive five thousand pounds a year for doing it. I shall now, for the first time in my life, enjoy that philosophical quiet, which, upon my word, I have long wished for. While I was able, that is, while I was young, I lived in a constant dissipation and tumult of pleasures ; the hurry and plague of business, either in or out of Court, succeeded, and continued till now. And it is now time to think of the only real comforts in the latter end of life, quiet, liberty, and health. Do not think, by the way, that by quiet and retirement I mean solitude and misanthropy ; far from it, my philosophy, as you know, is of a cheerful and social nature. My horse, my books, and my friends, will divide my time pretty equally ; I shall not keep less company, but only better, for I shall choose it. Therefore do not fear finding me, whenever you take a little turn here, morose and cynical : on the contrary, you will find me as gentle as a dove ; but, alas ! not so amorous. At least, whatever else you find me, you will always find me with the truest affection,

Yours."

[1] On February 6.

To Solomon Dayrolles,

London, February 9, O.S., 1748.

" As you will be asked a million of questions about my resignation, I have wrote you the letter in which this goes enclosed, by way of brief for you to talk out of ; and moreover, you may if you please (though with some seeming difficulty), show the letter itself to the curious.   Various and absurd reports will, I know, be stirring upon this event ; I cannot help that, and must pay that tax as well as other people.   One of those reports I am sure will be, and indeed in some measure already is, that my ambition was boundless, and that because I could not be everything, I would be nothing ; to which I shall only answer, that if such were my ambition, staying in Court was a much more likely way of gratifying it than going out ; and that my chance was far from being a bad one, if I would have tried it, as an ambitious man certainly would have done.   But upon my word, I gave you my true motives in my former letter, I told them to my friends here likewise, and as for the rest of the world, they are welcome to refine and speculate as much as ever they please for

Yours sincerely,

. *Point de Vivacité* ! Temper, Temper ! "

A Madame la Marquise de Monconseil.

à Bath, ce 15 Février, V.S.   1748.

" Il y a à cette heure douze jours que j'ai quitté mon poste de Secrétaire d'Etat ; vous l'aurez certainement su par les nouvelles publiques, mais vous n'en aurez certainement pas su les véritables raisons, que le public sait rarement, et n'allègue jamais : d'ailleurs, elles sont trop simples pour être crues ; elles ne sont donc véritablement que l'amour du repos, et le soin de ma santé, qui en exigeoit. Pour s'acquitter passablement de cet emploi, il faut un travail sans interruption, et une attention sans relâche, deux articles qui ne s'accordent nullement avec ma paresse naturelle, ni avec ma santé délicate.   Il y falloit aussi sacrifier toutes les douceurs de la société et de la vie privée, ce qui convenoit encore moins à mon humeur : enfin, après y avoir mûrement réfléchi, je me suis décidé en faveur du repos, et s'il eût été possible de me faire changer de sentiment, je dois avouer que la manière gracieuse et affectueuse, dont le Roi a tâché de me détourner du parti que j'avois pris, auroit plus que tout autre chose fait cet effect.

" Je jouis donc à présent d'un repos qui a d'autant plus de charmes, que je ne l'ai jamais goûté auparavant. Dans ma jeunesse, la dissipation, et le tumulte des plaisirs, auxquels je me livrai sans réserve, ne m'en laissoient point, et pendant ces dernières vingt années, les affaires m'en ont laissé aussi peu ; il étoit donc bien tems d'en jouir, et grace à Dieu j'en jouis pleinement à présent . . .."

To Solomon Dayrolles.

Bath, February 23, O.S., 1748.

" . . Without affectation, I feel most sensibly the comforts of my present free and quiet situation ; and if I had much vanity in my composition, of which I really think that I have less than most people, even that vanity would be fully gratified, by the voice of the public upon this occasion. But, upon my word, all the busy tumultuous passions have subsided in me ; and that not so much from philosophy, as from a little reflection upon a great deal of experience. I have been behind the scenes, both of pleasure and business. I have seen all the coarse pullies and dirty ropes, which exhibit and move all the gaudy machines ; and I have seen and smelt the tallow-candles which illuminate the whole decoration, to the astonishment and admiration of the ignorant audience . . ."

To the Bishop of Waterford.

Bath, March 1, 1748.

" I thank you for your kind letter, by which I am glad to find that you approve of my resignation, and of my resolution to enjoy the comforts of a private life ; indeed, I had enough both of the pageantry and hurry of public life, to see their futility, and I withdraw from them, *uti conviva satur*.[1] This conviction from experience secured me from regret ; those who have only seen the gaudy outside of great stations, languish for their hidden charms, which in my mind soon satiate after possession.[2]

---

[1] Horat. Sat. i. I, 119.

[2] " When I had the honour to see Lord Chesterfield, some time after his resignation, one reason he told me why he was glad he had resigned, was because it was very difficult, in the public station he was in, to be entirely free from doing things that were not quite right."—Note by the Bishop of Waterford in *Maty*, vol. II, p. 467.

To David Mallett.

Bath, March 9, 1748.

" . . . By this time I suppose that I am a little out of fashion, as a subject of political refinements ; and that new matter has shoved me off the coffee-house tables. I own I should not have been sorry to have heard, unseen, the various speculations thrown out, and facts asserted concerning myself of late ; which I daresay were full as near the truth, as those will be, which some solid historians of these times will transmit to posterity. Not one of them will allow the desire of ease and quiet to have had the least share in my determination ; but on the contrary will assert that it was only the pretence of disappointed ambition. Lord Chesterfield would be Cæsar or nothing, says a spirited politician ; there is something more in this affair than we yet know, says a deeper ; he expects to be called again, says a third ; while the silent pantomimical politician shrugs at every thing eventually, and is sure not to be disproved at last. They are all welcome ; let them account for my present situation how they please, this I know, and they do not, that I feel and enjoy the comfort of it . . ."

The cheerful forecast sketched out in these letters would have afforded Chesterfield somewhat bitter reflection in the years to come, had he ever allowed himself so to indulge. Of " the only real comforts in the latter end of life, quiet, liberty and health," [1] he obtained quiet four years later—the quiet of a deaf man. Liberty he also obtained, but it was the restricted liberty of an invalid, thankful to enjoy for short periods during the last twenty years of his life what he termed " negative health," a state in which he was " unwell," but free from any positive illness. " I shall not keep less company, but only better, for I shall choose it." [2] And the company he chose was " la seule compagnie à laquelle je ne suis pas à charge actuellement, c'est-à-dire mes choux." [3]

[1] Letter to Dayrolles, Feb. 9. 1748. See p. 127 *ante*.
[2] *Ibid.*
[3] Letter to Madame de Monconseil, May 3, 1753. Bradshaw, vol. III, p. 1060.

V

OLD AGE

C HESTERFIELD'S life from 1752, the year in which deafness overtook him, till his death in 1773, is a prolonged struggle against adversity in the form of ill-health and blasted hopes. He is by nature an optimist, and, while always utilizing his optimism to the full, never extends it beyond practical limits. His hopes continue until all remedies have been tried in vain, and then he abandons hope for philosophy. This philosophy we think can be best understood by extracts from his later letters which will be found at the end of this book, arranged chronologically in order to illustrate its growth and the growing force it had upon his character. It is important to remember that the philosophy itself is always under control, that he does not allow it to usurp the function of definite practical effort, any more than he allows his optimism to continue to the extent of false hopes. His philosophy is simple enough in itself, is, in fact, little more than seeing how to make the best of a bad job. It is its studied and successful application that we find not only admirable, but inspiring.

A fair indication of the way in which Chesterfield accepted his loss of social pleasures is given in the two following letters [1] written to the eccentric Anne Pitt, Chatham's sister.

January 17, 1754.

" By all I have heard of Monsieur de Gisors, his merit will leave me none, where I should wish to have a great deal, with you and Monsieur de Nivernois ; I could almost wish that he were a very unworthy object of your recommendations, that my attentions to him might be proofs of my regard to them. But why do I talk at all of atten-

---

[1] *Fortescue Papers at Dropmore.* Vol. I, Hist. MSS. Comm., 13th Report (1892). Appendix Part III, pp. 137–9. Though these letters are not entirely relevant to the context, we have omitted nothing in transcribing them on account of the characteristic grace of their contents and the fact that they are so little known.

tions so unavailing and so useless as mine must now be ?
Some philosophy, and perhaps more laziness, made retirement from both the polite and the busy world my choice
some years ago ; my deafness has now made it my only
and necessary refuge. I haunt my own house and seldom
any other ; I am a discreet ghost and, conscious that I
cannot be welcome, endeavour not to disturb. By this
account, which is a very true one, you see how improper
an introductor or companion I must be for a gay young
Frenchman of condition. But in all events Monsieur de
Gisors shall be master of my house and of my time, and
I shall think myself happy if either of them were sometimes of any use to him.

" I have received a letter from Monsieur de Nivernois
upon the same subject. You call M. de Gisors his Mr.
Stanhope : I wish with all my heart that I could call my
Mr. Stanhope his M. de Gisors. He was as kind to him
at Rome as if he really had been so, and, I fear, as partial
in the account he gave you of him as he could have been
had he been his own. For, notwithstanding all his travelling, he retains still a strong *goût du terroir*, and the
Westminster School roughness nor the true English
inurbanity are by no means worn out. I own I am so
superficial myself that I would give up a great deal of
what they call his sound knowledge for a little more
manners, attentions, and *tournure du monde*."

The second letter is undated, but was probably written
during the same year or the year following.

" This morning I *called upon you in my trouble that you
might deliver me out of my distress*, and my distress is this.
M. de Guerchy, intirely unprovoked on my part, took it
into his head to come to my house yesterday, and I, *comme
de raison*, was at his door this morning. But this is not
enough ; what must I do with Madame de Guerchy ?
Respect says, Go, make her a visit ; but deafness and
awkwardness say, Stay at home. This puzzles me so, I
can resolve on neither. Both my pride and my modesty
forbid me to exhibit my *chétive figure* in good company,
and a long disuse has totally disqualified me from doing
it. I can converse now with none but true British Johns
and Joans. Even cloaths, I mean dressed cloaths, are
as uneasy to me as they were to Humphrey Gubbin ; for

having dressed to-day in ceremony, *a l'intention de M. de Guerchy*, with my sword by my side, it has got between my legs, and has very near thrown me down twenty times. Now you could, if you would, turn a compliment for me to Madame de Guerchy that would satisfy us both much better than any visit I could make her, or anything I could say, for I do not believe I could now speak even prose to her. For God's sake, then, turn something very pretty for me, as you are the best or rather the only good turner in the kingdom. No matter for the substance, your *tournure* will make it do.

" I wish you would drop, accidentally, that, among many other oddnesses, I have that of never dining abroad, as it may prevent invitations which I should very unwillingly refuse, but which it would be absurd and impossible for me to comply with."

Our knowledge of Chesterfield as a young man is vague, and, though we get clearer glimpses of him in certain aspects during the turmoil of political life, it is not until we read his later letters that the picture becomes really vivid. But in these letters he stands out as prominently as Pepys in his Diary, or as Johnson in the pages of Boswell. We feel, in reading them, that we really know Chesterfield for the first time, know him as a brave, wise, kindly, humorous, lovable old man.

It is in these aspects that the aged earl is depicted in the admirable memoir prefixed to Lord Carnarvon's edition of the *Letters to his Godson*. We suggest that, had the letters to his son never been published, these later letters would have been hailed as perfect examples of charm and common-sense, and that Chesterfield would have taken his place in literary history as a most moral and fascinating instructor of youth.

It is impossible to read the Letters to the Godson without realizing that here is an altered Chesterfield. They breathe a kindlier, more tolerant atmosphere than that of the earlier series. The sentiments are for the most part the same ; in parts the very phraseology is identical ; but the voice is softened. As Lord Carnarvon says, " A careful reader will see changes in the spirit and general tone of thought. The affection shown to the Godson, as previously to the Son, is remarkable. The devotion of this cold man of the world to his son in the midst of public anxieties and labours, and his absolute faith in him, are among the most touching incidents I can recall ; but the gathering up afresh the broken threads of a life's hopes and ideas, and the concentration of them on another young life with undiminished passion, love, subordination of self, at the end of his earthly journey, seem still more pathetic." [1] But if, which is very doubtful, Chesterfield could ever have been fairly described as a " cold man of the world," it is impossible so to regard him in his old age.

To obtain the full value of these letters we should read them in conjunction with the contemporaneous letters to the boy's father, Arthur Charles Stanhope [2] first published in 1817, only three of which Mahon " deemed it desirable " to include in his edition of Chesterfield's *Letters*. [3] In this series, which was reprinted as an appendix to Lord Carnarvon's edition of the *Letters to his Godson*, Chesterfield is revealed in a more human and vivid light even than in his letters to Dayrolles and the Bishop of Waterford. We can hear the deaf, infirm old man instructing the seven-year-old child in the graces, watch him holding the wandering " *étourdi*'s " " head between my two hands to make him look at me whilst I was speaking to him or he to me, and now and then to tread upon his toes in order to make him stand still." [4]

The boy was sent at the age of six-and-a-half to a small private school in Marylebone kept by a Mr. Robert, and Chesterfield used to see him either there or at Blackheath almost weekly for some time, as well as write him numerous letters in French for his edification. His affection for the child is as touching as his pride in the child's affection for him. Yet he never allows himself to become maudlin, or in reality to spoil the future earl, which we understand Arthur Stanhope is at times afraid of his doing, being apparently himself of a decidedly heavy disposition, and unable to appreciate the lighter touches of his kinsman's letters. Thus, in his second letter to the father, Chesterfield says, " I must tell you for your entertainment only, that the rogue has found me out already : for having a mind to get up upon my little horse, Walsh told him that

[1] *Memoir*, p. lii.

[2] Chesterfield's third cousin.

[3] Preface, vol. I, p. xxvi.

[4] Letter to A. C. Stanhope, August 10, 1762. Carnarvon's Appendix, p. 9. See also *ibid.* p. 27.

he could not let him ride, because I should be angry at it.
'Why then,' says he, 'go and ask his leave; for, I am
sure, he will refuse me nothing.'"[1] But, despite the
observation that it was for his entertainment only, the
father needed reassurance, and Chesterfield explains in a
subsequent letter that, "Both he and you see that I can
refuse him any thing that is not proper for him; but why
refuse him any thing that is proper? I am very glad
that you was not at his elbow when he said he was sure
that I would refuse him nothing that he asked for."[2]

After the boy had been under his care for a year,
Chesterfield tells the father, "I have now by some means
or other got into all his secrets";[3] and this we have no
difficulty in believing, for the letters both to father and
son show an extraordinary sympathy with the child-mind.
We feel that the old man has entered into the little boy's
soul, understands all his childish feelings, prejudices,
levities and cares; and appreciates their values at the
child's actual appraisement. Thus, in one of the early
letters to the father :—" I gave the boy your letter, which
he said he could read when he got home, for that at present
he was too busy to do it. This great business was with
a pair of battledores, some shuttlecocks, two whips, and
tops, with which I provided him for his winter exercita-
tions, and with a very fine coach and six bays, which Lady
Chesterfield gave him. In such multiplicity of business
you cannot take it ill that your letter was postponed for
an hour."[4]

That Mahon, who must have been familiar with the
letters to A. C. Stanhope,[5] could have brought himself to
state that Chesterfield found his godson "uncongenial in
temper"[6] can be ascribed only to prejudice. The sole
authority he gives for this suggestion is that in his will
Chesterfield carefully guarded the estates he bequeathed
to his successor against waste or dilapidation as the result
of horse-racing, the keeping of a pack of hounds, betting,
or gambling.[7] The impression we receive from the letters

[1] Letter of July 23, 1762. *Ibid.* p. 8.
[2] Letter of August 10, 1762. *Ibid.* p. 9.
[3] Letter of November 28, 1763. *Ibid.* p. 34.
[4] Letter of October 30, 1762. *Ibid.* p. 16.
[5] He was of course unacquainted with the Letters to the Godson, which
were published some fifty years after his History.
[6] *History of England,* chap. xxx., vol. III, p. 342.
[7] Lord Carnarvon refutes Mahon's suggestion at some length in his
Memoir, p. lxx.

to parent and son is that Chesterfield obtained the entire confidence of his godson, and it is difficult to believe that the boy was not genuinely fond of his instructor, though Chesterfield's evidence on this point is from the very nature of the case not impartial.

" I guide him by love, not by fear, and can govern him absolutely by the eye, without saying one word to him. He is afraid of doing any thing to displease me, but is by no means afraid of me." [1]

" Though he loves me, he fears me more than he does anybody in the world : and I endeavour to keep those two sentiments alive in him." [2]

" I went to him yesterday at Marylebone, and in the course of a friendly conversation I asked him, if he loved me : he answered me, that he did. I then asked him why he loved me : he answered me honestly, because you love me. I asked him, how he knew it, and he replied, Oh, I can see that well enough ! He knows his power over me, but I must do him the justice to say that he never abuses it ; nor would I suffer him to do it to his own detriment, but I will indulge and gratify all his little harmless inclinations." [3]

" I think, we grow every day fonder of one another ; and indeed he very well deserves it from me : for he is upon the whole the best boy I ever knew, and I am very much mistaken, if he does not make the best man. I hope and believe that you will live to see him so, though I shall not : but I shall die in that faith." [4]

" He loves me as well as one creature can love another, and fears me as much, from love. I only regret that I probably shall not live to see him the man that I am persuaded he will be. You probably will, and I congratulate you before hand upon the just pleasure and pride which he will give you." [5]

[1] Letter to A. C. Stanhope, January 4, 1763. Carnarvon's Appendix, p. 19.
[2] Letter to A. C. Stanhope, January 26, 1764. *Ibid.* p. 37.
[3] Letter to A. C. Stanhope, July 24, 1764. *Ibid.* p. 42.
[4] Letter to A. C. Stanhope, October 25, 1764. *Ibid.* p. 45.
[5] Letter to A. C. Stanhope, April 22, 1766. *Ibid.* p. 64.

It is a sad commentary to make, but there is no doubt that Chesterfield was very much mistaken in his forecast. As Lord Carnarvon states, " Philip Stanhope was not the stuff out of which high eminence in statesmanship or letters could be carved ; and all that can be honestly said of him is that he was a sensible and kindly, if rather common-place man, whose life was the absolute opposite to that of his Godfather, and whose mental qualities were eclipsed by the brilliant memories of his predecessor." [1]

It is comforting to think that Chesterfield did not live to realize the non-fulfilment of his godson's early promise ; the more so, as he had already been made to realize only too acutely the mediocre abilities of the other Philip Stanhope from whom he had hoped so much. We need not recount in detail the successive disappointments that Chesterfield experienced with regard to his son ; his inability to acquire the graces essential to his success in society ; his failure in Parliament ; the objections to his birth raised in foreign courts, and the consequent handicap he suffered in his diplomatic career ; [2] all of which were met by the father with his customary philosophic fortitude. The crowning bitterness occurred in 1768, when the news of Philip's death at Avignon was followed by the personal announcement to the old man by Mrs. Eugenia Stanhope that she had been for some years secretly married to his son, by whom she had two sons, Charles and Philip.

In these circumstances Chesterfield behaved as one would expect a man to behave in whom apparently there was no trace of resentful feeling. His letters to Eugenia Stanhope are of a friendly, almost intimate nature, and the devotion he had felt for his son was extended to his grand-children, [3] to whom he wrote, eighteen months before his death, as follows :—

Bath, October 27, 1771.
" I received, a few days ago, two of the best written letters that I ever saw in my life ; the one signed Charles Stanhope, the other Philip Stanhope. As for you, Charles,

[1] *Memoir*, p. lxxi.
[2] See letters to Dayrolles, October 30, 1752, and August 16, 1753. *Brad-shaw*, vol. III, pp. 1042 and 1069.
[3] In his will, to each grandchild he leaves £100 yearly during his minority, and afterwards the interest of £10,000 ; a moiety of the corpus to be paid to each on his attaining the age of twenty-one.

I did not wonder at it ; for you will take pains, and are a lover of letters ; but you idle rogue, you Phil, how came you to write so well, that one can almost say of you two, *et cantare pares et respondere parati* ? Charles will explain this Latin to you.

" I am told, Phil, that you have got a nick-name at school, from your intimacy with Master Strangeways ; and that they call you Master *Strangerways* ; for to be sure, you are a strange boy. Is this true ?

" Tell me what you would have me bring you both from hence, and I will bring it you, when I come to town. In the mean time, God bless you both ! " [1]

It is difficult to believe that the author of that letter, or, moreover, of any of the letters to his godson, was a hard, cynical, worldly and selfish old man, which, as Lord Carnarvon suggests,[2] (with only too much reason) is the misconceived, though generally accepted, character of Chesterfield at that time. Slender evidence as it may seem, it is surely significant that Horace Walpole, who had probably said more bitter things about Chesterfield than had any of his contemporaries except Hervey, could write this note in his copy of Maty.[3]

" In the latter end of his life I frequently visited Lord Chesterfield, and received great civilities from him.[4] In 1770 he breakfasted with me at Strawberry Hill, where I made him the following compliment, which he found in the library printed at my own press.

> Few paces hence, beneath yon grottoed road,
> From dying Pope the last sweet accents flowed.
> O Twitnam ! would the friend of Pope but bless
> With some immortal strain thy favour'd press,
> The happier emblem would with truth depose,
> That where one Phoenix died, another rose ! "

What attractions could the deaf old invalid, a back number in society as in politics, offer to such a man as Horace Walpole, ever living abreast of the times, who had, moreover, perhaps better cause than anyone to dislike

---

[1] Bradshaw, vol. III, pp. 1398, 1399.
[2] *Memoir*, p. lxx.
[3] Vol. I, p. 223.
[4] See also Walpole's letter to Anne Pitt, March 6, 1766.

him ? Our suggestion is that they were the same attractions that his later letters have for us to-day, breathing as they do an atmosphere of wisdom, kindliness and charm. Dare we, in the face of long-established opinion, go further and suggest that, in his later years, by no means the least factor in Chesterfield's character was the charm of goodness ?

VI

GENERAL CHARACTERISTICS

WHILE it is clear that Chesterfield's later character differs in many respects from his earlier, it is by no means easy to draw a sharp distinction between the two. Broadly speaking, he may be said to have exhibited most of the faults of youth and none of the faults of old age. It may be useful to remember this as a guide to the development of his character, but the important fact to be realized is that, while the youthful faults may be attributed to " original sin," or, if it be preferred, to his natural temperament, the absence of the faults of age is due almost entirely to self-imposed virtue. Lord Carnarvon suggests in his *Memoir* [1] that the *Letters to his Godson* " show that private sorrows and public disappointments, and the heavy hand of age, and still more the natural kindliness of temper, which had been concealed under the polish of society, had led him in the sunset of life to a somewhat different estimate of right and wrong from that which he once professed." Churton Collins is at considerable pains to contradict this estimate. [2]

" Lord Carnarvon's remark that Chesterfield's ' estimate of right and wrong ' differed, and differed for the better, from the estimate which he had formed before he grew old, is, we venture to think, not quite just to him. For what the remark obviously implies is that the morality in the earlier correspondence is either less sound or less elevated than that in the later. . . . But Chesterfield was not, we submit, a reformed rake, except in the sense in which Aristippus and Horace were reformed rakes. He was a man of the world and a philosopher, consistent alike in his precepts and in his principles. What he preached at seventy was what he preached at fifty-seven, and what

[1] p. xiv. [2] *Essays and Studies*, pp. 218–223.

he preached at fifty-seven is what he would have preached at five-and-thirty. Of the follies and errors of his youth, of wasted opportunities, and of wasted time, he speaks with a regret common with men in all ages of the world. But the *lusus ac ludicra*, the inculcation of which has been so fatal to his reputation among his countrymen, were no more included in his remorse than they were included in the remorse of Horace. ' I do not regret,' he wrote to his son, ' the time that I passed in pleasures ; they were seasonable, they were the pleasures of youth, and I enjoyed them while young.' [1] On this point his sentiments were precisely those of the ancient moralists.[2] The licence which was allowed to youth, a proper sense of the becoming forbade to mature years. *Non lusisse pudet sed non incidere ludum.* The danger, as he well knew and has frequently remarked, lay in the possibility of the permanent corruption of character ; of the contamination, the essential contamination, of moral and intellectual energy ; of mischief alike to body and mind. As he did not, in accordance with those who thought with the ancients rather than with those who think with Christian teachers, press an austere morality on the young, so he saw no impropriety in endeavouring to render such indulgences as little harmful as possible."

In other words, so far as pleasure is concerned, Chesterfield had two moral standards, one for youth, and one for old age. He was, in fact, the last person in the world to compound for sins he was inclined to by damning those, which in his later years, he had no mind to. While, therefore, it is strictly true to say that Chesterfield was consistent in his precepts, and that what he preached to a youth at seventy was what he would have preached also to a youth at thirty-five, it must be remembered that the audience is of the same age in each case. Hence it does not follow that what he practised at seventy was what he practised at thirty-five.

It is difficult to trace the development of Chesterfield's character from youth up, as his actions are for so many

---

[1] February 16, 1748. Bradshaw, vol. I, p. 85. See also letters to his son, March 27, 1747, April 27, 1749, May 8, 1750, March 25, 1751 ; *ibid.*, pp. 48–50, 205, 339–341, 420, 421.

[2] "See particularly Cicero, *Pro Coelio, passim,* and especially chap. xii, if sentiments, which are commonplaces with the ancients, need illustration." (Collins's Note.)

years, to use Lord Carnarvon's happy phrase, " concealed under the polish of society." Chesterfield is often spoken of as " artificial," and in the broadest sense of the word no truer epithet could be applied. His life was artificial in the sense that he scorned the primitive, that he chose to be governed by a strict code of ethics rather than by his natural desires. How difficult he found it to conform to this code is as impossible for us to estimate as it was for him to say how much his cheerfulness depended on temperament, and how much on philosophy. Writing to Dayrolles of his deafness, he says, " I bear my misfortune better than I believe most other people would : whether from reason, philosophy, or constitution, I will not pretend to decide." [1] And again to Mme. de Monconseil, " Ma philosophie, ou peut-être mon tempérament, (car on s'y trompe souvent) me garantit des peines." [2]

That his natural temperament was a cheerful one we have already seen from his own admission,[3] but his later letters prove that natural cheerfulness alone was not enough to combat the host of troubles that beset him in his old age. Perhaps occasionally even his philosophy failed to come to the rescue. He was, after all, only human, and there is one unusually despairing cry in a letter to Mme. de Monconseil : " Il n'y a pas de philosophie qui tienne contre la surdité." [4]

Chesterfield is at pains to prove to his son that his own outward manners were artificially acquired : but to what a seemingly " natural " extent he trained them is admitted by all. To use an obvious paradox, the highest aim of artificiality is to appear natural. His belief was that the fundamental qualities of a gentleman (what he calls civility)[5] are innate and cannot be acquired, but that a coating of manners (what he calls good-breeding) must be artificially added before the perfect gentleman is produced ; in other words, that manners make a perfect out of a potential gentleman. Of his godson he writes to the father, A. C. Stanhope, " I will venture to promise you that he will be a gentleman. He has a natural fund of civility and good nature, upon which good breeding is

---

[1] October 18, 1752. Bradshaw, vol. III, p. 1038.
[2] September 13, 1753. *Ibid.*, p. 1071.
[3] Letter to Dayrolles, February 9, 1748. See p. 127 *ante.*
[4] December 7, 1762. Bradshaw, vol. III, p. 1286.
[5] See his Essay on Civility and Good-breeding. p. 247 *post.*

easily grafted." [1]   It is worth noting that he always uses the term "good-breeding" in a purely arbitrary and by no means a literal sense, that is to say that it has no relationship to "good birth," for which he had ever a profound contempt. [2]

That Chesterfield engrafted on his own natural "civility" the most perfect good-breeding is universally admitted; but it is not generally realized that he also engrafted on a naturally wayward and volatile temperament the high principles in which he always believed. What, in fact, impresses us most in Chesterfield's later life is the self-mastery he eventually obtained. We have seen the struggle he had in public life against what he so frequently refers to in his letters as his "natural idleness"—not idleness in the worst sense of the word, but a natural preference for a quiet, scholarly, sociable life to the turmoil, corruption, and vulgarity of eighteenth-century politics. His letters from the Hague and also to Newcastle from Ireland show that in this struggle he was not then the supreme victor; but in old age he had more than idleness to contend against, and the impression we receive from his later letters is that he had achieved a mastery over a sometimes hostile temperament, and almost invariably hostile circumstances, which betokens an ultimate realization by Chesterfield himself of the ideal of character that he had preached to his son and godson.   This ideal is taken from Cicero, who in his turn was indebted to the Greek philosophers, particularly Plato and Panaetius.   It is ably summarized by Churton Collins as follows :—" The perfection of character consists in the maintenance of an exquisite and absolute equilibrium of all the faculties and emotions of man, brought by culture to their utmost points of development and refinement in the case of the former, of refinement and temper in the case of the latter.   It is not merely completed self-mastery, but the harmony of the ordered whole, and a whole in which each part has been perfected. This is not all.   As man lives not for himself alone, but is a unit in society, the full and efficient discharge of his obligations to society, in the various relations in which he stands to it, is of equal importance.   These, then, are the two great ends of education, the perfection of the individual

---

[1] December 13, 1762. Carnarvon : Appendix p. 18.
[2] See pp. 10-11 *ante*.

character and the discipline of the individual with respect to social duties." [1]

After some pages of extracts from Chesterfield's letters to his son and godson illustrating the more important points in this summary, the same writer continues,

" On an impartial review, then, of Chesterfield's theory of education, how little fault is to be found with it ! Indeed, it would be difficult to see in what respect a character formed on such an ideal could be regarded as deficient. In what virtue, in what accomplishment, would he be lacking, either in his relation to public or in his relation to private life ? Where would he be weak, in what point unsound ? . . . The impress of sincerity is on every page of Chesterfield. The ideal he drew he had in himself realized. The unreality and unsatisfactoriness of his system lay in its attempt to revive an ideal which it is now impossible to revive, at all events popularly. It lay, to employ a word which has little to recommend it, but for which our language has no equivalent, in its pure paganism. His whole philosophy is of the world, worldly. Of the spiritual, of the transcendental, of the enthusiastic, it has nothing. He attaches, it is true, the very greatest importance to conventional religion, but he does so, it is evident, for the same reasons that the ancient legislators and moralists did so. The deference which he pays to Christianity is, we feel, no more than the deference which would have been paid to it by any wise and well-natured man of the old world, who knew the needs it was meeting and was aware of its virtues." [2]

After stating that " a philosophy of this kind is now an anachronism," that " the Religion which has revolutionised the world has made havoc of such ideals," Professor Collins points out that Chesterfield's philosophy is far from being anti-Christian.

" It is in the judgments of men like Chesterfield that conventional religious truths find their strongest collateral security.[3] Absolutely unprejudiced and absolutely

---

[1] *Essays and Studies*, pp. 243, 244.

[2] *Ibid.*, pp. 252, 253.

[3] A curiously exact counterpart to this sentiment occurs in Chesterfield's letter to his son of January 8, 1750 :—" You should by no means seem to

independent, he brings to bear on the facts of life, of which he had had a much wider and more varied experience than falls to the lot of many men, an intellect of extra-ordinary acuteness and sagacity, a judgment eminently discriminating and sober, and a temper strictly under the dominion of reason. He had studied, with minute and patient attention, the questions which are of the most vital interest to man and society, and the conclusions at which he arrived he has, regardless of anything but what he believed to be the truth, and with no object but the purest and most unselfish of all objects, both set forth and explained. That these conclusions should in so many important respects be identical with those of Christian moralists, that they should have convinced him of the wisdom of the strongest conservatism in what pertains to our religious system, and of the folly and wickedness of attempting to undermine it, is surely testimony not interesting merely, but of much value." [1]

It is doubtful whether this argument would be as generally accepted now as it probably was when written thirty years ago, but, for our part, we have no desire to disagree with its tenets in the main ; least of all do we wish to suggest that Chesterfield's philosophy is of as high an order as the Christian ethic, though in so far as the latter deals with the duty to one's neighbour there is little difference between the two teachings, as is clearly shown in the essay on Honour [2] and in many letters to his son and godson. Consider, for example, the following passage, which is worth quoting for its beauty of diction alone :

" Humanity inclines, religion requires, and our moral duty obliges us to relieve, as far as we are able, the distresses and misery of our fellow-creatures ; but this is not all, for a true heartfelt benevolence and tenderness will prompt us to contribute what we can to their ease, their amusement,

approve, encourage, or applaud, those libertine notions, which strike at religions equally, and which are the poor threadbare topics of half wits, and minute philosophers. Even those who are silly enough to laugh at their jokes, are still wise enough to distrust and detest their characters ; for, putting moral virtues at the highest, and religion at the lowest, religion must still be allowed to be a collateral security, at least, to virtue ; and every prudent man will sooner trust to two securities than to one."—Bradshaw, vol. I, p. 303.

[1] *Essays and Studies*, p. 255.
[2] No. 49 of the *World*, p. 233 *post*.

L

and their pleasure, as far as we innocently may. Let us then not only scatter benefits, but even strew flowers for our fellow-travellers, in the rugged ways of this wretched world." [1]

Of those moralists who cannot to-day accept Revelation or divine guidance, Chesterfield's ethic, except for its sexual laxity, would surely satisfy the sternest; therefore to call it an anachronism seems scarcely fair. [2] Moreover, while no Christian would be entirely satisfied with Chesterfield's philosophy, there are few who would fail to derive additional moral benefit from its wisdom.

Where we cannot help differing from Churton Collins is in his unqualified praise of Chesterfield's ideal, as apart from the pure ethic. When he asks, " In what accomplishment would he be lacking ? Where would he be weak, in what point unsound ? " we would refer him, *inter alia*, to this letter from Chesterfield to his son.

London.
April 19, O.S., 1749.

" Dear Boy,

This letter will, I believe, still find you at Venice, in all the dissipation of masquerades, ridottos, operas, etc. ; with all my heart ; they are decent evening amusements, and very properly succeed that serious application to which I am sure you devote your mornings. There are liberal and illiberal pleasures as well as liberal and illiberal arts. There are some pleasures that degrade a gentleman as much as some trades could do. Sottish drinking, indiscriminate gluttony, driving coaches, rustic sports, such as fox-chases, horse-races, etc., are, in my opinion, infinitely below the honest and industrious professions of a tailor and a shoemaker which are said to *déroger*.

As you are now in a musical country, where singing, fiddling, and piping are not only the common topics of conversation, but almost the principal objects of attention, I cannot help cautioning you against giving in to those (I will call them illiberal) pleasures (though music is commonly reckoned one of the liberal arts), to the degree

---

[1] To his Godson, November 7, 1765. (The second of the series on The Art of Pleasing). Carnarvon, p. 167.

[2] Perhaps it was more of an anachronism thirty years ago, when these words were written.

that most of your countrymen do when they travel in Italy. If you love music, hear it ; go to operas, concerts, and pay fiddlers to play to you ; but I insist upon your neither piping nor fiddling yourself. It puts a gentleman in a very frivolous, contemptible light ; brings him into a great deal of bad company ; and takes up a great deal of time which might be much better employed. Few things would mortify me more than to see you bearing a part in a concert, with a fiddle under your chin, or a pipe in your mouth." [1]

To take the question of music fist ; we feel that in this matter Chesterfield has for once allowed personal prejudice to get the better of his judgment. He must, of course, be judged to a certain extent by the standards of his time, and it would be perhaps rash to deny that when these words were written musical accomplishment put a gentleman in a very frivolous, contemptible light, and brought him into bad company. Doubtless it would have removed young Stanhope from the sort of company in Italy that his father felt it was necessary for him to frequent. But, making due allowance for *autres mœurs*, the fact remains that in this aspect Chesterfield falls definitely short of a true ideal.

With regard to " rustic sports," such as fox-hunting, there is perhaps more to be said in Chesterfield's defence. In a letter to his godson he writes : " Eat as much Game as you please, but I hope you will never kill any yourself ; and indeed, I think you are above any of those rustick illiberal sports, of guns, dogs, and horses, which characterize our English Bumpkin Country Gentlemen ; who are the most unlicked creatures in the world, unless sometimes by their hounds." [2]

At the present day it is not difficult to conceive an ideal of English manhood in which both fox-hunting and musical accomplishment would take their natural place. Indeed, one might go further and say that an ideal in which outdoor games and sport involving physical courage, and artistic attainments, involving something more than mere taste or appreciation, do not figure, is not entirely complete.

In Chesterfield's day conditions were different ; such

---

[1] Bradshaw, vol. I, p. 203.
[2] November 17, 1766. Carnarvon, p. 228. See also letter to his godson, November 17, 1767 : *ibid.*, p. 251.

versatility was practically impossible ; there was an almost total severance between town and country, and the result, as exemplified in the typical eighteenth-century fox-hunting squire, is well known. It would be wrong, therefore, to condemn Chesterfield for excluding " rustic sports " from the repertoire of the ideal gentleman. What we cannot, however, help entertaining is the suspicion that Chesterfield's ideal character is deficient in manly physical courage; that the man who attained it might be just a little namby-pamby, *un peu précieux* ; that if Chesterfield were writing at the present day he would recommend his son to play golf rather than Rugby football. It is not more than a suspicion, because in preaching to his son Chesterfield might quite possibly have felt that to urge physical courage was unnecessary. Moreover, we have the admirable ideal of manhood contained in the pen-portrait of his friend Richard Owen Cambridge, who " rides more miles in a year than the keenest sportsman, and with almost equal velocity." [1] The only reference to courage in his writings occurs in a letter to his son, where he says, " I thank you for your wild boar, who, now he is dead, I assure him *se laissera bien manger malgré qu'il en ait* ; though I am not sure that I should have had that personal valour which so successfully distinguished you in single combat with him, which made him bite the dust like Homer's heroes, and, to conclude my period sublimely, put him into that *pickle* from which I propose eating him. At the same time that I applaud your valour, I must do justice to your modesty, which candidly admits that you were not overmatched, and that your adversary was of about your own age and size." [2]

This latter point he makes also in an earlier letter, from which it is evident that he does not condemn hunting *per se*. " I suppose you have hunted at Compiègne. The King's hunting there, I am told, is a fine sight. The French manner of hunting is gentlemanlike ; ours is only for bumpkins and boobies. The poor beasts here are pursued and run down by much greater beasts than themselves ; and the true British fox-hunter is most undoubtedly a species appropriated and peculiar to this country, which no other part of the globe produces." [3]

[1] See p. 14 *ante*.
[2] January 15, 1754. Bradshaw, vol. II, p. 595.
[3] June 30, 1751. Bradshaw, vol. I, p. 463.

It is perhaps fairest to conclude that, since what corresponds in our day to healthy, manly exercise and sport could not easily be disassociated from much that was distinctly unwholesome, the father cannot be blamed for warning his son against such sports.   Chesterfield himself was assuredly no coward.   Mr. Sichel is alone in his opinion that he was " cautious to a fault, and timid by temperament " ; an opinion in support of which he not only adduces no evidence, but which he virtually contradicts in the same sentence, proceeding thus, " His *sangfroid* was eminent even in an age when *sangfroid* was the fashion." [1] There was certainly little caution in the anti-Hanoverian policy preached by him both in Parliament and in the Press, and his conduct in Ireland during the '45 Rebellion was scarcely that of a man lacking either physical or moral courage.

These are, however, minor points in comparison with the broader deficiencies in Chesterfield's ideal.   The proper study of mankind is man, and Chesterfield's study of man (though certainly not of woman) was perhaps as wise and sound as anyone's ; but man is not the universe.   To the voice of Nature he was deaf, and to her beauties blind : even when he took to gardening as a solace to his deaf old age, his interest lay almost entirely in the cultivation of melons and pineapples.   He had no love for the antique, and little for the picturesque.   To put it shortly, he was in many respects a Philistine, but it must be remembered that he lived in a Philistine age.   It would be unfair to judge him by present-day standards of æsthetic appraisement : on the other hand, these deficiencies, characteristic of his times though they doubtless were, remind us that the praise which Professor Collins bestows upon his ideal needs definite qualification.

It is hard to estimate clearly the eighteenth-century standard of appreciation of nature's beauties, but, low as it was, Chesterfield's was probably still lower, if not entirely non-existent.   He certainly had no love for the country, and says in a letter to Lord Huntingdon :—

" I have always been of your opinion as to long residence in the country, for I cannot look upon it as a scene of social life ; there are more people than men, and more

---

[1] *Bolingbroke and his Times*, vol. II, p. 241.   He is also alluded to as " the timorous Chesterfield ": *ibid*., p. 72.   See p. 173 *post*.

company than society. In fine weather I believe it is wholesome, and the spirits which exercise gives one, enables one for a time to bear the company, but *à la longue* there is nothing like a capital. St. Evremont says, ' qu'un honnête homme doit vivre et mourir dans une capitale, et qu'il n'y en a que trois au monde, qui sont Rome, Paris, et Londres.' I agree with him in both his propositions." [1]

Writing again to the same friend from Bath, he says :— " I have now, I think, got pretty near all the good that this place can or will afford me, so that I propose leaving it in about a fortnight for the Capital, which is my native air, and for which I have always had a sort of Swiss longing." [2]

Chesterfield's opinion of the importance of the arts in the equipment of a gentleman of his time can be best understood from the following pieces of advice contained in letters written to the young Lord Huntingdon during his travels in Europe between the years 1749 and 1756.

" I have heard that you intend to push your travels very far, and that, not content with going all over Europe, you propose visiting Greece and Egypt. Upon this occasion, my dear Lord, you will forgive me again if I assume the privilege of an old advising friend. The several countries and Courts of Europe, their characters, their constitutions, their politics and their manners, are very proper objects of your observation and attention, and will require all the time that you can well spare abroad. But the wild arabs in Egypt and the ignorant slaves of Greece are infinitely below your notice, and unworthy of the time they would take up. The broken pyramids and ruined temples of those desolated countries are below your attention, except in copper-plates, where they are to be seen with full as much advantage, and with much less time, trouble and danger . . . Great capitals are properer objects for you than a great variety of places ; take buildings and curiosities in your way, but go very little out of your way for them." [3]

---

[1] October 19, 1765. *Letters of Lord Chesterfield to Lord Huntingdon*, pp. 123–4.

[2] December 6, 1765 : *ibid.*, p. 129.

[3] March 3, 1751 : *ibid.*, pp. 40, 41.

" Leave pyramids, temples, sculpture and paintings to minds much below yours." [1]

" I take it for granted that you will pass the next winter at Rome, a place that well deserves your attention and observation ; I do not mean upon account of the music and the pictures, the sole objects of most of our wandering countrymen, but upon account of what it was once, and what it now is in other more important respects." [2]

" You are now My dear Lord at the seat of Arts, though perhaps not of Sciences, Florence, and by the pains you take to be a *Virtuoso*, I venture to pronounce that you will be *Virtuosissimo*, for you will always excel in whatever you undertake. A taste of painting, sculpture, architecture, and music is both an ornament and an amusement to a man of sense. But when carried by fools and blockheads into pedantry and affectation, becomes a just and inexhaustible object of ridicule, and that is commonly the case of most of our travelling countrymen. As they have more money than taste or manners, they lavish it equally ill in their *Virtu* and in their vices. The antiquities they purchase are often more modern than their mistresses and they are equally the bubbles of their *Ruffiani* and their *Ciceroni*." [3]

Chesterfield certainly spent much money on pictures, but, as is seen from his letters to Dayrolles, his attitude is that of a collector rather than of a true æsthetic appraiser. He buys Rubens or Teniers because they are Rubens or Teniers, not because they are beautiful. With regard to books his attitude is different. Here he feels himself on more familar, more solid ground, and he despises the mere bibliophile. " Buy good books, and read them ; the best books are the commonest, and the last editions are always the best, if the editors are not blockheads." [4] But at times his conscientious independence of taste is perhaps more to be admired than the taste itself. " Pour moi, je ne juge des ouvrages que par le plus ou le moins de plaisir qu'ils me donnent en mon petit particulier, et j'ose même dire, à la face de tous les pédans de l' univers, que les épîtres et les satires de Pope ont tout le bon sens

[1] April 8, 1751 : *ibid.*, p. 44.
[2] May 17, 1753 : *ibid.*, p. 77.
[3] February 21, 1755 : *ibid.*, p. 88.
[4] To his son, March 19, 1750. Bradshaw, vol. I, p. 330.

et toute la justesse, avec mille fois plus d'esprit que celles
d'Horace. Je dirai encore que le théâtre François est
infiniment supérieur au Grec ou au Latin. Je dirai aussi
que le divin Homère m'ennuye fort souvent, que le Docteur
Swift vaut mieux que Lucien, et que Tacite, de tous les
historiens du monde, est mon favori." [1]

Other literary confessions occur in the following letter
to his son of October 4, 1752. He is writing of Voltaire
and says :—

" In reading over all his works with more attention
I suppose than before, my former admiration of him is, I
own, turned into astonishment. There is no one kind of
writing in which he has not excelled. You are so severe
a classic that I question whether you will allow me to call
his *Henriade* an epic poem, for want of the proper number
of gods, devils, witches, and other absurdities requisite
for the machinery ; which machinery is (it seems) necessary
to constitute the *Epopée*. But whether you do or not,
I will declare (though possibly to my own shame) that I
never read any epic poem with near so much pleasure. I
am grown old, and have possibly lost a great deal of that
fire which formerly made me love fire in others at any
rate, and however attended with smoke ; but now I must
have all sense, and cannot for the sake of five righteous
lines forgive a thousand absurd ones.

" In this disposition of mind, judge whether I can read
all Homer through *tout de suite*. I admire his beauties ;
but, to tell you the truth, when he slumbers I sleep. Virgil,
I confess, is all sense, and therefore I like him better than
his model ; but he is often languid, especially in his five
or six last books, during which I am obliged to take a good
deal of snuff. Besides, I profess myself an ally of Turnus's
against the pious Aeneas, who, like many *soi disant* pious
people, does the most flagrant injustice and violence in
order to execute what they impudently call the will of
heaven. But what will you say, when I tell you truly,
that I cannot possibly read our countryman, Milton,
through ? I acknowledge him to have some most sublime
passages, some prodigious flashes of light ; but then you
must acknowledge that light is often followed by *darkness
visible*, to use his own expression. Besides, not having
the honour to be acquainted with any of the parties in

[1] To Baron de Kreuningen, July 7, 1752 : *ibid.*, vol. III, p. 1030.

his poem, except the man and the woman, the characters and speeches of a dozen or two of angels, and of as many devils, are as much above my reach as my entertainment. Keep this secret for me ; for if it should be known, I should be abused by every tasteless pedant, and every solid divine in England." [1]

Churton Collins puts a somewhat strained construction on this passage by remarking that Chesterfield " thought the *Henriade* a finer poem than the *Iliad* and the *Æneid.*" And the only possible authority for his succeeding statement—" He preferred Racine and Corneille to Shakespeare—" [2] is the inference to be drawn from these words of Chesterfield :—

" A gentleman should know those which I call classical works in every language—such as Boileau, Corneille, Racine, Molière, etc., in French ; Milton, Dryden, Pope, Swift, etc., in English. . . . " [3]

But though no direct evidence exists for this charge, it is possible that Chesterfield *did* consider Shakespeare inferior to Corneille and Racine. [4] The sentence we have just quoted is probably a fairly accurate estimate of the current educated taste, and it is at least doubtful whether Shakespeare at that date ranked as a classic. Blindness to nature's beauties was not the only æsthetic defect of this period. The national ear was still reacting to the Pope couplet, and had not become attuned to the subtler cadences of Shakespeare's blank verse. In the course of an enquiry into Voltaire's attack on Shakespeare, Mr. J. M. Robertson remarks :—" We may all agree, to begin with, that Voltaire *could not* in his day appreciate the unique greatness of Shakespeare as an artist. Hardly any Englishman adequately did, though Shakespeare had always been warmly praised " ; [5] and again :—" Many Englishmen eminent in that age for critical taste, Bolingbroke and Shaftesbury included, denied that there existed

[1] Bradshaw, vol. II, pp. 558, 559.
[2] *Essays and Studies*, p. 234.
[3] To his son, March 2, 1752. Bradshaw, vol. II, p. 500.
[4] Even in our own day Anatole France " saw fit to put the latter high above Shakespeare as a painter of women."—J. M. Robertson's *Voltaire*, p. 74.
[5] *Ibid.*, p. 92.

most foreign courts, and acquired all that was worth acquiring in them, a more extensive knowledge of mankind, the art of pleasing in conversation, the talent of speaking several languages, a select library, the best pictures to adorn his palace, and a knowledge to build it in the justest taste of architecture." [1]

Writing to Mann on April 2, 1750, Horace Walpole says:—" There is come from France a Madame Boccage who has translated Milton : my Lord Chesterfield prefers the copy to the original ; but that is not uncommon for him to do, who is the patron of bad authors and bad actors. She has written a play too, which was damned, and worthy my Lord's approbation."

This utterance has added some inconsiderable weight to the general low opinion of Chesterfield's literary judgment. Its value can be estimated from the fact that Chesterfield states in a letter to Madame de Monconseil, " le Milton de Madame du Boccage a, je vous en assure, beaucoup de mérite ; " upon which Mahon observes that, " This moderate praise, even to Madame du Boccage's friend sufficiently disproves the sarcasm of Horace Walpole." [2]

Still more unfair is the criticism of Elizabeth Montagu when replying to a letter from Lord Lyttelton with reference to some " Mémoires Littéraires de la Grande-Bretagne " written by a Frenchman in London, which had been strongly recommended by Chesterfield :—

" I am not surprized that Ld. Chesterfield should admire a french Coxcomb ; his Lordship has snipped his own witt into epigrams, and he always admires everyone who writes a kind of pert jargon. Some years ago, at the Bath, I took a particular course of study that he had recommended to a Lady ; if I had continued it for six months I should have been fit for nothing but playing at pictures and mottoes with boarding school Misses.

[1] *Letters concerning England, Holland and Italy by the celebrated Madame du Bocage . . . Written during her travels in those Countries. Translated from the French.* (London) 1770 ; vol. I, pp. 8, 9.
These letters are most readable, and shed on English society of 1750 a remarkably fresh and interesting light.

[2] Bradshaw, vol. III, p. 971 n.

" I will allow that Ld. C— has a great deal of parts, but a continual aiming at *bons mots* will ruin any understanding. The French admire him for his dexterity in twisting their fashionable jargon ; his address to the Academy of Belles Lettres [1] was the strongest satire upon the Society that ever I read, as it was the quintessence of their affectation in style. The illustrious Academicians of Louis the fourteenth wd have expell'd him for it." [2]

Speaking generally, it is difficult to believe that a man of Chesterfield's mental attainments and wide scholarship, a writer who possessed a perfect ear for prose cadence in French as well as English, had such deplorable literary taste as some critics would seem to suggest.[3] That there were certain peculiarities and serious deficiencies in his judgment is indisputable : the same could be said of every man of his time.[4] No critic that has ever lived is entirely free from the charge, though few have been so candid as Chesterfield in their confessions. Since, however, we have been at pains to cite what are generally considered his worst heresies of taste, it will be only fair to give two examples out of many from the du Boccage correspondence, which go to prove that his opinions were not purely arbitrary, but based to a large extent on sound canons of criticism.

" On dit que *Cléopâtre* [5] n'a pas réussi. La pièce manque sans doute de conduite ; j'ai peine à croire que l'auteur d'*Aristomène* et de *Denis le Tyran* ait fait une mauvaise pièce sur un si beau sujet. Il a sûrement du feu, du génie, de la verve ; mais n'importe, il aura manqué à quelque règle de théâtre ; il est proscrit. Vous vous êtes forgé des chaines poëtiques bien rudes, sous le poids desquelles tout bon auteur doit gémir, et souhaiter de les briser ; au lieu qu'un auteur sans feu, comme un amant sans vigueur, chérit ses chaines ; l'un devient régulier, et autre respec-

[1] August 8, 1755 : *ibid.*, pp. 1129–31.
[2] June 2, 1768. *Mrs. Montagu,* " *Queen of the Blues,*" by R. Blunt (1923), p. 173.
[3] *Cf.* " His literary taste, when it is not commonplace, is execrable."— Sir Leslie Stephen in the *Cornhill Magazine*, July, 1871, (p. 101).
[4] " His literary criticisms, in short, were the criticisms of most intelligent men in that age ; sensible enough as far as they went, but rarely going below the surface of things."—Sir M. E. Grant Duff in an excellent article on *Chesterfield's Letters to his Son* ; *Fortnightly Review*, June, 1879, (p. 829).
[5] A tragedy by Marmontel.

tueux, par impuissance. *Rome Sauvée* [1] ne réussira peut-être pas non plus. Voltaire veut se faire des règles nouvelles, et la mode, chez vous encore plus qu'ici, décide des ouvrages des poëtes comme de ceux des marchands. Je suis sûr pourtant que son *Cicéron* [2] ne ressemblera guères à celui de Crébillon, qui dans le plus bel endroit de sa vie est un imbécille. Enfin, quoiqu'en dise votre public, tout ce que Voltaire fait me charme. Toujours les plus beaux vers du monde, et des pensées brillantes et justes ; je n'en demande pas davantage ; *non paucis offendar maculis.*

" Sur l'échantillon que Madame de Graffigny a donné de la délicatesse de son esprit dans ses *Lettres Péruviennes,* j'augure bien de sa comédie,[3] quoique ces comédies tragiques et larmoyantes ne soient pas de mon goût. Qu'on me donne les choses pour ce qu'elles sont ; j'aime à rire et à pleurer dans les formes ; il y a pourtant quelque chose à dire en leur faveur. Horace permet à la comédie de s'élever de tems en tems ; et l'intérêt, les sentimens et les situations touchantes ne sont pas bornés aux rois et aux héros. La vie ordinaire les fournit. " [4]

" Nous ne méritons pas l'honneur, que vous nous faites de traduire nos pièces et nos romans. Votre théâtre est trop juste et trop châtié pour souffrir la plûpart de nos pièces, qui poussent non seulement la liberté, mais la licence, au-delà des bornes de la décence et de la vraisemblance. Je ne crois pas que nous en ayons six de présentables chez vous dans l'état où elles sont. Il faudroit nécessairement les refondre. Si Prévôt traduit notre *Clarice,*[5] il doit l'abréger d'une bonne moitié ; il y a un furieux superflu, et en même tems un intérêt touchant, et des situations intéressantes. Celui qui l'a écrite, qui est aussi l'auteur de *Pamela,* est un libraire, qui manque de savoir et de style, mais qui connoit le cœur. Des sept volumes il en faudroit faire trois." [6]

Chesterfield's æsthetic taste was probably very much the same as that of the average cultured person of his day. The same can scarcely be said of his opinion of women.

---

[1] Otherwise *Catiline.* Though not the best known, Voltaire is said to have preferred it to all his other tragedies.
[2] A character in *Rome Sauvée* played by Voltaire himself.
[3] *Cenie.* See Bradshaw, vol. II, p. 497.
[4] July 25, 1750. *Ibid.,* vol. III, pp. 960, 961.
[5] Richardson's *Clarissa.*
[6] October 13, 1750. Bradshaw, vol. III, p. 969.

In the excellent judgment of Churton Collins, " The contempt with which he speaks of women, and of the relation of women to life, has always appeared to us not merely the one great flaw in his writings, but indicative of the one unsound place in his judgment and temper." [1] It is, moreover, the one hard trait in his character which was not softened by old age. Indeed, in this respect the very opposite seems to have occurred, and the eccentricity become more pronounced with age and experience. It is to a certain extent reflected in his Will, [2] or at least current opinion believed that it was; and when that document was printed in the *Gentleman's Magazine* soon after his death, sympathy for the widow at once gave rise to a hostile feeling against one who during his life had for the most part been regarded with deep admiration and respect. Hence, when the *Letters to his Son* appeared in the following year the seed of reaction found favourable soil.

The following extracts from the letters of Mrs. Delany and Mrs. Montagu are probably fair indications of the feelings of fashionable society towards Chesterfield as a testator. Mrs. Delany was a lifelong friend of Lady Chesterfield, and on intimate terms with both her and her husband during the latter's Vice-Royalty of Ireland. Though her voluminous correspondence contains many references to Chesterfield, the first adverse one occurs in a letter written four months after his death.

" Tuesday morn[g] I went to see Lady Chesterfield and found her *very low* and very much alter'd. . . . She has been very ungratefully used by Ld. Chesterfield who has absolutely cheated her as much as he could, tho' she made him a most excellent wife." [3]

Writing to Bernard Granville on September 16, 1774, with reference to the new Earl she says :—

" Lord Chesterfield educated this boy and had an attention to him, not out of kindness, but because he was to keep up the name and title, and left him near twenty

---

[1] *Essays and Studies*, pp. 236, 237.
[2] Dated June 4, 1772.
[3] To the Rev. J. Dewes, July 22, 1773. *Autobiography and Correspondence of Mary Granville, Mrs. Delany*, vol. I, 2nd Series (ed. 1861), p. 259.

thousand pound a year. Lady Chesterfield's income is £4,000 a year, but chiefly her own money. It was hard, considering how good a wife she had been, and what a good fortune she was to him, *not* to leave her in *very* affluent circumstances for her own life. *He* even *left away* her jewels, which were *chiefly* purchased with her *own money*, and presents of the Duchess of Kendal's, but the *law* restored them to her as her own paraphanalia ! . . . So vanity, as you say, had taken possession of him, and drove out all gratitude and natural affection ; and such is the case with human frailty if not well guarded against." [1]

Mrs. Elizabeth Montagu, who never seems to have had much love for Chesterfield, writes on July 19, 1773 as follows :—

" Ld. Chesterfield had neither great talents nor solid virtues, and his will has disgraced him. It realy makes one sick to see him Coquetting with the World, and acting the grimacees and minauderies of virtue on so Solemn an occasion. He says, he looks on a Faithfull servant as an unfortunate friend, then leaves 40 pounds to the unfortunate friend that had lived with him 40 years. A humane sentiment ushering in an inhumane action is not to be endured. His neglect of his Friends and behaviour to his Lady in this Will convinces one he wanted principle." [2]

And again five months later :—

" People are so disgusted at Lord Chesterfield's will [3] that they speak slightly of his character, of which indeed he scratched the varnish at last ; which is a pity, for it was the best papier mache character I ever knew, and with good management might have preserved its gloss a great while." [4]

These extracts have been quoted as shedding light upon the origin of the popular prejudice against Chesterfield : that they have any valuable bearing on his character is improbable. To deduce a person's character from his

---

[1] *Autobiography and Correspondence of Mary Granville, Mrs. Delany,* vol. II, 2nd Series, p. 32.
[2] *Mrs. Montagu, "Queen of the Blues,"* by R. Blunt, vol. I, p. 273.
[3] This word appears as " witt " in the book—an obvious mistake.
[4] *Ibid.,* p. 281.

will is a rash proceeding, as everyone knows who has had experience in the drawing up of wills. Though in a will, bad qualities, such as spite, avarice, meanness, ingratitude can be and often are exhibited, the testamentary expression of correspondingly good qualities is more difficult, if not impossible. People may read of a testator's "munificent bequest" to some charity, and remain unaware that by this action a wife or sister has been left to end her days in penury. True generosity, which implies self-sacrifice, does not really come into the question at all, and, ethically speaking, the utmost a testator can hope to do is, in the words of Chesterfield's will, to dispose of his "worldly affairs not as humour may prompt, but as justice and equity seem to direct."

How far Chesterfield succeeded in this object it is impossible for us to say. We do not know how much of his property he was free to dispose of. Nor do we imagine that the public of his day were much wiser on this point. It is at least unfortunate that his wife is not mentioned in the account of Chesterfield's Will which appears as complete in the *Gentleman's Magazine*, and is the only printed version. As a matter of fact, both Chesterfield House and Blackheath together with the furniture they contained, as well as his horses, carriages etc., and an annuity of £1000, were left to her for life. The same abbreviated version of his will, from which it would seem that Mrs. Montagu and the general public must have drawn their conclusions, makes no mention of the numerous legacies left by Chesterfield to charities and friends. The servant whose legacy Mrs. Montagu describes as "an inhumane action" was an old groom to whom Chesterfield left forty guineas as well as two years wages : not a large reward, but probably more than most people would have received in similar circumstances at that time. Other servants of his in higher capacities received correspondingly larger legacies.

It may or may not have been true that Chesterfield left his godson more than justice and equity would seem to direct ; but, assuming he did, we are convinced that the sentiment prompting such an action was extreme love for young Philip rather than, as Mrs. Delany suggests, undue pride in the name and title, a feeling which Chesterfield was the last person in the world to entertain. Nevertheless, unjust and prejudiced as were the accusations of these ladies, and probably of public opinion at the time, it remains

M

true that women do not figure prominently in Chesterfield's Will, which fact is certainly consistent with his
later misogynistic sentiments. Reference has already
been made to the ideal of womanhood delineated by him in
Common Sense.[1] Yet the portrayer of this charming picture of unaffected woman wrote to his son eleven years
later as follows :—

" Women are only children of a larger growth ;[2] they
have an entertaining tattle and sometimes wit ; but for
solid, reasoning good-sense, I never in my life knew one
that had it, or who reasoned or acted consequentially for
four-and-twenty hours together. Some little passion or
humour always breaks in upon their best resolutions.
Their beauty neglected or controverted, their age increased,
or their supposed understandings depreciated, instantly
kindles their little passions, and overturns any system of
consequential conduct that in their most reasonable
moments they might have been capable of forming. A man
of sense only trifles with them, plays with them, humours
and flatters them, as he does with a sprightly, forward
child ; but he neither consults them about, nor trusts
them with, serious matters ; though he often makes them
believe that he does both ; which is the thing in the world
that they are proud of ; for they love mightily to be
dabbling in business (which by the way, they always spoil);
and, being justly distrustful that men in general look upon
them in a trifling light, they almost adore that man who
talks more seriously to them, and who seems to consult
and trust them ; I say, who seems, for weak men really
do, but wise ones only seem to do it. No flattery is either
too high or too low for them. They will greedily swallow
the highest, and gratefully accept of the lowest ; and you
may safely flatter any woman, from her understanding
down to the exquisite taste of her fan." [3]

There are other references to woman in the *Letters to
his Son*,[4] but the above passage contains the main counts
in his indictment against the opposite sex. We can trace,
however, throughout his life, a growing contempt for

---

[1] See pp. 14–15 *ante*.
[2] " Men are but children of a larger growth."—Dryden, *All for Love*,
iv, 1.
[3] September 5, 1748. Bradshaw, vol. I, pp. 141, 142.
[4] See particularly that of December 19, 1749. *Ibid.*, p. 296.

women in his attitude towards marriage. When he was thirty-eight years of age, Chesterfield figures in the rôle of match-maker, as appears from the letters to his friend, Baron Frederick William Torck of Gelderland, written towards the close of his first Embassy at the Hague. Exactly what Chesterfield did to promote the Baron's marriage does not appear, but soon after his return from the Hague he writes as follows :—

" Poursuivez cette affaire, car au bout du compte marriage pour marriage il n'y a pas à tout prendre, de si bon dans la République." [1]

And after the marriage has taken place there are sundry references in his later letters to the writer's pride in having helped to bring it about. The following letter, written a few weeks afterwards, is worth quoting since it throws an interesting light on his son's mother, Elizabeth du Bouchet.

" A Londres, ce 23 Juin, V.S. 1732.

MON CHER AMI,
  C'est avec bien du plaisir que j'apprends par votre dernière que votre marriage est en si bon train ; si un marriage peut être bon, c'est celuy cy ; car il y a le solide, à scavoir, L'Argent ; et c'est la fille que je connois, qui a le moins la mine de faire enrager son mari. Il est juste que le marriage paye les plaisirs passez car il n'en procure guères a l'Avenir. Et vous avez très bien fait de les endosser à Monsieur votre frère, et à votre famille, puis qu'à cette heure vous allez travailler pour eux ; et L'ouvrier, dit L'écriture, est digne de son salaire.
  Pour mon Marriage il ne va pas si vite, et la Bouchet me connoit trop bien pour vouloir de moy d'ailleurs qu'il nous convient mieux à tous deux, que je trouve quelque autre, sur laquelle je puisse aussi endosser mes plaisirs passez ; et qui fournisse un peu à l'Entretien de la Bouchet et de son Enfant, qui par parenthèse devient un gaillard ; et donne déjà tous les indices d'avoir un jour beaucoup de mérite." [2]

---

[1] " Some Unpublished Letters of Lord Chesterfield." Nineteenth Century,. August, 1912, p. 286. There are thirty-eight letters ranging from 1731 to 1747, all written from Chesterfield to Baron Torck, and dealing, for the most part, with current foreign affairs.
[2] Ibid., pp. 287, 288.

At the time this letter was written, the " *gaillard* " must have been less than four months old, [1] and the mother and son had evidently followed Chesterfield to London on his return from the Hague. Except that he gave her an allowance during her life, and a paltry legacy of £500 [2] in his will, " as some compensation for the injury I have done her," there is little known about the woman. It is unnecessary to relate the incredible story told by Lord Brougham in the *Quarterly Review* of September, 1845, in which Madame du Bouchet's downfall is ascribed to the result of a wild bet made by Chesterfield. Craig retells the story in his *Life*, [3] but is careful to point out the glaring improbabilities in which it abounds, and also that the Quarterly Reviewer " does not adduce a scrap of evidence " in support of it. The story has been significantly disregarded by all other commentators with the exception of Philarète Chasles, who relates it in his account of *Le Comte de Chesterfield* which first appeared in the *Revue des Deux Mondes* of December, 1845. Though the writer professes to cite his authorities in an introductory footnote, a perusal of his study of Chesterfield will show that a source to which he is in no small measure indebted is the unacknowledged one of Brougham's antecedent article in the *Quarterly*. His description of the library at Chesterfield House is, for instance, an almost literal translation of that which Brougham gives from first-hand knowledge. On the other hand, the account given by him of Madame du Bouchet's downfall, though agreeing in substance with Brougham's, bears little verbal resemblance to it, and was very likely taken from some other source.

Chasles is pleased to embellish his story with certain additions such as, " Chesterfield la fit peindre par la Rosalba, car elle était belle, et la plaça presque sans voiles et comme un trophée, dans un beau cadre doré, sur la cheminée de sa bibliothèque. Ce fut le seul honneur qu'il lui fit désormais." The sole foundation for these wildly improbable statements is, we are convinced, contained in

---

[1] As appears from a letter to his son of February 26, 1746. Bradshaw, vol. I, p. 29.

[2] " A sum which certain commentators, ignorant of the intimate history of the matter, have not hesitated to describe as disgracefully inadequate."— C. Strachey in Introduction to *Chesterfield's Letters to his Son*, p. xl. Craig also defends Chesterfield on this score in a footnote to p. 129 of his *Life of Lord Chesterfield*.

[3] pp. 126–128.

a letter from Chesterfield to Madame de Monconseil, describing his *boudoir* : " par dessus la cheminée, qui est de *Giallo di Sienna,* force glaces, sculptures, dorures, et au milieu le portrait d'une très belle femme, peint par la Rosalba." [1] Equally ridiculous is the following assertion which Chasles gives vent to in the fulness of his imagination: " La scène de Clarisse et de son séducteur était jouée d'avance ; c'était en 1727 [2] ; Richardson a tout simplement calqué son Lovelace sur l'ambassadeur anglais à la Haye, dont l'aventure était publique." [3]

Though Chesterfield frequently refers to the mother in writing to his son—always, be it noted, with deference and regard—the only other allusion to her worth mentioning is contained in a letter to Madame de Monconseil in which he says, " J'ai un garçon, qui à cette heure a treize ans ; je vous avouerai naturellement qu'il n'est pas légitime, mais sa mère est une personne bien née, et qui a eu des bontés pour moi que je ne méritois pas." [4]

The unromantic, not to say mercenary, sentiments that Chesterfield expressed with regard to a possible wife for himself are repeated in his next letter to Baron Torck, whom he congratulates on his recent marriage.

" A Brettby, ce 12 Sept. V.S. 1732.

. . Vous voicy donc à la fin marié, je vous jure que je vous en félicite du fond de mon cœur et j'en félicite tout autant Madame, qui aussi de son côté, n'a pas mal trouvé. Si le marriage peut être heureux, ce que je croy être possible mais pas ordinaire, le vôtre doit l'être, il n'y manque rien des deux cotez pour le [5] rendre bel ; et je vous proteste que si je trouvois un parti où les apparences fussent aussi bonnes que chez vous je franchirois le pas aussi. Mais je doute fort si je feray cette trouvaille, car je veux du mérite,

---

[1] Bradshaw, vol. II, p. 884.

[2] It would have been more correct to say 1731.

[3] An exhaustive account of how Richardson came to conceive the character of Lovelace is given by Austin Dobson in his study of the novelist. (English Men of Letters Series, pp. 88–91).   We need scarcely add that it contains no mention of Chesterfield, for whose opinion of *Clarissa* see p. 158 *ante.*

Further comment is, we hope, unnecessary : indeed, were it not for the author's literary eminence, we should not have called the reader's attention to this article, which is full of inaccuracies, and of no more critical than authoritative value.

[4] June 24, 1745.   Bradshaw, vol. II, p. 786.

[5] " *de* " in the text.

et je veux de l'argent, deux choses rarement unies. Le mérite feminin sans argent ne me suffiroit pas, et l'argent sans mérite auroit un furieux Alliage. Enfin je vous souhaitte ardemment tout le bonheur possible, et je n'en doute point." [1]

On January 2nd, 1733, Chesterfield writes again to his friend in the same strain.

" Vous me direz que . . . je suis à cette heure mariable ; il est vray, et si je pouvais aussi bien trouver que vous avez fait j'y serois très porté, mais voilà la difficulté ; car il m'en faudrait une, qui à tous égards, se contentât de donner beaucoup, et de recevoir peu ; et qui dans un mot, s'accommoderait d'un corps delabré, et raccommoderoit des affaires delabrées ; je crains fort que ce ne soit la femme de la Fontaine, qui ne fût et qui ne sera jamais." [2]

However, eight months later, Chesterfield found a wife with the necessary requirements in the person of Melusina de Schulenberg, a daughter of George I and the Duchess of Kendal, and writes to Torck as follows :—

" A Londres ce 14 Oct. V.S. 1733.
Voyez, Mon Cher Ami, le pouvoir que votre example a sur moy ; depuis que vous êtes marié, Je n'ay pas été en repos, que je ne le fusse aussi, et à la fin m'y voicy ; menant une vie réglée et domestique, et devenu le parfait modèle des maris en Angleterre, comme vous l'êtes dans les sept Provinces unies." [3]

Of Chesterfield's own marriage there is little to say. Churton Collins is alone, and, we are convinced, quite mistaken in his opinion, unsupported as it is by any evidence, that " there is every reason to believe that his marriage was a very unhappy one." [4] With regard to his wife, Maty says : " By her tenderness and virtues she merited all the returns he could make ; and by her prudent management she helped to retrieve and improve his long-neglected

---

[1] *Nineteenth Century*, August 1912.
[2] *Ibid.*, August, 1912.
[3] *Ibid.*, September, 1912. See also his letter to Lord Essex, November 29, 1733, p. 297 *post*.
[4] *Essays and Studies*, p. 239.

estate.[1] On changing her condition she did not leave the Duchess of Kendal ; and Lord Chesterfield, who was their next neighbour in Grosvenor Square, most constantly divided his time between his business in his own house, and his attentions and duties at the other." [2]

This arrangement, " which however odd it may appear to us, was not uncommon in those days," [3] apparently continued until her mother's death [4] some ten years later, for on May 12, 1743, Horace Walpole in a letter to Mann says, " The Duchess of Kendal is dead. . . . Her riches were immense ; but I believe my Lord Chesterfield will get nothing by her death—but his wife : she lived in the house with the duchess, where he had played away all his credit."

Lord Brougham, writing of Lady Chesterfield, asserts that " during the flower of her life and his own he was a most profligate husband. Nevertheless the Correspondence bears evidence that the childless Countess treated his son with almost maternal regard, and that in his infirm old age she watched over him with unwearied devotion. For his memory after he was gone she on all occasions showed an anxious concern. . . . We are, we suppose, to divide our admiration between the generosity of the sex which Chesterfield flattered, outraged, and despised—the clinging instincts of virgin love and conjugal pride—and the fascination of his habitual small courtesies." [5] This passage strikes us as being the reflection of early Victorian prudery rather than of sound judgment. " A most profligate husband " is a term scarcely justified by the single fact that " After his marriage, he had a long amour with Lady Fanny Shirley, a great beauty." [6] Since Craig, however, in a lengthy and badly-argued note [7] endeavours to disprove this statement of Walpole's, which he terms " unfounded," " ill-natured," and " highly improbable," it will be perhaps as well to state the evidence.

Lady Fanny Shirley was a daughter of the Earl of

[1] " Caused probably by his expensive tastes during his late embassy in Holland."—Ernst, p. 78.

[2] Vol. I, p. 71.

[3] Craig, p. 146.

[4] See Ernst on this point, p. 79.

[5] *Quarterly Review*, September, 1845.

[6] Horace Walpole's MS. note on Maty, vol. I, p. 71.

[7] pp. 145, 146.

Ferrers and lived at Twickenham. She was the subject of the well-known song,

> " When Fanny blooming fair
> First caught my ravish'd sight." [1]

Pope also wrote some verses, " On Receiving from the Lady Frances Shirley A Standish and Two Pens." She never married, and in a letter to the Rev. W. Mason, July 16, 1778, Horace Walpole writes from Twickenham, " ' Fanny, blooming fair,' died here yesterday of a stroke of palsy. . . . Being confined with only servants, she was continually lamenting, ' I to be abandoned that all the world used to adore ! ' She was seventy-two." [2] She was associated with Chesterfield in Sir C. H. Williams's poem, *Isabella or the Morning*.

> " Says Lovel—there were Chesterfield and Fanny
> In that eternal whisper which begun
> Ten years ago, and never will be done,
> For though you know he sees her every day,
> Still he has something ever new to say.
>
> Poor I ! am forc'd to keep my distance now,
> She won't ev'n curt'sy if I make a bow." [3]

According to Horace Walpole, " Thomas Coke, Lord Lovel, afterwards Earl of Leicester, Lord Chesterfield's rival for the favour of Lady Fanny Shirley," [4] was the original of the person described as follows by Chesterfield in an essay on affectation :—

" Fatuus, the most consummate coxcomb of this or any other age or country, has parts enough to have excelled in almost any one thing he would have applied himself to. But he must excel in all. He must be at once a wit, a lover, a scholar, and a statesman ; yet, conscious of the impracticability of the undertaking, he parcels out his

---

[1] It can be found attributed to Chesterfield in Dodsley's Collection and also in Maty, vol. III, p. 188 ; though " very strong reasons for supposing it was written by Mr. Thomas Philips, a dramatic writer " are stated by Isaac Reed in *Lysons' Environs*, vol. III, p. 599. See also *Wit and Wisdom of Lord Chesterfield*, p. 379 ; and Ernst, pp. 78, 79.

[2] See also his letter to Mann, August 4, 1778.

[3] *Works of Sir Charles Hanbury Williams*, (edit. 1822) vol. I, pp. 86, 87.

[4] MS. note on Maty, vol. I. Miscellaneous Pieces, p. 63.

accomplishments, and compounds to have the several branches of his merit admired in separate districts.

" Hence, he talks politics to his women, wit to ministers of state, displays his learning to beaux, and brags of his success in gallantry to his country neighbours. His caution is a proof of his guilt, and shews that he does not deceive himself, but only hopes to impose upon others. Fatuus's parts have undone him, and brought him to a bankruptcy of common sense and judgment ; as many have been ruined by great estates, which led them into expences they were not able to support." [1]

This estimate is certainly not inconsistent with that of Lovel in Sir C. H. Williams's same poem :

" Lovel,—the oddest character in town ;
A lover, statesman, connoisseur, buffoon ;
Extract him well, this is his quintessence,
Much folly, but more cunning, and some sense ;
To neither party is his heart inclin'd,
He steer'd twixt both with politics refin'd,
Voted with Walpole, and with Pulteney din'd."

Apropos of Lovel's voting may be mentioned the following story taken from the entertaining pages of Lord Egmont's Diary.[2]

" Monday, 26 [January, 1730]. This morning Mr. Capel Moore came to see me and made me smile at a story touching my Lord Lovel (Mr. Cook of Norfolk that was made a Baron when this King came to the Crown). My Lord, coming up to town against the meeting of Parliament, told the Earl of Chesterfield that now he was come he did not know how to vote. ' Why, with the Court, to be sure,' replied the Earl. ' Aye, but,' said Lovel, ' the Court is so divided that I don't know which way it leans. There are,' said he, ' in it a country party, a Spanish party, and a French party.' ' If you are under a difficulty,' replied the Earl, ' go to Sir Robert Walpole ; he will direct you.' " Says Lovel, ' If I vote with the Court, I expect to be paid for it.' ' How paid ? ' said Chesterfield. ' Why,' the other replied, ' I have an estate sufficient for an Earl or a Viscount at least, and I shall expect to be made one

[1] *Common Sense*, September 3, 1737. Maty, *ibid*.
[2] Vol. I (1730–33) p. 10, Hist. MSS. Comm. (1920).

of them.' 'That,' replied Chesterfield, 'is impossible ;
it is asking a thing the King cannot do.' Lovel replied
he did not understand him, that the King had made him
a Baron two years ago, and might make him a Viscount
if he pleased, for he was the fountain of honour and nothing
tied up his hands. To say, therefore, that it was impossible
implied something he did not comprehend, and he must
insist to know his lordship's meaning. 'Why, if you will
have it, ' replied the Earl, ' it is a maxim of our law that
the King can do no wrong. ' Which said, he left my Lord
Lovel to digest it as well as he could.''

We are, however, digressing. Let us hear Lovel himself
on the subject of his rivalry with Chesterfield for Lady
Fanny's heart. Writing from Holkham to the Earl of
Essex, he says :—

" You have open'd my wounds by speaking of Lady
Fanny ; she is quit lost to me ; that foul fiend Chesterfield has bewitch't her and, under pretence of serving me,
has intirely defeated me and is in full possession of the
Lady's soul ; as for her body, that is so glorifyed that I
presume none of our grosser mortal substance can ever
think of that. . . . I can with ease keep your secret, but as
for my own, since it is like never to be any secret at all,
I find great ease in discoursing of it, and tiring all my
acquaintance with my greif. My Rival triumphs so
publickly that I hear of nothing from London but his
success, all Summer, partly by water, rides in Bushy park,
etc. ; and Old Bitches begin to be censorious, which the
nice Lady however stands, and, since she herself knows
there is no harm, dos not mind what others say, This
plaguy peace that is like to unhinge the measures of the
seditious, and make them have nothing to do, will give
Chesterfield still more time to love. I cannot bear London
while things continue thus, tho' I must be there in about
3 weeks. . . . I shall remember you to all friends, even
Chesterfield, when I come to town.'' [1]

A month later he writes from London again to Essex :—

[1] December 21 O.S., 1735. Add. MSS. 27735, f. 1. Now first printed.
An earlier reference by Lovel to his rivalry with Chesterfield occurs in a
letter from him to the Hon. George Berkeley of July 23, 1735.—*Suffolk
Letters*, vol. II, pp. 125, 126.

" That beauty you think so cold shows herself warmer than any Lady in England, but not with me. . . . I attack't (tho' not boldly) in front ; dazzled by her beauty I could scarce approach, while that fly Chesterfield, like the toad in Milton, came privily behind and fastened on her ear, and that way found access to her heart . . . In short they live together, ride together, walk, go by water, etc., etc., in the face of the whole world, and this cold, shy beauty as you call'd her hears up, I do assure you, more than ever I yet saw either married or unmarried Lady. The great trouble they have is that when they ride out his Lordship is forced to stand on his stirrups while she makes her back ake with stooping to hear him ; but I am now in treaty for a monstrous tall horse that is shew'd at a show here, which I will present his Lordship. We are generous rivals, and good friends yet, and . . . he can't do less than give me his leavings, and that is all the hopes that now remain for me." [1]

It may be mentioned, in passing, that the two letters from which we have quoted were not the mere effusions of one young spark to another. Lovel and Essex were at that time middle-aged married men with children, both holding responsible posts ; [2] yet each letter deals at length with Lovel's endeavours to promote the interests of Essex in an intrigue between him and some lady in London [3]

There is no evidence to disprove Craig's suggestion that the intimacy between Chesterfield and Lady Fanny Shirley " never exceeded the bounds of friendship." [4] Lovel's surmises on the point are unfortunately quite unprintable, but even he is careful to profess that he does not *know* anything. [5] Mr. F. A. Steuart in his Introduction to *Chesterfield's Letters to Lord Huntingdon*, the great-

---

[1] January 25, O.S. 173 $\frac{5}{6}$ *Ibid.*, f. 66. Parts of this letter are quoted by W. Sichel in *Bolingbroke and His Times*, vol. II, pp. 72, 73.

[2] Lovel was Joint Postmaster-General, and Essex Envoy at Turin.

[3] " Lord Essex, universally esteemed, crams his correspondence with allusions to an inamorata at home, while he affectionately mentions his wife and children, who were with him during his envoyship at Turin. Henry Pelham, the most respectable of politicians, intersperses his private letters with allusions that would shock the social decency of to-day. There was certainly no squeamishness as regards these matters in society."—*Bolingbroke and his Times*, vol. II, p. 73.

[4] *Life of Lord Chesterfield*, p. 146 n.1.

[5] Letter to Lord Essex, January 25, 173 $\frac{5}{6}$.

nephew of Lady Fanny, deals at some length [1] with what he describes as "their wonderful friendship," which he does not suggest was anything more. We know of no other evidence in support of Lord Brougham's statement that Chesterfield was " a most profligate husband," though Mr. Sichel remarks that "his gallantries were common to his class," adding in a footnote, "With Mademoiselle du Bouchet, the mother of the son whom he devotedly trained in 1728[2]; and, not counting Lady Fanny Shirley, long afterwards with Walpole's eldest son's wife, whose giddiness was notorious in Florence, and whose sympathy with the heroes of 1745 is notorious. Stair was also one of her lovers. *Cf. H. Walpole's Letters*, vol. I, p. 149." [3] The reference is to a letter to Mann of April 29, 1742 which begins as follows :—

" By yours of April 17, N.S., and some of your last letters, I find my Lady Walpole is more mad than ever—why, there never was so wild a scheme as this of setting up an interest through Lord Chesterfield ! one who has no power; and, if he had, would think of, or serve her, one of the last persons upon earth. What connexion has he with, what interest could he have in obliging her ? and, but from views, what has he ever done, or will he ever do ? "

Mr. Sichel's motives are, we confess, inexplicable. Why, in actually making light of a man's "gallantries," should he go out of his way to invent one which is utterly refuted by the very authority he quotes for its existence ? [4]

---

[1] pp. vii-ix.

[2] 1731 is the date generally ascribed to this *amour*. The son was born in March, 1732.

[3] *Bolingbroke and His Times*, vol. II, p. 242.

[4] Another instance of Mr. Sichel's methods occurs on page 9 of the same volume where he achieves a neat "right and left" at the expense of Chesterfield and Stair. Referring to the latter, he says: " In 1733 Walpole punished him by depriving him both of his Scotch vice-admiralty and of his dragoon regiment, and in the same year Chesterfield—Chesterfield the ' Patriot '—was not ashamed to style him a malignant and a Jacobite." The authority given is " *Suffolk Letters*, II, p. 60," on reference to which we find these jesting words in a letter from Chesterfield to Lady Suffolk of August, 1733. He is writing from Scarborough, and says of the society there, " The grave people are mostly malignants, or, in ministerial language, notorious Jacobites, such as Lord Stair, Marchmont, Anglesea, and myself, not to mention many of the House of Commons of equal disaffection."

Mr. Sichel in his Preface to this volume (p. vii) claims that " In all cases we have striven to draw from the fountain instead of from the pitcher." We cannot help feeling that in some cases Mr. Sichel has striven not to draw

The same writer refers to Chesterfield's marriage as follows :—

" The timorous Chesterfield . . . wedded, with characteristic regret, the ' niece ' of the Schulemburg with her royal connection and immense dowry." To the word " regret " he subjoins this footnote : " Chesterfield writes to Lord Essex in April 1734 : ' I am married and out of court at the same time ; I am equally a stranger to the Busy and to the Polite part of mankind.' B.M. Add. MS. 27733, f. 55." [1]

It is surely putting a strained construction on this remark to say that it expresses regret of a " characteristic " or any other nature. Taken with the context, and punctuated as in the original,[2] it appears as nothing more than an excuse for lack of news in a dull letter. The phrase " characteristic regret," moreover, is as entirely inapplicable to Chesterfield's particular philosophic temper [3] as the epithet " timorous " is to a man with his political record of reckless disregard of self.[4] We know of no occasion on which Chesterfield ever expressed, and there seems no reason to believe that he ever felt, regret for his marriage, concerning which we believe the probable truth to be that it involved no more friction than it did romance, and that both parties were too sensible and calculating not to run smoothly in double harness.

Lady Chesterfield doubtless had a good deal to put up with, especially during the first ten years of her married life. Her feelings, while the amour with Lady Fanny was at its height, are hinted at in the following reflections made by Bolingbroke's second wife in a letter to the Countess of Denbigh, a Dutch lady.

" Je souhaitte a Mr. Charle Filding toutte sorte de

truth from the fountain, but to fill it with mud. It must be said in his favour, however, that, unlike most of Chesterfield's detractors, he is at least conscientious enough to put the reader on the track of his gratuitous inaccuracies, for other instances of which see pp. 218–220 *post*.

[1] *Bolingbroke and His Times*, vol. II, p. 72.

[2] The letter may be found transcribed in full on p. 298 *post*.

[3] As can be seen from nearly every letter in the section devoted to his Philosophy—pp. 272-290 *post*.

[4] See p. 149 *ante*.

bonheur,[1] mais il est rare que le mariage soit un chemin sur pour y arriver, sur tout a quelqu'on qui est acoutumé a vivre libre et pour luy. Il me semble que Madame de Chesterfield devroit estre plus blessée d'un amour platonique que de tout autre ; il n'est permi d'estre jalouse que des preferancs de sentiment." [2]

Writing again a week later, Lady Bolingbroke tells her friend that, " Lord Schesterfield des sept jours de la semaine a des affaires pour six a la ville, ce qui ne plaist ni a la tante ni a la niece." [3]

Some years later we find in a letter to Lady Denbigh from Elizabeth Wyndham [4] that Lady Chesterfield " a loué une petite maison a Hammersmith pour se desenuyer de l'absence de son epoux." [5] Where Chesterfield had gone in the Summer we do not know, but he had returned to town by the Autumn, as appears from an amusing letter to Lady Denbigh from her cousin J. de Pesters.

" . . . Si vous aviez été icy, vous m'auriez peutêtre empeché de reflechir et de voir comme dans un miroir tout ce qui se passera chez moy depuis quatre heures jusqu'a onze, je le sais par cœur. Lord Ches[terfield] dira des epigrames, sa bonne femme et votre sœur ne diront presque rien, ma voisine [Lady Lichfield ?] débitera des sottises auquelles Mr. Cook et Southcote repondront par des *quolibets* que Lady Jane [Coke] rêlevera avec son bon sens et son air de prude, tandis que dans un coin de la chambre, Lady Charlotte [Edwin] et sa bonne amie [Lady Townshend ?] se regaleront d'un petit tête a tête scandaleux ; le thé, les cartes, les bougies, et moy, nous ferons les honneurs.

" La ceremonie faite, chacun ira coucher, comme à l'enterement du Duc de Guise, ou si vous aimez une comparaison moderne, comme aux funerailles de la Duchesse de Marlborough,[6] car je suppose que ceux qui y

---

[1] He married Anne, Lady Bridges, on August 26, 1737.

[2] August 17, 1737. Hist. MSS. Comm. Report (1911) ; *Denbigh Papers* (Part V) p. 125.

[3] *I.e.* the Duchess of Kendal and Lady Chesterfield. *Ibid.*, p. 126. ' Niece ' was often used as a " courtesy title " for the illegitimate daughter of George I.

[4] She was the daughter of William Wyndham, and married George Grenville in 1748.

[5] July 21, 1744. *Denbigh Papers*, p. 252.

[6] She died on October 18, 1744.

assistoient se sont couchez. Vous a-t'on mandé qu'outre les vingt mille livres sterling cette Duchesse avoit encore laissé à Lord Chesterfield ses plus belles pierreries ? Je compte qu'il les donnera à sa femme, ce sera à la verité jetter de l'eau dans la mer, d'autres ne s'en soucieroient gueres à sa place, mais pour elle, elle en voudroit avoir autant que la Madonne de Lorette." [1]

It was some years before Chesterfield's views on matrimony underwent any change. We have seen him in 1731 figuring as a match-maker, and six years later he appears hypothetically, if not actually, in the same rôle, this time on behalf of his brother John,[2] who writes to Lady Denbigh with regard to his passion for a young lady (probably Elizabeth Wyndham) which he fears is not likely to be returned. In asking for her support in his cause he says that Lady Chesterfield is so good that she would, he is confident, do anything in her power for his happiness, but he does not wish to use this method. He adds that his brother, the Earl, is so anxious to see him settled that if this attempt fails, " nothing would be more natural than for him to say, ' I am glad to find you in this disposition ; since this has failed, we'll find somebody else,' " and so hurry him on more than he chooses.[3]

Chesterfield's soundest opinions on marriage are expressed in a letter to Lyttelton of June 19, 1742, beginning thus :—

" The newspapers inform me that you are married ; but what shall I say to you upon that occasion ? Is it necessary, or is it not rather superfluous, for me to tell you the wishes I form for you in this the most important period of your life, when you have so long known the sincere part I have taken in the most common occurrences of it ? To wish you joy were frivolous, that is certain and present ; but whenever that does decline, as from its nature

---

[1] November 6, 1744. *Denbigh Papers*, p. 185.

[2] It was this brother upon whose death in 1748 Chesterfield wrote to his son, 6th December :—" I am at present under very great concern for the loss of a most affectionate brother, with whom I had always lived in the closest friendship."—Bradshaw, vol. I, p. 176. In a letter to Dayrolles of the same date he says :—" By the death of poor John you have lost a true friend, and I a most affectionate brother and friend into the bargain."—*Ibid.*, vol. II, p. 898. See also letter to Madame de Monconseil of December 26, 1748.—*Ibid.*, p. 903.

[3] November, 1737. *Denbigh Papers*, p. 222.

it one day must, may all its sweetness turn to strength, or as Tompson [1] says, may it mellow into friendship, and may that serener and more lasting state so insensibly succeed your present tumultuous one, that the transition may not be perceived. This will and must happen, if Mrs. Lyttelton be (what for both your sakes I heartily wish her) like yourself, sex excepted, which for neither of your sakes, would I wish her. If she has a head to discern merit, and a heart to value it, and if she brings but with her the truth, the tenderness, and all the other virtues she will meet with, even my wishes for your mutual happiness can neither exceed nor survive it. Pray make my compliments to her, though I have not yet the honour of being known to her." [2]

Exactly what happened to disillusion Chesterfield on the subject of matrimony we cannot say, but it is clear that the sentiments so eloquently expressed in the above letter did not remain with him in his old age, when on more than one occasion he is found taking a decidedly different part from that of match-maker. His brother, Sir William Stanhope, at the age of sixty had married a girl of twenty-two, with the result that after four years we find Chesterfield telling his son that " I have at last done the best office that can be done, to most married people, that is, I have fixed the separation between my brother and his wife ; and the definitive treaty of peace will be proclaimed in about a fortnight : for the only solid and lasting peace, between a man and his wife, is doubtless a separation." [3]

Next month, writing to Arthur Charles Stanhope, the father of his godson and heir, he opens his mind still further on the subject :—

" In answer to the favour of your last letter, in which you desire my opinion concerning your third marriage, I must freely tell you, that in matters of religion and matrimony I never give any advice : [4] because I will not have any body's torments in this world or the next laid

---

[1] *Sic* in orig.—Mahon's note.
[2] June 19, 1742. Mahon, vol. V, pp. 446–7.
[3] September 1, 1763. Bradshaw, vol. III, pp. 1296–97.
[4] In making this claim, which is, by the way, hardly consistent with the remainder of the letter, Chesterfield seems to have forgotten some of his earlier ventures in the art of match-making. See pp. 163 and 175 *ante*.

to my charge. You say, that you find yourself lonely and melancholick at Mansfield, and I believe it : but then the point for your mature consideration is, whether it is not better to be alone than in bad company ; which may very probably be your case with a wife. I may possibly be in the wrong, but I tell you very sincerely, with all due regard to the sex, that I never thought a woman good company for a man tête-à-tête, unless for one purpose, which, I presume, is not yours now. You had singular good fortune with your last wife, who has left you two fine children, which are as many as any prudent man would desire. And how would you provide for more ? Suppose you should have five or six, what could you do with them? ... My brother gave me exactly the same reasons that you do for marrying his third wife. He was weary of being alone, and had by God's good providence found out a young woman of a retired disposition, and who had been bred up prudently under an old grandmother in the country ; she hated and dreaded a London life, and chose to amuse herself at home with her books, her drawing, and her music. How this fine prospect turned out, I need not tell you. . . . Upon the whole, you will marry or not marry, as you think best : but, to take a wife, merely as an agreable and rational companion, will commonly be found to be a great mistake. Shakespeare seems to be a good deal of my opinion, when he allows them only this department,

' To suckle fools, and chronicle small beer.' " [1]

As Churton Collins justly observes, when quoting this last sentence, " It would have been more correct to say Iago." The same writer goes on to say,

" Much of this is of course to be attributed to the age in which he lived and to the society in which he moved, and is to be regarded as simple deduction from his own experience. . . . But whatever may have been the reasons of Chesterfield's misogyny, it is undoubtedly a great blemish on his writings. It must not, however, mislead us. We are so much in the habit of reading other ages in the light of our own, and of assuming that what would apply to a man who acted and thought in a particular way among ourselves, would apply to a man who acted

[1] October 12, 1765. Carnarvon : Appendix pp. 57, 58.

N

and thought in the same way a century ago, that we very often arrive at most erroneous conclusions. A man who in our day spoke and wrote of women as Chesterfield has done, would justly be set down as a scoundrel and a fool. But Chesterfield, so far from being a fool, was in some respects one of the wisest men who have ever lived ; and, so far from being a scoundrel, practised as well as preached a morality which every gentleman in the world would aspire to emulate. The truth is, as it is only just to him to say, that he was generalising from his experience of women of fashion." [1]

This verdict strikes us as a remarkably fair one, and it is supported to a certain extent by the following passage from one of Chesterfield's later letters to his son :—

" One hears of nothing now, in town, but the separation of men and their wives. Will Finch the ex-Vice Chamberlain, Lord Warwick, your friend Lord Bolingbroke. I wonder at none of them for parting ; but I wonder at many for still living together ; for in this country it is certain that marriage is not well understood." [2]

Let it be noticed that in his attitude to matrimony Chesterfield does not stand aloof from mankind and sneer at the frailties of human nature, but simply states what he firmly believes is the truth, and what a study of contemporary French and English memoirs and letters leads us to realize was not very far removed therefrom. His attitude may have been distorted, but it is not the pose of a cynic, or indeed a pose of any kind. He despises cheap wit at the expense of the married, and warns his son against using matrimony as a topic for " false wit and cold raillery," wherein " every man and his wife hate each other cordially, whatever they may pretend in public to the contrary. The husband certainly wishes his wife at the devil, and the wife certainly cuckolds her husband. Whereas I presume that men and their wives neither love nor hate each other the more, upon account of the form of matrimony which has been said over them." [3]

It is probably his unfortunate attitude towards women

[1] *Essays and Studies*, pp. 239, 240.
[2] December 27, 1765. Bradshaw, vol. III, p. 1333.
[3] May 10, 1748. Bradshaw, vol. I, pp. 107, 108.

and matrimony that has given rise to the charge of cynicism so frequently brought against Chesterfield. We have cited above the most misogynistic passages that can be found in his writings, and, however misguided and unpleasant they may be, it cannot be denied that they ring of sincerity. Cynicism consists not so much in stating unpleasant truths as in stating them unpleasantly, or taking a pleasure in stating them. If, therefore, the above passages were written, as we think they were, mainly with a desire to help, and not for the pleasure of delivering an attack on womankind, the charge of cynicism almost entirely breaks down. But if it breaks down on the subject of woman it is difficult to find on what it can be supported to any important extent.

Is it not time that the " constant epithets " *hard* and *cynical* were given their proper value in relation to Chesterfield's character ? Hard he certainly was, in the sense that a person governed by a rigid ethical code must be hard ; but not hard in a narrow, unforgiving, selfish spirit : cynical at times, but his cynicism is for the most part of a playful, rather than a malicious order, as his essays and letters clearly show in their recurrent good-humour. This we maintain despite Hervey's oft-quoted portrait of Chesterfield, which, it must be said, the bitterest of his critics admit to be scandalously overdrawn.

" Lord Chesterfield was allowed by everybody to have more conversable entertaining table-wit than any man of his time ; his propensity to ridicule, in which he indulged himself with infinite humour and no distinction, and with inexhaustible spirits and no discretion, made him sought and feared, liked and not loved, by most of his acquaintance ; no sex, no relation, no rank, no power, no profession, no friendship, no obligation was a shield from those pointed, glittering weapons, that seemed to shine only to a standerby, but cut deep in those they touched. All his acquaintance were indifferently the objects of his satire,[1] and served promiscuously to feed that voracious appetite for abuse that made him fall on everything that came in his way, and treat every one of his companions in rotation

[1] Hervey himself was the object of " that well known and celebrated apothegm of Lord Chesterfield, that 'at the beginning God created three different species, men, women, and Herveys.' "—Lord Charlemont's Memoirs. *Charlemont Papers*, Hist. MSS. Comm., 12th Report, Appendix, Part X, p. 121.

at the expense of the rest. I remember two lines in a satire of Boileau's that fit him exactly :—

> Mais c'est un petit fou qui se croit tout permis,
> Et qui pour un bon mot va perdre vingt amis.

And as his lordship, for want of principle, often sacrificed his character to his interest, so by these means he as often, for want of prudence, sacrificed his interest to his vanity. With a person as disagreable as it was possible for a human figure to be without being deformed, he affected following many women of the first beauty and the most in fashion ; and if you would have taken his word for it, not without success ; whilst in fact and in truth, he never gained anyone above the venal rank of those whom an Adonis or a Vulcan might be equally well with, for a sum of money. He was very short, disproportioned, thick, and clumsily made ; had a broad, rough-featured, ugly face, with black teeth, and a head big enough for a Polyphemus.[1] One Ben Ashurst, who said few good things, though admired for many, told Lord Chesterfield once that he was like a stunted giant—which was a humourous idea and really apposite. Such a thing would disconcert Lord Chesterfield as much as it would have done anybody who had neither his wit nor his assurance on other occasions ; for though he could attack vigorously, he could defend but weakly, his quickness never showing itself in reply, any more than his understanding in argument.'' [2]

The only other contemporary estimate of Chesterfield's wit of any length is to be found in Colley Cibber's *Apology*, and, since it has never been previously cited in Chesterfield's favour, is worth quoting here for that reason alone, apart from the fact that it provides a wholesome antidote to Hervey's prejudiced account.

---

[1] " This is very different from his portraits, which represent a handsome and intellectual countenance, and indicate a fine, or at least an elegant, figure and air. Even admitting that the painters flattered, and that Lord Hervey caricatured, I am at a loss to account for so violent a contrast. He himself in his ' Letters ' (24th May, 1750) lets us know that his height was *under* 5 feet 8, but does not specify how much—perhaps an inch or two. He mentions also (15th February, 1754) the early discolour of his teeth.''—Croker's note. See also Brougham's lengthy and eloquent descriptions of the portraits of Chesterfield by Gainsborough and Rosalba. —*Quarterly Review*, September, 1845.

[2] *Memoirs of the Reign of George II*, vol. I, pp. 95–97.

" In Conversation he is seldom silent but when he is
attentive, nor ever speaks without exciting the Attention
of others ; and tho' no Man might with less Displeasure
to his Hearers engross the Talk of the Company, he has a
Patience in his Vivacity that chuses to divide it, and rather
gives more Freedom than he takes ; his sharpest Replies
having a mixture of Politeness that few have the command
of ; his Expression is easy, short, and clear ; a stiff or
studied word never comes from him ; it is in a simplicity
of Style that he gives the highest Surprize, and his Ideas
are always adapted to the Capacity and Taste of the
Person he speaks to. . . .

" Having often had the Honour to be my self the But of
his Raillery, I must own I have received more Pleasure
from his lively manner of raising the laugh against me,
than I could have felt from the smoothest flattery of a
serious Civility. Tho' Wit flows from him with as much
ease as common Sense from another, he is so little elated
with the Advantage he may have over you, that whenever
your good Fortune gives it against him, he seems more
pleased with it on your side than his own. The only
advantage he makes of his Superiority of Rank is, that
by always waving it himself, his inferior finds he is under
the greater obligation not to forget it." [1]

Allowing for Cibber's characteristic good-nature, and for
a certain degree of flattery, the many recorded sayings
of Chesterfield are in themselves enough to prove that this
is a far more accurate account than Hervey's. Lord
Carnarvon is perhaps nearer to the truth than either when
he says that, " In some of Lord Chesterfield's sayings
there is occasional sarcasm, but not much that can be
called malice. He constantly lays down the precept never
to offend by a witty saying, and he was generally true to
his rule." [2] Even Mrs. Elizabeth Montagu in the course
of a somewhat violent attack on Chesterfield's character,
written shortly after his death, goes so far as to admit
that, " He deserves some praise for never having made a
pernicious use of his Witt." [3]

Chesterfield himself says in a letter to his Godson, No.
VIII on *The Art of Pleasing* :—

[1] *Colley Cibber's Apology* (R. W. Lowe's edit. 1889) vol. I, pp. 14-16.
[2] *Memoir*, p. xliii.
[3] *Mrs. Montagu, Queen of the Blues*, by R. Blunt (1923) p. 273.

" MY DEAR LITTLE BOY,

If God gives you wit, which I am not sure that I wish you, unless He gives you at the same time an equal portion at least of judgment to keep it in good order, wear it like your sword in the scabbard, and do not brandish it to the terror of the whole company. If you have real wit, it will flow spontaneously, and you need not aim at it ; for, in that case, the rule of the Gospel is reversed, and it will prove—seek, and you shall not find. Wit is so shining a quality that everybody admires it ; most people aim at it, all people fear it, and few love it unless in themselves. A man must have a good share of wit himself to endure a great share of it in another. When wit exerts itself in satire, it is a most malignant distemper. Wit, it is true, may be shown in satire ; but satire does not constitute wit as most fools imagine it does. A man of real wit will find a thousand better occasions of showing it.

" Abstain, therefore, most carefully from satire, which, though it fall upon no particular person in company, and momentarily, from the malignity of the human heart, pleases all, upon reflection, it frightens all too ; they think it may be their turn next, and will hate you for what they find you could say of them, more than be obliged to you for what you do not say. Fear and hatred are next-door neighbours. The more wit you have, the more good-nature and politeness you must show, to induce people to pardon your superiority ; for that is no easy matter. Learn to shrink yourself to the size of the company you are in. Take their tone, whatever it may be, and excel in it if you can ; but never pretend to give the tone. A free conversation will no more bear a Dictator, than a free Government will.

" The character of a man of wit is a shining one that every man would have, if he could, though it is often attended by some inconveniences ; the dullest Alderman even aims at it, cracks his dull joke, and thinks, or at least hopes, that it is wit ; but the denomination of *a wit* is always formidable, and very often ridiculous. These titular *wits* have commonly much less wit than petulance and presumption ; they are at best *les rieurs de leur quartier*, in which narrow sphere they are at once feared and admired.

" You will perhaps ask me, and justly, how, considering the delusions of self-love and vanity, from which no man living is absolutely free, how you shall know whether you have wit or not. To which the best answer I can give you is, not to trust to the voice of your own judgment, for it will deceive you, nor to your ears, which will always greedily receive flattery, if you are worth being flattered ; but trust only to your eyes, and read in the countenance of good company their approbation or dislike of what you say. Observe, carefully, too, whether you are sought for, solicited, and in a manner pressed into good company. But even all this will not absolutely ascertain your wit ; therefore do not, upon this encouragement, flash your wit in people's faces à *ricochets*, in the shape of *bons mots*, epigrams, small repartees, etc.

" Appear to have rather less than more wit than you really have. A wise man will live as much within his wit as within his income. Content yourself with good sense and reason, which at long-run are sure to please everybody who has either. If wit comes into the bargain, welcome it, but never invite it. Bear this truth always in your mind, that you may be admired for your wit, if you have any ; but that nothing but good sense and good qualities can make you be loved ; they are substantial, every day's wear. Wit is for *les jours de Gala*, where people go chiefly to be stared at." [1]

It would be easy to read between the lines here and draw the conclusion that Chesterfield was writing in full consciousness of his past failings. We should certainly hesitate to say that this conclusion was wholly false. Chesterfield was the last person to be blind to his own failings, and is constantly in his letters holding himself as a young man up to his son as an example not to be followed in the paths of priggishness and gambling. That he does not confess to the practice of tactless or malicious wit is scarcely a proof that he was not conscious of this failing. Probably he could not bring himself to express regret for some of his jibes against the Hanoverians, since they were prompted more by national feeling than desire

[1] December 18, 1765. Carnarvon, pp. 180, 181 ; Bradshaw, vol. II, pp. 638–640. I have here followed in part Bradshaw's text, which is a compromise between that of the earlier inaccurate version (first published in the *Edinburgh Magazine and Review*, February to May, 1774, probably from copies made by Dr. Dodd, and reprinted in Maty's Supplementary Volume and Lord Mahon's edition of 1845) and that which is reprinted in Lord Carnarvon's edition from the originals, though " apparently with some inaccuracies," as Bradshaw remarks, we feel not without reason. See Carnarvon's *Memoir*, p. lxxvii and Bradshaw, vol. II, p. 627.

to obtain applause for their wit ; but he perhaps hoped that his godson would exercise a little more tact in the expression of his feelings than he himself had done.

It is certain that in the field of politics Chesterfield allowed little restraint either to his tongue or pen, and that both weapons were regarded with considerable awe by his opponents is clear from a brief sketch of him drawn by the Speaker, Arthur Onslow, who, after discussing the power of Bolingbroke, and Carteret's opposition to Walpole, goes on to say :—

" There was besides these two another person of great rank who came to have a considerable share in the design of ruining Sir Robert Walpole, I mean the Earl of Chesterfield. He was esteemed the wittiest man of his time, and of a sort that has scarcely been known since the reign of King Charles the Second, and revived the memory of the great wits of that age, to the liveliest of whom he was thought not to be unequal. He was besides this a very graceful speaker in public, had some knowledge of affairs, having been ambassador in Holland, and when he was engaged in debates always took pains to be well informed of the subject, so that no man's speaking was ever more admired or drew more audience to it than his did, but chiefly from those who either relished his wit or were pleased with seeing the Ministry exposed by his talent of ridicule and the bitterness of jest he was so much master of and never spared, and this made him so very terrible to the Ministers who were of the House of Lords that they dreaded his wit upon them there, and his writings too, for he sometimes, as it was thought, furnished the weekly paper of the Opposition with the most poignant pieces it had." [1]

What few traces of malice appear in his letters, writings, speeches and table-talk are in themselves scarcely enough to stamp Chesterfield as a cynic. In his actions, whether political or private, there is little or nothing to support the charge : on the other hand there are innumerable indications of its falsity. If adverse circumstances ever justified a man in adopting a cynical attitude towards life,

---

[1] *Onslow Papers*, Hist. MSS. Comm., 14th Report, Appendix Part IX, p. 472. See also Coxe's *Memoirs of Sir Robert Walpole*, vol. I, Appendix pp. 349, 350.

those which affected Chesterfield's old age may be said to have done so ; yet he bore disappointment after disappointment with increasing philosophical cheerfulness and fortitude.

To return to Chesterfield's wit ; what is most difficult for the modern reader to accept is the one point over which Hervey, Cibber, Onslow, and indeed all his contemporaries are in agreement—the excellence of his sayings. What strikes us to-day as being at the most a happy turn of phrase, enough to raise a passing smile on the hearer's face, was eagerly seized on by the expectant company and circulated round the town. As Horace Walpole observes,[1] " His great fame, and no man had more in his time, arose from his wit. . . . For a series of years nothing was more talked of than Lord Chesterfield's *bons mots*, and many of them were excellent ; but many, too, of others were ascribed to him." [2] Several of these *" bons mots "* are cited in Horace Walpole's racy notes on Maty, and as many more occur in his Letters, the first recorded one in which will serve as an example :—

" The opera does not succeed. . . . The dances are infamous and ordinary. Lord Chesterfield was told that the Viscontina said she was but four-and-twenty : he answered, ' I suppose she means four-and-twenty stone.' " [3]

At the risk of seeming partial, we suggest that even less praise is due to Walpole for repeating than to Chesterfield for uttering such a remark. Some of Chesterfield's recorded sayings are wittier than this : others are not. Perhaps the fairest thing that can be said about them is that they are as good as the sayings of other wits of the period, with the possible exception of George Selwyn's,[4] though some of

---

[1] In his MS. note on Maty, vol. I, p. 38.

[2] In a letter to the Countess of Suffolk written in the character of his footman, November, 1766 (Bradshaw, vol. III, p. 1350), by ascribing to himself the utterance of a particularly fatuous *bon mot*, " Lord Chesterfield rallies, with the good sense of his own and the coarseness of the assumed character, the fashion of attributing to him everything good, bad, or indifferent, which anybody said." (Note to the Suffolk Letters, vol. II, p. 336.) *Cf.* also " People have long thrown out their wit and humour under my name by way of trial ; if it takes, the true father owns his child ; if it does not, the foundling is mine."—Chesterfield to Sir Thomas Robinson, November 17, 1757. Bradshaw, vol. III, p. 1189.

[3] Letter to Horace Mann, November 12, 1741.

[4] In a note on Maty, vol. I, p. 43, Horace Walpole credits George Selwyn with more wit than Chesterfield.

his utterances, as recorded by Horace Walpole, sound remarkably fatuous to the modern ear. That Chesterfield was an eminently graceful conversationalist there is no reason to doubt : that many of his witticisms would pass muster in a modern drawing-room it is difficult to believe. We do not intend to relate here the dozen or so stock anecdotes exhibiting his humour that are faithfully cited in almost every article and book upon Chesterfield that has ever been written. It is our opinion that from the above letter to his godson half-a-dozen epigrams could be extracted, containing more wit than all his recorded sayings put together. Take this, for instance : " A wise man will live at least as much within his wit as within his income." [1] Probably Chesterfield had in his mind, at the time of writing, Pope's couplet,

> " There are whom Heaven has blest with store of wit,
>   Yet want as much again to manage it," [2]

which he quotes not quite accurately in a letter to his son of July 21st, 1752.[3] The above letter to his godson is the eighth of a series of fourteen on the Art of Pleasing, which, unlike the other letters to his godson, first appeared in print in 1774, and have been reprinted several times.[4] To read these fourteen letters, and also certain of Chesterfield's essays in the *World*, is like reading Pope in prose. The diction is as concise, and the subject matter as full of wisdom. Chesterfield at his best is, in fact, on the highest level of Pope, of whom he wrote to his son, " I used to think myself in company as much above me, when I was with Mr. Addison and Mr. Pope, as if I had been with all the Princes in Europe." [5] The appreciation was, moreover, reciprocated by Pope, in whose Epilogue to the Satires occurs the following :—

---

[1] *Cf.* " Woman's beauty, like men's wit, is generally fatal to the owners unless directed by a judgment, which seldom accompanies a great degree of either."—Chesterfield in *Common Sense*, No. 33. See p. 15 *ante*.

[2] Essay on Criticism, 80, 81. Pope's amended version was :—
" Some, to whom Heaven in wit has been profuse,
Want as much more to turn it to its use."

[3] Bradshaw, vol. II, p. 541.

[4] A full account of the curious manner of their publication is given in Carnarvon's *Memoir*, p. lxxvii.

[5] October 9, 1747. Bradshaw, vol. I, p. 63. And see letter to Baron de Kreuningen quoted on p. 152 *ante*.

" How can I Pult'ney, Chesterfield forget,
  While Roman Spirit charms, and Attic Wit." [1]

Maty tells us that " Mr. Pope often expressed the high
opinion he had of his noble friend," as an instance of which
he relates the following charming anecdote :—

" Being one day in company at Lord Cobham's with a
great number of persons of distinction, who were scribbling
verses on the glasses, he was desired by Lord Chesterfield
to oblige them with a distich *extempore*. ' Favour me with
your diamond, my Lord,' said the poet, and immediately
wrote on his glass :—

> " Accept a miracle instead of wit,
>   See two bad lines with Stanhope's pencil writ." [2]

One is tempted to add that, according to Pope's hypothesis, most of Chesterfield's verse is miraculous, for certainly
very little of it can be called good.   What Lord Carnarvon
regards as his best and neatest epigram was that which
he wrote upon the full-length portrait of Beau Nash, placed
in the Pump Room at Bath between the busts of Newton
and Pope :

> " Immortal Newton never spoke
>   More truth than here you'll find ;
>   Nor Pope himself e'er penned a joke
>   More cruel on mankind.
>
> This picture, plac'd the busts between,
>   Gives satire all its strength ;
> Wisdom and Wit are little seen
>   But Folly at full length." [3]

There is certainly little else in Chesterfield's verse
approaching this—dare we say ?—somewhat mediocre
standard.   But, as Lord Carnarvon wisely observes,
" It would be wrong to measure Lord Chesterfield's wit by

[1] Dialogue xi, 84. 85 : (written in 1738) to which Bishop Warburton
subjoins the following note, " Philip, Earl of Chesterfield, commonly given
by writers of all Parties for an Example to the Age he lives in, of *superior
talents*. and *public Virtue*."
[2] Maty, vol. I, pp. 133, 134.
[3] Maty gives a full account of the origin of this epigram (vol. I, pp. 88,
89), of which there are several versions discussed by Ernst in a foot-note
to p. 117 of his *Life of Lord Chesterfield*.

the merely smart sayings or graceful epigrams that have survived him. He conceived of wit in a much larger sense, and what the charm of his conversation must have been we can now only imagine from the general tradition that has come down to us, and from what he himself has left in writing." [1] To gain a proper idea of Chesterfield's wit and humour one must read his essays ; not the political ones, in which the satire is clumsy and tedious, and the humour merely a medium for the subject-matter, but those on more general subjects, in which the humour is less insistent and of a far higher order. It has long been the custom for writers on Chesterfield, and on eighteenth-century literature in general, to pass quickly over his essays by saying that they contain merit, but are of course far inferior to those of Addison and Steele.[2] One wonders at times whether all these critics have read all his essays. Dare we take a leaf out of Chesterfield's book and challenge " les pédans " to find eleven essays from the Tatler, Spectator and Guardian surpassing those reprinted at the end of this book in brilliance of style, wisdom of substance, and charm of expression ? For sheer humour, mingled with acute analysis and delicacy of satire, take No. 151 of The World [3]—an imaginary symposium on Fashion, reminiscent of Congreve's brilliance of dialogue and fun at his highest level. It contains, however, none of Congreve's extravagance, and, strangely enough, considering the nature of the subject under discussion, and its obsolete detail, is tinged throughout with a flavour arresting in its modernity.

It is curious, the thrill we experience on encountering " modern " humour in old writers. There is nothing exactly with which it can be compared, though a fanciful analogy might be drawn from Holbein's portraits, which produce the quaint effect of a kind of ante-dated realism. The standard of humour is strangely impermanent, as will be seen from a perusal of Punches not even more than a generation old, in which the humour is surprisingly antiquated, far more so than that of Sheridan's Critic, to take an example of an almost equally topical nature.

---

[1] Memoir, p. xliv.

[2] A pleasing exception to this custom occurs in The Periodical Essayist of the Eighteenth Century (1923) by Dr. G. S. Marr, in whose exhaustive survey Chesterfield is given his full meed of praise and is placed for the first time in what may be regarded as his lawful position amongst the essayists of that century. See particularly pp. 31, 81, 99–101, 144–5.

[3] See p. 250 post.

Or, consider the laughter of an audience at a Shakespeare comedy. How often is it the effect of a dutiful respect for the author's greatness, an acknowledgement rather than an appreciation ? Is the audience really amused ? We venture to say, not so on all occasions. Yet there are many scenes, many passages, which provoke spontaneous laughter and the accompanying thrill that " this might have been written to-day."

This comparison with a modern standard is a test of excellence that is applied to no æsthetic quality except humour ; rather do we in other forms of art test our modern achievements by comparison with earlier and generally accepted standards. It would seem that we regard, rightly or wrongly, the present day highest standard of humour as more subtle, more refined, than any previous standard, and that we are consequently surprised and charmed to find older writers occasionally reaching its heights. To give examples is perhaps unwise, since opinions vary so widely on the relative values of the comic authors, but, in this connection, *Don Quixote* may be cited as a great book at whose extravagances and whimsicalities we smile, but are not thrilled, while Sterne may be taken as an instance of an old writer with a distinctly modern vein of humour frequently cropping up in the midst of much that is obsolete. But whether we are justified or not in imposing this modern test, it is probably true that humour which evokes the thrill of modernity is, from the very spontaneity of its appeal, of the highest order, and ranks in reality not so much with modern humour as with humour for all time.

As we have already observed, it cannot be claimed that Chesterfield's humour always reaches this highest standard, but in certain respects he is supreme, notably in the refined expression of a coarse thought. How, for instance, could the following circumlocution be surpassed ? He is discussing in the first number of *Common Sense*[1] the merits of certain rival weekly papers.

" As for the *London Journal*, it cannot possibly interfere with me, as appears from the very title of my paper ; moreover I was informed, that paper of the same size and goodness as the *London Journal*, being to be had much

---

[1] February 5, 1737.

cheaper unprinted and unstamped, and yet as useful to all intents and purposes, was now universally preferred."

As can be seen from the essays at the end of this volume, Chesterfield had no profundity of thought : on the other hand, his reflections are never commonplace. His range of knowledge, though extensive, had distinct limitations ; but in charm, lucidity, and conciseness of expression he is unexcelled by any writer of the English language. No one, for example, could round off a letter with such neatness and apparent ease as Chesterfield. It may seem a trivial instance, but, since the pure artistry of expression appears in them without much simultaneous distraction of subject-matter, we will cite half-a-dozen examples taken from the many that occur in his letters.

" My head will not allow me to write any more ; it is my heart adds, that I am faithfully, Yours." [1]

" From a hermitage, this is, I think, a very long letter and full of news. You may very probably think the letter too long, and the news too old ; but I will conclude it with a piece of much staler and older news, which you have known these twenty years, that I am, affectionately and sincerely, Yours." [2]

" Adieu, Monsieur, je vois bien que je dois vous admirer de plus en plus tous les jours, mais aussi je sçais bien que rien ne pourra jamais ajouter à l'estime et à l'attachement avec lesquels je suis actuellement, Votre, etc." [3]

" The remaining pain in my right hand hinders me from troubling you with a longer letter ; but it is suspended while I have the pleasure of assuring you that I am, Yours, etc." [4]

" I am going next week to settle at Blackheath, in the quiet and obscurity that best become me now, where you and Lady Stanhope, when you have nothing better to do, will always find a very indifferent dinner, and
A very faithful servant." [5]

[1] To Solomon Dayrolles, June 23, 1749. Bradshaw, vol. II, p. 935.
[2] To the same, June 22, 1753. Bradshaw, vol. III, p. 1067.
[3] To Voltaire, August 27, 1752. Ibid., p. 1034.
[4] To the Bishop of Waterford, February 7, 1754. Ibid., p. 1085.
[5] To Earl Stanhope, May 13, 1758. Ibid., p. 1219.

" I have not been so long in writing this letter as I
have been trying, but in vain, to finish it with some
ingenious paragraph, that should neatly introduce my
being, with the utmost regard and attachment, Madam,
yours, etc." [1]

If this last example is an ingenious instance of *ars
ostendere artem*, are we to assume that the others are
nothing more than hollow compliments in the form of
verbal exercises? We think not. The fact that the
expression is artificial does not necessarily make the
sentiment expressed insincere. Chesterfield could do
nothing ungracefully, whether it were uttering a compliment or a rebuke, expressing admiration or contempt.
It is impossible to read his letters without becoming conscious that one of the most striking features of the writer's
temperament, perhaps the most striking feature, is its
affectionate nature. So powerful, however, is the prejudice
against Chesterfield, caused, we believe, almost entirely
by the unfortunate advice to his son, and the Johnson
episode, that this fact, despite its obvious truth, has never
been mentioned, or even recognised by the commentators.
Most writers on Chesterfield have made the admission
that the hard, worldly cynic, by some peculiar twist in
his character, had an extraordinary affection for his son,
just as some sour old character in fiction may be provided
with a dog, on which to lavish his sole affection, in order
that his misanthropic temperament may be the more
clearly contrasted.[2] Mr. Birrell, unlike the other critics,
seems disinclined to make even this admission.

" What, I have often wondered, induced Lord Chesterfield to write this enormously long and troublesome series
of letters to a son who was not even his heir? [3] Their
sincerity cannot be called in question. William Wilber-
force did not more fervently desire the conversion to God
of his infant Samuel than apparently did Lord Chesterfield
the transformation of his lumpish offspring into ' the all-
accomplished man ' he wished to have him. . . . But what
promoted the anxiety? Was it natural affection—a

---

[1] To the Countess of Suffolk, August 17, 1733. *Ibid.*, vol. II, p. 731.
[2] *Cf.* " This love of his son is the one sweet spring of natural affection
in the father's uncommonly stony bosom. It half softens us towards him."
—Sir Leslie Stephen in the *Cornhill Magazine*, July, 1871. (p. 91.)
[3] This question we have endeavoured to answer on pp. 25–26 *ante*.

father's love ? If it was, never before or since has that world-wide and homely emotion been so concealed. There is a detestable, a forbidding, an all-pervading harshness of tone throughout this correspondence that seems to banish affection, to murder love. Read Letter CLXXVIII,[1] and judge for yourselves. I will quote a passage :

' The more I love you now from the good opinion I have of you, the greater will be my indignation, if I should have reason to change it. Hitherto you have had every possible proof of my affection, because you have deserved it ; but when you cease to deserve it, you may expect every possible mark of my resentment. To leave nothing doubtful upon this important point, I will tell you fairly, beforehand, by what rule I shall judge of your conduct— by Mr. Harte's accounts. He will not, I am sure—nay, I will say more, he cannot be in the wrong with regard to you. He can have no other view but your good ; and you will, I am sure, allow that he must be a better judge of it than you can possibly be at your age. While he is satisfied, I shall be so too ; but whenever he is dissatisfied with you, I shall be much more so. If he complains, you must be guilty ; and I shall not have the least regard for anything that you may allege in your own defence.' [2]

" Ugh ! what a father ! Lord Chesterfield despised the Gospels and made little of St. Paul ; yet the New Testament could have taught him something concerning the nature of a father's love. His language is repulsive, repugnant, and yet how few fathers have taken the trouble to write 400 educational letters of great length to their sons ! All one can say is that Chesterfield's letters are without natural affection :

' If this be error and upon me proved,
I never writ, and no man ever loved.' " [3]

Despite the dire effects threatened in the couplet, we firmly believe that anyone familiar with Chesterfield's *Letters to his Son* will agree with us in saying that Mr. Birrell *is* in error. That it can be *proved* upon him is another matter, especially in view of the fact that Chester-

[1] In Strachey's edition. Undated. Bradshaw, vol. I, p. 198.
[2] We have quoted the passage in full from the text, in order to avoid an omission and slight inaccuracies in Mr. Birrell's quotation.
[3] *In the Name of the Bodleian*, pp. 77–79.

field, in answering Mr. Birrell's query as to what promoted the anxiety, himself pleads definitely guilty to the charge!

" Whatever my success may be, my anxiety and my care can only be the effects of that tender affection which I have for you and which you cannot represent to yourself greater than it really is. But do not mistake the nature of that affection, and think it of a kind that you may with impunity abuse. It is not natural affection, there being in reality no such thing ; for, if there were, some inward sentiment must necessarily and reciprocally discover the parent to the child, and the child to the parent, without any exterior indications, knowledge, or acquaintance, whatsoever ; which never happened since the creation of the world, whatever poets, romance or novel-writers, and such sentiment-mongers, may be pleased to say to the contrary. Neither is my affection for you that of a mother, of which the only, or at least the chief objects, are health and life : I wish you them both most heartily ; but, at the same time, I confess they are by no means my principal care." [1]

Upon this Churton Collins observes, " Like Lady Mary Wortley Montagu, to whom in constitution and temper he bore in some respects a singular resemblance, he was a philosopher even in his affections " ; adding in a footnote : " It is remarkable that they both speak in precisely the same way about natural affection. ' You are no more obliged to me for bringing you into the world,' writes Lady Mary to her daughter, ' than I am to you for coming into it, and I never made use of that commonplace (and like most commonplace, false), argument, as exacting any return of affection ' ; and then she goes on to say that what has formed the close bond of love between them has been the mutual interchange of what should unite reasonable beings. (*To the Countess of Bute : Works*, vol. IV, p. 61.)" [2]

Chesterfield continues :—

" My object is to have you fit to live ; which, if you are not, I do not desire that you should live at all.[3] My affection for you then is, and only will be, proportioned to

[1] To his son, December 18, 1747. Bradshaw, vol. I, p. 75.
[2] *Essays and Studies*, p. 214.
[3] " To his refined good sense the extinction of existence was preferable to its abuse, was preferable even to its misuse." Collins's note.

O

your merit, which is the only affection that one rational being ought to have for another. Hitherto, I have discovered nothing wrong in your heart or your head : on the contrary, I think I see sense in the one and sentiment in the other. This persuasion is the only motive of my present affection, which will either increase or diminish according to your merit or demerit. If you have the knowledge, the honour, and the probity which you may have, the marks and warmth of my affection shall amply reward them ; but if you have them not, my aversion and indignation will rise in the same proportion ; and in that case, remember, that I am under no further obligation than to give you the necessary means of subsisting. If ever we quarrel, do not expect or depend upon any weakness in my nature for a reconciliation, as children frequently do, and often meet with, from silly parents : I have no such weakness about me ; and, as I will never quarrel with you but upon some essential point, if once we quarrel I will never forgive. But I hope and believe, that this declaration, (for it is no threat) will prove unnecessary. You are no stranger to the principles of virtue ; and, surely, whoever knows virtue must love it." [1]

In this letter what Churton Collins terms " refined good sense " we cannot help thinking insincerely unnatural : what he regards as philosophical affection we suggest is nothing more than a hopeless attempt to rationalize what everyone knows will never admit of rationalization. Chesterfield's letters to his son are rational throughout. He lays down no dicta without giving accompanying reasons, asks his son to accept nothing on trust from him. He has, in fact, the utmost contempt for education on any other lines, and, in advising Dayrolles as to the upbringing of a son of his, to whom Chesterfield was godfather, says, " I am persuaded that a child of a year and a half old is to be reasoned with." [2] But the letter to his son we have just quoted is, we maintain, simply reasoning carried to excess in the form of a bluff. We cannot believe that Chesterfield really entertained the sentiments he uttered. Writing to Madame de Monconseil about his son he says, " je menace, je flatte, je fulmine, j'amadoue, tour à tour"; [3]

[1] Bradshaw, vol. I, pp. 75, 76.
[2] June 22, 1753. Bradshaw, vol. III, p. 1066.
[3] May 23, 1751. *Ibid.*, p. 989.

and this letter and the one cited by Mr. Birrell [1] should surely be regarded as instances of the first and third of these methods.

That both letters deserve the epithets " repulsive " and " repugnant ", or even stronger ones, no one could well dispute; but to deduce from them that " there is a detestable, a forbidding, an all-pervading harshness of tone throughout this correspondence that seems to banish affection, to murder love," is to be grossly unfair to Chesterfield. It is not overstating the case to say that there is more harshness of tone in these two passages than in all the other letters to his son put together. Stray sentences can be found in a few of the letters, in which certain sentiments expressed in these " repulsive " passages are repeated, but they are rare in occurrence, and generally softened by the context. Broadly speaking, the tone of these passages differs in marked degree from that of the rest of the correspondence, though the letters are seldom written in the strain that one would expect from a father to a son. They are, indeed, as Chesterfield is at continual trouble to point out, unpaternal in a deliberate and artificial sense. He believes that his son is more likely to adopt the reasonings of a friend than to obey the dictates of a father.

" As therefore it is plain that I can have no other motive than that of affection in whatever I say to you, you ought to look upon me as your best, and, for some years to come, your only friend.

" True friendship requires certain proportions of age and manners, and can never subsist where they are extremely different, except in the relations of parent and child ; where affection on one side, and regard on the other, make up the difference." [2]

Hence, carrying this idea to a logical conclusion, he ends his last letter of 1749 as follows :—

" Adieu, my dear friend, for such I shall call you, and

[1] Though we have no desire to justify the passage quoted by Mr. Birrell, it is only fair to mention that it is explained to a certain extent if the letter is taken as a whole. Stanhope was just going to make a prolonged stay at Turin, apropos of which Chesterfield gives many causes for his " anxiety for the consequences of your stay there, which must be either very good or very bad."—Bradshaw, vol. I, p. 199.
[2] November 24, 1747, *Ibid.*, p. 71.

as such I shall, for the future, live with you. I disclaim all titles which imply an authority that, I am persuaded, you will never give me occasion to exercise." [1]

His letters, which formerly began " Dear Boy," after the next one, accordingly, all begin " My dear friend," and a year later he ends one, " Adieu, my dear ; remember to write to me once a week, not as to a father, but without reserve as to a friend." [2]

Whether the friendship was ever reciprocated there is unfortunately no evidence to prove, but the fact that young Stanhope chose to preserve so many of his father's letters during his travels abroad, is at least an indication that he felt a considerable regard for him. That Chesterfield himself believed that his affection was returned is apparent from the following :—

" I am sure you love me so well, that you would be very sorry, when we meet, that I should be either disappointed or mortified ; and I love you so well, that I assure you I should be both if I should find you want any of those exterior accomplishments which are the indispensably necessary steps to that figure and fortune which I so earnestly wish you may one day make in the world." [3]

And again,

" You know my tenderness : I know your affection. . . . As fathers commonly go, it is seldom a misfortune to be fatherless ; [4] and, considering the general run of sons, as seldom a misfortune to be childless. You and I form, I believe, an exception to that rule ; for, I am persuaded, that we would neither of us change our relation, were it in our power. You will, I both hope and believe, be not only the comfort, but the pride of my age ; and, I am sure, I will be the support, the friend, the guide of your youth."[5]

Chesterfield is fond of telling his son what he conceives

---

[1] December 26, 1749. Bradshaw, vol. I, p. 302.

[2] January 3, 1751. *Ibid.*, p. 388.

[3] May 16, 1751. *Ibid.*, pp. 442, 443.

[4] As is well known, Chesterfield had been particularly unfortunate in his own father.

[5] July 15, 1751. *Ibid.*, pp. 470, 471.

to be the duties of a father, and the follies of carrying paternal love to excess.

" I have often thought, and still think, that there are few things which people in general know less, than how to love and how to hate. They hurt those they love, by a mistaken indulgence—by a blindness, nay, often a partiality to their faults. Where they hate, they hurt themselves, by ill-timed passion and rage. Fortunately for you, I never loved you in that mistaken manner; from your infancy, I made you the object of my most serious attention, and not my plaything; I consulted your real good, not your humours or fancies; and I shall continue to do so while you want it." [1]

Again,

" I long to see Lord and Lady Blessington (who are not yet arrived), because they have lately seen you; and I always fancy that I can fish out something new concerning you from those who have seen you last; not that I shall much rely upon their accounts, because I distrust the judgment of Lord and Lady Blessington in those matters about which I am most inquisitive. They have ruined their own son, by what they called and thought, loving him. They have made him believe that the world was made for him, not he for the world; and unless he stays abroad a great while, and falls into very good company, he will expect, what he will never find, the attentions and complaisance from others which he has hitherto been used to from Papa and Mamma. . . . However you may turn out, you can never make me any of these reproaches. I indulged no silly womanish fondness for you: instead of inflicting my tenderness upon you, I have taken all possible methods to make you deserve it; and, thank God, you do; at least, I know but one article in which you are different from what I could wish you, and you very well know what that is. I want that I and all the world should like you as well as I love you. Adieu." [2]

It would be very easy to cite many other passages in Chesterfield's letters expressing the affection he felt for

---

[1] November 26, 1749. Bradshaw, vol. I, pp. 279, 280.
[2] April 13, 1752. *Ibid.*, vol. II, p. 513.

his son,[1] but we feel that this last sentence, written as it so obviously is from the heart and not the mind, will suffice to disprove what both he and Mr. Birrell have written about his lack of natural affection. It must be added that the conclusion Mr. Birrell has drawn from the letter he quotes has led him to the equally erroneous conclusion that " Lord Chesterfield despised the Gospels, and made little of St. Paul " ; by which we can only assume that he is comparing the language of this particular letter with that of The Sermon on the Mount, and of 1 *Corinthians* xiii. To read this statement in a literal sense would be as unkind to Mr. Birrell as to Chesterfield himself ; for there is no particle of evidence in the whole of Chesterfield's writings to indicate that he ever expressed or even implied a contempt for the Gospels ; and the only references he makes to St. Paul are the following :—

" One must often yield, in order to prevail : one must humble oneself to be exalted ; one must, like St. Paul, become all things to all men, to gain some." [2]

" Business must not be sauntered and trifled with : and you must not say to it, as Felix did to Paul, ' at a more convenient season I will speak to thee.' " [3]

Mr. Birrell says that " the New Testament could have taught Chesterfield something concerning the nature of a father's love." Very possibly ; though we doubt whether any father has exhibited more devotion ; but the following letter to the Bishop of Waterford on the death of Mrs. Chenevix will show that Chesterfield was not entirely unacquainted with even the New Testament conception of a father's love. It is worth quoting in full as an example of a model letter of practical sympathy to a bereaved person.

" London, July 14, 1752.

My dear Lord,

I know the gentleness, the humanity, and the tenderness

---

[1] Whom he tells Madame de Monconseil, " j'aime infiniment."

[2] To his son : February 28, 1751. Bradshaw, vol. I, p. 409. (See 1 *Cor.* iv. 22.)

[3] To his son : March 5, 1752. Bradshaw, vol. II, p. 502. The same comparison and reference to *Acts* xxiv. 25, is made in letters to the Bishop of Waterford of June 26, 1755, and September 12, 1761, and in another letter to his son of June 10, 1751. In the two last-mentioned letters "Festus" is written in mistake for " Felix."

of your nature too well to doubt of your grief, and I know
the object of it too well to blame it.   No ; in such cases
it is a commendable, not a blameable passion, and is
always inseparable from a heart that is capable of friendship
or love.   I therefore offer you no trite, and always unavailing, arguments of consolation ; but, as any strong and
prevailing passion is apt to make us neglect or forget for
the time our most important duties, I must remind you
of two in particular, the neglect of which would render
your grief, instead of pious, criminal : I mean your duty
to your children as a father, and to your diocese as a
Bishop.   Your care of your children must be doubled,
in order to repair as far as possible their loss, and the
public trust of your flock must not suffer from a personal
and private concern.   These incumbent and necessary
duties will sometimes suspend, and at last mitigate, that
grief, which I confess mere reason would not : they are
equally moral and Christian duties, which I am sure no
consideration upon earth will ever make you neglect.   May
your assiduous discharge of them insensibly lessen that
affliction, which, if indulged, would prove as fatal to you
and your family, as it must be vain and unavailing to her
whose loss you justly lament ! I am, with the greatest
truth and affection, my dear Lord, Yours, etc." [1]

No man was, in fact, ever more acutely conscious of a
father's duties than Chesterfield, and, though few would
agree entirely with his conception of those duties, it is
impossible to conceive any father fulfilling them more
scrupulously.   But, though the exigencies of his moral
code were doubtless enough in themselves to effect such
fulfilment, the task was certainly rendered easier by natural
affection and fatherly instincts ; for Chesterfield was a
man in whose natural character the parental sense was
abnormally strong.   It may, in fact, be regarded as the
most distinctive *natural* trait in a character which was so
fashioned by the workings of a stern moral code that only
a few details of the original can be recognized.   These
fatherly instincts are manifested even more clearly in the
correspondence with his godson and A. C. Stanhope than
in the letters to his son.   They are also indicated in the

[1] Bradshaw, vol. III, pp. 1030–31.   See also his letter to A. C. Stanhope
on the death of the latter's wife : December 31, 1763. Carnarvon, Appendix
p. 36.

letters to the Earl of Essex [1] concerning Earl Stanhope and his brother George, " my two sons, for I look upon them as such " ; and in a letter advising his son to " form the most intimate connection with " the young Earl of Huntingdon, " who, next to you, is the truest object of my affection and esteem, and who (I am proud to say it) calls me and considers me as his adopted father." [2]

Further instances of the appeal which young men made to his fatherly disposition may be found in the letters to Edward Eliot [3] who was one of Dr. Harte's pupils and for some time a companion on the Continent with Philip Stanhope. He is constantly mentioned in Chesterfield's letters to his son and seems to have been of a particularly charming nature. Writing to his father Richard Eliot, he speaks of " Lord Chesterfield whose great and favourite object in this world is the education of his son " ; and in another letter written from Lausanne he says :—

" When you go to London after Christmas I hope some how or other you will meet his Lordship who was vastly Good to me when I was in Town, gave me a great deal of good Advice, and was at the Pains to write out a Catalogue of the Books He thought most proper for me to read, with the different Characters and Use of them All." [4]

At Dresden Sir Charles Hanbury Williams took much interest in the two pupils, and, when writing to Chesterfield, gave a very complimentary account of Eliot, which the earl in a spirit of parental sympathy copied out and sent to Richard Eliot with the following characteristically graceful letter.

London June y[e] 14th 1748.

S[r]

As the inclosed extract of S[r] Charles Williams's letter must give you the tenderest pleasure, I cannot refuse my

[1] See pp. 296–298 *post*. Note also the affectionate manner in which he writes, nearly forty years later, to his godson's friend Ernst, (pp. 312–314 *post*), and to his grandchildren (p. 137–38 *ante*).
[2] October 22, 1750. Bradshaw, vol. I, pp. 359, 360. See also his letter to Mme. de Monconseil recommending him to her care : September 25, 1750 ; *ibid.*, vol. III, pp. 966, 967. It was to this earl that Chesterfield wrote the series of letters (1749–69) published in 1923.
[3] Born in 1727 ; for many years M.P. for St. Germains, and in 1784 created Lord Eliot. He died in 1804.
[4] December 9, 1746. From the MSS. of the Earl of St. Germains at Port Eliot.

self the satisfaction of sending it you. I congratulate you upon the prospect which it presents you with, and am with the greatest truth

S^r, Your most faithfull humble servant

CHESTERFIELD.[1]

Chesterfield's genuine affection for the young can be realized to the full only by reading the letters to his son, godson, and Lord Huntingdon, and those to Lord Essex, Eliot and Ernst in the Appendix to this book. Some emphasis has to be laid on this point, partly because it has never previously been recognized, and partly because it might be thought that his letters to young friends were simply the outcome of an overweening desire to instruct. That Chesterfield was fond of acting the part of instructor is shown in these letters, as it is also in his contributions to *The World*; but this fact does little to support the extravagant theory thus put forward by Mr. Charles Whibley :—

" The enterprise, which he attempted, to make a fine gentleman of his son, failed . . . It is said that this obvious failure was a disappointment to Chesterfield. I cannot believe it, and there is no evidence which should justify such an opinion. Chesterfield was an artist in instruction, and he followed his art for its own sake. It was not his fault that the material which he chose was stubborn and unmalleable. In attempting to mould it, he had done what he was born to do, and success or failure meant far less to him than has been supposed. Had the end seemed greater to him than the design, he would have chosen his subjects with a finer tact. I can hardly believe that his good counsel was welcomed either by his godson or by Lord Huntingdon, whom presently he pressed into his service, and who profited as little as his son by the admonitions of the master. Wherefore he deserves the greater credit, due to the artist, who is content to do his work as well as he can, and is not too solicitous about the practical result which he attains." [2]

It might be suggested that this artistic ideal is of a somewhat mediocre nature, and that the true artist cannot be too solicitous about the practical result which he attains.

[1] From the MSS. of the Earl of St. Germains. Now first printed.
[2] " Lord Chesterfield."—*The Criterion*. April, 1924.

We are, however, not concerned with Mr. Whibley's theories on art. What does concern us is the fact that Chesterfield's extreme solicitude for the success of his enterprise is apparent in almost every letter of instruction he ever wrote to his son, or to others about him. If Chesterfield was simply an artist in instruction ; if the design seemed greater to him than the end ; if he was content to do his work as well as he could, and was not "too solicitous" about the practical result, how comes it that preparatory to and during the boy's visits to Paris, every letter from Chesterfield to Madame de Monconseil contains a request couched in the most urgent language that she should do her utmost to instruct him in the graces?[1] The artist, moreover, is fond of telling his deputy that she is entitled to what credit attaches to the boy's improvement in manners. "Ce n'est pas pour vous faire un fade compliment, mais c'est très-véritablement que je vous proteste, que je crois que sa réussite dans le monde dépendra plus de vous que de tout autre chose."[2] And again,

"Il vous est uniquement redevable, Madame, de ce qu'il a de passable : il le sent bien, je puis vous en assurer : et pour ma reconnoissance, soyez bien persuadée, qu'elle ne finira qu'avec mes jours."[3]

Mr. Whibley states that there is no evidence to justify the opinion that the failure of his enterprise was a disappointment to Chesterfield. We do not entirely agree, though for obvious reasons not much direct evidence exists. No man is likely to proclaim to the world that he has failed to make his son a gentleman, and Chesterfield of all men was the last to groan under a disappointment. When the King in 1753 refused to grant Stanhope a diplomatic post on which the father had "set his heart," Chesterfield says in a letter to Dayrolles, "I did not expect such a refusal of such a trifle. But it is over, and I have philosophy enough never unavailingly to regret what cannot be retrieved."[4]

When a man has toiled for ten years at a task which has eventually to be counted as a failure it seems fanciful

---

[1] See, for example, some twenty of the letters written to her in 1750–52. Bradshaw, vols. II and III, pp. 950–1044 *passim*.

[2] June 28, 1750. *Ibid.*, vol. III, p. 960.

[3] June 30, 1752. *Ibid.*, p. 1029.

[4] *Ibid.*, p. 1069.

to suggest that disappointment does not ensue. There
is, moreover, a mass of evidence in the letters both to his
son and to his friends of actual disappointment at the slow
progress made by the youth in acquiring the graces. To
quote a few stray passages from his letters to Madame de
Monconseil :—

" Après les soins que j'ai eu de son éducation, indé-
pendamment de ma tendresse pour lui, je me fais une
affaire, je me pique même de sa réussite dans le monde." [1]
" Il y a, dans le portrait que vous m'avez envoyé, et
qui, je suis bien sûr, est fort ressemblant, des traits qui
me choquent infiniment, et qui défigurent tout-à-fait
l'assemblage, malgré d'autres bons traits qui s'y trouvent.
Je crains même qu'il ne soit bien difficile de corriger l'original,
puisque jusqu'ici vous y avez perdu vos peines, et que,
depuis trois ans, j'y ai travaillé sans relâche, et comme il
paroit sans succès . . . Vous m'avouez, et je suis sûr que
vous mettez tout au mieux, que les progrès sont bien lents ;
c'est-à-dire qu'il n'en a point fait du tout. Ceci me fait
presque désesperer, et je n'attends de remède, si tant est
que j'en attende, que de votre part." [2]
" Je suis bien aise que votre petit galopin ait gagné
un peu du côté de l'air et des manières, mais je ne comprends
point comme quoi il n'a pas gagné beaucoup davantage, vu
qu'à présent il y a sept ans qu'il a été dans tous les pays
de l'Europe, et qu'il a réellement fréquenté tout ce qu'il
y a de mieux. Il devroit actuellement avoir, non seulement
l'air, la politesse, et les attentions nécessaires, mais même
le plus beau vernis, et tout ce qu'il y a de plus séduisant
dans l'art de plaire. Ce n'est pourtant rien moins que
cela ; et il a encore un furieux chemin à faire pour parvenir
au nécessaire . . . Mille personnes lui ont assez dit tout ce
qu'on peut dire sur ce sujet, et j'ai épuisé cette matière
dans les lettres que je lui ai écrites depuis quatre ans ; mais
il y a des propositions si évidentes en elles-mêmes, qu'il
n'y a pas moyen de les rendre plus claires." [3]

These were written while Philip Stanhope was still a
youth ; but when he was twenty-three years of age, and,

[1] June 28, 1750. Bradshaw, vol. III, pp. 959, 960.
[2] February 25, 1751. *Ibid.*, pp. 982, 983.
[3] December 18, 1752. *Ibid.*, p. 1049.

we may assume, past all hope of further polish, Chesterfield writes to Madame de Monconseil :—

" Vous voulez, Madame, que je vous rende compte de votre petit galopin de jadis . . . Il étudie, il s'applique, il s'informe ; à cet égard-là tout va bien ; il ne joue, ni ne boit, et pour le reste, je dois, et je veux l'ignorer." [1]

Mr. Whibley may or may not be able to believe it, but to our mind these words reveal a sense of disappointment, none the less intense for the delicacy with which it is expressed. *Je dois, et je veux l'ignorer !* One can almost hear the father's sigh. Madame, to judge from his subsequent letters to her, made no further enquiries concerning *le petit galopin de jadis.*

Mr. Whibley's conclusions are as fanciful as they are contrary to the evidence ; but when he suggests that, " Had the end seemed greater to him than the design he would have chosen his subjects with a finer tact," his fancy reaches a height of extravagance where it may conveniently be left. It is unnecessary to recount the motives which led Chesterfield to write at such length to his son and godson : nor can anyone determine with even approximate accuracy how far his efforts were due to a self-indulged desire for instructing the young, or to what extent the outcome of a sense of duty. The work that conscience dictates is not always of an uncongenial nature. But, easy as it is to supply adequate motives for Chesterfield's letters of instruction, let us not forget that they breathe a spirit of affection which reveals itself as not the least of the inspiring forces.

Chesterfield's affection was, however, by no means confined to the young, as can easily be seen from the miscellaneous letters to his friends, and, in particular, those to Madame de Monconseil ; Solomon Dayrolles, Minister at the Hague ; Dr. Chenevix, Bishop of Waterford ; George—afterwards Lord Lyttelton ; and Alderman George Faulkner, the Dublin printer and bookseller. Very dear as these friends were to him, there were doubtless others [2] to whom he was equally attached, but to whom, living in London, he had less occasion to write, or whose letters

---

[1] August 21, 1755. Bradshaw, vol. III, pp. 1133–34.

[2] For example, Sir Charles Hanbury Williams, Sir John Irwine, Dr. Arbuthnot, and Lady Hervey.

from him have not been preserved, as in the case of Montesquieu, with whom he " kept up a regular correspondence which only ended with Montesquieu's life." [1]

Among his intimate friends were Pope and Bolingbroke, but for these he had probably more regard than affection. The man whom he loved best in the world was the Earl of Scarborough, who, from all accounts, even Lord Hervey's, was a paragon of virtue. The friendship began in 1715, when Chesterfield was made one of the gentlemen of the bed-chamber to the Prince of Wales, and, to quote Maty,[2] " It was our young lord's peculiar good fortune to meet with a man whom Socrates would probably not have disowned as a disciple ; and he had the good sense to make that man his friend. Lord Lumley, afterwards so well known, so greatly esteemed, and so universally regretted, under the name of Lord Scarborough, was at this time lord of the bed-chamber, and master of the horse to the prince. The intimacy between these two noblemen was unreserved, notwithstanding the differences of characters and age, for Lord Scarborough was ten years older ; it continued unalterable amidst the conflict of interests and parties. We need no other test of the characters of these two lords, than that, though courtiers, they loved, trusted, and esteemed each other." From 1734 until shortly before his death in 1740 Lord Scarborough " supported the ministry against the efforts of those he was most intimately connected with, and lived upon the best terms both with Sir Robert Walpole and with Lord Chesterfield." [3] It was apparently his resignation from the ministry, caused by conscientious scruples, that led to his suicide on January 29, 1740. On the morning of this day, " he paid a long visit to Lord Chesterfield, and opened himself to him with great earnestness on many subjects. As he appeared somewhat discomposed, his friend pressed him in vain to stay and dine with him ; which he refused, but most tenderly embraced him at parting. It happened in the course of the conversation that something was spoken of which related to Sir William Temple's negociations, when the two friends not agreeing

[1] Maty, vol. I, p. 42. See also Chesterfield's short account of Montesquieu published in the London Evening Post, February, 1755 ; Bradshaw, vol. III, p. 1120.

[2] Vol. I, pp. 19, 20.

[3] Ibid., p. 94.

about the circumstances, Lord Chesterfield, whose memory was at all times remarkably good, referred Lord Scarborough to the page of Sir William's memoirs where the matter was mentioned. After his lordship's death, the book was found open at that very page. Thus he seems, in his last moments, to have been still attentive to his friend, and desirous that he should know he was so. This fatal catastrophe was universally lamented . . . but what must Lord Chesterfield's situation have been upon his being informed of this unfortunate event ? His excellent lady does not even now without the greatest emotion speak of the manner in which his lordship, on her return home at night, acquainted her with the loss of that amiable nobleman ; and he ever after lamented that he did not detain him at his house, saying he might perhaps have been saved, if he had not been left to himself that day." [1]

Nearly twenty years after Scarborough's death, Chesterfield wrote an eloquent character [2] of him, beginning as follows :—

" In drawing the character of Lord Scarborough, I will be strictly upon my guard against the partiality of that intimate and unreserved friendship, in which we lived for more than twenty years ; to which friendship, as well as to the public notoriety of it, I owe much more than my pride will let my gratitude own. If this may be suspected to have biassed my judgment, it must, at the same time, be allowed to have informed it ; for the most secret movements of his soul were, without disguise, communicated to me only " ; and ending thus ;—" I owed this small tribute of justice, such as it is, to the memory of the best man I ever knew, and of the dearest friend I ever had."

Next to Scarborough, perhaps the greatest of Chesterfield's earlier friends was William Hammond the poet, who lived with him during the greater period of his first

---

[1] *Ibid.*, pp. 95, 96. Interesting accounts of Scarborough's death can be found in the Diary of the Right Hon. William Wyndham, October 3, 1772 :—*Ketton Papers*, Hist. MSS. Comm., 12th Report, Appendix IX, p. 190 ; and also in a letter from Horatio Walpole to Robert Trevor, February 1, 1740, written shortly after it happened.—*Trevor Papers*, Hist. MSS. Comm., 14th Report, Appendix IX, p. 39.

[2] Bradshaw, vol. III, p. 1420.

Embassy at the Hague.[1] Hammond's early death is
deplored as a national loss by Thomson in his *Seasons*
(Winter), but whether he would ever have risen to any
literary eminence is very doubtful, and Johnson's adverse
verdict on his poems [2] will probably always remain the
final one. That Chesterfield had considerable faith in
Hammond's future is evident from the following letter to
Lyttelton of June 19, 1742.

" The death of poor Hammond was the only event that
disturbed the tranquillity of my mind. He died in the
beginning of a career which, if he had lived, I think he
would have finished with reputation and distinction.
But such is the folly, knavery, and futility of the world,
and such was his truth, fidelity, and attachment to me,
that in my opinion, I have lost more by his death than he
has." [3]

Chesterfield's love for Hammond is also expressed in
the preface he wrote for his *Love Elegies*, which he edited
and published a year after his friend's death.[4] These
poems were, for the most part, imitations of Tibullus ;
and Chesterfield, in speaking of " the influence of the
ancients " upon his style, says at the end of his preface :—

" He admired that justness, that noble simplicity of
thought and expression, which have distinguished and
preserved their writings to this day ; but he revered that
love of their country, that contempt of riches, that sacredness of friendship, and all those heroic and social virtues,
which marked them out as the objects of the veneration,
though not the imitation of succeeding ages ; and he looked
back with a kind of religious awe and delight upon those
glorious and happy times of Greece and Rome, when
wisdom, virtue and liberty formed the only triumvirates,
ere luxury invited corruption to taint, or corruption introduced slavery to destroy, all public and private virtues." [5]

[1] See Charles Holzendorf to George Tilson, February 19, 1732. *State
Papers* (Holland) vol. 316, f. 154.

[2] *Lives of the Poets*, edit. Birkbeck Hill, vol. II, p. 330. Johnson and
others incorrectly call the poet James Hammond.

[3] Mahon, vol. V, p. 447.

[4] See Maty, vol. I, pp. 47, 48, 133, 313. Ernst, pp. 183, 184. Bradshaw,
vol. III, p. 1007.

[5] Maty, vol. I, Miscellaneous Pieces, p. 283. Mahon, vol. V, p. 90.

We have cited this passage, not because we believe Hammond's name worthy of recall, but because we feel it expresses to a large extent Chesterfield's own ideal, which we have already said was founded directly on the *De Officiis*, and thus ultimately upon the Greek School. In most important respects it might be the panegyric of Chesterfield himself. " Simplicity of thought and expression " he admired and practised as few English writers have done before or since his time. The love he felt for his country and perhaps even more for Ireland, the country which he governed for eight difficult months under the principles of " wisdom, virtue and liberty," was profound. Above all he revered the " sacredness of friendship," and no man was more conscious of its obligations. In thanking one of his greatest friends, Madame de Monconseil, for offering her future services in the social upbringing of his son at Paris, he writes :—

" Vous entrez dans mes petits détails comme s'ils vous étoient personnels, et vous recherchez des soins, dont les amis vulgaires trouveroient bien moyen de s'excuser, sans pourtant blesser les apparences de l'amitié. J'y suis d'autant plus sensible, que je suis persuadé que la véritable amitié se distingue plus dans les petites choses que dans les grandes. On n'ose pas manquer aux grands devoirs de l'amitié, on y perdroit trop du côté de la réputation, mais aussi on les remplit souvent plus par intérêt, que par sentiment, au lieu qu'il y a mille prétextes honnêtes pour éviter les petites attentions, qui seroient très embarrassantes et incommodes, si le sentiment ne leur donnoit même des charmes." [1]

And again to the same lady :—

" Vous me reprochez, Madame, un silence que votre esprit ne peut pas regretter. Vos reproches me sont d'autant plus flatteurs que je les dois uniquement à vos sentimens d'amitié ; c'est par là seulement que je prétends vous tenir, et quoique vous ne vouliez pas m'accorder des sentimens en général, ayez la justice de faire une exception en votre faveur. Il est vrai, je ne suis pas ami banal ; si je l'étois, mon amitié seroit indigne de la vôtre. Il me faut premièrement bien connoître mes gens ; je ne

[1] July 26, 1745. Bradshaw, vol. II, p. 788.

veux point un ami sans sentimens, parcequ'il a de l'esprit, comme je ne veux pas non plus d'un ami à sentimens, qui n'a pas le sens commun. Il faut des sentimens réciproques pour former l'amitié, mais aussi il faut réciproquement de l'esprit pour la conduire." [1]

Because Chesterfield refused to allow sentiment to govern sense he has been credited with a cold, calculating temperament, in whose frigid atmosphere neither love nor hate could exist ; and with regard to the latter consideration this estimate is doubtless true. In a letter warning his son that when they next meet he " must expect the most critical *examen* that ever anybody underwent," he says :—"Hatred, jealousy, or envy, make most people attentive to discover the least defects of those they do not love ; they rejoice at every new discovery they make of that kind, and take care to publish it. I thank God, I do not know what those three ungenerous passions are, having never felt them in my own breast ; but love has just the same effect upon me, except that I conceal, instead of publishing, the defects which my attention makes me discover in those I love." [2] Nor was this any empty boast, uttered as an example for his son to follow. There is not a single recorded action in Chesterfield's life, whether public or private, which can in any sense be said to have been prompted by motives of hatred, jealousy, or envy. As we have seen, during his Secretaryship of State he was subjected to the most ungenerous and provoking treatment at the hands of Newcastle ; yet not a word of personal resentment escapes his pen even when he is explaining to his most intimate friends that this treatment has caused him to resign office. And within eight years from his resignation he becomes Newcastle's cherished political counsellor until the latter's death in 1768.

It may be said that, in thus returning good for evil, Chesterfield was prompted less by Christian motives than by a desire to promote the welfare of his son. Doubtless, in his relations with Newcastle, Chesterfield was always conscious of his son in the background ; yet there is nothing in his character to make us doubt whether he would have acted any differently had his son never been born. Perhaps his motives are expressed as clearly as they can be at the

---

[1] February 15, 1748. Bradshaw, vol. II, p. 849.
[2] March 11, 1751. *Ibid.*, vol. I, pp. 415, 416.

end of a paper [1] he wrote on the political situation shortly
after he had effected the famous coalition between Newcastle and Pitt in 1757.

" These are the sincere sentiments of a sincere friend of
the Duke of Newcastle, *qua* [sic] *censet amiculus*,[2] impartial
as to Men, and unconcerned, except as a Citizen, in events
unrelative to the bustle of the world, and Philosopher
enough to despise it."

It is perhaps this aloofness from human nature that has
made Chesterfield an unsympathetic character in the eyes
of so many readers of his letters, yet we cannot believe
that he was an unsympathetic character in reality, or
regarded as such by his contemporaries. There may not
be enough written evidence to disprove Hervey's dictum
that " he was liked and not loved by most of his acquaintances," though Scarborough's deep affection for him,
and his extreme popularity in Ireland, are strong indications of its falsity. But even without these instances, it
is difficult to believe that a man with the acknowledged
charm and sincerity of Chesterfield could lavish the
affection he did on so many friends without its being
reciprocated.

But, however lovable Chesterfield may have been to
those who knew him in his life, as a character he will
always command less affection than respect. What
personal charm and magnetism he had we get only the
merest glimpses of, and, posthumously, Chesterfield
becomes in our eyes a kind of moral ascetic, governed not
by human propensities, but by an inflexible code. If he
would only unbend occasionally ; allow his supreme
self-control a little latitude ; exhibit a few human weaknesses and foibles, a certain amount of Dr. Johnson's
spontaneity, our hearts would expand towards him. In
old age his pathetic and courageous figure does extract
our sympathy : we find him more human, and are gratified
to think that he may almost be guilty of spoiling his godson
at times—that perhaps he occasionally indulges in a little
sentiment at the expense of his eternal common sense.

---

[1] Add. MSS. 32872, f. 437. (*Newcastle Papers*). It is dated August 4,
1757, endorsed " Lord Chesterfield," and obviously, though not actually,
addressed to Newcastle.

[2] Hor. Ep. I., XVII, 3.

It remains true, however, that the principal feature in his character is self-control.   He was convinced from early middle age of the extreme plasticity of character.   It is to that conviction that we owe the letters to his son and godson, and, however much he failed objectively in moulding the characters of these two, he was entirely successful in the subjective moulding of his own.   (It is possible that, when writing to his son at such length and with such fervour, his deep sincerity compelled him to practise to the full what he preached, and that without these letters his ideal would have been less effectively realized.)

To what extent he changed his character in the course of this realization, it is impossible to say.   It was certainly no violent change, such as occurs in the case of one who alters his whole mode of living at the sudden call of some religious inspiration.   Rather should we describe it as the effect on character produced by the constant adherence to high principles—an adherence so habitually practised that, with a corresponding change of character, the reaction eventually became automatic, just as the branch of a climbing plant will come to grow naturally in the direction in which it has been forced.

Again, we are unable to estimate the difficulty of the task accomplished, though it was surely a more difficult one than that of the religious enthusiast, always acting under the urge of the strongest impulse and, *in rerum natura*, to a large extent divested of worldly temptations.   Chesterfield not only kept rigidly to the path of honour throughout the maze of eighteenth-century political intrigue and corruption, but pursued his ideals in the very midst of the world of fashion, the frothy, unethical atmosphere of London and Bath ;   and in so doing he was neither impelled nor protected by religious enthusiasm ;   he was inspired solely by the love of virtue for virtue's sake.

How far he succeeded in improving the tone of society we can only surmise, but the few essays at the end of this book will serve to indicate that his mind was not unoccupied in this direction.   The ideal of " gentleman " had become sadly distorted during the first half of the eighteenth century, and Chesterfield, by precept and example, did more than anyone to raise it to its proper level of morals and manners.   The value of this achievement for obvious reasons cannot even be approximately estimated, but, in view of the sanctity we attach to the ideal, and the impor-

212 CHESTERFIELD AND HIS CRITICS

tant part it has played in the formation of our present
national character, we should be inclined to reckon it as
very high. Certainly it was of greater value than anything
he accomplished in the sphere of politics, in which, by a
stroke of irony, his greatest definite achievement—the
Pitt-Newcastle coalition of 1757–1761—was rendered
possible of effect only by reason of the fact that he had
previously retired from political life. But circumstances
were against him throughout the whole of his Parliamentary
career. Had he been born a generation later, without
Newcastle and George II to hinder his projects at every
turn, he might have become one of our greatest statesmen.
At the same time, we believe that a man in his position,
practising the ideals he did, must have had a considerable
influence on the parliamentary standards of his time ;
that the force of his example did far more than is generally
recognized to purify our politics ; and that, despite the
conventional opinion on his morals, our country to-day
would be ethically the poorer, just as our literature would
be robbed of some of the choicest of its minor treasures,
had he never been born.

VII

ON THE AUTHENTICITY OF CHESTERFIELD'S ESSAYS

THE following are printed in Maty's edition of Chesterfield's Works, and reprinted by Mahon in vol. V of his edition of *Chesterfield's Letters.*

Fog's Journal. Nos. 376, 377, 388. (January 17, January 24, and April 10, 1736). Maty adds this footnote to No. 376 : " This was one of the weekly publications against Sir Robert Walpole's administration. It was first entitled *Mist's Journal.*[1] I suspect that Lord Chesterfield had, several times before, lent his hand to the writers of this witty paper ; but I have no authority to assert it. This, and the two following essays, were generally allowed to be his." [2]

Common Sense. Seventeen numbers ranging from No. 1 (February 5, 1737) to No. 103 (January 27, 1739).[3] To No. 1 Maty adds this footnote :—

" This paper, in which several persons of eminence were concerned, was partly political and on the side of opposition, but mostly moral, and calculated for the improvement of manners and taste. Lord Lyttelton was one of the writers, and the papers which fell from his pen have been inserted in the collection of his works.

" Those which are here given sufficiently shew, by the original turn and admirable management of irony discernible in them, the masterly hand from which they came. Our authority, however, for producing them as Lord

---

[1] " From the printer's name, and was afterwards continued under the punning title of Fog's."—Ernst, p. 88.

[2] Vol. I, *Miscellaneous Pieces*, p. 1.

[3] The eight numbers between April 30 and October 8, 1737, inclusive, are numbered incorrectly by Maty and Mahon.

Chesterfield's is that of one of his particular friends, to whom his lordship gave the list, which we have followed." [1]

Chesterfield's authorship of two of these numbers is, however, denied by Horace Walpole, who says in a MS. note [2] to No. 18 (wrongly numbered 19 by Maty) : " This paper of June 4th (1737) was not written by Lord Chesterfield, and is not worthy of him."

Despite Maty's strong authority, it is probable that Walpole is correct. The number in question is in the form of a letter addressed " To the Author of Common Sense," and is signed " A. Z." Only one other of the seventeen alleged contributions is in the form of a letter, and that (No. 103) is signed " Anglo-Germanicus," a pseudonym in keeping with the irony of its contents.

The letter is an attack on the Bill for Licensing Theatres, debated in the House of Lords on June 2, 1737, two days before the date of this number. It was on this occasion that Chesterfield made one of his most celebrated speeches,[3] which, on comparison, it is difficult to believe could have been by the author of the essay. Exactly when the latter was written we cannot tell, but it would be reasonable to assume that it was not long before the speech was delivered. Of the various points made in both, however, not one is duplicated. The arguments are entirely distinct, and there is not, in short, the faintest resemblance between the two in treatment. Moreover, the style and vocabulary in the paper are less simple than Chesterfield's.

Horace Walpole says in another MS. note [4] that No. 24, July 16, 1737 (incorrectly numbered 25 by Maty) was not written by Chesterfield, a statement with which we are also inclined to agree, though on less certain grounds. The style is not so unlike Chesterfield's as is that of No. 18 but the subject-matter, an attack on parties and party factions, is treated by him with so much greater skill in *Old England* No. 1 (February 5, 1743) that it is difficult to imagine the two productions to be by the same hand.

The essay begins as follows :—

" It is the complaint of most men who have lived any time in the world that the present age is much degenerated

---

[1] Vol. I, *Miscellaneous Pieces*, p. 20. [2] *Ibid.*, p. 46.
[3] A full report of which appears in *ibid.*, pp. 228–241. [4] *Ibid.*, p. 51.

in its morals within the memory of man. I am afraid this complaint is not altogether without foundation. That there has been a gradual decay of public spirit for some years cannot be denied ; and which owes its original, if I am not very much mistaken, to our party divisions."

It is not easy to believe Chesterfield guilty of the last ill-expressed sentence, and the fallacious sentiment contained in the passage is exposed by him in his last contribution to the *World*.[1]

Old England or the Constitutional Journal. Nos. 1 and 3, February 5 and 19, 1743, to the first of which Maty adds this footnote :—

" This paper . . . made a great deal of noise, and the supposed author and printer were taken into custody. Lord Chesterfield owned himself repeatedly to his chaplain, the present bishop of Waterford, author of the first number; and I think there can be no doubt but that the third came from the same hand." [2]

It would appear from the following extracts from Lord Marchmont's Diary that Chesterfield had at least a share in the number of *Old England* of November 3, 1744.

" Nov. 8th [1744] Thursday. Lord Bolingbroke told me . . . that the Duke of Newcastle and his brother were both piqued at last Saturday's *Old England* ridiculing 'em, at the very time they were doing all the opposition could desire of 'em."

" Nov. 10th Saturday. Lord Bolingbroke said . . . that when he blamed Lord Chesterfield for last Saturday's paper, revolting those whom he was labouring to conciliate, Lord Chesterfield said only that he thought all was over." [3]

Unfortunately, no copy of this particular number exists in either the British Museum or the Bodleian.

---

[1] October 7, 1756. See p. 267 *post*.

[2] Vol. I, *Miscellaneous Pieces*, p. 108.

[3] *Marchmont Papers*, vol. I, pp. 75–80. As a matter of fact the coalition was soon after effected, and Chesterfield appointed Lord Lieutenant of Ireland on December 22.

The World. Twenty-three numbers ranging from No. 18 (May 3, 1753) to No. 197 (October 7, 1756). There seems no reason to doubt the authenticity of these, all of which are ascribed to Chesterfield in editions of the *World* reprinted in book form.

OTHER ESSAYS ASCRIBED TO CHESTERFIELD

Common Sense. Nos. 16, 17, 37, 40 and 52 are ascribed to Chesterfield by Horace Walpole, whose authority is given in the following MS. note which appears in his copy of Maty [1] at the end of *Common Sense*, May 14, 1737.

" The paper of May 21st was also written by Lord Chesterfield, but is omitted here. Lady Hervey allowed me to mark in my edition of *Common Sense* all the papers written by Lord Chesterfield which she had marked in her own copy, and which from her living at the time, and from her intimacy with the author, she must have known well. The paper of May 28th was also Lord Chesterfield's." [2]

Excellent as this authority may sound, there are strong reasons for supposing Walpole's statements to be incorrect, apart from the unexplained omission of the numbers by Maty, whose authority is equally good, if not better. To take the five numbers in order : with regard to the authorship of No. 16, it is necessary first to mention that not long before its publication Fielding, under the name of " Pasquin " had written two plays, *The Historical Register for the Year* 1736 and *Eurydice Hiss'd,* in which the Government was made the subject of much ridicule. They are, in fact, generally supposed to have given rise to the introduction and passing of the Licensing Act, and were, together with their author, severely attacked in a Government publication, *The Daily Gazeteer* of May 7, 1737.
The number of *Common Sense,* May 21, 1737, which Walpole ascribes to Chesterfield begins as follows :—

---

[1] Vol. I, *Miscellaneous Pieces,* p. 46.
[2] A list of the same five omissions with a similar but shorter reference to Lady Hervey's authority occurs in Horace Walpole's *Noble Authors.*

" To the Author of *Common Sense*.

SIR,

As I have yet no vehicle of my own, I shall be obliged to you if you will give the following a Place in the next Stage, and am,

Your humble servant."

The remainder of the paper consists of a violent letter addressed to " The Author of the *Gazeteer* of May 7," and signed " Pasquin." [1]

There seems, then, no reason for supposing that the author was not Fielding, who is generally believed to have spent a certain portion of the years 1737-40 in writing essays to periodicals, none of which has been identified.[2]

The author of No. 17 (May 28, 1737) seems clearly to have been a Dr. William King (1685-1763), according to the following extract from the article on him in the Dictionary of National Biography.

" About April 1737 King wrote a witty political paper called *Common Sense*, in which he proposed a new scheme of government to the people of Corsica (*i.e.* Great Britain) advising them to make their king of the same stuff of which the Indians fashion their gods.[3] He enclosed a copy in a letter to Swift, but both were intercepted at the post-office. (SWIFT, *Works*, ed. Scott, 1824, XIX, 81.) It seems to be identical with " Antonietti ducis Corseorum epistola ad Corseos de rege eligendo " included in King's collected writings."

Of the next two numbers, whose omission Walpole notes in Maty,[4] No. 37 (October 15, 1737) is commonly attributed to George (Lord) Lyttelton, at the end of whose works it appears, together with No. 10, as an example of his powers as an essayist : [5] the other one, No. 40 (November 5, 1737) is a continuation of No. 37, and manifestly by the same writer.

[1] See also "Dedication to the Publick" written for *The Historical Register* and *Eurydice Hiss'd*, 1737.
[2] See Austin Dobson's *Fielding* p. 62.
[3] This is a manifest reference to *Common Sense* of May 28, 1737.
[4] Vol. I, *Miscellaneous Pieces*, p. 76.
[5] Ayscough edit. (1774), p. 755. See also article on Lyttelton in the *Dictionary of National Biography*.

Horace Walpole writes of No. 52 in Maty[1] as follows :—

" The paper of January 21st, 1738, consisted of two parts, the latter of which was most indecent and was written by Lord Chesterfield, but I suppose was omitted for its great indecency."

If this paper, a long and tedious exercise in the *double entendre*, was really by Chesterfield, Maty certainly had good cause for omitting it. We feel bound to add, however, that it bears little resemblance in style or matter to any other of Chesterfield's essays.

Bellchambers in his edition of Colley Cibber's *Apology* states that, " To Cibber's passive valour Lord Chesterfield ironically alludes in a weekly paper called *Common Sense*," from which he proceeds to quote the following :—

" Of all the Comedians who have appeared upon the stage within my memory, no one has taking [sic] a kicking with so much Humour as our present most excellent Laureat." In the latest edition of this work [2] occurs the same quotation from " *Common Sense* for 11th June, 1737, a paper attributed to Lord Chesterfield."

The paper in question is very much longer than and of inferior merit to Chesterfield's other contributions to *Common Sense*, from which it differs considerably in style and general manner. It is moreover unlikely that Maty and Horace Walpole would have each omitted it from his list.

The Craftsman. Mr. Walter Sichel, in the course of a lengthy enquiry into the authorship of the articles in the *Craftsman*, says :—

" The series of papers beginning with Nos. 24 and 64 and resumed in Nos. 111 and 113, and in each instance signed ' A ', we should ascribe to Chesterfield. They are samples of the " Opera-politics " which they brought into vogue. Faustina typifies Spain and Cuzzoni England ; and just before the Congress of Soissons, Cuzzoni, despite Senesino's moderating endeavours, is drolly left singing alone on the stage." [3]

---

[1] Vol. I, *Miscellaneous Pieces*, p. 83.
[2] By R. W. Lowe (Nimmo) 1889, p. 71 n.
[3] *Bolingbroke and His Times*, vol. II, pp. 253-4.

This statement lacks accuracy in some respects.

Of the four numbers mentioned only No. 113 is signed"A."
No. 24 (signed "C") contains a passing reference to the
Opera, but does not touch on what Mr. Sichel terms
" Opera-politics."

No. 64 (signed "D") is in no way concerned with the
Opera : nor is either part of No. 111, the first part of which
(signed "O") is also attributed by Mr. Sichel " most
certainly " to Bolingbroke on p. 250, while on pp. 251-252 he
ranks it under the head of " such as display every quality
of Swift."

To turn for a moment to plain fact, the series to which
Mr. Sichel alludes is comprised in Nos. 49, 54, 85 and 113,
all of which deal with disputes between Cuzzoni and
Faustina, and, except for No. 113, are in the form of letters
from " Phil-Harmonicus."   No. 49 is signed "C" and the
rest "A."   These earlier three would certainly seem to be
by the same hand, and it would perhaps be difficult to
prove that it was not Chesterfield's ; but Mr. Sichel has
removed the difficulty by pointing out on p. 250 that No.
54 seems to be " unquestionably by Bolingbroke," while
he " discerns " Arbuthnot in No. 85, (p. 252).

We do not profess to aspire to the discernment of Mr.
Sichel, by means of which he claims " to set on a new
footing the real contributors to the *Craftsman*." [1] With
regard to No. 113, however, which it must be admitted
Mr. Sichel ascribes to no other writer, we would venture
to point out the following facts.

It is dated August 31, 1728.   On the previous 23rd of
April Chesterfield set out on his first embassy to Holland,
where he remained for nearly four years.   From letters
written by him to Mrs. Howard [2] in May, July and August
of that year, we learn that his life at the Hague was
exceptionally busy, and that he was endeavouring to
ingratiate himself with Queen Caroline, to whom he sent
in August a present of china.   On August 31, N.S. 1728
(*i.e.* eleven days before the date of No. 113), we find him
making his request for the Garter to Lord Townshend. [3]
Altogether, neither place nor period seems a likely one in
which to find him engaged in writing a satirical article to

[1] Preface p. vii.   *Cf.* also " We shall prove that these conjectures are
baseless, that under all these initials many authors lay alternately concealed,
and that both Arbuthnot and Swift were constant contributors."   p. 248.
[2] Afterwards the Countess of Suffolk.   Bradshaw, vol. II pp. 677-684.
[3] *Ibid.*, pp. 684-5.   See pp. 77-78 *ante*.

an Opposition newspaper; and with all respect to Mr. Sichel we feel he might have made a happier choice. His comments on Chesterfield, however, as we have already seen,[1] are not always of the most fortunate nature.

The Economy of Human Life. It is perhaps advisable to add here a short note on the authorship of *The Economy of Human Life,* the first part of which has often been attributed to Chesterfield, and is assigned to him in Italian, Spanish and Portuguese translations.[2] Other writers have ascribed it to Robert Dodsley who first published it in 1750.

In *Notes and Queries* (1st Series, vol X, pp. 8, 74, 318) may be found three somewhat violent protests against Chesterfield's being " robbed of the honour of composing this admirable epitome of morals," (p. 8). None of these, however, contains any actual evidence or even argument either in support of Chesterfield's authorship or in disproof of Dodsley's. One writer claims (p. 74) that " the morals and reflections are obviously the same as Chesterfield inculcated in his writings." The general truth of this statement it would be difficult to dispute for the simple reason that these " reflections," expressed in semi-biblical language, are as ethically unimpeachable as they are commonplace in character, and can be regarded as consistent with those of nearly every accepted teacher of morals who has ever lived. With regard, however, to the subject of Woman and sex morality in general, the reflections Chesterfield inculcated in his writings sink to a distinctly lower ethical level than and are by no means " obviously the same " as those expressed in the *Economy of Human Life.*[3]

In short, there seems no satisfactory evidence to prove that Chesterfield was responsible for the book—Maty and Horace Walpole are both silent on the point—and for our part we find it impossible to believe that he could have written anything so unoriginal in substance and conventional in manner.

---

[1] Pp. 172–173 *ante.*

[2] See the *Dictionary of National Biography,* where it is assigned definitely to Chesterfield in the articles both on him and on Dodsley.

[3] Contrast, for example, the following passage from the chapter on " Woman " with the sentiments expressed in Chesterfield's letter to A. C. Stanhope of October 12, 1765, quoted on pp. 176–177 *ante.* " Remember that thou art made man's reasonable companion, not the slave of his passion ; the end of thy being is not merely to gratify his loose desire, but to assist him in the toils of life, to sooth him with thy tenderness, and recompense his care with soft endearments."

VIII

ELEVEN SELECTED ESSAYS

" COMMON SENSE "

Saturday, Feb. 11, 1738.   No. 54.[1]

" Ne vitam transeant, veluti pecora ; quae natura prona, atque ventri obedientia finxit."—*Sallust.*

[Lest they should pass their time like the beasts, which are by nature disposed to grovel upon this earth, and be slaves to their bellies.]

TASTE is now the fashionable word of the fashionable world. Every thing must be done with taste : that is settled ; but where and what that taste is, is not quite so certain, for, after all the pains I have taken to find out what was meant by the word, and whether those who use it oftnest had any clear idea annexed to it, I have only been able negatively to discover that they do not mean their own natural taste ; but, on the contrary, that they have sacrificed it to an imaginary one, of which they can give no account. They build houses in taste, which they can't live in with conveniency ; [2] they suffer with impatience the music they pretend to hear with rapture, and they even eat nothing they like, for the sake of eating in taste.

[1] Of this essay Dr. G. S. Marr observes, " This is the kind of essay that is too seldom given, but is just right both in style and manner. It is light and amusing, and yet has an ulterior purpose in view which is made abundantly clear as the paper draws to a close."—*The Periodical Essayists of the Eighteenth Century,* p. 101.

[2] An allusion to the house built by the Earl of Burlington for Field-Marshal Wade in Burlington Street, concerning which Horace Walpole wrote to George Montagu as follows : " I went yesterday to see Marshal Wade's house which is selling by auction; it is worse contrived on the inside than is conceivable, all to humour the beauty of the front. My Lord Chesterfield said that to be sure he could not live in it, but intended to take the house over against it to look at it."—May 18th, 1748.

Maty relates that Chesterfield on seeing the house said to Wade : " If I had your house I would hire the opposite one to live in, and enjoy the prospect." Vol. I, *Miscellaneous Pieces,* p. 84. See also Ernst p. 168 ; *Wit and Wisdom of Lord Chesterfield,* p. 192 ; Cunningham's *Handbook of London,* p. 140 ; *Round about Piccadilly,* p. 78.

" Not for himself, he sees, or hears, or eats,
Artists must chuse his pictures, music, meats."

Pope.[1]

It is certain the Commandments, now so much neglected, if not abrogated, might be observed with much less self-denial, than these imaginary laws of taste, to which so exact and scrupulous an obedience is paid.

I take taste, when not used for the sensation of the palate, which is its proper signification, to be a metaphor to express that judgment each man forms to himself of those things, which are not contained in any certain rules, and which admit of no demonstration ; thus circles and equilateral triangles allow of no taste, they must be as they are ; but the colors they are drawn in, or the materials they are made of, depend upon fancy or taste.—In building, there are certain necessary rules founded upon nature, as, that the stronger must support the weaker, etc., but the ornamental and convenient parts are the objects of taste. Hence arises the propriety of the metaphor, because taste in everything is undetermined and personal, as in the palate and all our other senses ; nay, even our minds are as differently affected as our palates, by the same things, when those things are not of a nature to be ascertained and demonstrated.

However, this right of tasting for one's self, which seems to be the natural privilege of mankind, is now totally surrendered even in the proper sense of the word ; and if a man would be well received in good company, he must eat, though with reluctance, according to the laws of some eminent glutton at Paris, promulgated here by the last-imported French cook, wishing all the while within himself, that he durst avow his natural taste for good native beef and pudding.[2]

---

[1] *Moral Essays*, Epistle IV, 5, 6.

[2] Chesterfield apparently did not himself conform to these excellent sentiments. In a letter from Madame du Boccage (see p. 155 n. 1 *ante*) to her sister, written during her stay in England (twelve years after the date of this article), we find the following interesting commentary on French cooking.

" You know what high favour Voltaire and Montesquieu are in with the English ; yesterday we drank their healths at the Earl of Chesterfield's, after a meal which was by no means philosophical, that is to say frugal : this learned Nobleman has the misfortune of having a *French* cook. Noblemen, in all probability by the advice of Physicians, whose interest it is to destroy their stomachs, have recourse to these poisoners. Our senseless luxury will by degrees corrupt all nations, but we shall not see them in the

The absurdity, as well as the real ill consequences, of this prevailing affectation, has, I confess, excited my wrath; and I resolved that the nobility and gentry of this kingdom should not go on to ruin their fortunes and constitutions, without hearing at least the representations and admonitions of common sense.

Eating, itself, seems to me, to be rather a subject of humiliation than of pride, since the imperfection of our nature appears in the daily necessity we lie under of recruiting it in that manner. So that one would think the only care of a rational being should be, to repair his decaying fabric as substantially and as cheap as possible. But the present fashion is directly contrary : and eating, now, is the greatest pride, business, and expence of life, and that, too, not to support, but to destroy nature.

The frugal meal was antiently the time of unbending the mind by chearful and improving conversation, and the table-talk of ingenious men has been thought worth transmitting to posterity. The meal is now at once the most frivolous and most serious part of life. The mind is bent to the utmost, and all the attention exerted, for what ? The critical examination of compound dishes : and if any two or three people happen to start some useful or agreeable subject of conversation, they are soon interrupted, and overpowered by the extatic interjections of, " Excellent ! Exquisite ! Delicious ! Pray taste this, you never eat a better thing in your life.   Is that good ? Is it tender ? Is it seasoned enough ? Would it have been better so ? " Of such wretched stuff as this does the present table-talk wholly consist, in open defiance of all conversation and common sense. I could heartily wish that a collection of it were to be published for the honour and glory of the performers ; but for want of that, I shall give my readers a short specimen of the most ingenious table-talk I have lately heard carried on with most wit and spirit.

My lord, having tasted and duly considered the *Bechamele*, shook his head, and then offered as his opinion to the company, that the garlick was not enough concealed, but earnestly desired to know their sentiments, and begged they would taste it with attention.

The company, after proper deliberation, replied that

they were of his lordship's opinion, and that the garlick did indeed distinguish itself too much : but the *maître d'hôtel* interposing, represented that they were now stronger than ever in garlick at Paris ; upon which the company one and all said that altered the case.

My lord, having sagaciously smelt at the breech of a rabbit, wiped his nose, gave a shrug of some dissatisfaction, and then informed the company that it was not absolutely a bad one, but that he heartily wished it had been kept a day longer. " Ay," said Sir Thomas, with an emphasis, " a rabbit must be kept." " And with the guts in too," added the colonel, " or the devil could not eat it." Here the *maître d'hôtel* again interposed, and said that they eat their rabbits much sooner now than they used to do at Paris. " Are you sure of that ? " said my lord, with some vivacity. " Yes," replied the *maître d'hôtel*, " the cook had a letter about it last night." " I am not sorry for that," rejoined my lord ; " for, to tell you the truth, I naturally love to eat my meat before it stinks." The rest of the company, and even the colonel himself, confessed the same.

This ingenious and edifying kind of conversation continued, without the least interruption from common sense, through four courses which lasted four hours, till the company could neither swallow nor utter any thing more.

A very great person among the antients was very properly asked if he was not ashamed to play so well upon the fiddle ? And one may surely with as much reason ask these illustrious moderns if they are not ashamed of being such good cooks.

It is really not to be imagined with what profound knowledge and erudition our men of quality now treat these culinary subjects, and I cannot but hope that such excellent critics will at last turn authors themselves ; nay, I daily expect to see a digest of the whole art of cookery by some person of honor.[1]

I cannot help hinting, by the way, to these accurate kitchen critics, that it does not become them to be facetious and satyrical upon those dissertations which ladies sometimes hold upon their dress, the subject being by no means so low nor so trifling.

---

[1] " The Duc de Nevers, father of the Duc de Nivernois, did actually publish a book on cookery."—Horace Walpole's MS. note in Maty, vol. I, *Miscellaneous Pieces*, p. 87.

Though such a degree of affected gluttony, accompanied with such frivolous discourses, is pardonable in those who are little superior to the animals they devour, and who are only *fruges consumere nati*, I am surprized and hurt when I see men of parts fall into it, since it not only suspends the exercise of their parts for the present, but impairs them, together with their health, for the future ; and if fools could contrive, I should think they had contrived this method of bringing men of sense down to them ; for it is certain, that when a company is thus gorged, glutted, and loaded, there is not the least difference between the most stupid and the wittiest man in it.

> What life in all that ample body, say
> What heavenly particle inspires the clay ?
> The soul subsides, and wickedly inclines
> To seem but mortal even in sound divines.
>
> *Pope.*[1]

Though an excess in wine is highly blameable, it is surely much more pardonable, as the progressive steps to it are chearful, animating, and seducing : the melancholy are for a while relieved, the grave are enlivened, and the witty and the gay seem almost inspired ; whereas in eating, after nature is once satisfied, which she soon is, every additional morsel carries dulness and stupidity along with it. Moreover, these glorious toils are crowned with the just rewards of all chronical distempers ; the gout, the stone, the scurvy, and the palsy are the never-failing trophies of their achievements. Were these honors, like simple knighthood, only to be enjoyed by those who had merited them, it would be no great matter ; but unfortunately, like baronetship, they descend to and visit their innocent children. It is already very easy to distinguish at sight the puny son of a compound *entremets*, from the lusty offspring of beef and pudding : and I am persuaded, the next generation of the nobility will be a race of pale-faced, spindle-shanked Lilliputians, the most vigorous of whom will not come up to an abortion of John of Gaunt's. Nor does the mischief even stop here, for as the men of fashion frequently condescend to communicate themselves

---

[1] *Imitations of Horace*, Satire II, Book 2. The quotation becomes more intelligible if it is begun with the two preceding lines :—
"How pale each worshipful and rev'rend guest
Rise from a clergy or a city feast ! "

Q

to families of inferior rank, but better constitutions, they enervate those families too, and present them with sickly helpless children, to the great prejudice of the trade and manufactures of this kingdom.

Some people have imagined, and not without some degree of probability, that animal food communicates its qualities with its nourishment. In this supposition it was, that Achilles, who was not only born, and bred, but fed up too for a Hero, was nourished with the marrow of lions ; and we all know what a fine lion he turned out at last. Should this rule hold, it must be a melancholy reflection to consider, that the principal ingredients in the food of our principal nobility, is essence of swine.

The Egyptians, who were a wise nation, thought so much depended upon diet, that they dieted their kings, and prescribed by law both the quality and quantity of their food. It is much to be lamented, that those bills of fare are not preserved to this time, since they might have been of singular use in all monarchical governments ; but it is reasonable to be conjectured, from the wisdom of that people, that they allowed their kings no aliments of a bilious or a choleric nature, and only such as sweetened their juices, cooled their blood, and enlivened their faculties, if they had any.

The common people of this kingdom are dieted by laws ; for, by an act passed about two years ago, not less advantageous to the crown than to the people, the use of a liquor, which destroyed both their minds and their bodies, was wisely prohibited, and, by repeated Acts of Parliament their food is reduced to a very modest and wholesome proportion. Surely then the nobility and gentry of the kingdom deserve some attention too, not so much indeed for their own sakes, as for the sake of the public, which is in some measure under their care : for if a porter, when full of gin, could not do his business, I am apt to think a privy counsellor, when loaded with four courses, will but bungle at his.

Suppose, for instance, a number of persons, not over-lively at best, should meet of an evening to concert and deliberate upon public measures of the utmost consequence, grunting under the load and repletion of the strongest meats, panting almost in vain for breath, but quite in vain for thought, and reminded only of their existence by the unsavory returns of an olio ; what good could be expected from such a consultation ?[1] The best one could hope for would be that they were only assembled for shew, and not for use ; not to propose or advise, but silently to submit to the orders of some one man there, who, feeding like a rational creature, might have the use of his understanding.

I would therefore recommend it to the consideration of the legislature, whether it may not be necessary to pass an act to restrain the licentiousness of eating, and assign certain diets to certain ranks and stations. I would humbly suggest the strict vegetable as the properest ministerial diet, being exceedingly tender of those faculties in which the public is so highly interested, and very unwilling they should be clogged or incumbered.

But I do most seriously recommend it to those who, from their rank and situation in life, settle the fashions, and whose examples will in these sorts of things always be followed, that they will by their example, which will be more effectual than any law, not only put a stop to, but reform, the ridiculous, expensive, and pernicious luxury of tables ; they are the people whom all inferior ranks imitate, as far as they are able, and commonly much farther. It is their fatal example that has seduced the gentry, and people of smaller fortunes, into this nasty and ruinous excess. Let their example then, at last, reclaim them ; let those who are able to bear the expence, and known not to grudge it, give the first blow to this extravagant folly ; let them avow their own natural taste, for nature is in everything plain and simple, and gratify it decently, at a frugal and wholesome table, instead of purchasing stupidity and distempers at the expence of their time and their estates. And they may depend upon it that a fashion so convenient to the fortunes and the constitutions of their fellow subjects, will chearfully be followed, and universally prevail, to the great advantage of the public.

[1] " The Cabinet Council. The Duke of Newcastle had a famous French cook called *Cloe*."—Horace Walpole's MS. note in Maty, vol. I, *Miscellaneous Pieces*, p. 89. Upon this Ernst makes the following comment :—" But Lord Chesterfield could appreciate the favourable influence on the mind to be obtained by good living. Writing from the Hague to the Duke of Newcastle, on March 20, 1745, he says :—' Mr. Van de Poll's son, of Amsterdam, goes to England by the next packett boat. Hop will present him at Court and to your Grace. I beg you will let Chloe stuff him once or twice, and let him know that I procur'd him the stuffing . . .' *Newcastle Papers*, 804, f. 249."—*Life of Lord Chesterfield*, p. 170.

"Common Sense"

Saturday, Nov. 11, 1738. No. 93.

EVERY age has its fashionable follies, as well as its fashionable vices : but, as follies are more numerous than vices, they change oftner, and every four or five years produce a new one. I will indulge my fellow-subjects in the full enjoyment of such follies as are inoffensive in themselves, and in their consequences. Men, as well as children, must have their play-things : but when *hae nugae seria ducunt in mala,* I shall take the liberty to interpose, represent, and censure.

Fashion, which is always at first the offspring of little minds, and the child of levity, gains strength and support by the great number of its relations, till at length it is received and adopted by better understandings, who either conform to it to avoid singularity, or who are surprized into it, from want of attention to an object, which they look upon as indifferent in itself, and so dignify and establish the folly.

This is the case of a present prevailing extravagancy, I mean the absurd and ridiculous imitation of the French, which is now become the epidemical distemper of this kingdom : not confined to those only from whom one expects no better, but it has even infected those whom one should have thought much above such weaknesses ; and I behold with indignation the sturdy conquerors of France shrunk and dwindled into the imperfect mimics, or ridiculous *caricaturas*, of all its levity. The travesty is universal ; poor England produces nothing fit to eat, or drink, or wear. Our cloaths, our furniture, nay our food too, all is to come from France, and I am credibly informed that a poulterer at Calais now actually supplies our polite tables with half their provisions.

I don't mean to undervalue the French ; I know their merit ; they are a chearful, industrious, ingenious, polite people, and have many things in which I wish we did imitate them. But, like true mimics, we only ape their imperfections, and awkwardly copy those parts which all reasonable Frenchmen themselves contemn in the originals.

If this folly went no farther than disguising both our meats and our selves in the French modes, I should bear it with more patience, and content myself with representing only to my country folks that the one would make them sick, and the other ridiculous : but when even the materials for the folly are to be brought over from France too, it becomes a much more serious consideration. Our trade and manufactures are at stake, and what seems at first sight only very silly, is in truth a great national evil, and a piece of civil immorality.

There is surely some obedience due to the laws of the land, which strictly prohibit the importation of these fooleries, and, independently of those laws, there is a strong obligation upon every member of a society to contribute all he can to the benefit of that society from which he himself receives so many advantages : these are moral duties, if I know what moral duties are, but I presume they are awkward ones, and not fit to restrain the un-bounded fancy of fine gentlemen and fine ladies in their dress and manner of living ; and it is, certainly, much more reasonable, that our trade should decay, and our manufacturers starve, than that people of taste and condition should content themselves with the wretched produce of their own country.

Methinks there is something very mean in being such avowed plagiaries, and I wonder the British spirit will submit to it. Why will our countrymen thus distrust themselves ? Let them exert their own genius and invention, and I make no doubt but they will be able to produce as many original extravagancies, as all the mareschals of France can do. How much more glorious would it be for those ladies who establish the fashion here, to consider at the same time their own dignity and the public good ! Let them not servilely copy or translate French edicts, but let them enact original laws of their own. I look upon the birth-day cloaths of a fine woman to be the statute of dress for that year : and, by the way, the only statute which is complied with. I therefore humbly intreat that it may be enacted in English. Seriously, if three or four ladies, at the head of the fashion, would but value them-selves upon being cloathed entirely with the manufactures of their own country, and from the plenitude of their own power, pronounce all foreign manufactures ungenteel, awkward, and frippery, the legions, who dress under their banner, would soon be as much ashamed of dressing against their country, as they are now of being thought even natives of it. This would be moreover the real imitation of the French, who like nothing but their own.

What I have said with relation to my fair country-women holds equally true as to my fine countrymen, to whom I cannot help hinting, over and above, that they make very ridiculous Frenchmen, and might be very valuable Englishmen. Every nation has its distinguishing mark and characteristic. If we have a solidity, which the French have not, they most certainly have an elasticity, which we have not ; and the imitation is mutually awkward. Horace justly calls imitators *servum pecus* ; and, to do him justice, he is himself an original. If my country-men would be thought to be conversant with Horace, as they most of them would be, I am sure they will find in him no instance of foppery, luxury, or profusion.

We have heard with satisfaction that some considerable persons in this kingdom, from a just and becoming concern for our distressed tradesmen and manufacturers, discountenance, as far as possible, this pernicious folly. And, though I make no doubt but, at the end of this long mourning,[1] by which trade has suffered so immensely, some measures will be taken to this effect elsewhere, this would be the most likely way of eradicating the evil, and, as it is by no means unprecedented to annex certain conditions to the honor and privilege of subjects appearing in the presence of their sovereign, surely none can be juster nor more reasonable than that they should conform to the laws, and contribute to the good of their country.

But the mischief does not stop here neither ; for now we are not content with receiving our fashions and the materials for them from France, but we even export ourselves in order to import them. The matter, it seems, is of too great consequence to trust to hearsay evidence for ; but we must go ourselves to view those great originals, be able to say, of our own knowledge, how such a glutton eats, and how such a fool dresses, and return loaded with the prohibited tinsel and frippery of the *Palais*.[2] Half the private families in England take a trip, as they call it,

---

[1] " For Queen Caroline who had died on the 20th of November in the previous year." (Mahon's note.) See pp. 69–70 *ante*.

[2] " The place where the courts of justice and parliament are held at Paris, answering to Westminster Hall. Milliners and toymen are allowed to have shops and stalls ; and know how to dispose of their trinkets, to young lawyers, foreigners, and other persons, whom curiosity or idleness draws to this place."—Maty's note.

every summer to Paris ; and I am assured that near four hundred thousand pounds have been remitted thither in one year to supply this extravagancy. Should this rage continue, the act of parliament, proposed in one of Mr. Congreve's comedies, to prohibit the exportation of fools, will in reality become necessary. Travelling is, unquestionably, a very proper part of the education of our youth ; and, like our bullion, I would allow them to be exported. But people of a certain age beyond refining, and once stamped here, like our coin, should be confined within the kingdom. The impressions they have received make them current here, but obstruct their currency any where else, and they only return disguised, defaced, and probably much lessened in the weight.

The sober and well-regulated family of a country gentleman is a very valuable part of the community ; they keep up good neighbourhood by decent hospitality, they promote good manners by their example, and encourage labour and industry by their consumption. But when once they run French, if I may use the expression, and are to be polished by this trip to Paris, I will venture to assure them that they may, from that day, date their being ridiculous for ever afterwards. They are laughed at in France, for not being like the French, they are laughed at here, for endeavouring to be like them ; and, what is worse, their mimicking their luxury brings them into their necessity, which ends in a most compleat imitation indeed, of their mean and servile dependance upon the court.

I could point out to these itinerant spirits a much shorter, less expensive, and more effectual method of travelling and frenchifying themselves, which is, if they would but travel to *old Soho*, and stay two or three months in *le quartier des Grecs ;* [1] lodgings and *legumes* are very cheap there, and the people very civil to strangers. There, too, they might possibly get acquainted with some French people, which they never do at Paris, and, it may be, learn a little French, which they never do in France neither: and I appeal to any one, who has seen those venerable personages of both sexes, of the refugees, if they are not

---

[1] " The place where most of the descendants of the French refugees then lived. Their chapel, in which divine service was, and still continues to be, performed according to the rites of the Church of England, had formerly belonged to a congregation of Greeks, and has given its name to all the *environs* of Soho square."—Maty's note.

infinitely more genteel, easier, and better dressed in the French manner, than any of their modern English mimics.

As for our fair countrywomen in particular, they are so valuable, so beautiful a part of our own produce, and [one] in which we so eminently excel all other nations, that I can by no means allow of their exportation : they are surely, if I may say so, much more valuable commodities than wool or fuller's earth, the exportation of which is so strictly prohibited by our laws, lest foreigners should have the manufacturing of them ; which reasoning holds stronger, upon many accounts, in this case, than in the two others.

Let it not be urged, that the loss arising from these follies is but a trifling object with relation to our trade in general. This for aught I know, might have been true some years ago : but such is the present unhappy state of our trade, that I doubt no object is now a trifling one, or below the attention of every individual. After six-and-twenty years peace, we labour under every one of the taxes which subsisted at the conclusion of the last expensive war, without reckoning some new ones laid on since ; while other nations, gradually eased of that burthen, under-work and under-sell us in every foreign market. The last valuable part of our trade, how has it been attacked for these many years ! and how has it been protected ! It would be unreasonable to expect that the administration, ingrossed by much greater cares, should attend to so trifling a consideration as trade ; nor can one wonder that it has intirely escaped the attention of parliaments, when one considers that so many affairs of a much higher nature have, of late, so advantageously employed them. But it therefore becomes more peculiarly the care of every individual ; and if, from the reformation only of those follies here mentioned, five or six hundred thousand pounds a year may be saved to the nation, which I am convinced is the case, how incumbent is it upon every one to sacrifice a little private folly to so much public good ! It may at least be a reprieve to our trade and manufactures from that ruin which, at best, seems to be too near them ; and possibly, too, the examples of some private people may, at least, shame others, whose more immediate care it ought to be, into some degree of attention to what they have so long seemed to neglect and despise.

" The World "

December 6, 1753. No. 49.

Though I am an old fellow, I am neither sour nor silly enough yet to be a snarling *laudator temporis acti,* and to hate or despise the present age because it *is* the present. I cannot, like many of my contemporaries, rail at the wonderful degeneracy and corruption of these times, nor, by sneering compliments to the ingenious, the sagacious moderns, intimate that they have not common sense. I really do not think that the present age is marked out by any new and distinguished vices and follies unknown to former ages. On the contrary, I am apt to suspect that human nature was always very like what it is at this day, and that men, from the time of my great progenitor down to this moment, have always had in them the same seeds of virtue and vice, wisdom and folly, of which only the modes have varied from climate, education, and a thousand other conspiring causes. . . .[1]

With modes, the signification of words also varies and, in the course of these variations, convey ideas very different from those, which they were originally intended to express. I could give numberless instances of this kind, but at present I shall content myself with this single one.

The word honour, in its proper signification, doubtless implies the united sentiments of virtue, truth, and justice, carried by a generous mind beyond those mere moral obligations which the laws require or can punish the violation of. A true man of honour will not content himself with the literal discharge of the duties of a man and a citizen ; he raises and dignifies them into magnanimity. He gives where he may with justice refuse ; he forgives where he may with justice resent, and his whole conduct is directed by the noble sentiments of his own unvitiated heart ; surer and more scrupulous guides than the laws of the land, which, being calculated for the generality of mankind, must necessarily be more a restraint upon vices in general, than an invitation and reward of particular virtues. But these extensive and compound notions of honour have been long contracted and reduced to the single one of personal courage. Among the Romans,

---

[1] A long passage of a topical nature, dealing with the insufficient circulation of the *World,* is here omitted.

honour meant no more than contempt of dangers and death in the service, whether just or unjust, of their country. Their successors and conquerors the Goths and Vandals, who did not deal much in complex ideas, simplified those of honour, and reduced them to this plain and single one, of fighting for fighting's sake, upon any or all, no matter what, occasions.

Our present mode of honour is something more compounded, as will appear by the true character which I shall now give of a fashionable man of honour.

A gentleman,[1] which is now the genteel synonymous term for a man of honour, must, like his Gothic ancestors, be ready for and rather desirous of single combat. And if by a proper degree of wrong-headedness he provokes it, he is only so much the more jealous of his honour, and more of a gentleman.

He may lie with impunity, if he is neither detected nor accused of it, for it is not the lie he tells, but the lie he is told of, that dishonours him. In that case he demonstrates his veracity by his sword, or his pistol, and either kills or is killed with the greatest honour.

He may abuse and starve his own wife, daughters or sisters, and he may seduce those of other men, particularly his friends, with inviolate honour, because, as Sir John Brute [2] very justly observes, *he wears a sword*.

By the laws of honour he is not obliged to pay his servants or his tradesmen ; for, as they are a pack of scoundrels, they cannot without insolence demand their due of a gentleman ; but he must punctually pay his gaming debts to the sharpers who have cheated him ; for those debts are really debts of honour.

He lies under one disagreeable restraint ; for he must not cheat at play, unless in a horse-match ; but then he may with great honour defraud in an office, or betray a trust.

In public affairs, he may, not only with honour, but even with some degree of lustre, be in the same session a turbulent patriot, opposing the best measures, and a servile courtier, promoting the worst ; provided a very

---

[1] A gentleman is every man who, with a tolerable suit of clothes, a sword by his side, and a watch and snuff-box in his pockets, asserts himself to be a gentleman, swears with energy that he will be treated as such, and that he will cut the throat of any man who presumes to say the contrary.

[2] In *The Provoked Wife* of Vanbrugh.

lucrative consideration be known to be the motive of his conversion : for in that case the point of honour turns singly upon the *quantum*.

From these premises, which the more they are considered the truer they will be found, it appears that there are but two things which a man of the nicest honour may not do ; which are declining single combat, and cheating at play. Strange, that virtue should be so difficult, and honour, its superior, so easy to attain to !

The uninformed herd of mankind are governed by words and names, which they implicitly receive without either knowing or asking their meaning. Even the philosophical and religious controversies, for the last three or four thousand years, have turned much more upon words and names, unascertained and misunderstood, than upon things fairly stated. The polite world, to save time and trouble, receive, adapt and use words in the signification of the day ; not having leisure nor inclination to examine and analyse them ; and thus, often misled by sounds, and not always secured by sense, they are hurried into fatal errors, which they do not give their understandings fair play enough to prevent.

In explaining words, therefore, and bringing them back to their true signification, one may sometimes happen to expose and explode those errors, which the abuse of them both occasions and protects. May that be the good fortune of this day's paper ! How many unthinking and unhappy men really take themselves to be men of honour, upon these mistaken ideas of that word ! And how fatal to others, especially the young and unexperienced, is their example and success in the world ! I could heartily wish that some good dramatic poet would exhibit at full length, and in lively colours, upon the stage, this modish character of a man of honour, of which I have but slightly and hastily chalked the outlines. Upon such a subject I am apt to think that a good poet might be more useful than a good preacher, as perhaps his audiences would be more numerous, and his matter more attended to. Besides,

> "Segnius irritant animos, demissa per aurem,
> Quam quæ sunt oculis subjecta fidelibus, et quæ
> Ipse sibi tradit spectator."[1]

[1] Horace, *De Arte Poetica*, 180–183.

P.S. To prevent mistakes, I must observe that there is a great difference between a *Man of honour*, and a *Person of honour*. By *Persons of honour*, were meant, in the latter end of the last century, bad authors and poets of noble birth, who were but just not fools enough to prefix their names in great letters to the prologues, epilogues and sometimes even the plays with which they entertained the public. But now that our nobility are too generous to interfere in the trade of us poor professed authors, or to eclipse our performances by the distinguished and superior excellency and lustre of theirs ; the meaning at present of a person of honour is reduced to the simple idea of a person of illustrious birth.

"THE WORLD"

February 20, 1755. No. 112.

A LATE noble author has most justly and elegantly defined custom to be " The result of the passions and prejudices of many, and of the designs of a few ; the ape of reason who usurps her seat, exercises her power, and is obeyed by mankind in her stead." [1]

This definition enables us to account for the various absurd and wicked customs which have severally and successively prevailed in all ages and countries, and also for those which unfortunately prevail in this ; for they may all be traced up to the passions and prejudices of many and to the designs of a few.

It is certain, however, that there has not been a time when the prerogative of human reason was more freely asserted, nor errors and prejudices more ably attacked and exposed by the best writers, than now. But may not the principle of enquiry and detection be carried too far, or at least made too general ? And should not a prudent discrimination of cases be attended to ?

A prejudice is by no means necessarily (though generally thought so) an error. On the contrary, it may be a most unquestioned truth, though it be still a prejudice in those who, without any examination, take it upon trust, and entertain it by habit.

There are even some prejudices, founded upon error,

[1] Lord Bolingbroke's Letter to Lord Bathurst, " Of the True Use of Retirement and Study."—*Bolingbroke's Works*, Edit. 1809, IV, p. 163.

which ought to be connived at, or perhaps encouraged ; their effects being more beneficial to society than their detection can possibly be. Human reason, even when improved by knowledge, and undisturbed by the passions, is not an infallible, though it is our best, guide : but unimproved by knowledge, and adulterated by passion, it becomes the most dangerous one ; constituting obstinate wrongheadedness, and dignifying, nay, almost sanctifying, error.

The bulk of mankind have neither leisure nor knowledge sufficient to reason right : why then should they be taught to reason at all ? Will not honest instinct prompt, and wholesome prejudices guide them much better than half-reasoning ?

The power of the magistrate to punish bad, and the authority of those of superior rank to set good examples, properly exerted, would probably be of more diffusive advantage to society than the most learned theological, philosophical, moral, and casuistical dissertations. As for instance :—

An honest cobbler in his stall, thinks and calls himself a good protestant ; and, if he lives at the city end of the town, probably goes to his parish church on Sundays. Would it be honest, would it be wise, to say to this cobbler,

" Friend, you only think yourself a member of the Church of England ; but in reality you are not one, since you are only so from habit and prejudice, not from examination and reflection. But study the ablest controversial writers of the popish and reformed churches ; read Bellarmine, Chillingworth, and Stillingfleet, and then you may justly call yourself, what in truth you are not now, a protestant."?

Should our mender of shoes follow this advice (which I hope he would not), a useful cobbler would most certainly be lost, in a useless polemic, and a scurvy logician.

It would be just the same thing in morals. Our cobbler received from his parents, that best and shortest of all Christian and moral precepts, " Do as you would be done by." He adopted it without much examination, and scrupulously practised it in general, though with some few exceptions perhaps in his own trade. But should some philosopher, for the advancement of truth and knowledge, assure this cobbler, " That his honesty was mere prejudice and habit, because he had never sufficiently considered the relation and fitness of things, nor contemplated the beauty of virtue ; but that if he would carefully study the Characteristics, the Moral Philosopher, and thirty or forty volumes more upon that subject, he might then, and not till then, justly call himself an honest man " ; what would become of the honesty of the cobbler after this useful discovery, I do not know ; but this I very well know, that he should no longer be *my* cobbler.

I shall borrow him in two instances more, and then leave him to his honest, useful, home-spun prejudices, which half-knowledge and less reasoning will, I hope, never tempt him to lay aside.

My cobbler is also a politician. He reads the first news-paper he can get, desirous to be informed of the state of affairs in Europe, and of the street robberies in London. He has not, I presume, analysed the interests of the respective countries of Europe, nor deeply considered those of his own : still less is he systematically informed of the political duties of a citizen and a subject. But his heart and his habits supply those defects. He glows with zeal for the honour and prosperity of old England, he will fight for it, if there be occasion, and drink to it perhaps a little too often, and too much. However, is it not to be wished that there were in this country six millions of such honest and zealous, though uninformed, citizens ?

All these unreflected and unexamined opinions of our cobbler, though prejudices in him, are in themselves undoubted and demonstrable truths, and ought therefore to be cherished even in their coarsest dress. But I shall now give an instance of a common prejudice in this country, which is the result of error, and which yet I believe no man in his senses would desire should be exposed or removed.

Our honest cobbler is thoroughly convinced, as his forefathers were for many centuries, that one Englishman can beat three Frenchmen ; and, in that persuasion, he would by no means decline the trial. Now, though in my own private opinion, deduced from physical principles, I am apt to believe that one Englishman could beat no more than two Frenchmen of equal strength and size with himself, I should, however, be very unwilling to undeceive him of that useful and sanguine error, which certainly made his countrymen triumph in the fields of Poictiers and Crecy.

But there are prejudices of a very different nature from

these ; prejudices not only founded on original error, but that give birth and sanction to the most absurd, extravagant, impious, and immoral customs.

Honour, that sacred name, which ought to mean the spirit, the supererogation of virtue, is, by custom, profaned, reduced, and shrunk to mean only a readiness to fight a duel upon either a real or an imaginary affront, and not to cheat at play. No vices nor immoralities whatsoever blast this fashionable character, but rather, on the contrary, dignify and adorn it : and what should banish a man from all society, recommends him in general to the best. He may, with great honour, starve the tradesmen, who by their industry supply not only his wants but his luxury. He may debauch his friend's wife, daughter, or sister ; he may, in short, unboundedly gratify every appetite, passion, and interest, and scatter desolation round him, if he be but ready for single combat, and a scrupulous observer of all the moral obligations of a gamester.

These are the prejudices for wit to ridicule, for satire to lash, for the rigour of the law to punish, and (which would be the most effectual of all) for fashion to discountenance and proscribe. And these shall in their turns be the subjects of some future papers.[1]

" THE WORLD "
March 6, 1755. No. 114.

THE notion of Birth, as it is commonly called and established by custom, is also the manifest result " of the prejudices of the many, and of the designs of a few." [2] It is the child of Pride and Folly, coupled together by that industrious pander Self-love. It is surely the strongest instance and the weakest prop of human vanity. If it means any thing, it means a long lineal descent from a founder, whose industry or good fortune, whose merit, or perhaps whose guilt, has enabled his posterity to live useless to society, and to transmit to theirs their pride and their patrimony. However, this extravagant notion, this chimerical advantage, the effect of blind chance, where prudence and option cannot even pretend

[1] The next number of the World Chesterfield devoted to a satire on duelling.
[2] See p. 236 ante.

to have the least share, is that fly which, by a kind of Egyptian superstition, custom all over Europe has deified, and at whose tawdry shrine good sense, good manners, and good nature are daily sacrificed.

The vulgar distinction between people of birth and people of no birth will probably puzzle the critics and antiquarians of the thirtieth or fortieth centuries, when, in their judicious and laborious researches into the customs and manners of these present times, they shall have reason to suppose that in the sixteenth, seventeenth and eighteenth centuries, the island of Great Britain was inhabited by two sorts of people, some born, but the much greater number unborn. The fact will appear so incredible that it will certainly be believed ; the only difficulty will be how to account for it ; and that, as it commonly does, will engross the attention of the learned. The case of Cadmus's men will doubtless be urged as a case in point to prove the possibility of the thing, and the truth of it will be confirmed by the records of the University of Oxford, where it will appear that an unborn person, called for that reason " Terrae Filius ", annually entertained that university with an oration in the theatre.

I therefore take with pleasure this opportunity of explaining and clearing up this difficulty to my remotest successors in the republic of letters, by giving them the true meaning of the several expressions of great birth, noble birth, birth, and no birth at all.

Great and illustrious birth is ascertained and authenticated by a pedigree carefully preserved in the family, which takes at least an hour's time to unroll, and when unrolled, discloses twenty inter-marriages of valiant and puissant Geoffreys and Hildebrands, with as many chaste and pious Blanches and Mauds, before the Conquest, not without here and there a dash of the Plantagenets. But if unfortunately the insolent worms should have devoured the pedigree as well as the persons of the illustrious family, that defect may be supplied by the authentic records of the herald's office, that inestimable repository of good sense and useful knowledge. If this great birth is graced with a peerage, so much the better, but if not, it is no great matter ; for being so solid a good in itself, it wants no borrowed advantages, and is unquestionably the most pleasing sentiment that a truly generous mind is capable of feeling.

Noble birth implies only a peerage in the family. Ancestors are by no means necessary for this kind of birth ; the patent is the midwife of it, and the very first descent is noble. The family arms, however modern, are dignified by the coronet and mantle ; but the family livery is sometimes, for very good reasons, laid aside.

Birth, singly, and without an epithet, extends, I cannot positively say how far, but negatively, it stops where useful arts and industry begin. Merchants, tradesmen, yeomen, farmers, and ploughmen, are not born, or at least, in so mean a way as not to deserve that name ; and it is perhaps for that reason that their mothers are said to be delivered, rather than brought to bed of them. But baronets, knights, and esquires have the honour of being born.

I must confess that, before I got the key to this fashionable language, I was a good deal puzzled myself with the distinction between birth and no birth ; and having no other guide but my own weak reason, I mistook the matter most grossly. I foolishly imagined that *well-born* meant born with a sound mind in a sound body ; a healthy, strong constitution, joined to a good heart and a good understanding. But I never suspected that it could possibly mean the shrivelled tasteless fruit of an old genealogical tree. I communicated my doubts, and applied for information to my late worthy and curious friend, the celebrated Mrs. Kennon, whose valuable collection of fossils and minerals, lately sold,[1] sufficiently proves her skill and researches in the most recondite parts of nature. She, with that frankness and humanity which were natural to her, assured me that it was all a vulgar error, in which however the nobility and gentry prided themselves : but that in truth she had never observed the children of the quality to be wholesomer or stronger than others, but rather the contrary ; which difference she imputed to certain causes which I shall not here specify. This natural (and, I dare say, to the best of her observation, true) account confirmed me in my former philosophical error.

---

[1] " You would laugh if you saw in the midst of what trumpery I am writing. Two porters have just brought home my purchases from Mrs. Kennon the midwife's sale : Brobdignag combs, old broken pots, pans, and pipkins, a lantern of scraped oyster-shells, scimitars, Turkish pipes, Chinese baskets, etc, etc. My servants think my head is turned : I hope not : it is all to be called the personal estate and moveables of my great-great-grandmother, and to be reposited at Strawberry."—Horace Walpole to H. S. Conway, February 12, 1756.

R

242 CHESTERFIELD AND HIS CRITICS

But still not thoroughly satisfied with it, and thinking that there must be something more in what was so universally valued, I determined to get some farther information by addressing myself to a person of vast, immense, prodigious birth, and descended *atavis regibus*, with whom I have the honour of being acquainted. As he expatiates willingly upon that subject, it was very easy for me to set him agoing upon it, insomuch that upon some few doubts which I humbly suggested to him, he spoke to me in the following manner.

" I believe, Mr. Fitz-Adam, you are not (for no body is) ignorant of the antiquity of my family, which by authentic records I can trace up to King Alfred, some of whose blood runs at this moment in my veins ; and I will not conceal from you that I find infinite inward comfort and satisfaction in that reflection. Let people of no birth laugh as much as they please at these notions ; they are not imaginary ; they are real ; they are solid ; and whoever is well-born is glad that he is so. A merchant, a tradesman, a yeoman, a farmer, and such sort of people, may perhaps have common honesty and vulgar virtues ; but, take my word for it, the more refined and generous sentiments of honour, courage and magnanimity, can only flow in ancient and noble blood. What shall animate a tradesman, or mean-born man to any great and heroic virtues ? Shall it be examples of his ancestors ? He has none. Or shall it be that impure blood that rather stagnates than circulates in his veins ? No ; ancient birth and noble blood are the only true sources of great virtues. This truth appears even among brutes, who we may observe never degenerate, except in cases of mis-alliances with their inferiors. Are not the pedigrees of horses, cocks, dogs, etc., carefully preserved, as the never-failing proofs of their swiftness and courage ? I repeat it again, birth is an inestimable advantage, not to be adequately understood but by those who have it."

My friend was going on, and, to say the truth, growing dull, when I took the liberty of interrupting him by acknowledging that the cogency of his arguments, and the self-evidence of his facts, had entirely removed all my doubts, and convinced me of the unspeakable advantages of illustrious birth ; and unfortunately I added, that my own vanity was greatly flattered by it, in consequence of my being lineally descended from the first man.[1] Upon this my friend looked grave, and seemed rather displeased ; whether from a suspicion that I was jesting, or upon an apprehension that I meant to *out-descend* him, I cannot determine ; for he contented himself with saying, " That is not a necessary consequence neither, Mr. Fitz-Adam, since I have read somewhere or other of pre-adamites, which opinion did not seem to me an absurd one."

Here I took my leave of him, and went home full of reflections upon the astonishing powers of self-love that can extract comfort and pleasure from such groundless, absurd and extravagant prejudices. In all other respects my friend is neither a fool nor a madman, and can talk very rationally upon any rational subject. But such is the inconsistency, both of the human mind and the human heart, that one must not form a general judgment of either, from one glaring error, or one shining excellence.

" THE WORLD "

April 17, 1755. No. 120

MOST people complain of fortune ; few of nature ; and the kinder they think the latter has been to them, the more they murmur at what they call the injustice of the former.

Why have not I the riches, the rank, the power of such and such is the common expostulation with fortune : but why have not I the merit, the talents, the wit, or the beauty of such and such others is a reproach rarely or never made to nature.

The truth is that nature, seldom profuse, and seldom niggardly, has distributed her gifts more equally than she is generally supposed to have done. Education and situations make the great difference. Culture improves, and occasions elicit natural talents. I make no doubt but that there are potentially (if I may use that pedantic

---

[1] *Cf.* " I have had the old Vere pedigree lately in my hands, which derives that house from Lucius Verus ; but I am now grown to bear no descent but my Lord Chesterfield's, who has placed among the portraits of his ancestors two old heads, inscribed *Adam de Stanhope* and *Eve de Stanhope* ; the ridicule is admirable."—Horace Walpole to Mann, September 1, 1750.

word) many Bacons, Lockes, Newtons, Caesars, Cromwells, and Marlboroughs at the ploughtail, behind counters, and, perhaps, even among the nobility ; but the soil must be cultivated, and the seasons favourable, for the fruit to have all its spirit and flavour.

If sometimes our common parent has been a little partial, and not kept the scales quite even ; if one preponderates too much, we throw into the lighter a due counterpoise of vanity, which never fails to set all right. Hence it happens that hardly any one man would, without reserve, and in every particular, change with any other.

Though all are thus satisfied with the dispensations of nature, how few listen to her voice ! How few follow her as their guide ! In vain she points out to us the plain and direct way to truth ; vanity, fancy, affectation, and fashion assume her shape, and wind us through fairy-ground to folly and error.

These deviations from nature are often attended by serious consequences, and always by ridiculous ones : for there is nothing truer than the trite observation, " that people are never ridiculous for being what they really are, but for affecting to appear what they really are not." [1] Affectation is the only source and, at the same time, the only justifiable object of ridicule. No man whatever, be his pretensions what they will, has a natural right to be ridiculous : it is an acquired right, and not to be acquired without some industry ; which perhaps is the reason why so many people are so jealous and tenacious of it.

Even some people's *vices* are not their own, but affected and adopted (though at the same time unenjoyed) in hopes of shining in those fashionable societies, where the reputation of certain vices gives lustre. In these cases, the execution is commonly as awkward, as the design is absurd; and the ridicule equals the guilt.

This calls to my mind a thing that really happened not many years ago.[2] A young fellow of some rank and fortune, just let loose from the university, resolved, in order to make a figure in the world, to assume the shining

[1] " On n'est jamais si ridicule par les qualités que l'on a que par celles que l'on affecte d'avoir."—de la Rochefoucault *Maximes*, cxxxiv. See also Chesterfield's essay on Affectation, *Common Sense*, No. 32.

[2] Chesterfield tells the same story in a letter to his son of May 8, O.S., 1750.—Bradshaw, vol. I, p. 339.

character of, what he called, a rake. By way of learning the rudiments of his intended profession, he frequented the theatres, where he was often drunk, and always noisy. Being one night at the representation of that most absurd play, the *Libertine Destroyed*, he was so charmed with the profligacy of the hero of the piece, that, to the edification of the audience, he swore many oaths that he would be the Libertine *destroyed*. A discreet friend of his, who sat by him, kindly represented to him that to be the *Libertine* was a laudable design, which he greatly approved of ; but that to be the Libertine *destroyed* seemed to him an unnecessary part of his plan, and rather rash. He persisted, however, in his first resolution, and insisted upon being the Libertine, and *destroyed*. Probably he was so ; at least the presumption is in his favour. There are, I am persuaded, so many cases of this nature, that, for my own part, I would desire no greater step towards the reformation of manners for the next twenty years, than that people should have no vices but their own.

The blockhead who affects wisdom, because nature has given him dulness, becomes ridiculous only by his adopted character ; whereas he might have stagnated unobserved in his native mud, or perhaps have engrossed deeds, collected shells, and studied heraldry, or logic, with some success.

The shining coxcomb aims at all, and decides finally upon every thing, because nature has given him pertness. The degree of parts and animal spirits, necessary to constitute that character, if properly applied, might have made him useful in many parts of life : but his affectation and presumption make him useless in most, and ridiculous in all.

The septuagenary fine gentleman might probably, from his long experience and knowledge of the world, be esteemed and respected in the several relations of domestic life, which, at his age, nature points out to him : but he will most ridiculously spin out the rotten thread of his former gallantries. He dresses, languishes, ogles, as he did at five-and-twenty ; and modestly intimates that he is not without a *bonne fortune* ; which *bonne fortune* at last appears to be the prostitute he had long kept (not to himself), whom he marries and owns, because " the poor girl was so fond of him, and so desirous to be made an honest woman."

The sexagenary widow remembers that she was handsome, but forgets that it was thirty years ago, and thinks herself so, or at least very *likeable*, still. The pardonable affectations of her youth and beauty unpardonably continue, increase even with her years, and are doubly exerted, in hopes of concealing the number. All the gaudy, glittering parts of dress, which rather degraded than adorned her beauty in its bloom, now expose to the highest and the justest ridicule her shrivelled or her overgrown carcase. She totters or sweats under the load of her jewels, embroideries, and brocades, which, like so many Egyptian hieroglyphics, serve only to authenticate the venerable antiquity of her august mummy. Her eyes dimly twinkle tenderness, or leer desire ; their language, however inelegant, is intelligible ; and the half-pay captain understands it. He addresses his vows to her vanity, which assures her that they are sincere. She pities him, and prefers him to credit, decency, and every social duty. He tenderly prefers her (though not without some hesitation) to a jail.

Self-love, kept within due bounds, is a natural and useful sentiment. It is, in truth, social love too, as Mr. Pope has very justly observed [1] : it is the spring of many good actions, and of no ridiculous ones. But self-flattery is only the ape or caricatura of self-love, and resembles it no more than is absolutely necessary to heighten the ridicule. Like other flattery, it is the most profusely bestowed and greedily swallowed, where it is the least deserved. I will conclude this subject with the substance of a fable of the ingenious Monsieur de la Motte, which seems not unapplicable to it.

Jupiter made a lottery in heaven, in which mortals, as well as gods, were allowed to have tickets. The prize was *Wisdom*, and Minerva got it. The mortals murmured and accused the gods of foul play. Jupiter, to wipe off this aspersion, declared another lottery for mortals singly, and exclusively of the gods. The prize was *Folly*. They got it, and shared it among themselves. All were satisfied. The loss of *Wisdom* was neither regretted nor remembered ; *Folly* supplied its place, and those who had the largest share of it thought themselves the wisest.

---

[1] " That true self-love and social are the same."—*Essay on Man*, Ep. iv. 396.

" The World "
October 30, 1755. No. 148.[1]

CIVILITY and good-breeding are generally thought, and often used, as synonymous terms, but are by no means so.

Good-breeding necessarily implies civility ; but civility does not reciprocally imply good-breeding. The former has its intrinsic weight and value, which the latter always adorns, and often doubles by its workmanship.

To sacrifice one's own self-love to other people's is a short, but, I believe, a true definition of civility : to do it with ease, propriety, and grace, is good-breeding. The one is the result of good-nature ; the other of good-sense joined to experience, observation, and attention.

A ploughman will be civil, if he is good-natured, but cannot be well-bred. A courtier will be well-bred, though perhaps without good nature, if he have but good-sense.

Flattery is the disgrace of good-breeding, as brutality often is of truth and sincerity. Good-breeding is the middle point between those two odious extremes.

Ceremony is the superstition of good-breeding, as well as of religion ; but yet, being an out-work to both, should not be absolutely demolished. It is always, to a certain degree, to be complied with, though despised by those who think, because admired and respected by those who do not.

The most perfect degree of good-breeding, as I have already hinted, is only to be acquired by great knowledge of the world, and keeping the best company. It is not the object of mere speculation, and cannot be exactly defined, as it consists in a fitness, a propriety of words, actions, and even looks, adapted to the infinite variety and combinations of persons, places, and things. It is a mode, not a substance : for what is good-breeding at

---

[1] " Lord Chesterfield, being at Bath, shewed one of his last *Worlds* to his friend General Irwine, who dined with him almost every day. The general, in the course of the conversation, mentioned good-breeding, as distinguished from mere civility, as a subject that deserved to be treated by him. His lordship at first declined it, but on his friend's insisting, and urging the singular propriety of its being undertaken by a man who was so perfect a master of the thing, he suddenly called for pen and ink, and wrote this excellent piece off hand, as he did all the others, without any erasure or interlineation. The paper, ever after, went by the name of General Irwine's paper."—Maty's note, vol. I, *Miscellaneous Pieces*, p 203. See, however, p. 22 *ante*.

St. James's would pass for foppery or banter in a remote village ; and the homespun civility of that village, would be considered as brutality at court.

A cloistered pedant may form true notions of civility ; but if, amidst the cobwebs of his cell, he pretends to spin a speculative system of good-breeding, he will not be less absurd than his predecessor, who judiciously undertook to instruct Hannibal in the art of war. The most ridiculous and most awkward of men are, therefore, the speculatively well-bred monks of all religions and all professions.

Good-breeding, like charity, not only covers a multitude of faults, but, to a certain degree, supplies the want of some virtues. In the common intercourse of life, it acts good-nature, and often does what good-nature will not always do ; it keeps both wits and fools within those bounds of decency, which the former are too apt to transgress, and which the latter never know.

Courts are unquestionably the seats of good-breeding ; and must necessarily be so ; otherwise they would be the seats of violence and desolation.[1] There, all the passions are in their highest state of fermentation. All pursue what but few can obtain, and many seek what but one can enjoy. Good-breeding alone restrains their excesses. There, if enemies did not embrace, they would stab. There, smiles are often put on, to conceal tears. There, mutual services are professed, while mutual injuries are intended ; and there, the guile of the serpent simulates [2] the gentleness of the dove : all this, it is true, at the expense of sincerity ; but, upon the whole, to the advantage of social intercourse in general.

I would not be misapprehended, and supposed to recommend good-breeding, thus profaned and prostituted to the purposes of guilt and perfidy ; but I think I may justly infer from it, to what a degree the accomplishment of good-breeding must adorn and enforce virtue and truth, when it can thus soften the outrages and deformity of vice and falsehood.

I am sorry to be obliged to confess that my native country is not perhaps the seat of the most perfect good-breeding, though I really believe that it yields to none in

---

[1] " Courts are unquestionably the seats of politeness and good-breeding ; were they not so, they would be the seats of slaughter and desolation."— Chesterfield to his son, August 21, 1749. Bradshaw, vol. I, pp. 232, 233.

[2] As in Maty and Mahon. In the original it is " stimulates."

hearty and sincere civility, as far as civility is (and to a certain degree it is) an inferior moral duty of doing as one would be done by. If France exceeds us in that particular, the incomparable author of *L'Esprit des Loix* accounts for it very impartially, and I believe very truly. " If my countrymen," says he, " are the best bred people in the world, it is only because they are the vainest." It is certain that their good-breeding and attentions, by flattering the vanity and self-love of others, repay their own with interest. It is a general commerce, usually carried on by a barter of attentions, and often without one grain of solid merit, by way of medium, to make up the balance.

It were to be wished that good-breeding were in general thought a more essential part of the education of our youth, especially of distinction, than at present it seems to be. It might even be substituted in the room of some academical studies that take up a great deal of time to very little purpose ; or at least, it might usefully share some of those many hours that are so frequently employed upon a coach-box, or in stables. Surely those who, by their rank and fortune, are called to adorn courts, ought at least not to disgrace them by their manners.

But I observe with concern that it is the fashion for our youth of both sexes to brand good-breeding with the name of ceremony and formality. As such, they ridicule and explode it, and adopt in its stead an offensive carelessness and inattention, to the diminution, I will venture to say, even of their own pleasures, if they know what true pleasures are.

Love and friendship necessarily produce, and justly authorize familiarity : but then good-breeding must mark out its bounds, and say, thus far shalt thou go, and no farther ; for I have known many a passion and many a friendship degraded, weakened, and at last (if I may use the expression) wholly *slatterned* away, by an unguarded and illiberal familiarity. Nor is good-breeding less the ornament and cement of common social life : it connects, it endears, and, at the same time that it indulges the just liberty, restrains that indecent licentiousness of conversation, which alienates and provokes.[1] Great talents make

[1] " There is a third sort of good-breeding, in which people are the most apt to fail, from a very mistaken notion that they cannot fail at all ; I mean, with regard to one's most familiar friends and acquaintances, or those who really are our inferiors ; and there, undoubtedly, a greater degree of ease is not only allowed, but proper, and contributes much to the comforts of

a man famous, great merit makes him respected, and great learning makes him esteemed ; but good-breeding alone can make him be loved.

I recommend it in a more particular manner to my country-women, as the greatest ornament to such of them as have beauty, and the safest refuge for those who have not. It facilitates the victories, decorates the triumphs, and secures the conquests of beauty ; or in some degree atones for the want of it. It almost deifies a fine woman, and procures respect at least to those who have not charms enough to be admired.

Upon the whole, though good-breeding cannot, strictly speaking, be called a virtue, yet it is productive of so many good effects, that, in my opinion, it may justly be reckoned more than a mere accomplishment.

" THE WORLD "

November 20, 1755. No. 151.

I WAS lately subpœnaed by a card to a general assembly at Lady Townly's, where I went so awkwardly early, that I found nobody but the five or six people who had dined there, and who, for want of hands enough for play, were reduced to the cruel necessity of conversing, till something better should offer. Lady Townly observed with concern and impatience that people of fashion now came intolerably late, and in a glut at once, which laid the lady of the house under great difficulties to make the parties properly. "That, no doubt," said Manly, "is to be lamented ; and the more so, as it seems to give your ladyship some concern : but in the meantime, for want of something better to do, I should be glad to know the true meaning of a term that you have just made use of, *people of fashion*. I confess I have never yet had a precise and clear idea of it ; and I am sure I cannot apply more properly for information than to this company, which is most unquestionably composed of *people of fashion*, whatever *people of*

a private, social life. But that ease and freedom have their bounds too, which must by no means be violated. A certain degree of negligence and carelessness becomes injurious and insulting, from the real or supposed inferiority of the persons ; and that delightful liberty of conversation among a few friends is soon destroyed, as liberty often has been, by being carried to licentiousness."—Chesterfield to his son, November 3, 1749. Bradshaw, vol. I, pp. 265, 266.

fashion may be. I therefore beg to know the meaning of that term : what are they, who are they, and what constitutes, I had almost said, anoints them, *people of fashion ?* "

These questions, instead of receiving immediate answers, occasioned a general silence of above a minute, which perhaps was the result of the whole company's having discovered, for the first time, that they had long and often made use of a term which they had never understood : for a little reflection frequently produces those discoveries. Belinda first broke this silence by saying, " One knows well enough who are meant by *people of fashion*, though one does not just know how to describe them : they are those that one generally lives with ; they are people of a certain sort." " They certainly are so," interrupted Manly, " but the point is of what sort ? If you mean by people of a certain sort, yourself, which is commonly the meaning of those who make use of that expression, you are indisputably in the right, as you have all the qualifications that can, or at least, ought to constitute and adorn a *woman of fashion*. But pray, must all *women of fashion* have all your accomplishments ? If so, the myriads of them which I had imagined from what I heard every day, and every where, will dwindle into a handful." " Without having those accomplishments which you so partially allow me," answered Belinda, " I still pretend to be a *woman of fashion* ; a character, which I cannot think requires an uncommon share of talents or merit." " That is the very point," replied Manly," which I want to come at ; and therefore give me leave to question you a little more particularly. You have some advantages, which even your modesty will not allow you to disclaim, such as your birth and fortune : do they constitute you a *woman of fashion ?* " As Belinda was going to answer, Bellair pertly interposed, and said, " Neither, to be sure, Mr. Manly : if birth constituted *fashion*, we must look for it in that inestimable treasure of useful knowledge, the peerage of England ; or if wealth, we should find the very best at the Bank, and at Garraway's." " Well then, Bellair," said Manly, " since you have taken upon you to be Belinda's sponsor, let me ask you two or three questions, which you can more properly answer than she could. Is it her beauty ? " " By no means neither," replied Bellair, " for at that rate there might perhaps be a *woman of fashion* with a gold chain about her neck in the city, or with a fat amber necklace in the country ; prodigies, as yet unheard of and unseen." " Is it then her wit and good-breeding ? " continued Manly. " Each contributes," answered Bellair, " but both would not be sufficient without a certain *je ne scay quoy*, a something or other that I feel better than I can explain."

Here Dorimant, who had sat all this time silent, but looked mischievous, said, " I could say something."—" Ay, and something very impertinent, according to custom," answered Belinda ; " so hold your tongue, I charge you." " You are singularly charitable, Belinda," replied Dorimant, " in being so sure that I was going to be impertinent, only because I was going to speak. Why this suspicion of me?"

" Why ! because I know you to be an odious, abominable creature, upon all subjects of this kind."

This amicable quarrel was put to an end by Harriet, who, on a sudden, and with her usual vivacity, cried out, " I am sure I have it now, and can tell you exactly what *people of fashion* are : they are just the reverse of your *odd people*." " Very possibly, madam," answered Manly, " and therefore I could wish that you would give yourself the trouble of defining *odd people* ; and so, by the rule of contraries, help us to a true notion of *people of fashion*."

" Ay, that I can very easily do. In the first place, your *odd people* are those that one never lets in, unless one is at home to the whole town."

" A little more particular, dear Harriet," interrupted Manly. " So I will," said Harriet, " for I hate them all. There are several sorts of them. Your prudes, for instance, who respect and value themselves upon the unblemished purity of their characters ; who rail at the indecency of the times, censure the most innocent freedoms, and suspect the Lord knows what, if they do but observe a close and familiar whisper between a man and a woman, in a remote corner of the room. There are, too, a sober, formal sort of married women, insipid creatures, who lead domestic lives, and who can be merry, as they think, at home, with their own and their husband's relations, particularly at Christmas. Like turtles, they are true and tender to their lawful mates, and breed like rabbits to beggar and perpetuate their families. These are very *odd women*, to be sure ; but deliver me from your severe and august dowagers, who are the scourges of *people of fashion*, by infesting all public places in order to make their spiteful remarks. One meets them every where, and they seem to have the secret of multiplying themselves into ten different places at once. Their poor horses, like those of the sun, go round the world every day, baiting only at eleven in the morning, and six in the evening, at their parish churches. They speak as movingly of their *poor late lords*, as if they had ever cared for one another ; and, to do them honour, repeat some of the many silly things they used to say. Lastly, there are your maiden ladies of riper years, orphans of distinction, who live together by twos and threes, who club their stocks for a neat little house, a light-bodied coach, and a foot-boy—." "And," added Bellair, "quarrel every day about the dividend." "True," said Harriet, "they are not the sweetest-tempered creatures in the world ; but, after all, one must forgive them some malignity, in consideration of their disappointments. Well, have I now described *odd people* to your satisfaction?" "Admirably," answered Manly ; "and so well, that one can, to a great degree at least, judge of their antipodes, the *people of fashion*. But still there seems something wanting ; for the present account, by the rule of contraries, stands only thus : that *women of fashion* must not care for their husbands, must not go to church, and must not have unblemished, or at least unsuspected, reputations. Now, though all these are very commendable qualifications, it must be owned they are but negative ones, and consequently there must be some positive ones necessary to complete so amiable a character." "I was going to add," interrupted Harriet, "which, by the way, was more than I engaged for, that *people of fashion* were properly those who set the fashions, and who gave the tone of dress, language, manners, and pleasures to the town."

"I admit it," said Manly ; "but what I want still to know is, who gave them that power, or did they usurp it ? For, by the nature of that power, it does not seem to me to admit of a succession by hereditary and divine right." "Were I allowed to speak," said Dorimant, "perhaps I could both shorten and clear up this case. But I dare not, unless Belinda, to whom I profess implicit obedience, gives me leave." "E'en let him speak, Belinda," said Harriet ; "I know he will abuse us, but we are used to him." "Well, say your say then," said Belinda. "See what an impertinent sneer he has already." Upon this, Dorimant, addressing himself more particularly to Belinda, and smiling, said,

> " Then think
> That he, who thus commanded, dares to speak,
> Unless commanded, would have died in silence."

" O, your servant, Sir," said Belinda ; " that fit of humility will, I am sure, not last long ; but however, go on." " I will, to answer Manly's question," said Dorimant, " which, by the way, has something the air of a catechism. Who made these *people of fashion ?* I give this short and plain answer ; they made one another. The men, by their attentions and credit, make the *women of fashion* ; and the women, by either their supposed or real favours, make the *men* such. They are mutually necessary to each other."

" Impertinent enough, of all conscience," said Belinda. " So, without the assistance of you fashionable men, what should we poor women be ? " " Why faith," replied Dorimant, " but *odd women* I doubt, as we should be but odd fellows without your friendly aid to fashion us. In one word, a frequent and reciprocal collision of the two sexes is absolutely necessary to give each that high polish, which is properly called *fashion*."

" Mr. Dorimant has, I own," said Manly, " opened new and important matter ; and my scattered and confused notions seem now to take some form, and tend to a point. But, as examples always best clear up abstruse matters, let us now propose some examples of both sorts, and take the opinions of the company upon them. For instance, I will offer one to your consideration. Is Berynthia a *woman of fashion* or not ? " The whole company readily and almost at once answered, " Doubtless she is." " That may be," said Manly, " but why ? For she has neither birth nor fortune, and but small remains of beauty." " All that is true, I confess," said Belinda : " but she is well dressed, well bred, good humoured, and always ready to go with one any where." " Might I presume," said Dorimant, " to add a title, and perhaps the best, to her claims of *fashion*, I should say that she was of Belville's creation, who is the very fountain of honour of that sort. He dignified her by his addresses ; and those who have the good fortune to share his reputation—." " Have," said Belinda, with some warmth, " the misfortune to lose their own. I told you," turning to Harriet, " what would happen if we allowed him to speak : and just so it has happened ; for the gentleman has almost in plain terms asserted that a woman cannot be a *woman of fashion* till she has lost her reputation." " Fye, Belinda, how you wrong me!" replied Dorimant. " Lost her reputation ! Such a thought never entered into my head ; I only meant, mislaid it. With a very little care she will find it again." " There you are in the right," said Bellair ; " for it is most certain that the reputation of a *woman of fashion* should not be too muddy." " True," replied Dorimant, " nor too limpid neither ; it must not be mere rock water, cold and clear ; it should sparkle a little."

" Well," said Harriet, " now that Berynthia is unanimously voted a *woman of fashion*, what think you of Loveit? Is she, or is she not one ? " " If she is one," answered Dorimant, " I am very much mistaken if it is not of Mirabel's creation—." " By *writ*, I believe," said Bellair ; " for I saw him give her a letter one night at the opera." " But she has other good claims too," added Dorimant. " Her fortune, though not large, is easy ; and nobody fears certain applications from her. She has a small house of her own, which she has fitted up very prettily, and is often *at home*, not to crowds indeed, but to people of the best fashion, from twenty, occasionally down to two ; and let me tell you, that nothing makes a woman of Loveit's sort better received abroad, than being often *at home*." " I own," said Bellair, " that I looked upon her rather as a genteel led-captain, a postscript to *women of fashion*." " Perhaps, too, sometimes the cover," answered Dorimant, " and if so, an equal. You may joke as much as you please upon poor Loveit ; but she is the best-humoured creature in the world ; and I maintain her to be a *woman of fashion* ; for, in short, we all roll with her, as the soldiers say."

" I want to know," said Belinda, " what you will determine upon a character very different from the two last, I mean Lady Loveless : is she a *woman of fashion ?* " " Dear Belinda," answered Harriet hastily, " how could she possibly come into your head ? " " Very naturally," said Belinda ; " she has birth, beauty, and fortune ; she is genteel and well bred." " I own it," said Harriet ; " but still, she is handsome without meaning, well shaped without air, genteel without graces, and well dressed without taste. She is such an insipid creature, she seldom comes about, but lives at home with her lord, and so domestically tame that she eats out of his hand, and teaches her young ones to peck out of her own. Odd, very odd, take my word for it." " Ay, mere rock water," said Dorimant, " and, as I told you an hour ago, that will not do." " No, most certainly," added Bellair, " all that reserve, simplicity, and coldness can never do. It seems to me rather that the true composition of *people of fashion*, like that of Venice Treacle, consists of an infinite number of fine ingredients, but all of the warm kind."

" Truce with your filthy treacle, Bellair ; and since the conversation has hitherto chiefly turned upon us poor women, I think we have a right to insist upon the definition of you *men of fashion*." " No doubt on't," said Dorimant ; " nothing is more just, and nothing is more easy. Allowing some small differences for modes and habits, the *men* and the *women of fashion* are in truth the counterparts of each other : they fit like tallies, are made of the same wood, and are cut out for one another."

As Dorimant was going on, probably to illustrate his assertion, a valet de chambre proclaimed in a solemn manner the arrival of the duchess dowager of Mattadore and her three daughters, who were immediately followed by Lord Formal, Sir Peter Plausible, and divers others of both sexes, and of equal importance. The lady of the house, with infinite skill and indefatigable pains, soon peopled the several card-tables with the greatest propriety, and to universal satisfaction ; and the night concluded with slams, honours, best-games,[1] pairs, pair-royals, and all other such rational demonstrations of joy.

For my own part, I made my escape as soon as I possibly could, with my head full of that most extraordinary conversation which I had just heard, and which, from having taken no part in it, I had attended to the more, and retained the better. I went straight home, and immediately reduced it into writing, as I here offer it for the present edification of my readers. But, as it has furnished me with great and new lights, I propose, as soon as possible, to give the public a new and complete system of ethics, founded upon these principles of *people of fashion* ; as, in my opinion, they are better calculated than any others, for the use and instruction of all private families.

[1] See p. 260 *post*.

"THE WORLD"
August 12, 1756. No. 189.

WE are accused by the French, and perhaps but too justly, of having no word in our language which answers to their word *police*, which therefore we have been obliged to adopt, not having, as they say, the thing.

It does not occur to me that we have any one word in our language (I hope not from the same reason) to express the ideas which they comprehend under their word "*les mœurs.*" *Manners* are too little, *morals* too much. I should define it thus ; *a general exterior decency, fitness and propriety of conduct in the common intercourse of life.*[1]

Cicero, in his *Offices*, makes use of the word *decorum* in this sense, to express what he tells us the Greeks signified by their word (I will not shock the eyes of my polite readers with Greek types) *to prepon.*[2]

The thing however is unquestionably of importance by whatever word it may be dignified or degraded, distinguished or mistaken ; it shall therefore be the subject of this paper to explain and recommend it ; and upon this occasion I shall adopt the word *decorum.*

But, as I have some private reasons for desiring not to lessen the sale of these my lucubrations, I must premise, that, notwithstanding this serious introduction, I am not going to preach either religious or moral duties. On the contrary, it is a scheme of interest which I mean to communicate, and which, if the supposed characteristic of the present age be true, must, I should apprehend, be highly acceptable to the generality of my readers.

[1] " Discretion will teach you to have particular attention to your *Mœurs* which we have no one word in our language to express exactly. *Morals* are too much, Manners too little ; Decency comes the nearest to it, though rather short of it. Cicero's word *Decorum* is properly the thing, and I see no reason why that expressive word should not be adopted, and naturalised in our language ; I have never scrupled using it in that sense."—Chesterfield to his godson (undated), No. xiv of the series on *The Art of Pleasing.* Carnarvon, pp. 194, 195. Bradshaw, vol. II, p. 650.
Since this letter was written the word *decorum* has, without doubt, become naturalised in our language, perhaps largely through Chesterfield's influence. The two earlier sentences of this extract are described by Churton Collins as " fine and exquisite, with the precision and subtilty of La Bruyère at his best."—*Essays and Studies,* p. 229.

[2] " Pray read frequently and with the utmost attention ; nay, get by heart, if you can, that incomparable chapter [XXVII] in Cicero's *Offices* upon the τὸ πρέπον, or the *Decorum.* It contains whatever is necessary for the dignity of manners."—Chesterfield to his son, August 10, 1749. Bradshaw, vol. I, p. 231.

I take it for granted that the most sensible and informed part of mankind, I mean people of fashion, pursue singly their own interests and pleasures ; that they desire as far as possible to enjoy them exclusively, and to avail themselves of the simplicity, the ignorance, and the prejudices of the vulgar, who have neither the same strength of mind, nor the same advantages of education. Now it is certain that nothing would more contribute to that desirable end than a strict observance of this *decorum*, which, as I have already hinted, does not extend to religious or moral duties, does not prohibit the solid enjoyments of vice, but only throws a veil of decency between it and the vulgar, conceals part of its native deformity, and prevents scandal and bad example. It is a sort of pepper-corn quit-rent paid to virtue, as an acknowledgement of its superiority ; but, according to our present constitution, is the easy price of freedom, not the tribute of vassalage.

Those who would be respected by others, must first respect themselves. A certain exterior purity, and dignity of character, command respect, procure credit, and invite confidence ; but the public exercise and ostentation of vice has all the contrary effects.

The middling class of people in this country, though generally straining to imitate their betters, have not yet shaken off the prejudices of their education ; very many of them still believe in a Supreme Being, in a future state of rewards and punishments, and retain some coarse home-spun notions of moral good and evil. The rational system of materialism has not yet reached them, and, in my opinion, it may be full as well it never should ; for, as I am not of levelling principles, I am for preserving a due subordination from inferiors to superiors, which an equality of profligacy must totally destroy.

A fair character is a more lucrative thing than people are generally aware of ; and I am informed that an eminent money-scrivener has lately calculated with great accuracy the advantage of it, and that it has turned out a clear profit of thirteen and a half per cent. in the general transactions of life ; which advantage, frequently repeated, as it must be in the course of the year, amounts to a very considerable object.

To proceed to a few instances. If the courtier would but wear the appearance of truth, promise less, and perform more, he would acquire such a degree of trust and confidence, as would enable him to strike on a sudden, and with success, some splendid stroke of perfidy, to the infinite advantage of himself and his party.

A patriot, of all people, should be a strict observer of this *decorum*, if he would (as it is to be presumed he would) bear a good price at the court market. The love of his dear country, well acted and little felt, will certainly get him into good keeping, and perhaps procure him a hand- some settlement for life ; but, if his prostitution be flagrant, he is only made use of in cases of the utmost necessity, and even then only by cullies. I must observe, by the by, that of late the market has been a little glutted with patriots, and consequently they do not sell quite so well.

Few masters of families are, I should presume, desirous to be robbed indiscriminately by all their servants ; and, as servants in general are more afraid of the devil, and less of the gallows, than their masters, it seems to be as imprudent as indecent to remove that wholesome fear, either by their examples, or their philosophical disserta- tions, exploding in their presence, though ever so justly, all the idle notions of future punishments, or of moral good and evil. At present, honest faithful servants rob their masters conscientiously only in their respective stations ; but, take away those checks and restraints which the prejudices of their education have laid them under, they will soon rob indiscriminately, and out of their several departments ; which would probably create some little confusion in families, especially in numerous ones.

I cannot omit observing that this *decorum* extends to the little trifling offices of common life ; such as seeming to take a tender and affectionate part in the health or fortune of your acquaintance, and a readiness and alacrity to serve them in things of little consequence to them, and of none at all to you. These attentions bring in good interest ; the weak and the ignorant mistake them for the real sentiments of your heart, and give you their esteem and friendship in return. The wise, indeed, pay you in your own coin, or by a truck of commodities of equal value, upon which however there is no loss ; so that, upon the whole, this commerce, skilfully carried on, is a very lucrative one.

In all my schemes for the general good of mankind I have always a particular attention to the utility that may arise from them to my fair fellow-subjects, for whom I have the tenderest and most unfeigned concern ; and I lay hold of this opportunity most earnestly to recommend to them the strictest observance of this *decorum*. I will admit that a fine woman of a certain rank, cannot have too many real vices ; but, at the same time, I do insist upon it, that it is essentially her interest, not to have the appearance of any one. This *decorum*, I confess, will conceal her conquests, and prevent her triumphs ; but, on the other hand, if she will be pleased to reflect that those conquests are known, sooner or later, always to end in her total defeat, she will not upon an average find herself a loser. There are indeed some husbands of such humane and hospitable dispositions, that they seem determined to share all their happiness with their friends and acquaintance ; so that, with regard to such husbands singly, this *decorum* were useless ; but the far greater number are of a churlish and uncommunicative disposition, troublesome upon bare suspicions, and brutal upon proofs. These are capable of inflicting upon the fair delinquent the pains and penalties of exile and imprisonment at the dreadful mansion-seat, notwithstanding the most solemn protestations and oaths, backed with the most moving tears, that nothing really criminal has passed. But it must be owned that, of all negatives, that is much the hardest to be proved.

Though deep play be a very innocent and even commendable amusement in itself, it is, however, as things are yet constituted, a great breach, nay perhaps the highest violation possible, of the *decorum* in the fair sex. If generally fortunate, it induces some suspicion of dexterity ; if unfortunate, of debt ; and in this latter case, the ways and means for raising the supplies necessary for the current year, are sometimes supposed to be unwarrantable. But what is still much more important is that the agonies of an ill run will disfigure the finest face in the world, and cause most ungraceful emotions. I have known a best game,[1] suddenly produced upon a good game, for a deep stake at bragg or commerce, almost make the vermillion turn pale, and elicit from lips, where the sweets of Hybla dwelt, and where the loves and graces played, some mur-

[1] As in the original. In Maty, Mahon and *Parson's Classics* it is given as " bad," which we think is a mistake. *Best-game* was a term used in card games of that period (see p. 256 *ante*), and signified a winning hand or win ; the meaning here being roughly, " I have known a good hand, on which a deep stake has been made, defeated." Brag was a game very similar to poker.

mured oaths, which, though minced and mitigated a little in their terminations, seemed to me, upon the whole, to be rather unbecoming.

Another singular advantage, which will arise to my fair countrywomen of distinction from the observance of this *decorum*, is that they will never want some creditable led-captain to attend them at a minute's warning to operas, plays, Ranelagh, and Vauxhall ; whereas I have known some women of extreme condition, who, by neglecting the *decorum*, had slatterned away their characters to such a degree, as to be obliged upon those emergencies to take up with mere toad-eaters of very equivocal rank and character, who by no means graced their entry into public places.

To the young unmarried ladies I beg leave to represent that this *decorum* will make a difference of at least five-and-twenty, if not fifty per cent. in their fortunes. The pretty men, who have commonly the honour of attending them, are not in general the marrying kind of men ; they love them too much, or too little, know them too well, or not well enough, to think of marrying them. The husband-like men are a set of awkward fellows with good estates, and who, not having got the better of vulgar prejudices, lay some stress upon the characters of their wives, and the legitimacy of the heirs to their estates and titles. These are to be caught only by *les mœurs* ; the hook must be baited with the *decorum* ; the naked one will not do.

I must own that it seems too severe to deny young ladies the innocent amusements of the present times, but I beg of them to recollect that I mean only with regard to outward appearances ; and I should presume that *tête-à-têtes* with the pretty men might be contrived and brought about in places less public than Kensington-gardens, the two parks, the high roads, or the streets of London.

Having thus combined, as I flatter myself that I have, the solid enjoyments of vice, with the useful appearances of virtue, I think myself entitled to the thanks of my country in general, and to that just praise which Horace gives to the author, " qui miscuit utile dulci " ; or, in English, who joins the useful with the agreeable.

"THE WORLD"

September 30, 1756. No. 196.[1]

IT is a vulgar notion, and worthy of the vulgar, for it is both false and absurd, that passionate people are the best-natured people in the world. *They are a little hasty, it is true ; a trifle will put them in a fury ; and while they are in that fury, they neither know nor care what they say or do : but then as soon as it is over, they are extremely sorry and penitent for any injury or mischief they did.* This panegyric of these choleric good-natured people, when examined and simplified, amounts in plain common sense and English to this : that they are good-natured when they are not ill-natured ; and that when, in their fits of rage, they have said or done things that have brought them to gaol or the gallows, they are extremely sorry for it. It is indeed highly probable that they are ; but where is the reparation to those whose reputations, limbs, or lives, they have either wounded or destroyed ? This concern comes too late, and is only for themselves. Self-love was the cause of the injury, and is the only motive of the repentance.

Had these furious people real good-nature, their first offence would be their last, and they would resolve at all events never to relapse. The moment they felt their choler rising, they would enjoin themselves an absolute silence and inaction, and, by that sudden check, rather expose themselves to a momentary ridicule (which, by the way, would be followed by universal applause) than run the least risk of being irreparably mischievous.

I know it is said in their behalf that this impulse to wrath is constitutionally so sudden and so strong, that they cannot stifle it, even in its birth : but experience shows us that this allegation is notoriously false ; for we daily observe that these stormy persons both can and do lay those gusts of passion, when awed by respect, restrained by interest, or intimidated by fear. The most outrageous furioso does not give a loose to his anger in presence of his sovereign, or his mistress ; nor the expectant heir in presence of the peevish dotard from whom he hopes for an inheritance. The soliciting courtier, though perhaps

---

[1] " Those who like to observe the different methods of various writers in treating the same subjects, may compare this paper with No. 11 of *The Rambler.*"—*Wit and Wisdom of Lord Chesterfield*, p. 295.

under the strongest provocations from unjust delays and broken promises, calmly swallows his unavailing wrath, disguises it even under smiles, and gently waits for more favourable moments : nor does the criminal fly in a passion at his judge or his jury.

There is then but one solid excuse to be alleged in favour of these people ; and, if they will frankly urge it, I will candidly admit it, because it points out its own remedy. I mean, let them fairly confess themselves mad, as they most unquestionably are : for what plea can those that are frantic ten times a day bring against shaving, bleeding, and a dark room, when so many much more harmless madmen are confined in their cells at Bedlam, for being mad only once in a moon ? Nay, I have been assured by the late ingenious Doctor Monro, that such of his patients who were really of a good-natured disposition, and who, in their lucid intervals, were allowed the liberty of walking about the hospital, would frequently, when they found the previous symptoms of their returning madness, voluntarily apply for confinement, conscious of the mischief which they might possibly do, if at liberty. If those who pretend not to be mad, but who really are so, had the same fund of good-nature, they would make the same application to their friends, if they have any.

There is in the Menagiana a very pretty story of one of these angry gentlemen, which sets their extravagancy in a very ridiculous light.

Two gentlemen were riding together, one of whom, who was a choleric one, happened to be mounted upon a high-mettled horse. The horse grew a little troublesome, at which the rider grew very angry, and whipped and spurred him with great fury ; to which the horse, almost as wrong-headed as his master, replied with kicking and plunging. The companion, concerned for the danger, and ashamed of the folly of his friend, said to him coolly, " Be quiet, be quiet, and shew yourself the wiser of the two."

This sort of madness, for I will call it by no other name, flows from various causes, of which I shall now enumerate the most general.

Light unballasted heads are very apt to be overset by every gust, or even breeze, of passion ; they appreciate things wrong, and think every thing of importance, but what really is so ; hence those frequent and sudden transitions from silly joy to sillier anger, according as the present silly humor is gratified or thwarted. This is the never-failing characteristic of the uneducated vulgar, who often in the same half-hour fight with fury and shake hands with affection. Such heads give themselves no time to reason ; and, if you attempt to reason with them, they think you rally them, and resent the affront. They are, in short, overgrown children, and continue so, in the most advanced age. Far be it from me to insinuate, what some ill-bred authors have bluntly asserted, that this is in general the case of the fairest part of our species, whose great vivacity does not always allow them time to reason consequentially, but hurries them into testiness upon the least opposition to their will. But, at the same time, with all the partiality which I have for them, and nobody can have more than I have, I must confess that, in all their debates, I have much more admired the copiousness of their rhetoric, than the conclusiveness of their logic.

People of strong animal spirits, warm constitutions, and a cold genius (a most unfortunate and ridiculous, though common compound) are most irascible animals, and very dangerous in their wrath. They are active, puzzling, blundering, and petulantly enterprising and persevering. They are impatient of the least contradiction, having neither arguments nor words to reply with ; and the animal part of their composition bursts out into furious explosions, which have often mischievous consequences. Nothing is too outrageous or criminal for them to say or do in these fits ; but, as the beginning of their frenzy is easily discoverable by their glaring eyes, inflamed countenances, and rapid motions, the company, as conservators of the peace (which, by the way, every man is, till the authority of a magistrate can be procured), should forcibly seize these madmen, and confine them, in the mean time, in some dark closet, vault or coal-hole.

Men of nice honour, without one grain of common honesty (for such there are), are wonderfully combustible. The honourable is to support and protect the dishonest part of their character. The consciousness of their guilt makes them both sore and jealous.

There is another very irascible sort of human animals, whose madness proceeds from pride. These are generally the people, who, having just fortunes sufficient to live idle, and useless to society, create themselves gentlemen, and are scrupulously tender of the rank and dignity which they have not. They require the more respect, from being conscious that they have no right to any. They construe every thing into a slight, ask explanations with heat, and misunderstand them with fury. " Who are you ? What are you ? Do you know who you speak to ? I'll teach you to be insolent to a gentleman," are their daily idioms of speech, which frequently end in assault and battery, to the great emolument of the Round-house and Crown-office.

I have known many young fellows, who, at their first setting out in the world, or in the army, have simulated a passion which they did not feel, merely as an indication of *spirit*, which word is falsely looked upon as synonymous with courage. They dress and look fierce, swear enormously, and rage furiously, seduced by that popular word *spirit*. But I beg leave to inform these mistaken young gentlemen, whose error I compassionate, that the true spirit of a rational being consists in cool and steady resolution, which can only be the result of reflection and virtue.

I am very sorry to be obliged to own that there is not a more irritable part of the species than my brother authors. Criticism, censure, or even the slightest disapprobation of their immortal works, excite their most furious indignation. It is true, indeed, that they express their resentment in a manner less dangerous both to others and to themselves. Like incensed porcupines, they dart their quills at the objects of their wrath. The wounds given by these shafts are not mortal, and only painful in proportion to the distance from whence they fly. Those which are discharged (as by much the greatest numbers are) from great heights, such as garrets, or four-pair-of-stair rooms, are puffed away by the wind, and never hit the mark ; but those which are let off from a first or second floor, are apt to occasion a little smarting, and sometimes festering, especially if the party wounded be unsound.

Our Great Creator has wisely given us passions to rouse us into action, and to engage our gratitude to Him by the pleasures they procure us ; but, at the same time, He has kindly given us reason sufficient, if we will but give that reason fair play, to control those passions ; and has delegated authority to say to them, as He said to the waters, " Thus far shall ye go, and no farther." The angry man is his own severest tormentor ; his breast knows no peace, while his raging passions are restrained by no sense of either religious or moral duties. What would be his case, if his unforgiving example (if I may use such an expression) were followed by his All-merciful Maker, whose forgiveness he can only hope for, in proportion as he himself forgives and loves his fellow-creatures ?

[NOTE.—This essay may be compared with the following passages which occur in two characteristic letters from Chesterfield to his godson's father, A. C. Stanhope.]

9th July, 1763.

" Our boy was very thoughtful and grave upon account of your last letter to him, and Mr. Robert's [1] letter to you, which, by Mr. Robert's order, he brought me, though very unwillingly to read. I must say that he acted contrition very well to me ; but when my back was turned, he was very cheerful. I read him a grave and strong lecture upon sudden passion : for what Mr. Robert wrote to you is very true, that he is subject to too sudden gusts of passion : but it is as true, too, that they are very soon over. However, they must be got the better of ; for I know nothing in the common course of the world more prejudicial, and often more fatal, than those sudden starts of passion . . . This disposition is only to be cured by time and by reasoning, ridicule and shame, but not by anger and passion ; which, instead of curing, would authorize his own hastiness. Therefore, I must desire you not to write him any angry letters upon this subject, which would dispirit and deject him too much, but to ridicule and shame him by the feigned examples of third persons. That he can check this humour is evident ; for I am sure that the whole world could not provoke him to be in a passion in my presence ; so that you may depend upon it that I will cure him in time, and by fair means."

20th July, 1763.

" I joked with our boy about the name of Cacafogo, but promised him, at the same time, that I would keep it a secret, because, if it should be known, he would never get rid of it, and that it would be a ridiculous thing, when he came to be a man, to be called Cacafogo Stanhope ; which would certainly be the case if he gave way to those

[1] The schoolmaster with whom the godson lived. See p. 134 *ante*.

little starts of passion. He took it immediately, and I dare say it will have some effect upon him; for he is exceedingly afraid of ridicule. But, indeed, you take this matter too seriously. Would you have a boy of seven years old be a stoic? For my own part, I should be very sorry he were one at that age. His little ebullitions of wrath are only the result of spirit and vivacity, which must gradually be calmed by ridicule and reasoning, but not punished like mortal sins. Do you know any grown man that is not sometimes in a passion—and do you expect that the child should not? When I was much older than he is, I was infinitely more passionate, and nothing but experience and reasoning cured me of it." Carnarvon, Appendix, pp. 26, 27.

"THE WORLD"

October 7, 1756. No. 197.

IF we give credit to the vulgar opinion, or even to the assertions of some reputable authors, both ancient and modern, poor human nature was not originally formed for keeping; every age has degenerated; and from the fall of the first man, my unfortunate ancestor, our species has been tumbling on, century by century, from bad to worse, for about six thousand years.

Considering this progressive state of deterioration, it is a very great mercy that things are no worse with us at present; since, geometrically speaking, the human ought by this time to have sunk infinitely below the brute and the vegetable species, which are neither of them supposed to have dwindled or degenerated considerably, except in a very few instances; for it must be owned that our modern oaks are inferior to those of Dodona, our breed of horses to that of the Centaurs, and our breed of fowls to that of the Phoenixes.

But is this really the case? Certainly not. It is only one of those many errors which are artfully scattered by the designs of a few, and blindly adopted by the ignorance and folly of the many. The moving exclamations of— *these sad times! this degenerate age!* the affecting lamentations over *declining virtue* and *triumphant vice*, and the tender and final farewell bidden every day to unrewarded and discouraged public spirit, arts and sciences, are the commonplace topics of the pride, the envy, and the malignity of, the human heart, that can more easily forgive, and even commend, antiquated and remote, than bear cotemporary and contiguous merit. Men of these mean sentiments have always been the satirists of their own, and the panegyrists of former times. They give this tone, which fools, like birds in the dark, catch by ear, and whistle all day long.

As it has constantly been my endeavour to root out, if I could, or, if I could not, to expose the vices of the human heart, it shall be the object of this day's paper to examine this strange inverted entail of virtue and merit upwards, according to priority of birth, and seniority of age. I shall prove it to be forged, and consequently null and void to all intents and purposes whatsoever.

If I loved to jingle, I would say that human nature has always been invariably the same, though always varying ; that is, the same in substance, but varying in forms and modes, from many concurrent causes, of which perhaps we know but few. Climate, education, accidents, severally contribute to change those modes ; but in all climates, and in all ages, we discover through them the same passions, affections, and appetites, and the same degree of virtues and vices.

This being unquestionably the true state of the case, which it would be endless to bring instances to prove from the histories of all times and of all nations, I shall, by way of warning to the incautious, and of reproof to the designing, proceed to explain the reasons, which I have but just hinted at above, why the human nature of the time being has always been reckoned the worst and most degenerate.

Authors, especially poets, though great men, are, alas ! but men ; and, like other men, subject to the weaknesses of human nature, though perhaps in a less degree : but it is, however, certain that their breasts are not absolutely strangers to the passions of jealousy, pride, and envy. Hence it is that they are very apt to measure merit by the century, to love dead authors better than living ones, and to love them the better the longer they have been dead. The Augustan age is therefore their favourite era, being at least seventeen hundred years distant from the present. That emperor was not only a judge of wit, but, for an emperor, a tolerable performer too ; and Maecenas, his first minister, was both a patron and a poet : he not only

encouraged and protected, but fed and fattened men of
wit at his own table, as appears from Horace : no small
encouragement for panegyric. Those were times indeed
for genius to display itself in ! It was honoured, tasted
and rewarded. But now—" *O tempora ! O mores !* One
must, however, do justice to the authors, who thus declaim
against their own times, by acknowledging that they are
seldom the aggressors ; their own times have commonly
begun with them. It is their resentment, not their judgement (if they have any) that speaks this language. Anger
and despair make them endeavour to lower that merit,
which, till brought very low indeed, they are conscious
they cannot equal.

There is another and much more numerous set of much
greater men, who still more loudly complain of the
ignorance, the corruption, and the degeneracy of the present
age. These are the consummate volunteer, but unregarded
and unrewarded politicians, who, at a modest computation,
amount to at least three millions of souls in this political
country, and who are all of them both able and willing to
steer the great vessel of the state, and to take upon themselves the whole load of business and burthen of *employments* for the service of their dear country. The
administration for the time being is always the worst,
the most incapable, the most corrupt, that ever was, and
negligent of every thing but their own interest. " *Where
are now your Cecils and your Walsinghams ?* " Those who
ask that question could answer it, if they would speak out,
Themselves : for they are all that, and more too.

I stepped the other day, in order only to enquire how
my poor country did, into a coffee-house that is without
dispute the seat of the soundest politics in this great
metropolis, and sat myself down within ear-shot of the
principal council-table. Fortunately for me, the president,
a person of age, dignity, and becoming gravity, had just
begun to speak. He stated, with infinite perspicuity and
knowledge, the present state of affairs in other countries,
and the lamentable situation of our own. He traced with
his finger upon the table, by the help of some coffee which
he had spilt in the warmth of his exordium, the whole
course of the Ohio, and the boundaries of the Russian,
Prussian, Austrian, and Saxon dominions ; foresaw a long
and bloody war upon the continent, calculated the supplies
necessary for carrying it on, and pointed out the best

methods of raising them, which, for that very reason, he intimated would not be pursued. He wound up his discourse with a most pathetic peroration, which he concluded with saying, " Things were not carried on in this way in Queen Elizabeth's days ; the public was considered, and able men were consulted and employed. Those were days!" " Aye, Sir, and nights too, I presume," said a young fellow who stood near him, " some longer and some shorter, according to the variation of the seasons ; pretty much like ours."

Mr. President was a little surprised at the suddenness and pertness of this interruption ; but, recomposing himself, answered with that cool contempt that becomes a great man, " I did not mean astronomical days, but political ones." The young fellow replied, " Oh then, Sir, I am your servant," and went off in a laugh.

Thus informed and edified, I went off too, but could not help reflecting in my way upon the singular ill-luck of this, my dear country, which, as long as ever I remember it, and as far back as I have read, has always been governed by the only two or three people, out of two or three millions, totally incapable of governing, and unfit to be trusted. But these reflections were soon interrupted by numbers of people whom I observed crowding into a public house. Among them I discovered my worthy friend and taylor, that industrious mechanic, Mr. Regnier. I applied to him to know the meaning of that concourse ; to which, with his usual humanity, he answered, " We are the master-taylors, who are to meet to-night to consider what is to be done about our journeymen, who insult and impose upon us, to the great detriment of trade." I asked him whether, under his protection, I might slip in and hear their deliberations. He said, yes, and welcome ; for that they should do nothing to be ashamed of.

I profited of this permission, and, following him into the room, found a considerable number of these ingenious artists assembled, and waiting only for the arrival of my friend, who it seems was too considerable for business to begin without him. He accordingly took the lead, opened the meeting with a very handsome speech, in which he gave many instances of the insolence, the unreasonableness, and the exorbitant demands of the journeymen taylors, and concluded with observing, " that if the government minded any thing now-a-days but themselves, such abuses would not have been suffered ; and had they been but attempted in Queen Elizabeth's days, she would have *worked* them with a witness." Another orator then rose up to speak, but as I was sure that he could say nothing better than what had just fallen from my worthy friend, I stole off unobserved, and was pursuing my way home, when in the very next street I discovered a much greater number of people (though by their dress of seemingly inferior note) rushing into another public-house. As numbers always excite my curiosity, almost as much as they mutually do each other's passions, I crowded in with them, in order to discover the object of this meeting, not without some suspicion that this frequent senate might be composed of the journeymen taylors, and convened in opposition to that which I had just left. My suspicion was soon confirmed by the eloquence of a journeyman, a finisher, I presume, who expatiated with equal warmth and dignity, upon the injustice and oppression of the master-taylors, to the utter ruin of thousands of poor journeymen and their families ; and concluded with asserting, " it was a shame that the government and the parliament did not take notice of such abuses ; and that, had the master-taylors done these things in Queen Elizabeth's days, she would have *mastered* them with a vengeance, so she would."

I confess I could not help smiling at this singular conformity of sentiments, and almost of expressions, of the master politicians, the master-taylors, and the journeymen taylors. I am convinced that the two latter really and honestly believed what they said , it not being in the least improbable that their understandings should be the dupes of their interests : but I will not so peremptorily answer for the interior conviction of the political orator, though at the same time I must do him the justice to say, that he seemed full dull enough to be very much in earnest.

The several scenes of this day suggested to me when I got home, various reflections, which perhaps I may communicate to my readers in some future paper.[1]

---

[1] This was, however, the last of Chesterfield's contributions ; the paper came to a close at the end of 1756.

IX

CHESTERFIELD'S PHILOSOPHY AS ILLUSTRATED IN HIS LATER LETTERS [1]

To the Earl of Huntingdon.

London, September 3, O.S. 1750.

. . . I have sauntered away good part of this summer at Blackheath, in those amusements of gardening, and idle reading, which my former youth and spirits would have despised, but which now stand in the stead of pleasures with me. The different stages of life fortunately bring with them different ways of thinking, and upon the whole such a proportion of good and bad, that none of them are either to be envied or pitied by the others. [2]

To the Earl of Huntingdon.

Bath, September 24, O.S. 1750.

I should pity those poor enthusiasts you have lately seen at La Trappe, if I did not know that enthusiasm carries along with it, not only it's comforts but it's joys. It is the source of a thousand ills to society, but of a thousand pleasures to the enthusiasts themselves. What strange notions must those distempered brains have formed of an all-wise and omnipotent Being, to suppose that he placed us here, to be a burden to ourselves, and at least useless, if not prejudicial to society. But whoever has lived much in the world and read much of it, will wonder at none of those absurdities and extravagancies, which the mind of man intimidated by fear, invited by interest, or perverted by vanity, is capable of entertaining very seriously, and even with warmth and acrimony. Witness, most of the systems of philosophy, and most sects of religion. [3]

---

[1] See p. 131 *ante*.
[2] *Letters of Lord Chesterfield to Lord Huntingdon*, p. 17.
[3] *Ibid.*, pp. 21, 22.

To Solomon Dayrolles Esq.,
Greenwich, June 30, O.S. 1752.
. . . I am here in my hermitage, very deaf, and consequently alone. I read as much as my eyes will let me, and I walk and ride as often as the worst weather I ever knew will allow me. *D'ailleurs*, good health, natural good spirits, some philosophy, and long experience of the world, make me much less dejected and melancholy than most people in my situation would be, or than I should have been myself some years ago. I comfort myself with the reflection that I did not lose the power, till after I had very near lost the desire, of hearing. I have been long and voluntarily deaf to the voice of ambition, and to the noise of business, so that I lose nothing upon that head ; and when I consider how much of my life is passed, and how little of it, according to the course of nature, remains, I can almost persuade myself that I am no loser at all. By all this, you see that I am neither a dejected nor a sour deaf man. . .[1]

A Madame La Marquise De Monconseil.
à Londres, ce 30 Juin, V.S. 1752.
.   Il faut profiter de nos goûts pendant que nous le pouvons, avec le ménagement nécessaire pour leur durée. Je suis devenu plus gourmand qu'à mon ordinaire, et, ayant actuellement un sens de moins, je tire tout le parti que je puis de ceux qui me restent : ma surdité continue, et par conséquent mon ennui augmente. J'ai beau philosopher, et tâcher de m'en dédommager par la lecture, la promenade, et la table ; Il reste, à mon âge, un furieux vuide, quand on ne jouit plus des douceurs de la société. Dans la dissipation, et le tumulte de la jeunesse, on n'en connoît pas tout le prix ; c'est à mon âge qu'elle devient un véritable et presque le seul bien, et c'est justement à cette heure que je m'en vois privé. Je vous avoue que j'en suis extrêmement abbattu, malgré tout ce que ma raison, ou mes amis, peuvent m'offrir de consolations sur ce sujet.[2]

To Solomon Dayrolles, Esq.,
Bath, October 18, 1752.
. . . I bear my misfortune better than I believe most other people would ; whether from reason, philosophy, or constitution, I will not pretend to decide. If I have no

[1] Bradshaw, vol. III, p. 1027.   [2] *Ibid.*, p. 1029.

T

very cheerful, at least I have no melancholy, moments. Books employ most of my hours agreeably ; and some few objects, within my own narrow circle, excite my attention enough to preserve me from *ennui* . . . [1]

A Madame La Marquise De Monconseil.

à Londres, ce 11 Novembre, V.S. 1752.

. . . Que mon sort seroit triste, si je n'avois pas du goût pour la lecture, qui me fait souvent oublier, pendant que j'y suis, que je ne suis plus bon à autre chose. A tout âge, il faut chérir les illusions consolantes ou agréables ; dans la jeunesse, elles se présentent, dans la vieillesse, il les faut chercher, ou même en faire, et avec tout cela, l'ennui en est l'appanage. [2]

To the Bishop of Waterford.

Bath, November 11, 1752.

. . . I stay here a fortnight longer, in hopes of more benefit, which my physician promises me strongly ; as I do not expect it, if I receive it, it will be the more welcome. If not, I have both philosophy and religion enough to submit to my fate without either melancholy or murmur ; for though I can by no means account why there is either moral or physical evil in the world, yet, conscious of the narrow bounds of human understanding, and convinced of the wisdom and justice of the Eternal Divine Being, who placed them here, I am persuaded that it is fit and right that they should be here . . . [3]

To Solomon Dayrolles, Esq.,

London, April 6, O.S. 1753.

. . . I am now, for the first time in my life, impatient for the summer, that I may go and hide myself at Blackheath, and converse with my vegetables *d'égal à égal*, which is all that a deaf man can pretend to. I propose to migrate there in about three weeks, and idle away the summer, without fearing or wishing the return of winter. Deaf as I am, I would not change the interior quiet and tranquillity of my mind for the full possession of all the objects of my former pursuits. I know their futility, and I know now that one can only find real happiness within one's self . . . [4]

---

[1] Bradshaw. vol. III, p. 1038.   [2] *Ibid.*, p. 1044.
[3] *Ibid.*, pp. 1047–8.   [4] *Ibid.*, p. 1059.

A Madame La Marquise de Monconseil.

à Londres, ce 3 Mai, 1753.

. . . Nous sommes, plus que nous ne le croyons généralement, les maîtres des sentimens de notre coeur, et des
mouvemens de notre esprit ; il leur faut nécessairement
un objet, mais en prenant un peu sur nous, nous pouvons
en grande partie leur choisir ces objets, et en substituer
d'agréables aux désagréables.   Au moins je prêche d'exemple, puis-qu'au lieu de succomber sous le plus grand
malheur qui pouvoit m'arriver à mon âge, la surdité, je
m'occupe à en chercher tous les dédommagemens possibles,
et je me prête d'autant plus à tous les amusemens, qui
sont à ma portée.   Voilà, Madame, la véritable philosophie,
je vous la recommande . . . [1]

To Solomon Dayrolles, Esq.,

Blackheath, June 22, 1753.

. . . It is very true, that I am very well in health ; but
I can assure you that my deafness is much more than a
thickness of hearing, and that I am very far from being a
social animal.   I will never be an unsocial one, however,
and I will wish my fellow creatures as well as if I heard
them.   I have natural good spirits to support me under
this misfortune, and philosophy enough not to grieve
under any that I cannot remove, bodily pain excepted, of
which, thank God, I have had as small a share as anybody
of my age, perhaps even a smaller.   My only society is
the person, who, for the time being, sits near me.   It is a
great satisfaction to me to reflect that I retired from
business to the comforts of a quiet and private life before
my unfortunate deafness reduced me to the necessity of
doing it ; or it would never have been thought choice, had
it been ever so truly so, the generality of mankind not
having the least notion of giving up power or profit . . . [2]

To the Bishop of Waterford.

Bath, October 10, 1753.

. . . I belong no more to social life, which, when I quitted
busy public life, I flattered myself would be the comfort
of my declining days ; but that, it seems, is not given
me.   I neither murmur nor despair ; the lot of millions
of my fellow creatures is still worse than mine.   Exquisite
pains of the body, and still greater of the mind, conspire

[1] Bradshaw, vol. III, p. 1061.   [2] *Ibid.*, pp. 1064–5.

to torture many of them. I thank God I am free from both, and I look upon the privation of those ills as a real good. A prouder being than I am—a Lord, or if you will, a stately Duke, of the whole creation—would place this singly to the account of his reason ; but I am humble enough to allow my constitution its share. I am naturally of a cheerful disposition ; I view things in their most comfortable light, and I unavailingly repine at nothing that cannot be retrieved . . . [1]

To Solomon Dayrolles, Esq.,

Blackheath, September 25, 1754.
. . . All the infirmities of an age, still more advanced than mine, crowd in upon me. I must bear them as well as I can ; they are more or less the lot of humanity, and I have no claim to an exclusive privilege against them. In this situation you will easily suppose that I have no very pleasant hours ; but on the other hand, thank God, I have not one melancholy one ; and I rather think that my philosophy increases with my infirmities. Pleasures I think of no more ; let those run after them that can over-take them, but I will not hobble and halt after them in vain. My comfort and amusements must be internal ; and by good luck, I am not afraid of looking inwards.— Some reading, some writing, some trifling in my garden, and some contemplation, concur in making me never less alone than when alone. But this letter runs too much in the moral essay of a *solitaire*. *Changeons de thèse*.

I shall go to London in November, upon the account of Lady Chesterfield, and even of my servants, who, not having the resources that I have, would be very miserable here in the winter. The difference will be but little to me, it would be great to them, which in my mind makes it a social duty . . . [2]

To Solomon Dayrolles, Esq.,

London, December 17, 1754.
. . . As I know my ill to be incurable, I bear it the better from a philosophy of my own, very different from most other people's ; for while I have both hopes and fears I am anxious ; but when I have no hope I take *mon parti*, and am easy . . . [3]

A Madame La Marquise de Monconseil.

à Londres, ce 10 Janvier, 1755.

. . . Il faut donc prendre patience, c'est le seul remède qui me reste ; triste remède, à la vérité, et qui ne guérit point, mais qui mitige un peu les maux, qu'elle ne peut pas guérir.   Je ne fais pas le philosophe Stoïcien ; je sens mon mal, et je conviens que c'en est un, mais en même tems je sens par expérience qu'on peut prendre beaucoup plus sur moi-même, qu'on ne croit généralement.   En voulant s'aider, on s'aide à un certain point ; je cherche tout ce qui peut m'amuser, et faire diversion aux tristes réflexions, que mon malheur autrement m'inspireroit.   Je me prête aux moindres amusemens ; je tâche de les grossir, et d'en faire objet, moyennant quoi, et avec le secours d'un tempérament naturellement gai, je suis encore à l'abri de la mélancolie ; je ne me divertis guères, mais aussi je ne m'attriste point . . . [1]

To the Bishop of Waterford.

London, March 12, 1755.

White [2] was puzzled what account to give you of me, and therefore gave you none ; and, to say the truth, I am pretty much in the same case myself, only resolved to answer as well as I can your kind enquiries after me.   I am tolerably well one day, ill the next, and well again perhaps the third ; that is, my disorders in my stomach, and my giddiness in my head, return frequently and unexpectedly.   Proper care and medicines remove them for the time, but none will prevent them.   My deafness grows gradually worse, which in my mind implies a total one before it be long.   In this unhappy situation, which I have reason to suppose will every day grow worse, I still keep up my spirits tolerably ; that is, I am free from melancholy, which I think is all that can be expected.   This I impute to that degree of philosophy, which I have acquired by long experience of the world.   I have enjoyed all its pleasures and consequently know their futility, and do not regret their loss.   I appraise them at their real value, which in truth is very low ; whereas those who have not experienced, always over-rate them.   They only see their gay outside, and are dazzled with their glare ; but I have been behind the scenes.   It is a common notion, and like

[1] Bradshaw, vol. III, p. 1115.
[2] An old and faithful servant of Lord Chesterfield.

many common ones a very false one, that those, who have led a life of pleasure and business, can never be easy in retirement ; whereas I am persuaded that they are the only people who can, if they have any sense and reflection. They can look back *oculo irretorto* upon what they from knowledge despise ; others have always a hankering after what they are not acquainted with. I look upon all that has passed as one of those romantic dreams that opium commonly occasions, and I do by no means desire to repeat the nauseous dose, for the sake of the fugitive dream. When I say that I have no regret, I do not mean that I have no remorse ; for a life of either business, or still more pleasure, never was, nor never will be, a state of innocence. But God, who knows the strength of human passions, and the weakness of human reason, will, it is to be hoped, rather mercifully pardon, than justly punish, acknowledged errors. . . [1]

To the Bishop of Waterford.

Blackheath, June 26, 1755.

. . . One cannot think of one's own existence, without thinking of the Eternal Author of it ; and one cannot consider his physical or moral attributes, without some fear, though in my mind, still more hopes. It is true we can have no adequate notions of the attributes of a Being, so infinitely superior to us ; but, according to the best notions we are capable of forming of his justice and mercy, the latter, which is the comfortable scale, seems necessarily to preponderate . . [2]

To Solomon Dayrolles, Esq.,

Blackheath, July 10, 1755.

. . . I find that I am got half-way down hill, and then you know the velocity increases very considerably. But what is to be done ? Nothing but patience. Whatever the purest air, constant moderate exercise, and strict regimen can do, I have here ; but they serve only to prolong, for a little time, an irksome situation, which my reason tells me the sooner it is ended, the better.

My deafness is extremely increased, and daily increasing ; this cuts me wholly off from the society of others, and my other complaints deny me the society with

---

[1] Bradshaw, vol. III, pp. 1121–2.   [2] *Ibid.*, p. 1126.

myself, which I proposed when I came here. I have brought down with me a provision of pens, ink and paper, in hopes of amusing myself, and perhaps entertaining or informing posterity by some historical tracts of my own times, which I intended to write with the strictest regard to truth, and none to persons ; myself not excepted. But I have not yet employed my pen, because my mind refused to do its part ; and in writing, as well as in other performances, whatever is not done with spirit and desire, will be very ill done. All my amusements are therefore reduced to the idle business of my little garden, and to the reading of idle books where the mind is seldom called upon. Notwithstanding this unfortunate situation, my old philosophy comes to my assistance, and enables me to repulse the attacks of melancholy, for I never have one melancholic moment. I have seen and appraised everything in its true light, and at its intrinsic value. While others are outbidding one another at the auction, exulting in their acquisitions, or grieving at their disappointments, I am easy, both from reflection and experience of the futility of all that is to be got or lost.

But *trève de réflexions morales*. A man may be too sober as well as too drunk to go into company, and his philosophical reflections may be as troublesome in one case, as his extravagancies in the other . . . [1]

To the Bishop of Waterford.

Blackheath, August 30, 1755.
. . . Hawkins brought me the other day your kind present of Dr. Seed's *Sermons*. I have read some of them and like them very well ; but I have neither read nor intend to read those which are meant to prove the existence of God, because it seems to me too great a disparagement of that reason which He has given us, to require any other proofs of His existence than those which the whole and every part of the creation afford us. If I believe my own existence, I must believe His ; it cannot be proved *a priori*, as some have idly attempted to do, and cannot be doubted of *a posteriori*. Cato says, very justly, " *And that He is, all nature cries aloud.*" . . . [2]

[1] Bradshaw, vol. III, pp. 1127–8.
[2] *Ibid.*, pp. 1134–5.

A Madame La Marquise de Monconseil.

à Londres, ce 25 Décembre 1755.

Je n'ai garde, Madame, de vous faire les complimens usés de la saison, que la fausseté du cœur a depuis longtems rendu suspects, et qu'une politesse prostituée a avilis. Bon jour, bon an, donc, et voilà qui est fait. Je ne puis pourtant pas m'empêcher de vous assurer des vœux que je fais pour votre santé ; aussi bien c'est tout ce qui peut vous manquer. Mes propres maux m'ont attendri sur ce sujet, et à peine puis-je comprendre qu'il y en ait d'autres que la mauvaise santé et la surdité. Il me semble que le mal physique attendrit, autant que le mal moral endurcit, le cœur. Je ne donne plus aux pauvres, qui paroissent se bien porter, je les envie trop ; mais je me ruine en médecines et en aumônes pour les malades. C'est une bricole de l'amour-propre, il est vrai, mais c'est l'humanité, et aussi cet amour-propre produit de bons comme de mauvais effets. . . .[1]

To the Bishop of Waterford.

Blackheath, October 11, 1756.

What can a hermit send you from the deserts of Blackheath, in return for your kind letter, but his hearty thanks ? I see nobody here by choice, and I hear nobody anywhere by fatal necessity ; and as for the thoughts of a deaf, solitary, sick man, they cannot be entertaining for one in health, as I hope you are. Those thoughts which relate to you are such as you would desire—that is, such as you deserve. My others seem to be a succession of dreams, but with this comfortable circumstance, that I have no gloomy ones. No passions agitate me, no fears disturb me, and no silly hopes gull me any longer. I have done with this world, and think of my journey to another, which I believe is not very remote. In the meantime, I shall next week take one to Bath, which the skilful say may perhaps do me good : *à la bonne heure*, I will try. I only ask for negative health, and if those waters will procure me that, I shall be abundantly satisfied . . .[2]

To the Earl of Huntingdon.

Blackheath, August 2, 1757.

. . . We owe the greatest part of our pleasures and our pains to the imagination ; true wisdom encourages and

[1] Bradshaw, vol. III, p. 1145.　　　[2] *Ibid.*, pp. 1155–6.

assists it in the former case, corrects and checks it in the latter. The happiest, and the unhappiest men in the world are those who severally think themselves such, no matter why.[1]

To Dr. Monsey.

Bath, November 8, 1757.

. . . Your faculty will, I hope, pardon me, if, not having the vivacity of ladies, I have not their faith neither. I must own that they always reason right in general ; but I am sorry to say at the same time, that they are commonly wrong in every particular. I stick to that middle point, which their alacrity makes them leap over.

I am persuaded that you can do more than other people ; but then give me leave to add that I fear *that more* is not a great deal. In the famous great fog, some years ago, the blind men were the best guides, having been long used to the streets ; but still they only groped their way ; they did not see it. You have, I am sure, too much of the skill, and too little of the craft, of your profession, to be offended with this image. I heartily wish that it was not so just a one.

Why physical ills exist at all, I do not know ; and I am very sure that no Doctor of Divinity has ever yet given me a satisfactory reason for it : but if there be a reason, that same reason, be it what it will, must necessarily make the art of medicine precarious, and imperfect : otherwise the end of the former would be defeated by the latter.[2]

To the Bishop of Waterford.

Bath, November 22, 1757.

. . . All mineral waters, and the whole *materia medica*, lose their efficacy upon my shattered carcase ; and the enemy within is too hard for them. I bear it all with patience and without melancholy, because I must bear it whether I will or no. Physical ills are the taxes laid upon this wretched life ; some are taxed higher, and some lower, but all pay something. My philosophy teaches me to reflect how much higher, rather than how much lower, I might have been taxed. How gentle are my physical ills

---

[1] *Letters of Lord Chesterfield to Lord Huntingdon*, p. 119.

[2] *Censura Literaria*, vol. IX, (1815), p. 107. Art. DCCLXXI. " Original Letter of the late Lord Chesterfield. (The Superscription lost, but probably addressed to Dr. Monsey)."

compared with the exquisite torments of gout, stone, etc !
The faculties of my mind are, thank God, not yet much
impaired ; and they comfort me in my worst moments,
and amuse me in the best.

I read with more pleasure than ever ; perhaps, because
it is the only pleasure I have left. For since I am struck
out of living company by my deafness, I have recourse to
the dead, whom alone I can hear ; and I have assigned them
their stated hours of audience. Solid *folios* are the people
of business with whom I converse in the morning. *Quartos*
(not *quarts*, pardon the quibble) are the easier mixed
company with whom I sit after dinner ; and I pass my
evenings in the light, and often frivolous, *chit-chat* of small
octavos and *duodecimos*.[1] This, upon the whole, hinders
me from wishing for death, while other considerations
hinder me from fearing it.[2]

To the Bishop of Waterford.
Blackheath, August 29, 1758.

I cannot return such an answer as we could either of us
wish to your frequent and friendly enquiries after my
weakened and decaying body and mind. I am at least
unwell, often worse, and never quite well. My deafness,
which is considerably increased, deprives me of that
consolation which sickness commonly admits of—the
conversation of a few friends ; and my illness deprives
me of the chief consolation under deafness, which is reading
and writing. My head will seldom let me read, and seldomer let me think ; consequently still seldomer let me
write. Shall I tell you that I bear this melancholy situation
with that meritorious constancy and resignation which
most people boast of ? No, for I really cannot help it ;
if I could, I certainly would ; and, since I cannot, I have
common sense and reason enough not to make my situation
worse by unavailing restlessness and regret . . . [3]

To his Son.
London, April 27, 1759.

I have received your two letters of the 10th and 13th
by the last mail ; and I will begin my answer to them by
observing to you, that a wise man, without being a Stoic,
considers, in all misfortunes that befall him, their best as

---

[1] See Letter to his Son, November 4, 1757. Bradshaw, vol. III, p. 1188.
[2] *Ibid.*, pp. 1192-3.   [3] *Ibid.*, p. 1232.

well as their worst side ; and everything has a better and a worst side.   I have strictly observed that rule for many years, and have found by experience that some comfort is to be extracted, under most moral ills, by considering them in every light, instead of dwelling, as people are apt to do, upon the gloomy side of the object.   Thank God, the disappointment that you so pathetically groan under, is not a calamity which admits of no consolation.   Let us simplify it, and see what it amounts to.   You were pleased with the expectation of coming here next month, to see those who would have been pleased with seeing you.   That, from very natural causes, cannot be ; and you must pass this summer at Hamburgh, and next winter in England, instead of passing this summer in England, and next winter at Hamburgh.   Now, estimating things fairly, is not the change rather to your advantage ?   Is not the summer more eligible, both for health and pleasure, than the winter, in that northern frozen zone ?—and will not the winter in England supply you with more pleasures than the summer in an empty capital could have done ?   So far then it appears you are rather a gainer by your misfortune.

The *tour*, too, which you propose making to Lubeck, Altona, etc., will both amuse and inform you ; for, at your age, one cannot see too many different places and people, since at the age you are now of, I take it for granted that you will not see them superficially, as you did when you first went abroad.

This whole matter then, summed up, amounts to no more than this—that you will be here next winter, instead of this summer.   Do not think that all I have said is the consolation only of an old philosophical fellow, almost insensible of pleasure or pain, offered to a young fellow, who has quick sensations of both.   No ; it is the rational philosophy taught me by experience and knowledge of the world, and which I have practised above thirty years. I always made the best of the best, and never made bad worse by fretting.   This enabled me to go through the various scenes of life, in which I have been an actor, with more pleasure and less pain than most people.   You will say perhaps—One cannot change one's nature ; and that, if a person is born of a very sensible [1] gloomy temper,

---

[1] *Sensible* is used in its eighteenth-century sense of "sensitive." Its present meaning was only "in low conversation" according to Johnson's *Dictionary*.—Bradshaw's note.

and apt to see things in the worst light, they cannot help it, nor new-make themselves. I will admit it to a certain degree, and but to a certain degree ; for, though we cannot totally change our nature, we may in a great measure correct it, by reflection and philosophy ; and some philosophy is a very necessary companion in this world, where, even to the most fortunate, the chances are greatly against happiness.

I am not old enough, nor tenacious enough, to pretend not to understand the main purport of your last letter ; and to show you that I do, you may draw upon me for two hundred pounds, which I hope will more than clear you.

Good-night ! *aequam memento rebus in arduis servare mentem* ; be neither transported nor depressed by the accidents of life.[1]

To the Bishop of Waterford.

London, December 9, 1759.

I have been often within these three months, not only too ill to write, but too ill to speak, think or move. I have now a favourable moment of negative health, and that is the most that I must ever expect ; and I think I cannot employ it better than in thanking you for your friendship, and in assuring you of mine. When I reflect upon the poor remainder of my life, I look upon it as a burden that must every day grow heavier and heavier, from the natural progression of physical ills, the usual companions of increasing years ; and my reason tells me that I should wish for the end of it ; but instinct, often stronger than reason, and perhaps oftener in the right, makes me take all proper methods to put it off. This innate sentiment alone makes me bear life with patience ; for I assure you I have no farther hopes ; but, on the contrary, many fears from it. None of the primitive Anchorets in the *Thebais* could be more detached from life than I am. I consider it as one who is wholly unconcerned in it ; and, even when I reflect back upon what I have seen, what I have heard, and what I have done myself, I can hardly persuade myself that all that frivolous hurry and bustle, and pleasures of the world, had any reality ; but they seem to have been the dreams of restless nights. This philosophy, however, I thank God, neither makes me sour nor melancholic ; I see the folly and absurdity of mankind, without

[1] Bradshaw, vol. III, pp. 1254-6.

indignation or peevishness. I wish them wiser, and consequently better than they are. I pity the weak and the wicked, without envying the wise and good, but endeavouring to the utmost of my abilities to be one of that minority . . . [1]

To the Bishop of Waterford.

London, January 22, 1760.

When I received your last letter, I was not in a condition to answer, and hardly to read it ; I was so extremely ill, that I little thought that I should live to the date of this letter. I have within these few months more than once seen death very near ; and when one does see it near, let the best or the worst people say what they please, it is a very serious consideration. I thank God I saw it without very great terrors ; but, at the same time, the divine attribute of mercy, which gives us comfort, cannot make us forget, nor ought it, His attribute of justice, which must blend some fears with our hopes.

The Faculty tell me that I am now much better, and to be sure I am so, compared with what I was a fortnight ago ; but, however, still in a very weak and lingering condition, not likely in my opinion to hold out long ; but whether my end be more or less remote, I know I am tottering upon the brink of this world, and my thoughts are employed about the other. However, while I crawl upon this planet, I think myself obliged to do what good I can, in my narrow domestic sphere, to my fellow-creatures, and to wish them all the good I cannot do . . . [2]

Upon these last two letters Churton Collins comments as follows :—" He so abhorred anything which savours of cant, and especially of theological cant, that he seldom touches on religious subjects. But he does so sometimes, and that with an earnestness which will surprise every one who knows him only as people in general know him."

After quoting the last two sentences in each of the two preceding passages, he continues, " It is the reflection of all this, of this mingled sadness and cheerfulness, good sense and good temper, mild wisdom and wise mildness, which is perhaps the chief attraction of these Letters. The voice which is speaking is, we feel, the voice of one without faith and with little hope, but at peace with

[1] *Ibid.*, p. 1262.   [2] *Ibid.*, p. 1263.

himself and at peace with the world, grateful to Nature for having called him into life, and to Philosophy for having taught him how to live. Much experience and reflection had enabled him to estimate at its true value what it is in the power of man to attain and enjoy. He had reckoned with existence and struck the balance. The delusions of the brute and the fool had never misguided or perplexed him : to the visions of the transcendentalist he was constitutionally blind, but he had found the secret which had escaped equally the ascetic and the sensualist—the art of living, the true use of fortune. He knew how little of what constitutes human happiness and contentment depends on man's mere capacities and externals ; he knew of how much which constitutes both they may be made the means."—*Essays and Studies*, pp. 212-214.

To the Bishop of Waterford.

London, April 29, 1760.

. . . I now read Solomon with a sort of sympathetic feeling. I have been as wicked and as vain, though not so wise as he ; but am now at last wise enough to feel and attest the truth of his reflection, that all is vanity and vexation of spirit. This truth is never sufficiently discovered or felt by mere speculation ; experience in this case is necessary for conviction, though perhaps at the expense of some morality. . .

My stay in this world cannot be long. God, who placed me here, only knows when He will order me out of it ; but whenever He does, I shall most willingly obey His command, with confidence in His mercy . . . [1]

To the Bishop of Waterford.

Blackheath, August 28, 1760.

. . . I am now a little better, but this better moment is no security that the next will not be a very bad one, for I am more than *journalier* in my complaints ; even hours make great variations in them. This, you must allow, is an unfortunate latter end of my life, and consequently a tiresome one ; but I must own, too, that perhaps it is a very just one, and a sort of balance to the tumultuous and imaginary pleasures of the former part of it. In the general course of things there seems to be, upon the whole, a pretty equal distribution of physical good and evil, some extra-

[1] Bradshaw, vol. III, pp. 1265-6.

ordinary cases excepted ; and even moral good and evil seem mixed to a certain degree ; for one never sees any body so perfectly good, or so perfectly bad as they might be. Why this is so, it is in vain for us upon this subject to inquire, for it is not given us yet to know. I behold it with a respectful admiration, and cry out *O altitudo!* . . . [1]

To the Bishop of Waterford.

Blackheath, Sept. 4, 1762.

. . . God has sent physical as well as moral ills into the world ; and for good and wise reasons of His own, I am convinced, which I do not pretend to know ; nor do I at all admit those reasons which men are pleased to assign for it. I wish mankind would condescend to be respectfully ignorant of many things, which it is impossible they can ever know whilst in this world. But no, we must know every thing ; and our pride will not let us own our ignorance . . . [2]

To his Son.

Blackheath, September 30, 1763.

. . . The present inaction, I believe, gives you leisure enough for *ennui*, but it gives you time enough too for better things ; I mean, reading useful books ; and, what is still more useful, conversing with yourself some part of every day. Lord Shaftesbury recommends self-conversation[3] to all authors ; and I would recommend it to all men ; they would be the better for it. Some people have not time, and fewer have inclination, to enter into that conversation ; nay, very many dread it, and fly to the most trifling dissipations in order to avoid it ; but if a man would allot half an hour every night, for this self-conversation, and recapitulate with himself whatever he has done, right or wrong, in the course of the day, he would be both the better and the wiser for it.[4] My deafness gives me more than sufficient time for self-conversation ; and I have found great advantages from it.[5]

The advice contained in this letter was probably derived

---

[1] Bradshaw, vol. III, pp. 1266–7.   [2] *Ibid.*, pp. 1279–80.
[3] Shaftesbury uses the words " self-examine " and " self-inspection " (*Characteristics*, I, 168 and 196), but not, I think, " self-conversation."— Note by Dr. Hill in *The Worldly Wisdom of Lord Chesterfield*.
[4] *Cf.* Letter to his Son, October 26, 1757. Bradshaw, vol. III, p. 1184.
[5] *Ibid.*, p. 1297.

from Cicero, *de Senectute* XI. " Pythagoreorum more exercendae memoriae gratia, quid quoque die dixerim, audierim, egerim, commemoro vesperi " ; upon which Melmoth observes :—

" It was not in order to exercise and improve the memory, that Pythagoras enjoined his disciples the practice of this nightly recollection ; it was for a much more useful and important purpose. The object of the philosopher's precept is indeed wholly of a moral nature, as appears from that noble summary of his Ethics, supposed to be drawn up by one of his disciples, and known by the name of the ' Golden Verses of Pythagoras ':—

' Μηδ' ὕπνον μαλακοισι ἐπ' ὄμμασι ' etc.

' Nightly forbear to close thine eyes to rest
Ere thou hast questioned well thy conscious breast
What sacred duty thou hast left undone—
What act committed which thou ought 'st to shun.
And, as fair truth or error marks the deed,
Let sweet applause, or sharp reproach succeed :
So shall thy steps, while this great rule is thine,
Undevious lead in Virtue's paths divine.'

" It is not a little surprising that Cicero should have considered this great precept merely in its *mechanical* operation upon one of the faculties of the human mind, and have passed over unnoticed its most important intent and efficacy ; especially as he had so fair an occasion of pointing out its nobler purpose. Perhaps there never was a rule of conduct delivered by any uninspired moralist which hath so powerful a tendency to promote the interests of virtue as the present precept."

A Madame La Marquise de Monconseil.

à Londres, ce 23 Avril, 1764.

. . . *Job de mille maux atteint* [1] n'avoit pas plus de patience, que ma philosophie ne m'en procure ; la lecture m'occupe et m'amuse : d'ailleurs, j'ai le loisir d'avoir plusieurs tête-à-têtes avec moi-même, dont je me flatte d'avoir profité, et auxquels je n'avois jamais pensé, pendant que j'étois rapidement emporté par le tourbillon des

---

[1] The beginning of a well-known sonnet by Benserade.—Bradshaw's note.

affaires, ou des plaisirs ; de sorte que, graces à Dieu, je n'ai ni mélancolie ni humeur, et nonobstant tous mes maux, *j'en connois de plus misérables* . . . [1]

To the Bishop of Waterford.

Blackheath, October 1, 1764.

. . . I am never free from physical ills of one kind or another, but use and patience make them supportable ; and I own this obligation to them, that they have cured me of worse ills than themselves, I mean moral ills, for they have given me leisure to examine, and reflection to subdue all my passions. I think only of doing my duty to my Creator, and to my fellow-created beings, and *omnis in hoc sum* . . . [2]

To the Bishop of Waterford.

Blackheath, October 10, 1766.

I am conscious that I have been long in your debt ; and, were my letters of any value, I would make you my excuses for non-payment. The mind unfortunately keeps pace in decay with the body, and age and infirmities weaken them equally. I feel it most sensibly ; my body totters, and my understanding stutters ; but, I thank God, I am wise enough still not to put either of them upon attempting what neither of them could probably perform. I have run the silly rounds both of pleasure and business, and have done with them all. I think there is some merit in knowing when to have done. I have lived here at my hermitage in peaceful retirement all this summer without any grievous physical ills, but at the same time never quite free from some of the lesser ones. Upon the whole I have no reason to murmur at my lot ; it is better than I have deserved ; and, as I have generally observed, that there is a compensation of good and ill, even in this world, I ought not to complain, considering the former part of my life, that the latter part of it is as wretched as it now is, I mean relative to my deafness . . . [3]

To the Bishop of Waterford.

London, August 12, 1771.

. . . I am most prodigiously old, and every month of the calendar adds at least a year to my age. My hand trembles

---

[1] Bradshaw, vol. III, p. 1306. [2] *Ibid.*, p. 1313. [3] *Ibid.*, pp. 1346–7.

U

to that degree that I can hardly hold my pen,[1] my understanding stutters, and my memory fumbles. I have exhausted all the physical ills of Pandora's box, without finding hope at the bottom of it ; but who can hope at seventy-seven ? One must only seek for little comforts at that age. One of mine is that all my complaints are rather teasing than torturing ; and my lot, compared with that of many other people's, who deserve a better, seems rather favourable. Philosophy, and confidence in the mercy of my Creator, mutually assist me in bearing my share of physical ills, without murmuring . . . [2]

[1] " The original of this is written in a very trembling hand."—Note in Maty's edition.
[2] Bradshaw, vol. III, p. 1397.

X

A SHORT BIBLIOGRAPHICAL NOTE ON CHESTERFIELD'S LETTERS

Letters to his Son.

The best edition is that with an Introduction by Charles Strachey (72 pp.) and notes by Annette Calthrop, Methuen and Co., 1901 ; 2 vols. ; the prefatory note to which begins as follows :—" In these Letters, as originally published, a large number of proper names were left blank, and many passages (especially in the later letters) were omitted. The blanks remained, and the existence of the omitted passages was unsuspected, until the original manuscript came into Lord Mahon's possession—unfortunately too late to be utilised in his collected edition of Lord Chesterfield's *Letters and Works*, which appeared in 1845. A supplementary volume, however, was issued by him in 1853, wherein, in an Appendix, he printed the omitted names and passages with references to the places where they should properly appear. Subsequent editors have, oddly enough, ignored these interesting emendations, with the exception of Mr. Bradshaw, who, on the other hand, omits a large number of the letters (those addressed to a little boy) altogether, and follows Lord Mahon in distributing the later ones chronologically among Lord Chesterfield's letters to persons other than his son. The present edition, which embodies all Lord Mahon's *Addenda* and omits no letters, may therefore claim to be the most complete that has yet appeared."

Letters to his Godson.

The only edition is *Letters of Philip Dormer fourth Earl of Chesterfield to his Godson and Successor now first edited from the originals with a Memoir of Lord Chesterfield by the Earl of Carnarvon*, Clarendon Press, 1890 ; to which there is an appendix consisting of *Letters from the Earl of Chesterfield to Arthur Charles Stanhope Esq.*, etc., etc.

(*First Printed in* 1817). There are 236 letters to the Godson. In the Appendix are 96 letters from Chesterfield to A. C. Stanhope and one from Chesterfield to Dodd. There are also three letters from A. C. Stanhope to Chesterfield, one from Philip Stanhope to Chesterfield, and one from him to his father, A. C. Stanhope.

Letters to Lord Huntingdon.

These were discovered in the archives of the Countess of Loudoun, and published for the first time in 1923 under the title of *Letters of Lord Chesterfield to Lord Huntingdon with Introduction and Notes by A. Francis Steuart*, Medici Society. They consist of 46 letters written to Lord Huntingdon, ranging from 1749 to 1769, and one to Chesterfield's brother, Sir William Stanhope, March 2, 1756.

Miscellaneous Letters.

These are at present in an unsatisfactory state of collection. The first attempt at a complete collection after Maty's editions was made by Mahon in his four-volume edition of 1845, containing also the *Letters to his Son*, but only 15 of those to his godson,[1] and three of the letters to A. C. Stanhope. In the supplementary volume of 1853, alluded to above by C. Strachey, appear, besides the *addenda* to the *Letters to his Son*, several pages of omitted passages in the letters to the Bishop of Waterford ; the earlier letters to his son, omitted by him in his previous volumes ; and 16 other letters, including 11 to Lord Lyttelton.

The only other edition purporting to be complete is *The Letters of Philip Dormer Stanhope, Earl of Chesterfield, with the Characters*. Edited by John Bradshaw, M.A. LL.D. ; Swan, Sonnenschein and Co., 1892. (Republished by George Allen and Co., 1913.) 3 vols. Bradshaw states in his preface that " This edition of Chesterfield's ' Letters and Characters ' contains all that was published by Lord Mahon in his four-volume edition of 1845, together with the ' omitted passages ' in the letters to the Bishop of Waterford and to Chesterfield's son, which were supplied in the supplemental volume in 1853, and now first appear in their proper places."

---

[1] *I.e.* the series of 14 on *The Art of Pleasing* and the letter to be delivered to him after Chesterfield's death.

This statement is not strictly accurate. It would appear that Bradshaw was unaware of the contents of Mahon's supplementary volume until his first two volumes were in print. Whether this surmise is correct or not, the fact is that the only " omitted passages " which he inserts are in his third volume. The first omission in the letters to the Bishop of Waterford, and the first eight in those to his son have been disregarded. It may be added that in the passages that he has inserted occur at least eight departures from Mahon's text, most of them misprints. But these are relatively unimportant points. What is unfortunate is that Bradshaw has not inserted the 16 additional letters appearing in Mahon vol. V, of which he makes no mention at all in his preface. On the other hand, it may be claimed for Bradshaw that the Waterford correspondence is practically complete in his edition, and that it contains five letters not in Mahon : namely, one to the Lords Justices of Ireland, November 18, 1746 ; three to George Faulkner, April, 1746, May 11, 1758, December 3, 1761 ; and one to Solomon Dayrolles, January 7, 1758.

The only other non-political letters of any interest that I have been able to find, besides the twenty-six which appear in the following section, are :—

One to Dr. Monsey dated November 8, 1757, which appears in *Censura Literaria* (edit. 1815), vol. IX, p. 107. Art. DCCLXXXI. Part of this letter will be found on p, 281 *ante*.

One to Dr. Samuel Squire dated October 29, 1758. Add. MSS. (*Newcastle Papers*) 32885, f. 192. This is printed in full in Ernst's *Life*, pp. 506–8.

One to Lord Lyttelton dated May 7, 1760, thanking him for sending Chesterfield a copy of the *Dialogues of the Dead*. It is printed in full in *Elizabeth Montagu, The Queen of the Blue Stockings* (ed. Emily J. Climenson, 1906), vol. II, pp. 181–182.

Partially printed Letters.

Thirty-eight to Baron Torck (1731–47), long extracts from which appear in " Some Unpublished Letters of Lord Chesterfield," *Nineteenth Century*, August and September, 1912. (See pp. 49 and 163 *ante*.)

Two printed in the *English Historical Review*, October,

1889 : vol. IV, pp. 750–3. The name of the recipient in neither case appears. One, from which an extract is given on p. 86 *ante*, is dated July 23, 1745, a month before Chesterfield's arrival in Ireland. The other, dated March 5, 1745–6 (*i.e.* seven weeks before his departure from Ireland) gives an entertaining account (doubtless from Newcastle's information) of the resignation of the Pelham Government in the previous month, and its successful return forty hours later, after Granville's failure to form a ministry.

Two which appear in Coxe's *Memoirs of Lord Walpole*, vol. II,—namely, one to Sir C. H. Williams of December 8, 1747 (pp. 284–5) and one to Horace (Lord) Walpole of March 22, 1748–9 (p. 239).

About twenty in various volumes of the Historical MSS. Commission, extracts from the more interesting of which have appeared in these pages.

Unpublished Letters.

The most important of those in private collections referred to but not printed in *Reports of the Historical MSS. Commission* would seem to be :—

Letters to Sarah, Duchess of Marlborough.—*Marlborough Papers.* 8th Report (1881), Appendix I, p. 18. To these I have been unable to obtain access.

Letter to the Earl of Dartmouth, February 20, 1766, expressing his abhorrence of the Stamp Act.—*Dartmouth Papers.* 14th Report. Appendix Part X, p. 36.

Besides these, there are in the British Museum and Public Record Office some hundreds of official letters written by Chesterfield in the various capacities of Ambassador at the Hague (1728–32 and 1745) ; Lord Lieutenant of Ireland (1745–6) ; and Secretary of State (1746–8). The most interesting are those written in the years 1745 and 1746, extracts from which appear in the *Life of Lord Chesterfield* by W. Ernst, who has made his selections with much skill and judgment. The rest deal for the most part with current diplomatic affairs and are of no general interest. Some forty of them occur in the editions of Mahon and Bradshaw under the years 1728–31 and 1745–47. Except for the historical student these letters can be said to have little value, and appear as excrescences on the pages of Chesterfield's personal correspondence.

XI

UNPUBLISHED LETTERS

To the Hon. Mrs. Howard.[1]

Tunbridge, July 22nd.[2]

MADAM,

Tho' I hope you can't suspect me of negligence where you are concern'd, yett, being disappointed of the pleasure of obeying your commands, I must take the liberty to assure you that nothing but an utter impossibility should have hinder'd me. Here are yett no wheatears, but I have bespoke the first that come, and shall not fail to send them.

I have found no diversions here that have hinder'd my regretting of Richmond, but I believe my last week at Richmond may have made me partial against any other place. Who that is owing to, I leave you to guess, and if you find them out, begg you would tell them, in a better manner than I am able, how sensible I am of their goodness. I hope it is unnecessary to assure you that I am, with the greatest respect and sincerity,

Your most obedient humble servant, STANHOPE.[3]

To The Hon. Mrs. Howard.

Hague, Sept. 23rd, N.S. 1729.

MADAM,

Had I been as lately at Paris as Lord Herbert, I should be better able to thank you, as I ought, for the ring Lady Albemarle brought me ; and a string of compliments, as well turn'd and as neatly sett as the Ring itself, would have expressed my thanks for it ; but from a place where I am now in a manner naturaliz'd, and where we content our selves with speaking our real thoughts without art or ornament, you must accept of the plain, hearty Dutch acknowledgment of *Ick bedanck u mevrouw*.

I confess I hear'd with some surprize that my noble Lord, in his travels to Paris, had discover'd that a very great bagg to a wigg was less troublesome than two very

---

[1] Henrietta, eldest daughter of Sir Henry Hobart, Bart. : married, about 1708, the Hon. Charles Howard who succeeded in 1731 to the earldom of Suffolk. There are sixteen other letters to her from Chesterfield, first published in an abridged form by J. W. Croker in his edition of the *Suffolk Letters* and reprinted in the same form in Mahon and Bradshaw.

[2] Before 1725. [3] Add. MSS. 22626, f. 86 (*Suffolk Papers*).

little knotts ; till I was credibly inform'd afterwards that
his Lordship, who always unites use and ornament, had
very good reasons for what he did ; that that bagg was in
reality his knapp-sack, that, instead of hair, it was fill'd
with water cresses and Beet root, and that my Lord had
victuall'd himself for six months in it, in hopes of a campaign
against the King of Prussia ; and they added, too, that
some waggs had therefore call'd it My Lord's Campaign
wigg. How true these informations are, you, who are
upon the place, are best able to judge, but I own they have
the air of probability. You'l see Lady Albemarle again,
as soon as the Yatcht can come here and return, for she
begins already to be very weary of the tranquillity of this
place, which at present is really very empty. It was lucky
she came as she did, or else his Majesty would have had
ne're a Yatcht to have carried him to England, where I
reckon and hope that he arriv'd safely yesterday. By the
King's early return your winter will begin early this year.
I could wish I were to take a share of it, and at least
prevent my being quite forgott in England ; but, since I
can hardly expect such a pleasure, I must content my self
with that of assuring you, at this distance, that it is impossible to be with greater truth and respect,

Your most obedient, humble servant, CHESTERFIELD.[1]

To the Earl of Essex.[2]

London, June y° 21st, 1733.

MY DEAR LORD,

Your friendship to me and the kindness you have show'd
Earl Stanhope,[3] will, I am sure, make you forgive the
liberty I take of recommending the bearer, his brother,[4]
to you. He is to stay a year at the Academy at Turin,
and during that time flatters himself with having your
protection, which I am perswaded he will endeavour to
deserve. Unless he is very much alter'd, he is a fine,
sprightly, idle boy with very good parts and no application.

---

[1] Add. MSS. 22626, f. 100. As a matter of fact, Chesterfield applied
for leave a fortnight later, and left the Hague for ten months on October
31, 1729. See p. 35 ante.

[2] William Capel, 3rd Earl of Essex (1697-1743). At this time ambassador
to the King of Sardinia at Turin.

[3] 2nd Earl Stanhope (1714-1786) and second cousin of Chesterfield's
father. For his character see Mahon's History of England, chap. xxv.

[4] George Stanhope, for whom Chesterfield tried unsuccessfully to obtain
a colonelcy in 1748. See p. 120 ante.

And, unless your Lordship is very much alter'd, I flatter myself these qualifications will not make him very disagreable to you. I don't know whether it may not seem impertinent, in a disgrac'd Courtier,[1] to apply for a favour to a person who represents his late Master, but, however, I have some hopes of success from having previously applied to Monsieur Villette,[2] your first Minister, in a manner I could not find in my heart to do to some other body's. In short, raillerie apart, I shall always expect every thing from your friendship and good nature, as I desire you will be perswaded of the attachment of, My Dear Lord,

Your most faithfull humble servant, CHESTERFIELD.[3]

To the Earl of Essex.

London, Nov. ye 29th, 1733. O.S.

MY DEAR LORD,

Though my acknowledgements for the favour of your letter come late, they are not, I assure you, the less sincere ; and nobody can be more sensible than I am of your kindness

To a man who marrys for the first time with fear and trembling the congratulations of a friend, who has try'd that state twice with success, are exceedingly comfortable as well as obliging, and give one reason to hope it may not be so bad as it is generally represented. For my own part, I found both my constitution and my fortune so much the worse for wearing that they would neither of 'em pay at sight ; from whence I concluded it was high time to lay aside the fine gentleman, and to think of repairing them.[4]

I have by this post wrote to Mr. Vilette, concerning George Stanhope, in whose name I must again thank you for all your civilitys to him, which I look upon as so many marks of your friendship to, My Dear Lord, Your most faithfull and most obedient servant, CHESTERFIELD.

I begg my respects to Lady Essex.[5]

---

[1] Chesterfield had been dismissed from his post as Lord Steward in April 1732. See p. 59 *ante*.

[2] A Swiss ; afterwards minister in Switzerland. See *Marchmont Papers*, vol. I, p. 217.

[3] Add. MSS. 27732, f. 180.

[4] Chesterfield had married on the 5th of September previously. See p. 166 *ante*.

[5] Add. MSS. 27732, f. 286.

To the Earl of Essex.

London, April ye 8th, O.S. 1734.

MY DEAR LORD,

I don't know what to say to you for your kindness to my two sons, for I look upon them as such.[1] All I can offerr you in return is, about eighteen years hence, by which time there may be possibly a change of Affairs, to send Earl Stanhope Ambassador to what Court you like best, to take the same care of Lord Capel.[2] In the mean time I heartily thank you, and that's all I can do. I have, according to your directions, writt to Earl Stanhope to approve extreamly of his attending you this summer, which letter I take the liberty of inclosing here. I am sure he cannot be any where so well, to my satisfaction, nor, by his account, to his own.

You frighten us Country gentlemen out of our wits with your wars and rumours of wars, and, as we are in a state of ignorance, we tremble at the terrors of troops and taxes. My apprehensions are still the greater, because your Honour did not use to pass for a peace maker in this part of the world.

I suppose you expect no news from one so much out of all parts of the world as I am. Married and out of Court at the same time, I am equally a stranger to the busy and to the Polite part of Mankind.[3] The best I can expect is that you will excuse a dull letter in consideration of [the] truth and regard, with which the writer is, My Dear Lord,

Your most faithfull humble servant, CHESTERFIELD.

I begg my respects to Lady Essex.[4]

To Dr. William Warburton.[5]

London, May 15th, 1742.

SIR,

I must thank you doubly, both for your remembrance of me, and the pleasing mark you give me of it, your book.[6]

---

[1] Both their parents had died before the eldest son was eight years old.

[2] The eldest son of Lord Essex.

[3] This sentence is quoted by Mr. Sichel in *Bolingbroke and His Times*, vol. II, p. 72. See p. 173 *ante*.

[4] Add. MSS. 27733, f. 55.

[5] (1698-1779). Theologian and Bishop of Gloucester. Friend and literary executor of Pope whose works he edited.

[6] A new edition of *A Critical and Philosophical Commentary on Mr. Pope's " Essay on Man."*

Those who can judge of the merit of the latter will have the just value for the former ; and I don't know which will give me the most pleasure, reading your book, or writing upon the first page of it, that it was given me by the Author.

I hope you have entirely recovered your health, and that you are able to pursue your studys with as much pleasure as they give to others, and particularly to

Your faithfull humble servant, CHESTERFIELD.[1]

To the Earl of Stair.

London, January 6th, 1743.

MY DEAR LORD,

I waited for some better opportunity than that of the common post to have returned you my thanks for your letter which, in the variety of affairs you must have upon your hands, I lookt upon as a flattering mark of your remembrance and friendship ; but, not finding any body that was going to you, I would delay no longer ; and the curious, if they think proper to open my letter, may know, what I am proud to own, that you have not a more faithfull servant in the world.

I wish I could tell you that things on this side of the Water were in a situation of adding weight to operations on the other side ; but that is not the case. The publick dissatisfaction is certainly greater than ever. The Nation sees with uneasyness that the change of a few men has not produced the least change of domestick measures, but rather the contrary ; and those very men are the avow'd screens of former men and measures which they so much condemned, and tread in the paths of their predecessors even with rather more vehemence.

They oppose without shame whatever is proposed in favour of the Constitution, though they themselves had formerly been the proposers of those very constitutional measures ; and the nation, thus disappointed by those they confided in, you will easily believe must be exasperated in proportion. The Person [2] you mention has been too much the cause ever to be the cure of these evils ; nor has he now any weight any where if he would use it well.

---

[1] Egerton MSS. 1955, f. 3.
[2] Probably Carteret. See p. 19 *ante*.

I heartily wish the affairs in your department[1] may go better. As far as they depend upon you I am sure they will, but as it has been of late the fashion for ministers to become immediately, *virtute officii*, both generals and admirals, the abilitys of either are no security for success.[2] I do not know whether this fashion is now more alter'd or not ; if it be, it is the only one.

George Stanhope gives me such accounts of your kindness to him that I must return you my thanks for it, and do him the justice to say that he is extremely sensible of it.

Adieu, my dear Lord ; all happyness and success attend you, and believe me with inviolable attachment

Your most humble faithfull servant, CHESTERFIELD.[3]

To Dr. William Warburton.

London, June y⁰ 4th, 1745.

SIR,

It is with great pleasure that I can now offer you to be one of my Domestic Chaplains in Ireland, if you approve of that situation. I hope it will soon enable me to put you in a better. Your merit has long since entitl'd you to much more than your fortune has done for you, and I shall be very glad to do justice to the former, and supply the defects of the latter. If this proposal is not disagreable to you, you will be at Dublin the 25th of next August where you will meet,

Your faithfull humble servant, CHESTERFIELD.[4]

To Dr. William Warburton.

London, June y⁰ 20th, 1745.

SIR,

Though I regret the loss of your company to Ireland, the reasons that deprive me of it are so just, and so uncommon, that they add to my esteem for you.

[1] He was then in command of the British army in Flanders.

[2] Chesterfield's gloomy forebodings proved only too true. The victory at Dettingen was turned to little advantage. "The King's camp was distracted with jarring counsels and rival pretensions : Lord Stair, above all, complained with bitterness that his advice had been slighted ; and he delivered to His Majesty an angry memorial, reflecting on past transactions, hinting at Hanoverian partialities, and asking permission to retire, as he expressed it, to his plough. His resignation was immediately accepted, not without some marks of the Royal displeasure at the language in which it was tendered." Mahon's *History of England*, vol. III, chap. 25, p. 152 ? See also Stone to Harrington, September 11, 1743. (Coxe's *Pelham*.)

[3] Add. MSS. 35455, f. 62.

[4] Egerton MSS. 1955, f. 5.

The offices of filial duty and friendship are so seldom proof against the views of private interest, that where they do prevail over it they deserve particular distinction. I shall therefore always wish and endeavour to show you here, since I can't in Ireland, the esteem and friendship with which I am,

Your most faithfull, humble servant, CHESTERFIELD.[1]

To Sir Thomas Robinson.[2]

London, July 9th, O.S. 1745.

SIR,

I receiv'd the favour of your letter of the 19th June N.S. with all the satisfaction that such expressions of friendship and esteem can give to one who has the same sentiments for the person from whom he receives 'em, however undeservedly. *Laudari a laudato viro* was always reckon'd a pardonable piece of vanity, and by that rule I am sure my vanity could not be better flatter'd, nor less blameable.

I know Dr. Cornabé a little personally, and have always hear'd him very well spoken of ; but your recommendation alone is sufficient to make me impatient to do him any service I can, and I wish I had a Prospect of serving him sooner, but I must tell you, what you will easily conceive to be my case, that I lye under many previous engagements to some clergymen from old and long acquaintance, and to others from the early importunity of their sollicitations, and the weight of their patrons. I can therefore only promise you that I will not forget Dr. Cornabé, when my present engagements set me at liberty to show him the weight your recommendation, independently of his own merit, will always have with me.

We wait here with impatience for some good news from the Rhine ; from Flanders we can expect none ; from Bohemia we rather wish that [than ?] hope some ; and from Italy we have yet no little prelude to teach us what to expect. Our Cordial (and indeed we want one) must come from the Rhine. We have had several reports of

---

[1] Egerton MSS. 1955, f. 7.

[2] (1695–1770). Ambassador at Vienna 1730–1748. Afterwards Secretary of State. Created Lord Grantham 1761. There are six letters from Chesterfield to Robinson in the Miscellaneous Letters, and many unpublished ones on diplomatic matters written to him at Vienna when Chesterfield was at the Hague in 1731–32.—Add. MSS. 23781–23784 *passim*. (*Robinson Papers*.) See pp. 47–54 *ante*.

advantages gain'd over the prince of Conti, but hitherto they have all prov'd groundless. I cannot help suspecting the Court of Dresden, which is as apt to Gallicize as ever Pythia was to Phillipize ; [1] and distress added to coquettry has made many a whore of women naturally as virtuous at least as that Court.

This is certainly a period big with great and decisive events ; a few weeks more must necessarily draw up the curtain, till when all speculations are vain. I'll trouble you with no more of mine, which I own give me no great pleasure. I have much more in assuring you of one plain simple truth, which is that I am with the most perfect esteem and regard,

Sir, Your most faithfull and obedient servant,

CHESTERFIELD.[2]

To Lord Hardwicke.[3]

Dublin Castle, Nov. y⁰ 28th, 1745.

MY LORD,

Mr. Belcher brought me this morning the honour of your Lordship's letter, by which I find he has been misinform'd as to the promotion of Mr. Tennison, of which there is not the least probability, there being no vacancy upon the Bench at present, nor any likelyhood of there being any soon, I can, with truth, assure your Lordship that I am desirous, and even impatient to serve Mr. Belcher, but your Lordship knows very well that sometimes a certain concurrence of circumstances will make it impossible for one to do what one has the greatest mind to do. This was my case with regard to the place of Commissioner of Appeals which I lately dispos'd of. The Lord Chancellor here, a man of great worth, sollicited it strongly for the

[1] During the Sacred War, Philip of Macedon was entrusted with the care of Apollo's Temple at Delphi, the shrine of the Pythian Oracle. (See Grote's *History of Greece*, Part II, chap. 89.)

How far Chesterfield's suspicions with regard to the Court of Dresden were justified, it is impossible to say. By the Quadruple Alliance, concluded in January, 1745, between England, Holland, Austria, and Saxony, the latter Power undertook the defence of Bohemia in return for a subsidy of £150,000. Soon after the date of this letter, however, Frederick of Prussia, then in alliance with the French; overran Saxony, and, after defeating the Austrians and Saxons at Pirna on December 15th, imposed terms on the Elector (Frederick Augustus II, King of Poland) by the Treaty of Dresden signed on Christmas Day, 1745.

[2] Add. MSS. 23820, f. 367. (*Robinson Papers.*)

[3] Philip Yorke, 1st Earl of Hardwicke (1690–1764). Lord Chancellor 1737–1756.

person to whom I gave it, the son of the Lord Chief Justice Marlay. Here are partys, though not of Whigg and Tory, and they insult each other, and are consider'd by the public as supported or disgrac'd in proportion as the favours of the Government are granted or refus'd to each. And Lord Chancellor happen'd to be in such a situation that a refusal of that small favour would have stamp'd the disgrace of the Government upon him, and would have made many think, and more say that every thing was thrown into the hands of another set of people. I have troubl'd your Lordship with this little detail only to justify my self from the least suspicion of negligence in obeying your commands. I have heard with great concern of the still unsettl'd state of both foreign and domestic affairs, and agree intirely with your Lordship that till a strong and right connection is form'd at home, nothing can be done abroad. But I say it with sorrow as to my self, and with shame for other people, places only can (I see), form that connection. A certain degree of force *somewhere* can alone extort those places, and bring about the foreign measures necessary, in consequence of the connection form'd by those places. What those foreign measures will or can be, God knows, but from the present situation and disposition of all those powers, who either are, or call themselves our Allys, as well as from our own circumstances, the continuation of the war seems to me impossible.

Your Lordship does me a great deal too much honour in thinking that my presence could be of any use : though I am sensible of the contrary, I am doubly proud of your Lordship's error, as it is the first I have ever known you entertain, and as it can therefore only proceed from your partiality to

Your Lordship's most obedient humble servant,

CHESTERFIELD.[1]

To Edward Eliot.[2]

London, June ye 9th, O.S. 1747.

S^r,

I am very much oblig'd to you for the favour of your letter which I receiv'd yesterday ; and I flatter my self that the arrangement which I have now made for your

---

[1] Add. MSS. 35588, f. 166 (*Hardwicke Papers*).
[2] See p. 200 *ante*.

young fellow-traveller, will so co-incide with your intentions, that it will continue to him for some time longer the pleasure and advantage of your company. It is no compliment to you to assure you, that that advantage, is the principal motive of the disposition I have made, for the particulars of which, I referr you to my letter by this Post to Mr. Harte. The best German is spoke, and the best Professors in Germany are now at Leipsig, two objects that seem to make part of yours, and your Father's plan. I wish the Boy may deserve the Character which you are pleas'd to give me of him, but I am sure that the best chance he has to deserve it, is to follow both your advice and example. I am with the greatest truth and esteem S^r

Your most obedient humble servant

CHESTERFIELD.[1]

To Dr. William Warburton

London. Dec. ye 31st, 1747.

SIR,

I return you my sincerest thanks for the last edition of your " Alliance Between Church and State," [2] which was sent me a few days ago by your orders.

I had read the former edition with attention and pleasure, and am sure that I shall read this with more, in proportion as it is enlarged. One may say of Church and State what our late friend Pope said of wit and judgement

" . . . ever are at strife
Though meant each other's aid like man and wife." [3]

But you have shown the utility and means of their agreement, an agreement which I have always thought so necessary, both for their mutuall interest and the advantage of the whole, that I am particularly flattered by your thinking me worthy to be the patron of so useful a work. I wish I were more worthy of what your partial friendship makes you say in the dedication, but, to tell you the truth, I am not the less pleased with it ; for as one fears Satyr, though ever so groundless, in the apprehension that some

---

[1] From the MSS. of the Earl of St. Germains.

[2] His most important work, first published in 1736. This new edition was dedicated to Chesterfield out of gratitude for his offer to take Warburton as his chaplain in 1745.

[3] *Essay on Criticism*, Part I, 82, 83. " Ever " should be " often."

of it may be believed, why may not one like flattery, though ever so undeserved, in the hopes that some of it will be believed ? Your testimony at least gives me the best chance that I can have for it. I wish it were in my power to give you as publick a testimony of that perfect truth and distinguished esteem with which I am, Sir,

Your most faithfull humble servant,

CHESTERFIELD.

Pray make my compliments to Mr. Allen.[1]

To Edward Eliot.

London, Sept. y⁰ 29th, 1748.

Sʳ,

As this is about the time when you proposed being in Town, and as I should be very much concerned if I were not to have the pleasure of seeing you before your return to Leipsig, you will (I am sure) excuse the precaution which I now take to prevent, if possible, that disappointment.

The worse than indifferent state of my health obliges me to go to the Bath, for which place I shall set out on this day seven-night the 6th of Oct. and consequently be there on the 9th. Though I am in hopes still of seeing you in Town before I leave it, yet if I should not have that good fortune, I take the Bath to be almost in your way from Cornwall to London, or at least so little out of your road, that I will venture to propose that digression to you, if we do not meet here by the 6th. I can offerr you no other inducement to it, than the pleasure which it will give to one, who knows and values your merit, who desires your friendship, and who wishes for every opportunity to prove to you the truth and esteem, with which he is

Your most faithfull humble servant

CHESTERFIELD.[2]

To Edward Eliot.

Monday morning. [Nov. 21st, 1748.]

Sʳ,

I will not trouble you with any professions of my concern for your loss of a very good Father,[3] as the part which I

[1] Egerton MSS. 1955, f. 9. Ralph Allen of Bath, Warburton's benefactor, to whom he was introduced by Pope in 1741, and whose favourite niece Warburton married.

[2] From the MSS. of the Earl of St. Germains.

[3] Richard Eliot, bapt. 1694; died 19th November and was buried at St. Germains 3rd December, 1748.

X

dare say you believe that I take in every thing that relates to you, would render such assurances unnecessary ; this therefore is only to offerr you most sincerely my best services, if it is in my power to do you any, and to assure you that I am with the warmest sentiments of Esteem and Friendship

Your most faithfull humble servant CHESTERFIELD.

I will have the pleasure of waiting upon you, when you shall let me know, that I shall not be troublesome, and not till then ; but in the meantime, I will venture to advise you not to take hastily, any Political Engagements, with any Person whatsoever ; You will be tryed by more than one upon that Subject ; but the previous arrangement of your own Domestick affairs is a just answer to every body.[1]

To Dr. William Warburton.

London, Sep. ye 14th, 1749.

SIR,

I have but two livings in my gift worth anybody's taking, and they are both in Nottinghamshire.

The best is the living of Bingham, worth three hundred pounds a year, of which my father was pleased to sell the then next presentation, and the then incumbent is still alive, so that with regard to that, and to my own age, I look upon myself to be out of the question. The other is the living of Gedling, worth about one hundred pounds a year, and that I disposed of five years ago to a man not forty years old ; consequently there is little probability of my disposing of it again. But should it, by great chance, be vacant in my time, I have one engagement, and but one in the world, to a clergyman of great want and merit, to whom (if at that time unprovided for) I must give it. This is the true state of my Ecclesiastical Affairs, which I am very sorry gives me no better hopes of serving you. As for my interest with the Administration, either in these or other matters, my situation tells you how considerable it must be. Retirement is not in the road that leads to Interest at Court, and he who will enjoy the former (as I am determined to do) must renounce the latter. The Political road is (by the by) not one jot cleaner than the Ecclesiastical one. I know it by long experience ; for,

---

[1] From the MSS. of the Earl of St. Germains.

though I endeavoured to keep as clean as I could, I found that if I did not bemire myself, I was sure to be bespattered at least by others who rode full speed either to overtake or to jostle me. I have therefore put an end to my journey, instead of drudging on to my journey's end.

Thus you see that I am a very useless, though your very sincere friend and humble servant,

CHESTERFIELD.

Pray make my compliments to the most worthy Mr. Allen.[1]

In 1750 Chesterfield wrote two letters to Edward Eliot with a view to procuring a benefice for Dr. Harte. They are of no general interest and are here omitted except for the following conclusion to the second one.

London, Nov. ye 29th, 1750.

. . . I believe that very few things could have given either you or me more pleasure than the opportunitys we have both had of showing the truth of our regard to one who so well deserves it, and of procuring him a comfortable Wellcome at his return to his own Country. I am now too old and too insignificant to hope to be of any farther use to him, though while I live I will endeavour it ; but it is a comfort to me to reflect that he has in you a friend who will most probably be as able as now willing to serve him. I am with the greatest truth and esteam

S^r, Your most faithfull humble servant

CHESTERFIELD.[2]

To the Duke of Newcastle.

Bath, Feb. ye 14th, 1756.

MY LORD,

There is, it seems, a man in the world wretched enough to imagine that he wants, and may be the better for, my assistance, and, as I know his necessity and honesty, I could not refuse him to bear my testimony of both. I take the liberty of inclosing to Your Grace his own letter to me, which I received this morning. In that he states

---

[1] Egerton MSS. 1955, f. 11. " This was in answer to one I wrote him to desire a living for my nephew, if ever he had one fall that way disengaged, What he says of the Eccl. and Pol. Road alludes to something I said in mine."—Note by W. Warburton.

[2] From the MSS. of the Earl of St. Germains.

his own case which I submitt to Your Grace's compassion, and, I may add, Charity.

I am etc.[1]

On February 24th 1764, Newcastle sent Chesterfield the following note :—

The Duke of Newcastle sends his compliments to the Earl of Chesterfield, and should be very much obliged to his Lordship if he would be so good as to use his interest with Mr. Lyon of Pembroke Hall to be for My Lord Royston[2] to be High Steward of the University of Cambridge, in case we should be so unhappy as to have a vacancy.

The Duke of Newcastle begs pardon for troubling My Lord Chesterfield in this manner. He intends to do himself the honor to wait upon his Lordship very soon. He has lately been very much employed, and particularly in waiting upon a *Lady*[3] with the gout ; but, thank God, *she is in a very good way.*[4]

To this Chesterfield made the following reply :—

Feb. 25th, 1764.

My Dear Lord,

Three months ago, at Bath, I received an application from Lord Sandwich, through a third person, to the same effect as the letter with which your Grace honoured me yesterday. My answer was that I had no interest in the University, and that if I had I should not use it for or against any body. This declaration, therefore, I must observe, even with Lord Sandwich, and I can the more easily do it as there is not a single vote in the whole University that I can influence. Mr. Lyon will certainly be guided by his brother, Lord Strathmore, who will as certainly, according to the Scotch custom, *gang with the Prerogative.* Though I have a very indifferent opinion of my Alma Mater,

[1] Add. MSS. 32862, f. 486. (*Newcastle Papers.*)

[2] Afterwards 2nd Earl of Hardwicke ; see p. 315 *post.* He was elected High Steward in 1764, and retained the post till his death in 1790.

[3] This is a reference to Chatham, whom Chesterfield often humorously alludes to as Newcastle's wife. Writing to Dayrolles on July 4, 1757, he says, " I look upon his Grace and Pitt to be rather married than united ; the former will be a very jealous husband, and the latter a very haughty imperious wife."—Bradshaw, vol. III, p. 1170.

[4] Add. MSS. 32956, f. 91. (*Newcastle Papers.*)

I can hardly think that she will stain her annals with the name of Lord Sandwich, when she may adorn them with that of Lord Royston. But if she does, I shall, and I believe many others will, look upon her in the honourable light of the *Catch Club*. I am, with the greatest truth and respect, etc.

I am very glad to hear that your gouty patient is so much better.[1]

To Mr. Harte.[2]

Blackheath, Aug. 10, 1764.

SIR,

I give you a thousand thanks for your book,[3] of which I've read ev'ry word with great pleasure, and full as great astonishment. When in the name of God could you have found time to read the ten or twenty thousand authors whom you quote of all countries and all times, from Hesiod to du Hamel? Where have you plough'd, sown, harrow'd, drill'd and dug the earth for at least these forty years ; for less time couldn't have made you such a complete master of the practical part of Husbandry? I can only account for it from the Pythagorean doctrine of the transmigration of souls, and the supposition that Hartlib's soul has animated your body, with a small alteration of name. Seriously, your book entertains me exceedingly, and has made me quite a *Dilettante*, tho' too late to make me a *Virtuoso* in the usefull and agreable Arts of Agriculture. I own myself ignorant of them all, but am nevertheless sensible of their utility and the pleasure it must afford those who pursue them. Moreover, you've scattered so many graces over them that one wishes to be better acquainted with them, and that one reads your book with almost as much pleasure as if one were. It is the only prose Georgic that I know, as agreable, and I dare say much more usefull in this climate than Virgil. Why have you

---

[1] Add MSS. 32956, f. 112.

[2] Formerly tutor to Chesterfield's son.

[3] *Essays on Husbandry.* Writing to his son on September 3, 1764, he says, " I have received a book for you, and one for myself, from Harte. It is upon agriculture, and will surprise you, as, I confess, it did me. This work is not only in English, but good and elegant English ; he has even scattered graces upon his subject ; and, in prose, has come very near Virgil's *Georgics* in verse. I have written to him to congratulate his happy transformation. As soon as I can find an opportunity, I will send you your copy. You (though no Agricola) will read it with pleasure."—Bradshaw, vol. III, p. 1311.

not put your name to it ? For tho' some passages in it
point you out to be the author here, they will not do so
in other countries ; and, as I am persuaded that your
book will be translated into most modern languages, and
be a polyglott of husbandry, I could have wish'd your
name had been to it.

How goes the Flavabilious complaint ; has not the Bath
waters wash'd it away yet ? I heartily wish it was, as I
sincerely wish you whatever can give you ease or pleasure,
for I am with great truth

Your faithfull friend and servant, CHESTERFIELD.

P.S. Tho' I can be as partial as another to my friend,
I cannot be quite blind to their omissions ; for tho' you
have enumerated so many sorts of grass, with a particular
panegyrick on your dear Lucerne, you have not describ'd,
nor so much as mention'd that *particular sort of grass
which, while it grows* the steed starves.[1]

Your Elève is very well at Dresden. I will send him
his book when I can find a good opportunity.[2]

To — Yorke.[3]

March 28th, Friday, 1766.

Lord Chesterfield is extremely flattered by the undeserved
attention of one whose character he honours and esteems,
as he does Mr. Yorke's. He will think himself very happy
in sharing some of those few moments which Mr. Yorke
has to throw away upon idle acquaintances, and is almost
always at home till one o'clock.

Lord Chesterfield would have had the pleasure of preven-
ting Mr. Yorke by attending him at his own house, but
that he supposed he should break in upon business.[4]

To his Godson.

Monday. [October, 1766.]

MY DEAR LITTLE BOY,

As I believe that we shall reciprocally be glad to meet,
I will send the Coach next Sunday about one o'clock to

---

[1] An old proverb. *Cf.* "'While the grass grows'—the proverb is
something musty."—*Hamlet*, III, 2.

[2] Add. MSS. 35126, f. 6. Correspondence of Arthur Young.

[3] Charles Yorke (1722–1770) second son of 1st Lord Hardwicke. After
repeated refusals he accepted the Great Seal in 1770, thus deserting his
Whig friends. He died a few days later. At the time of this letter he
was Attorney General in the Rockingham Ministry.

[4] Add. MSS. 35430, f. 260. (*Hardwicke Papers.*)

bring your little body to dinner at my House. I hope you are now so well settled in your new habitation [1] (all but the bureau) [2] that you can persue your studies without interruption, for a day's interruption does more mischief with such a giddy head as yours, than a week's application can do good.

As I was dipping the other day among Mr. Addison's *Spectators*, which you shall in time be better acquainted with, I met with one upon the judgements often formed of people from their Physiognomy and air ; upon which that excellent writer says, " We are no sooner presented to anyone we never saw before, but we are immediately struck with the idea of a proud, a reserved, an affable or a good-natured Man and upon our first going into a company of strangers, our benevolence or aversion rises naturally towards several particular persons, before we have heard them speak one single word, or so much as know who they are." This observation is most unquestionably true, and I dare say you have found it so by your own little experience. Therefore, as the general air and countenance are of such consequence in the common intercourse of Life, it is very well worth your while to make the best of yours. Wear a chearfull and affable countenance, and take your air from Mr. Gherardi's [3] instructions. In the same *Spectator*, which is, if I mistake not, No. 86, there is a very pretty epigram of Martial upon a strange, awkward, ill-looking fellow :

" Crine ruber niger ore, brevis pede, lumine laesus ;
Rem magnam praestas Loile,[4] si bonus es." [5]

The translation is subjoyned in English, but it is not a very faithfull one.

[1] " The Doctor [Dodd] and he go at Michaelmas to settle in their new house in Great Russell Street, Bloomsbury."—Chesterfield to the father, A. C. Stanhope, 6th September, 1766. Carnarvon's *Appendix* p. 70.

[2] " He told me t'other day that he intended to buy a bureau with a bookcase over it, to keep his papers and books in good order. I asked him if he had money to pay it : he answered, No : but that he should draw upon his banker for the money. I told him I was glad to hear that he had a banker, and asked him who it might be ? He answered without hesitation, that I was his banker. In return for this mark of confidence, I could not possibly protest his draught, and so the bureau was paid for."—Chesterfield to A. C. Stanhope, 23rd October, 1766 ; *ibid.* See also letter to godson, July. 1766. (Carnarvon, p. 211.)

[3] Philp Stanhope's dancing master.

[4] Should be " Zoile."

[5] Epig. XII, 54.

" Thy beard and head are of a different Die ;
Short of one foot, distorted in one [1] Eye
With all these tokens of a knave compleat,
Should'st thou be honest, thou'rt a Devilish Cheat."

If you should not be honest, as I am sure you will be,
you would be still a more devilish cheat, for you have an
honest open countenance. Adieu a Dimanche prochain.[2]

To the Duke of Newcastle.

Jan. 24th, 1768.

Lord Chesterfield sends his best compliments to the
Duke of Newcastle, with his most sincere congratulations
upon his Grace's recovery, which gives him as real a joy
as his illness gave him concern. Weakness in the limbs
is a common consequence of a violent fever. Lord
Chesterfield experiences it at this moment, not being able
to go up or down stairs without assistance, though he has
been cured of the fever these five months. The following
receipt has been known to contribute more to convalescence
than any other medicine.

Rx [= Recipe] otium dies noctesque procul a negotiis.[3]

To Monsieur Ernst, fils.[4]

London, Jan. 25th, 1771.

MY DEAR FRIEND,

I have double thanks to return you for the prettiest
snuff-box accompanyed by as pretty a letter as possible :
but it lyes a little upon my conscience that I have put

[1] Should be " an."

[2] Add. MSS. 26053, f. 12. It is endorsed " Chesterfield to his Godson
circa 1766." Philip Stanhope was then eleven years old.

[3] Add. MSS. 33072, f. 65. (Newcastle Papers.)

[4] A pupil with Chesterfield's godson at Dr. Dodd's. There are many
references to him in the Letters to the Godson, the first of which occurs
in a letter of November 17, 1766 :—" I know your young companion Mr.
Ernst very well, and am very glad that you have him with you, for he is
a very well-bred pretty Boy."—Carnarvon, p. 227.
He took part with young Stanhope in a dramatic entertainment, of
which Chesterfield wrote to his father as follows :—" 8th April, 1767. Our
theatrical performance went off to admiration, before a numerous audience
of both sexes, who applauded loudly. My boy . . . was clapped several
times, and, indeed, he deserved it. His friend, who was two years older,
has greater powers of voice, but not greater propriety of action. They are
of great use to each other, for there is an amicable emulation between
them, and without the least envy, which shows the generosity of both
their minds."—Carnarvon's Appendix, p. 74.

you to the expence of two boxes, which is rather too much for a Student of Leipsig. If you have any commissions of any kind in this country I hope you will make me your Commissioner *par preference*. There goes to you with this letter a little deal box which I have desired your unkle to forward to you. What the box contains I know not, but I was required to send it to you.

How do you like Leipsig? Have you good Professors there of the Law of Nature and Nations? If they can teach I am sure you can and will learn. You may chance to see your friend Stanhope there in a little more than a year. I am sure I wish it and will endeavour to contrive it if I can. Your example did him a great deal of good while you was here, and will do him still more if you meet abroad.

I am with true esteem,

Your most faithfull humble servant CHESTERFIELD.[1]

To Monsieur Ernst.

London, April 22, 1771.

MY DEAR FRIEND,

From the real part that I take in whatever concerns you, I cannot hesitate one moment to advise you to accept gladly the offer that Colonel [*sic*] has made you. The department of foreign affairs and you were made for each other ; whereas you have neither lungs nor impudence for Westminster Hall : your uncle seems to agree in opinion with me. I speak against my private interest, for, as I propose sending your little friend to Leipsig in about a year, I should have been very glad that he had found you there to have been his mentor. Apropos of Leipsig, pray inform me in the next letter which you favour me with what allowance will be sufficient for your friend during his stay there. He will have a Governor, a Valet de chambre, and a footman, and a coach, if coaches are used there commonly. I would have him live decently and with some dignity, but without an idle, ridiculous profusion. I sollemnly promise you secrecy.

You see pretty plainly by my letter[2] that I am far from being quite recovered yet from my last fit of illness, in

---

[1] Add. MSS. 35350, f. 39. (*Hardwicke Papers.*)
[2] Both this and the next letter are written in a very trembling hand.

which I was, during a fortnight, given over by the Faculty.
I am with great truth, Sir,

Your faithfull humble servant, CHESTERFIELD.[1]

A Monsieur Keith,[2] Secretaire de Legation de S.M. Brittque
à Copenhague.

Blackheath, Aug. yᵉ 4th, 1771.

MY VERY GOOD FRIEND,

I did not acknowledge your last letter so soon as otherwise I should have done because I was not sure of the time
of your arrival at Copenhagen, and also because I chose to
let you turn your self in your Office before I troubled you
with such frivolous letters as mine must be. But now to
the business of your last letter. You have informed me
so fully of every circumstance relative to Leipsig [3] that I
have nothing to do but to send your young friend [4] there
whenever I please, which I think will be about April or
May next. You and I differ but upon one point which is
his dining in his own room ; whereas I would always have
him eat in the most numerous company of the place where
he resides, for I send him abroad not to see things, but
Persons with their various characters and manners ; and
I will venture to give you the same advice for your own
conduct in the several courts where you probably will go.

I am sure you apply your self diligently to your present
business, for which Nature seems to have particularly
formed you ; but, however, I will venture to give you one
word of advice, which is this. Let Modern History be
both your study and amusement : by Modern History
from 1500 to your own time, from which æra Europe took
that colour which to a great degree it retains at this day ;
and let Alexander and Julius Caesar shift for themselves :
you are enough acquainted with them already.

I am grown at least twenty years older than when you
saw me last, having had a long and dangerous fit of illness
last Spring which has irrecoverably weakened my wretched
carcase, as you see by my trembling hand, and my old
decayed understanding, as you will perceive by the sub-

---

[1] Add. MSS. 35503, f. 195. (*Hardwicke Papers.*)

[2] Lieut.-General Sir Robert Murray Keith (1730–1795).

[3] In 1769 he had been appointed British Minister at the Court of Saxony,
whence he was transferred to Copenhagen in 1771.

[4] Chesterfield's godson.

stance of this letter ; but I assure you has not the least diminished the friendship and esteem with which I am,

Your faithfull friend and humble servant,

CHESTERFIELD.[1]

To Lord Hardwicke.[2] (Dictated).

Chesterfield House, 2nd Jan., 1773.

Lord Chesterfield, incapable of holding a pen, and still more so of inditing a letter, returns his sincerest thanks to Lord Hardwicke for his good wishes, and assures him that he is not behindhand with him in whatever can contribute to the prosperity and satisfaction of Lord Hardwicke and his family.

Since Lord Hardwicke commands it, there shall be a picture of Lord Chesterfield : otherways it could not be imagined that there would have been one of him drawn at seventy-eight years of age, and in the manifest decline of his health.[3]

[1] Add. MSS. 35503, f. 197. (*Hardwicke Papers*).

[2] Philip Yorke, 2nd Earl of Hardwicke (1720–1790). Sat in House of Commons as Lord Royston for some years. Succeeded to title on death of his father in 1764 and was a member of the Rockingham Ministry in 1765. High Steward of Cambridge from 1764 (see p. 308 *ante*). It was doubtless in this latter official capacity that he had asked for a picture of Chesterfield to be given to Cambridge University.

[3] Add. MSS. 35611, f. 3. (*Hardwicke Papers.*) Chesterfield died on the 24th March following.

INDEX